Official Proceedings Of The Democratic National Convention Held In Chicago, Ill., July 7Th, 8Th, 9Th, 10Th And 11Th, 1896

Containing Also, The Preliminary Proceedings Of The Democratic National Committee. Etc. With An Appendix Containing The Proceeding Of The Committee Of Notification Organization Of The Democratic National Committee Of 1896, And The Letters Of Acceptance Of William J. Bryan And Arthur Sewall

Edward B. Dickinson

Alpha Editions

This Edition Published in 2021

ISBN: 9789354485244

Design and Setting By
Alpha Editions
www.alphaedis.com
Email – info@alphaedis.com

As per information held with us this book is in Public Domain.
This book is a reproduction of an important historical work. Alpha Editions uses the best technology to reproduce historical work in the same manner it was first published to preserve its original nature. Any marks or number seen are left intentionally to preserve its true form.

OFFICIAL PROCEEDINGS

OF THE

DEMOCRATIC NATIONAL CONVENTION

HELD IN CHICAGO, ILL., JULY 7th, 8th, 9th, 10th and 11th, 1896;

CONTAINING, ALSO, THE

PRELIMINARY PROCEEDINGS OF THE DEMOCRATIC
NATIONAL COMMITTEE, ETC.

WITH AN APPENDIX CONTAINING THE

PROCEEDINGS OF THE COMMITTEE OF NOTIFICATION
ORGANIZATION OF THE DEMOCRATIC NATIONAL
COMMITTEE OF 1896, AND THE LETTERS OF
ACCEPTANCE OF WILLIAM J. BRYAN
AND ARTHUR SEWALL.

REPORTED FOR THE CONVENTION BY

EDWARD B. DICKINSON,

OFFICIAL STENOGRAPHER

LOGANSPORT, IND.
WILSON, HUMPHREYS & CO., 200-204 FOURTH STREET.
1896.

INDEX.

Address of—

Altgeld, J. P. (Ill.), By invitation of Convention	125
Atwood, J. H. (Kansas), On report on Credentials	132–136
Blackburn, J. C. S. (Ky.), By invitation of Convention	121
Bailey, J. W. (Texas), Seconding Bland's nomination	291
Blake, T. W. (Texas), On report on Credentials	149
Bragg, Edward (Wis.), on State privilege	329
Brennan, John L. (Wis.), On report on Credentials	137
Brice, Calvin S. (Ohio), On contracts offered by cities	52–56
Brucker, Ferdinand (Mich.), On report on Credentials	153
Bryan, William J. (Neb.), On Resolutions	227
Bryan, William J. (Neb.), Speech of acceptance	391
Burk, William R. Cal.), nominating Sewall	343
Clayton, Henry D. (Ala.), On Report Committee on Temporary Organization	92
Clayton, Henry D. (Ala.), On resolutions to Harrity and Sheerin	388
Crain, T. C. T. (N. Y.), Presenting claims of New York	38
Crosby, J. C. (Mass.), On report on Credentials	136
Culbertson, C. A. (Texas), Nominating Bland	344
Cummings, Amos (N. Y.), Withdrawing Sibley's name	359
Currie, J. H. (N. C.), Nominating Clarke	338
Daniel, John W. (Va.), Accepting temporary chairmanship	99
Dockery, E. J. (Wis.), Seconding Bryan's nomination	296
Dockery, E. J. (Wis.), Regarding Unit Rule	308
Duncan, John M. (Texas), On Report Committee Temporary Organization	87
Fellows, John R. (N.Y.), Presenting claims of New York	40
Fellows, John R. (N. Y.), On report on Temporary Organization	81
Fithian, George (Ill.), Seconding Sibley's nomination	349
Follett, John F. (Ohio), Presenting claims of Cincinnati	31
Foote, W. W. (Cal.), Seconding Blackburn's nomination	286
Ford, Simeon (N. Y.), Presenting claims of New York	36
Francis, David R. (Mo.), Presenting claims of St. Louis	44
Goodrich, Adams A. (Ill.), Presenting claims of Chicago	27
Gorman, A. P. (Md.), To National Committee	20
Grady, Thomas F. (N. Y.), On report on Credentials	157
Green, Rev. Thos. E. (Iowa), prayer	113–190 297
Harrity, William F. (Penn.), Calling Convention to order	69
Harrity, William F. (Penn.), Nominating Pattison	298
Harrity, William F. (Penn.), To National Committee	381

iv   INDEX.

Address of
Harrity, William F. (Penn.), On Resolution of thanks............ 386
Hill, David B. (N. Y.), Supporting minority report on resolution.. 210
Hogg, J. S. (Tex.), By invitation of Convention.................. 114
Howell, Clark, Jr. (Ga.), To National Committee.................. 23
Howry, C. B. (Miss.), On date for Convention 6
Ingalls, M. E. (Ohio), Presenting claims of Cincinnati........... 29
James, Ollie (Ky.), Withdrawing Blackburn's name................. 322
Johnson, Thomas (Ohio), Nominating Fithian....................... 340
Jones, Paul (Ark.), Nominating Bland............................. 287
Jones, J. K. (Ark.), On report of Committee on Resolutions....... 209
Jones, W. A. (Va.), Withdrawing Daniel's name.................... 346
Kernan, T. J. (La.), Seconding Bryan's nomination................ 267
Klutz, T. K. (N. C.), Seconding Bryan's nomination............... 267
Ladd, C. K. (Ill.), On report on temporary organization.......... 89
Lewis, H. T. (Ga.), Nominating Bryan............................. 265
Long, G. S. (Ohio), Withdrawing McLean's name.................... 365
Maloney, Thomas (Wash.), Nominating Lewis........................ 338
Marston, B. W. (La.), On report on temporary organization........ 86
Marston, B. W. (La.), Nominating McLean.......................... 337
Mattingly, Robert E. (D. of C.), Seconding McLean's nomination.. 298
McDermott, Allen L. (N. J.), On report on temporary organization 73
McKnight, W. F. (Mich.), On report on Credentials................ 151
McLaurin, A. J. (Miss.), On report on Credentials................ 140
Miller, M. A. (Ore.), Nominating Pennoyer................... 298-340
Morgan, J. T. (Ala.), On date for Convention..................... 11
Morris, Free P. (Ill.), Seconding Sibley's nomination............ 346
O'Donnell, T. J. (Colo.), On report on Credentials............... 161
O'Sullivan, J. T. (Mass.), Nominating George F. Williams......... 335
Overmeyer, David (Kans.), By invitation of Convention............ 125
Overmeyer, David (Kans.), Seconding Bland's nomination........... 260
Owen, Robert L. (I. T.), On representation of Territories........ 22
Pasco, Samuel (Fla.), On date for Convention..................... 7
Patrick, A. W. (Ohio), Nominating McLean......................... 298
Powers, O. W. (Utah), By invitation of Convention................ 156
Powers, O. W. (Utah), Nominating Daniel for Vice-President...... 346
Russell, William E. (Mass.), supporting minority report on resolutions.. 224
Rhea, John S. (Ky.), nominating Blackburn........................ 283
Rawlins, J. L. (Utah), seconding nomination of Bland............. 293
Saulsbury, John F. (Del.), On report on Credentials.............. 146
Scott, John (Me.), Seconding Sewall's nomination................. 350
Sewall, Arthur P. (Me.), Acceptance.............................. 438
Sheehan, William F. (N. Y.), On report on Credentials............ 148
Sheerin, Simon P. (Ind.), On resolutions of thanks............... 387
Sherley, T. H. (Ky.), On date for Convention..................... 6
Shewalter, J. D. (Mo.), Nominating Sibley........................ 342
Sloan, Ulric (Ohio), On John R. McLean 347

INDEX.   v

Address of—

Smith, G. Waldo (N. Y.), Presenting claims of New York........   33
Smith, T. A. (Minn.), Seconding nomination of Boies............ 281
St. Claire, J. W. (W. Va.), On report on temporary organization...   90
St. Clair, J. W. (W. Va.), seconding nomination of Blackburn..... 295
Stevenson, E. G. (Mich.), On report on Credentials.............. 146
Stires, Rev. Ernest M. (Ill.), prayer...........................   69
Stone, William J. (Mo.), Presenting claims of St. Louis.........   48
Stone, William J. (Mo.), Withdrawing Bland's name........ 323, 361
Stone, William J. (Mo.), Advocating adjournment................. 330
Tarpey, M. F. (Cal.), On report on temporary organization....... 281
Taylor, S. M. (Ark.), On report on Credentials.................. 139
Thomas, C. S. (Colo.), On date for Convention...................   9
Thomas, C. S. (Colo.) On report on temporary organization.......   78
Thomas, C. S. (Colo.), On report on Credentials................. 154
Thomas, C. S. (Colo.), Seconding Sewall's nomination............ 344
Thomas, C. S. (Colo.), Seconding motion for vote of thanks to Har-
    rity and Sheerin.. 385
Thurman, Allen W. (N. M.), On date for Convention..............   15
Tillman, B. R. (S. C.), On report Committee on Resolutions...... 199
Trippett, O. A. (Cal.), Seconding Matthews' nomination.......... 275
Turpie, David (Ind.), Nominating Matthews...................... 269
Turpie, David (Ind.), Withdrawing Matthews' name............... 325
Van Wagenen, A. (Iowa), Withdrawing Boies' name................ 355
Vest, G. G. (Mo.), Presenting claims of St. Louis..............   49
Vest, G. G. (Mo.), Nominating Bland............................ 257
Vilas, W. F. (Wis.), On report on Resolutions.................. 220
Walbridge, C. P. (Mo.), Presenting claims of St. Louis.........   47
Wallace, Hugh C. (Wash.), On date for Convention...............   9
Waller, T. M. (Conn.), On report on temporary organization.....   75
Waller, C. E. (Ala.), on report on temporary organization......   80
Weadock, T. E. (Mich.), On report on Credentials............... 160
White, Frederick (Iowa), Nominating Boies...................... 276
White, S. M. (Cal.), Permanent chairman........................ 171
Williams, George Fred (Mass.), On invitation of Convention..... 131
Williams, J. R. (Ill.), Nominating Bland....................... 263

Ballot on—

Date for Convention..   19
Place for Convention.. 58, 64
Report Committee on Credentials................................ 166
Resolutions....................................... 241, 247, 248, 249
President..................................... 311, 361, 319, 321, 327
Vice-President................................ 354, 359, 361, 365, 368, 371
Blackburn, Joseph, Nominated for President..................... 283
Bland, Richard P., Nominated for President..................... 257
Bland, Richard P., Nominated for Vice-President................ 344
Bryan, William J., Nominated for President..................... 265

Index.

Bryan, William J., nominated for Presidency, unanimously....... 328
Bryan, William J., Speech of acceptance............................ 391
Bryan, William J., Letter of acceptance............................ 429
Boies, Horace, Nominated for President............................. 276
Call for National Committee meetings........................... 3, 335
Call for Convention.. 65
Campau, Daniel J., Chairman Campaign Committee.................... 390
Canda, F. E., Vote of thanks to................................... 385
Chicago, chosen unanimously for Convention......................... 64
Clark, W. A., Presenting silver gavel to Convention............... 172
Clarke, Walter, Nominated for Vice-President...................... 338
Cogan, T. J., Made Permanent Secretary............................ 167
Coliseum Harden Amusement Company's invitation to America......... 365

Committees—
    National Committee of 1892.................................... 1–68
    Consideration of permanent hall for conventions report........... 3
    On Convention arrangements............................... 32-3-67
    To escort Temporary Chairman to Chair........................... 98
    On Credentials.. 109–136
    On Permanent Organization........................... 110–167–170
    On Rules... 108–110
    On Resolutions.............................. 111, 191, 196, 198
National Committee of 1892, last meeting.......................... 382
National Committee of 1896, organization of....................... 389
    Notification Committee... 376
    Executive Committee of National Committee of 1896.............. 390
    Campaign Committee of National Committee of 1896............... 390
Communications to National Committee................................ 5
Contract of Chicago Committee...................................... 54

Convention—
    First day.. 54
    Second day... 69–113
    Third day... 136–190
    Fourth day.. 297–329
    Fifth day... 334
Daniel, J. W... 72, 97, 346
Delegates, List of.. 174
Dickinson, Edward B., Official Stenographer........................ 71
Finley, E. E., Member committee to escort White to chair.......... 171
Fithian, George, Nominated for Vice-President..................... 340
Gordon, Basil B., Resignation from National Committee.............. 2
Harrity, William F., Resolutions thanking......................... 370
Hill, David B., Nominated for temporary chairman................... 71
Hirsheimer, Louis D., Made permanent assistant secretary.......... 167
Hosford, Frank, Secretary Campaign Committee...................... 390
Jones, James K., Member committee to escort Daniel to chair........ 98

INDEX.

Jones, James K., Elected chairman of National Committee of 1896.. 389
Keating, R. P., Member committee to escort Daniel to chair........ 98
Letter of acceptance of William J. Bryan....................... 429
Letter of acceptance of Arthur P. Sewall....................... 441
Lewis, James Hamilton, Nominated for Vice-President............ 338
Martin, John I., Sergeant-at-Arms........................... 71-167
Matthews, Claude, Nominated for President..................... 269
McConnell, Samuel P., Member committee to escort White to chair. 171
McLean, John R, Nominated for President and Vice-President. 289, 337
Nelson, John C., Principal (temporary) Reading Clerk 71
Pattison, Robert E., nominated for President.................... 298
Pennoyer, Sylvester, nominated for President and Vice President. 298-340
Permanent Organization...................................... 167

Platform—
  Majority Report.. 191
  Minority Report.. 196
  Hill's Amendments... 198
  Official Platform.. 250

Resolution of Thanks to—
  William F. Harrity....................................108-370
  John W. Daniel, S. M. White and James M. Richardson......... 369
  Secretaries and Assistant Secretaries........................ 369
  Chicago and citizens....................................... 370
  William F. Harrity, on behalf of free silver people............ 370
  William F. Harrity, by National Committee of 1892............ 384
  Simon P. Sheerin, by National Committee of 1892............. 384

Resolutions in Reference to—
  Rules... 108
  Representation from Territories.............................. 19
  Roll Call of States for naming Committees................... 109
  Tickets for Nebraska delegation............................. 173
  Authority to fix time and place for next convention........... 369
  Preparation of proceedings by official stenographer........... 369
Secretary and assistants of Convention (temporary).............. 71
Secretaries Convention (permanent)........................... 445
Sewall, A. P., nominated for Vice-President.................... 343
Sewall, A. P., nomination made unanimous..................... 369
Sewall, A. P., speech of acceptance........................... 438
Sewall, A. P., letter of acceptance............................ 441
Sheerin, Simon P., Temporary Secretary....................... 71
Sibley, Joseph, nominated for Vice-President................... 342
Signatures of Cincinnati, New York and St. Louis Committees.... 55
St. John, Wm. P., selected Treasurer of National Committee of 1896, 389
Temporary Organization, Minority Report...................... 71
Temporary Organization, Majority Report...................... 72

Two-thirds Rule, Chairman's Decision 322
Vest, G. G., Member of Committee to escort White to chair......... 171
Vice-Presidents of Convention.................................... 445
Wade, E. B., Permanent Reading Clerk............................. 167
Walsh, Chas. A., selected Secretary of National Committee of 1896.. 389
White, Stephen M., Member of Committee to escort Daniel to chair, 98
White, Stephen M., Permanent Chairman 171

THE COLISEUM

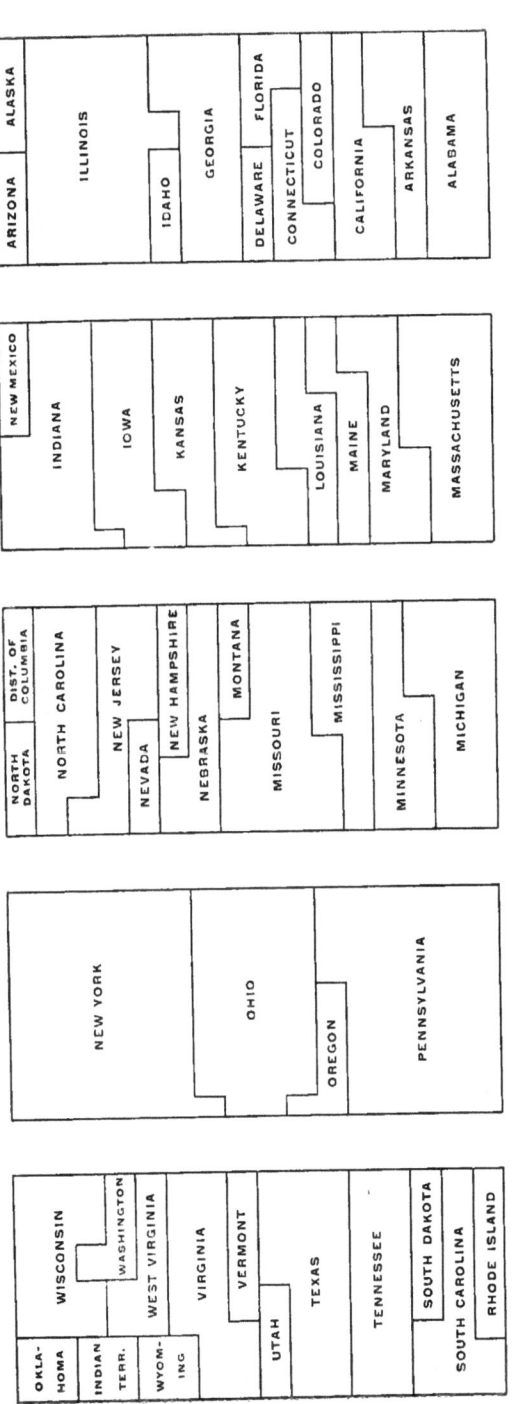

SEATING ARRANGEMENT OF DELEGATIONS

DEMOCRATIC NATIONAL COMMITTEE.

MEETING, JANUARY 16, 1896.

The Democratic National Committee met on the 16th day of January, 1896, pursuant to call, at the Arlington Hotel, in the City of Washington, D. C., at 12 o'clock noon.

THE CHAIR (William F. Harrity, of Pennsylvania:) The meeting will be in order. Gentlemen who are not members of the Committee will be kind enough to retire, as this is to be an executive or private session of the Committee.

Gentlemen of the Committee: There is a gentleman here who wants a snap shot at you; the sooner that is taken, the sooner we will be rid of him.

The Secretary will proceed to call the roll and note substitutions or corrections, if any are to be made.

The Secretary (S. P. Sheerin, of Indiana) then proceeded to call the roll of States and Territories, which were represented by members of the Committee in person or by proxy, as follows:

Alabama,	John T. Morgan	(Proxy for Henry D. Clayton).
Arkansas.	W. L. Terry	(Proxy for U. M. Rose).
California,	Stephen M. White	(Proxy for M. F. Tarpey),
Colorado,	Chas. S. Thomas.	
Connecticut,	Carlos French.	

Delaware,	Chas. W. McFee	(Proxy for Lewis C. Vandergrift).
Florida,	Samuel Pasco.	
Georgia,	Clark Howell, Jr.	
Idaho,	J. C. Edwards	(Proxy for Frank W. Beane).
Illinois,	Ben T. Cable.	
Indiana,	Simon P. Sheerin.	
Iowa,	J. J. Richardson.	
Kansas,	Chas. W. Blair.	
Kentucky,	Thos. W. Sherley.	
Louisiana,	James Jeffries.	
Maine,	Arthur Sewall.	
Maryland,	Arthur P. Gorman.	
Massachusetts,	John W. Corcoran	(Proxy for Josiah Quincy).
Michigan,	Daniel J. Campau.	
Minnesota,	(Absent).	
Mississippi,	Chas B. Howry.	
Missouri,	John G. Prather.	
Montana,	A. J. Davidson.	
Nebraska,	Tobias Castor.	
Nevada,	Clinton B. Davis	(Proxy for R. P. Keating).
New Hampshire,	A. W. Sulloway.	
New Jersey,	Willard F. Ross	(Proxy for Miles Ross).
New York,	William F. Sheehan.	
North Carolina,	M. W. Ransom.	
North Dakota,	W. N. Roach	(Proxy for Wm. C. Leistikow).
Ohio,	Calvin S. Brice.	
Oregon,	Henry C. Grady	(Proxy for E. D. McKee).
Pennsylvania,	William F. Harrity.	
Rhode Island,	John D. Crimmins	(Proxy for Samuel R. Honey).
South Carolina,	M. L. Donaldson.	
South Dakota,	James M. Woods.	
Tennessee,	Holmes Cummins,	
Texas,	Roger Q. Mills	(Proxy for O. T. Holt).
Utah,	Caleb W. West	(Proxy for Samuel A. Merritt).
Vermont,	Bradley B. Smalley.	
Virginia,	....	

THE CHAIR: The resignation of Mr. Basil B. Gordon, as a member of this Committee from Virginia, has been duly tendered and the officers of the Committee advised of that fact. At the same time, they were also advised that the Chairman of the Democratic State Central Committee, of Virginia, Mr. J. Taylor Ellyson, had been recommended by that committee, as the successor of Mr. Gordon. What is the pleasure of the Committee?

SENATOR GORMAN, of Maryland: I move that his name be entered as a member upon the roll of the Committee.

This motion being duly seconded, was put to a vote and carried.

The Secretary continued the roll call as follows:

Virginia,	J. Taylor Ellyson.	
Washington,	Hugh C. Wallace.	
West Virginia,	John Sheridan.	
Wisconsin	E. C. Wall.	
Wyoming,	Wm. Thomas	(Proxy for W. L. Kuykendall).
Alaska,	L. W. Nieman	(Proxy for A. L. Delaney).
Arizona,	Chas. M. Shannon.	
District of Columbia,	James L. Norris.	
New Mexico,	Allen W. Thurman	(Proxy for H. B. Ferguson).
Oklahoma,	Leslie G. Niblack	(Proxy for T. M. Richardson.)
Indian Territory,	Robert L. Owen.	

THE CHAIR: The Secretary will now read the official call for the meeting.

The Secretary then read the official call for the meeting, as follows:

DEMOCRATIC NATIONAL COMMITTEE.

LOGANSPORT, INDIANA, December 14, 1895.

DEAR SIR:

A meeting of the Democratic National Committee will be held at the Arlington Hotel, in the City of Washington, D. C., on Thursday, the 16th of January, 1896, at 12 o'clock M., to fix the time and place of holding the Democratic National Convention for the nomination of candidates for President and Vice-President of the United States, and for such other business as may come before the Committee.

Yours respectfully,
SIMON P. SHEERIN,
Secretary.

THE CHAIR: Under the provision of the call, it would seem to the Chair to be in order to make report from the sub-committee which was charged with the consideration of the resolution offered by Gen. P. A. Collins, of Massachusetts, in the Democratic National Convention of 1892, looking to arrangements for holding the Convention in a permanent hall, which would accommodate only the delegates, alternates, members of the National Committee and the press. The Committee, after consideration of the subject, is unanimously of the opinion that there is no occasion for a departure from what has been the practice in the past, of having accommodations for a reasonable number of spectators, as well as delegates, alternates, etc., and for so many as is consistent with the orderly conduct of proceedings in the Convention. What is the pleasure of the Committee?

It was moved and seconded that the report of the Sub-Committee be adopted. The motion was put to a vote and carried.

Mr. Wallace, of Washington: I move that we proceed to fix a time for holding the next Democratic National Convention, and in order to ascertain the sense of this meeting, I move that Tuesday, June 30, 1896, at 12 o'clock, noon, be fixed as the time for holding the Convention.

The Chair: The gentleman from Washington moves that Tuesday, June 30, 1896, be fixed as the time for holding the next Democratic National Convention. Before discussion of the question the Chair would like the opportunity of saying that communications have been received, during the past three months, from many different commerical bodies and trade organizations, advising in favor of a late Convention. The Chair thinks that it would be proper, under the circumstances, to read the list of the organizations from which such communications have been received; and then it will be for the Committee to say whether or not they desire that all of the communications shall be read.

Senator Pasco, of Florida: Will the Chair state the time for the Republican Convention?

The Chair: June 16. The Secretary will read the names of those bodies from which communications have been received. The communications are all of the same general tenor and effect.

The Secretary then read to the Committee the following list of commercial and trade organizations, viz.:

The Cleveland Chamber of Commerce.
Detroit Chamber of Commerce.
The Commercial Club of Kansas City.
Commercial Club (Webb City, Missouri).
The Denver Chamber of Commerce.

The Board of Trade of the City of Mankato, Minnesota.
Buffalo Real Estate Exchange.
The Board of Trade of the City of Baltimore.
Scranton Board of Trade (Scranton, Pennsylvania).
The Galveston Chamber of Commerce.
The Board of Trade of the City of Fall River, Massachusetts.
Los Angeles Chamber of Commerce.
Chamber of Commerce, Nashville, Tennessee.
Jackson General Welfare Association (Jackson, Michigan).
Boston Chamber of Commerce.
Board of Trade of San Francisco.
New Bedford Board of Trade (Massachusetts).
Keokuk Business Men's Association (Iowa).
Buffalo Merchants' Exchange.
The National Live Stock Exchange (Chicago).
The Wheeling Chamber of Commerce (West Virginia).
The National Hardware Association of the United States (Philadelphia).

THE CHAIR: What is the pleasure of the Committee with reference to the communications themselves?

MR. SMALLEY, of Vermont: I move that they be placed on file.

THE CHAIR: You have heard the motion made by the gentleman from Vermont, that the communications be placed on file.

Which motion, duly seconded, was put to a vote and carried.

THE CHAIR: The question is now upon the motion offered by the gentleman from Washington, Mr. Wallace.

MR. ELLYSON, of Virginia: I would like to say to the Committee that the time would be very inconvenient for many of us in the South, for the reason that on that very day there will be assembled in Richmond a convention of the United Confederate Veterans, which includes representatives from all the Southern States. We expect a very large attendance upon that occasion. It would certainly be impossible for many of us, who had expected to have the pleasure of attending both Conventions, to be away from Richmond at that time. Those of you who are from the Southern States will know that the United Confederate Veterans embrace representatives from all of the Southern States. If some other day could be fixed, which would be as equally agreeable to the members of the Committee, it would certainly be a gratification to us in Virginia, and in some of the other Southern States as well.

Mr. THOMAS, of Colorado: I move as an amendment to the motion made by the member from Washington, that the date of the Convention be fixed for Tuesday, the 9th day of June.

THE CHAIR: The gentleman from Colorado, Mr. Thomas, moves to amend by substituting the date of Tuesday, the 9th of June.

Mr. SHERLEY, of Kentucky: Having only in view the interests of the party, I think the date to be selected ought to be one after the Republican Convention, and that sufficient length of time should elapse to enable us to see the result upon the public of their platform and their selection of candidates. I think instead of making it earlier than the 30th day of June, it ought surely be later than that. The 15th day of July, to me, would be a more appropriate date, giving sufficient time after the Republican Convention; but, as I am not desiring to be an extremist at all I will offer as a substitute Tuesday, July 7. I think Tuesday comes on the 7th of July—or is it on the 6th?

THE CHAIR: The Chair thinks that July 7 will fall on Tuesday; June 30, being Tuesday, July 7, seven days later, will be Tuesday.

Mr. SHERLEY, of Kentucky: I offer as a substitute that it be fixed Tuesday, the 7th day of July.

THE CHAIR: You have heard the further amendment offered by the gentleman from Kentucky.

Mr. HOWRY, of Mississippi: I do not know what may be embraced in these petitions, resolutions or communications from the different trade organizations; but so far as the people in the South are concerned I think that they favor an early Convention. It may be it would be better to have it a week or so after the Republican Convention. I think a decided sentiment in the Southern country, so far as I can gather it from the newspapers, is in favor of an early Convention. I think we would be doing good service to the Democratic party to have an early Convention; therefore, I favor an early Convention. Perhaps the motion of the gentleman from Colorado, which fixes it before the Republican Convention, ought not to prevail. Under all the circumstances, we had better come a little after the Republicans this time, although we ought to have it as early after their Convention as possible.

I move as a substitute for the motion offered by the gentleman from Washington, Tuesday, June 23rd. In this day of telegraphic and rapid intercommunication, the effects of any platform and the results of any Republican Convention are soon taken in by the country. In order to accommodate all the interests, I move Tuesday, the 23rd day of June, be fixed as the date.

THE CHAIR: The Chair is not entirely clear as to whether it is exactly in order to further amend the motion, two amendments having been already offered.

MR. HOWRY, of Mississippi: My motion is a substitute.

MR GORMAN, of Maryland: The vote should be taken on the latest date first.

THE CHAIR: The gentleman from Maryland suggests that when the vote comes to be taken, that it ought to be taken on the latest date first.

MR. PASCO, of Florida: I am entirely in favor of an early Convention, but an early Convention now is very different from what would have been an early Convention a few years ago. I think July is abundantly early, and I would have it the second rather than the first Tuesday.

If the Democratic Convention is held immediately after the Republican Convention, there will be no time for the people throughout the country to confer with their delegates after the adjournment of that Convention, because in distant States the delegates will have to start from their homes before the Republican Convention has actually adjourned. It is very important that the effect of the Republican nominations and the Republican platform should go before the country, and that its influence be felt before we attempt to take any action. We shall need all the assistance we can get during the coming year. We need all the advantages that may come to us from any mistakes that may be made, and the circumstances attending the nominations and their platform should be known to the people all over the country before our Convention meets. If there are any weak spots in their armor we ought to have the advantage of preparing for a fair attack upon them and finding those weak spots. Two or three week's deliberation after they have adjourned will give us time and opportunity to prepare for such attacks. Instead of holding our Convention on the first Tuesday in July, I think it should be put as far in advance, say, as the second Tuesday, and would give us longer time. So far as the 7th is concerned, unless some one moves to change it to a later time, I shall vote for that date; my judgment would be rather in favor of the 14th of July than the 7th, or any other earlier date. Then we can have time for deliberation after the Republicans have spread their plans before the country, nominated their candidates and announced their platform, and if there is any hope of making successful nominations it will be greater with these facts before the people than if we rush into the fight unprepared and act hastily directly after their nominations have been made. I do not at all share in the view suggested by my friend from Colorado that we should meet first. I think it would be suicidal to do so. The Republicans have charge now of the two Houses of Congress, and have assumed control of the legislation of the country, and it is right and proper for them to make the first nominations, and when they have laid down their line of battle let us see how we can best meet it. Let us take a little time for deliberation so that our attack may not be a hasty one. Perhaps time for deliberation may help to repair some of the errors of the past and we may be better able to go forth united and make a successful attack upon them.

THE CHAIR : Does the Chair understand the gentleman from Florida to make a motion to that effect?

MR. PASCO, of Florida : I will not press that unless my views are favorably regarded by the gentleman who has offered the motion for the 7th of July. I shall vote for that date if nothing better is offered ; but if the view I have presented is favored by the gentleman who made that motion, it can be offered as a substitute.

Mr. Wallace, of Washington: It seems very clear that there is a very strong sentiment throughout the country in favor of a late Convention. It also seems clear that if we hold our Convention at a later time, so that we can take advantage of any mistake which may be made by the Republican Convention, we will have to hold a late Convention. * * * Now an election in Alabama, as I understand, occurs in August, and that election may be one of great import to our party. Following that there is an election in Maine and one in Vermont, and these States wish their speakers and they wish aid. So it seems to me, while it is desirable to hold a late Convention, to hold it later than from the first to the seventh of July, might embarrass the Campaign Committee very much. In view of the suggestion of this meeting of the Confederate Veterans—rather the Confederate reunion—that is to be held in Richmond on the 30th of June, I am willing to accept the amendment, the one suggesting the 7th of July as the date.

Mr. Sherley, of Kentucky: I hope you will; because it was offered as a compromise between the 23rd of June and the 14th of July.

Mr. Howry, of Mississippi: I withdraw my motion.

The Chair: That leaves but two dates before the Committee, namely: July 7th, as now accepted by the gentleman from Washington, and June 9th, as offered by the gentleman from Colorado.

Mr. Thomas, of Colorado: Mr. Chairman, my purpose in suggesting that date, was due entirely to the fact that I believe a long campaign and a vigorous one is absolutely essential to success if we are going to succeed in this campaign. As a matter of fact, unless I am greatly misinformed, it is a sort of unwritten custom that the National party of the country in control of the administration shall hold the first convention. I think that that has been the custom for a very long time, and if we now depart from that custom it seems to me that we begin our campaign with a confession of weakness. We may be weak—we probably are weak—but it is not for this Committee, in my judgment, to do anything which virtually amounts to or is tantamount to a confession of weakness. In other words, if we reverse the precedents of many years past, we go into the campaign handicapped with a sort of a tacit admission that we are the under dog in the fight. I am aware, as doubtless all the members of the Committee are, as they have been deluged with letters from different commercial organizations throughout the country, that those organizations are in favor of a short campaign. The reason why they claim to be in favor of a short campaign is that a long one will interfere with business, and business with them is the paramount object and purpose of civil government. Of course this is a subject to which we ought to give attention, but the people, as far as my limited observation goes, are in favor of a long campaign. It may be that the Republican party, when it meets in St. Louis, will make some mistakes. It may be that we can take advantage of them, but the history of the Democratic party for the last twenty-five years shows that mistakes of the Republican party made by virtue of its platform and the holding of early conventions, have not redounded very much to the benefit of the Democratic party. When we have succeeded, we have succeeded on positive platforms based on positive principles. My own judgment is that this next campaign, whether we wish it or not, is bound to turn upon the financial questions which are at present agitating the country, and the Democratic party is bound to take a positive stand upon them whether it waits until after the other Convention is held or holds its own first. I believe that if we can decide upon our platform and nominate our candidates without reference to the action of the Republican party, we will stand a much better chance of winning. In consequence, I am in favor of an early campaign. Personally I would be in favor of June 2, rather than June 9. If we can nominate our candidates and get our campaign started, and get everything ready and equipped as rapidly as possible, then we can go into the fight, to win or lose, as the case may be, with some chance of success. I believe an early campaign—as early a Convention as possible—is absolutely essential to success if we can succeed at all. I now renew my motion for the 9th of June. There is no use disguising the fact that there are very serious differences in the ranks of the Democracy. It must be recollected that we must do something to get together, and the more time we have in which to get together, the better it is going to be for us. I think we better have an early Convention. Whatever the result of that Convention, there is going to be dissatisfaction, and I think we will be needing all the time we can get for the purpose of harmonizing our differences and presenting an united front to the common enemy.

THE CHAIR: The motion of Mr. Thomas has been renewed.

MR. MORGAN, of Alabama: I think it my duty as one of the delegates from Alabama to make a statement which I think ought to have some effect upon the Committee. Alabama stands at the head of the column alphabetically. She also may take a place at the head for a persistent and unvarying course always in the election of Democratic electors. Her record is particularly clear on the subject and has been maintained for many years. The result of the next election, held the first week in August for Governor and members of the legislature, who will elect a senator, will necessarily have a very profound effect upon the feelings and the situation of Democrats throughout the State and throughout the country. I do not know whether the election in Maine comes earlier than ours or not.

THE CHAIR: That will be held in September.

MR. MORGAN: Alabama's election probably is the first one. The state of Alabama is in a very unsettled condition politically and it is in serious danger of being thrown into the category of the doubtful States. In other words, the Democratic party of the United States is in serious danger of losing the electoral vote in Alabama through its unfortunate troubles, and I hope that this Committee will give to us an opportunity to bring the Democrats of Alabama from their retreats, and assemble them together on the old lines of the party, which I think will not be a difficult task, if we show them that we are in harmony with and courteous to them. I hope this committee will give us an opportunity to do that. Now a late Convention will not produce that effect. We must have a chance, if possible, of following the lead of the men who are to be selected as the candidates for President and Vice-president. They are to become the rallying point of the Democracy of that State. If we have to go into a late campaign which will make it difficult to prevent these various differences from crystallizing into antagonistic forces, a campaign without national leadership and without our being able to bring our Democrats in harmony with the Democracy of the United States, we are going to have a hard fight and to need every assistance in our efforts to save that State. It has been charged against Alabama upon the floor of the Senate and sent to all the newspapers in the North that the results of our last elections, including the Presidential election, were obtained through manipulations of the ballot box. Such accusations have been made freely in the Senate of the United States upon Populist authority, but the Senators from that State have not as yet felt called upon to respond to the charge. The truth is that we have a clear Democratic majority of good, sound, honest Democrats in Alabama of not less than 60,000. That is the truth, and it is also true that while there may have been some irregularities—I believe there were in some counties—yet in all these elections to which I have referred, including that of the President, we have had a decisive and strong majority of Democrats in that State, so that we know and feel that we stand upon no uncertain ground at all in respect to our ability to carry the State except that uncertainty which has been produced by the trouble among the people over the subject of the currency. The Populists have made some inroads upon us and twice have claimed that they have elected their Governor. The claim was not answered nor was it believed in or insisted upon with seriousness. At the same time they have given us a great amount of annoyance. The methods of our party have been denounced in the management of the ballot box. The same thing, I think, has occurred in North Carolina. The Senators recently elected from that State arose in their seats recently and said that the loss of the State of North Carolina to the Democracy was because of the fusion between the Populists and the Republicans. That is what they say. Of course I do not believe it. That surely is not the fact, but that is the reason why they say they lost the State. Now there is a very large body of very sincere, good, honest Democrats in Alabama who have been either driven off or their power neutralized by these accusations. Whether true or untrue it makes no difference. When you get the popular mind in a condition amounting to conviction, you have got to remove it by some pretty earnest means; otherwise you will be snowed under. You have got to check it in time. It is very probable, Mr. Chairman, that, if these obstinate gentlemen in Alabama, who are now openly flirting with the Republicans, can produce a demonstration in that State amounting really to the opening of the campaign before our Convention meets, we shall be in very serious difficulties. Then you can very well understand what the effect upon the Democrats of the United States would be with an adverse vote to the Democratic party in Alabama. While latterly I have not had much to do with the active politics of the Democratic party there, yet I have been identified with the party for over fifty years without a break, and never have I struck a blow for myself. I have been fighting for the Democratic party because I believe in its principles and I rejoice in the glory of its traditions. I believe in the wonderful results that it has accomplished for the people of the United States. Those are the reasons why I am a Democrat. I glory in the party and no man in the world can drive me out of it, not even if the coming Convention should establish a platform entirely inconsistent or unwise. While I might kick, I would stay with my party because it is the best party in the world. (Applause.) The members of the Democratic party really do their own thinking and fight their own battles, and that is the real strength of the Democratic party. This country has never yet found and never will find any real national trouble for which, when it throws itself upon the bosom of the Democratic party, that party will not give absolute and speedy relief.

After the Civil war was over, what did we do? We found ourselves ready to march back again into the Union, because the doctrine of States' rights controlled influential public opinion in the United States. But people of our sort need no cowardly leader. He can not possibly have their votes and be untrue to the principles of the party. Above all, he must have courage; a coward can not lead the Democratic party to victory. Take a mediocre man, a man of ordinary reputation and abilities, and let him have a reputation for courage, consistent honor, and a reputation for faithful, conscientious adherence to the Democratic creed and principles, and the people will support him with joy.

So I think, Mr. Chairman, when the Committee undertakes to outline this campaign by the action we are about to take here now, we ought in our conduct to rely upon ourselves as Democrats, and that action, it seems to me, ought to be attended with firmness and courage. There are as many Democrats in the United States as voted for Mr. Cleveland four years ago. This year by reason of all the difficulties we have had, they have not voted, they have not all gone into the Populist party; they have not surrendered to the Republicans. They have taken to the woods. Now, the Populist party has not gone over to the Republicans. The Republican party is not any stronger in the United States today; it is not as strong as when it elected Mr. Harrison or when it voted for him the last time and got defeated. The Democratic party is as strong as it was then, excepting a few outlying men who are anxious to come home and who see the failure of their course.

I understand it to be a fact that the Democratic party heretofore has been accustomed to taking the lead in the time of holding a convention. They have said to the people of the United States, "Here is our creed; here are our men," for the purpose of making a gallant, aggressive, intense, thorough and honest campaign. We are not afraid to address the people of the United States and avow what we believe to be our duty. We are not going to hold off merely for the purpose of taking such advantages as might fall to us by some inconsiderate action on the part of the opposition. We do not expect to win a campaign by playing their tricks at the card table. We want to win by our own strength. We want a fair fight. The people will sustain you if you step to the front and furnish them with men and measures that they can unite upon, and they will go a great way to get both the men and the measures with which they can come to the front in advance of the Republicans. (Applause.) Then the people will understand that they have got a party with convictions which does not depend upon whether anybody else believes in them or not, but upon what the party believes and feels to be for the best interests of the country.

Therefore, Mr. Chairman, I am in favor of an early Convention. More than that, as I understand it, and I think I do understand it, the Southern people are in a more serious state of mind than I have ever known them. I never had anything like the requests made upon me for information connected with the financial question that I have had within the last two years. The newspaper press of the country has been immensely influential in distributing information and the people are taking a great deal more interest than they ever did formerly in the study of this question. I can honestly say that both on account of the state of the Democracy in the South and the duty which I think we owe to Democrats everywhere, the party should hold its Convention at an early date and before the Republican Convention is held.

MR. THURMAN, of New Mexico. Mr. Chairman: We might as well all recognize the fact that the Democratic party of the United States is in a rather disorganized condition.

The last two general elections have thrown us into a state of semi-collapse. I feel, however, that it is within the power of this Committee to assist us in retrieving our fortunes. I feel that if this Committee will give us an early Convention, and in a Western city, you will have an enthusiastic one which will give Democrats courage and hope of success. On the other hand if the time be fixed at a late date, and the place selected be in the East, the impression that is now abroad, especially throughout the West and South, will only be intensified, namely: that the National Democratic organization does not intend giving the Democrats of the West and South, who differ from their brethren and their gospel in the East, a fair, square opportunity to present their cause before a Democratic National Convention.

You may think this is an over statement, but it is absolutely true, gentlemen, that there is an impression in the West, that if this Convention is put off until a late date, it will be done for the purpose of controlling it, by manipulation, against Democrats who are in favor of the free coinage of both gold and silver.

You might as well look this matter straight in the face That is the impression, and if it be decided to put off the date until away into July, the rank and file of the Democratic party in those states to which I have referred, and who have always been true to the principles of the Democratic party, will at once lose all heart and hope. They will feel just as they did concerning the State Conventions which were held in the West during the last year. They will fear that the power of the Administration will be so used that it will control the delegates to that Convention. We fear this, because having felt the power of official patronage in thus controlling delegates to Conventions, we know what it means, and I assure you we do not want another practical example of such a pure (?) exalted (?) and clear conception (?) of civil service reform as was displayed upon those occasions. And what is more, I want to say, as much as you may dislike to hear it, that the Democrats who believe in the free coinage of both gold and silver will not stand any more of such work. If this is done you will simply drive them away from the Democratic party. If they do not go into the Populist party, you will, as Senator Morgan has said, drive them into the bushes, and when there you can not get them out; and if you can not get them out it is just as utterly impossible for the Democratic party to elect the next President of the United States as it is for any man here to jump over Washington's Monument.

We have anything other than a sure thing upon this election. New York, Connecticut and New Jersey with the South, even should we carry them, will no longer elect a Democratic President. We will have to have several of the Western States in addition; and if by your action you do not make those people to whom I have referred believe that you are giving them an equal chance to control the delegates to the National Convention, you can not get a single, solitary one of those States. Any action on your part other than this will be sure to bring about the election of a Republican President, either by securing to that party a majority of the electoral votes, or by the election being thrown into the House of Representatives, and that body would of course elect a Republican President. Therefore, gentlemen of the Committee, I beg of you in the name of the Democrats of the West and South, who honestly believe in the free coinage of both gold and silver, who believe that the Constitution of the United States guarantees that they shall be both coined into money; who believe just as sincerely and honestly in their position as you do in yours, not only to listen but to heed. If you do not, we will all go down together.

Firmly believing this, Mr. Chairman, I hope that instead of

having a late Convention, that this committee will select the date of holding the same not later than the first day of June. And I move to amend by striking out the date we are now considering and to substitute therefor the first day of June—I learn the second day will be on Tuesday. That would be a better day of the week; therefore, I name the second day of June instead of the first.

MR. THOMAS: Mr. Chairman, with the consent of my second, I will accept the suggestion of the gentleman representing New Mexico, making the date the second day of June instead of the 9th.

THE CHAIR: The motion to fix June 9th has been withdrawn. As the Chair recalls it, the only dates now before the Committee are June 2d and July 7th.

MR. CABLE, of Illinois: In view of the fact that June 30th has been withdrawn, I would like to offer July 14th.

THE CHAIR: July 14th has been named.

MR. GORMAN, of Maryland: Mr. Chairman, I have listened attentively to the remarks of Mr. Thurman who represents New Mexico and it seems to me they show the importance of great deliberation on our part, and the necessity for fixing the time for holding the Convention at as late a period as possible with the view of organizing a successful campaign in order that we may, if possible, by counseling each other bring about greater harmony than seems to exist today. If the party were united, it would make but little difference when the Convention should be held. But it seems to me that we must take into account the fact, as stated by the different members of this committee, that there are serious differences of opinion upon questions of importance.

We are in a minority in Congress in part because of these divisions, but Mr. Chairman we all wish the Democratic party to come back into power. We will get back when we make up our minds to harmonize these little differences upon mere questions of detail. There must be great liberty of action permitted to members of the party. So long as we agree upon the cardinal principles, we can tolerate minor differences. I have but little respect for the judgment or action of any Democrat who would leave his party or refuse to abide by his party's nominee because of some difference upon some detail of a financial policy. I hope that when our Convention shall have assembled we may all harmonize upon a platform and agree upon a candidate that every Democrat in the Union can vote for.

The Convention should be held at such time as will give ample opportunity after the nomination to prepare for the contest. I do not believe that you could make nominations in the latter part of July or the first of August and then make the campaign an effective one, and I believe it would be folly to fix the date of the Convention prior to the time agreed upon for the Republican Convention at St. Louis. But if we shall meet early in July we can take advantage of whatever mistakes the Republicans may make. Let us have ample time to prepare for this fight and not go into battle until we are ready There can be no disadvantage in giving Democrats an opportunity to deliberate together.

Mr. Chairman, while I will not be a delegate to the Convention, at the same time I have great interest that the gathering will be a harmonious one. I believe that the Democratic creed is broad enough and liberal enough to permit every Democrat, East, West, North and South, to come into the fold and take an active part in the support of whoever we may nominate.

While the outlook today is against us, I think that if we shall meet each other in a spirit of fairness and frankness the clouds will pass away before October next. With a sound platform, broad and liberal, and with good nominations and a united party we can make such a contest as ought to insure success.

Mr. CABLE, of Illinois: Mr. Chairman, I wish to withdraw the amendment I offered of the 14th of July.

THE CHAIR: The date of July 14th is withdrawn.

Mr. SMALLEY, of Vermont: I would like to make a suggestion that can only be taken up by unanimous consent, and that is, that the Secretary be directed to call the roll of States and let each State name the time when it would prefer the Convention to be held.

THE CHAIR: The question has practically resolved itself

MEETING, JANUARY 16, 1896. 19

into one of two dates, June 2 and July 7: The Secretary will proceed to call the roll and, as the Chair understands it, the date receiving the majority vote, will be regarded as the date fixed for holding the Convention.

MR. RANSOM, of North Carolina: Would not the proper way of putting the question be, first, to have the vote on July 7? That will leave an opportunity for further discussion as to the other date.

THE CHAIR: The suggestion is accepted by the Chair; and the vote will be taken on the question whether July 7 shall be the date selected.

The Secretary called the roll of the States and Territories, and the vote resulted as follows:

YEAS—Connecticut, Florida, Idaho, Illinois, Indiana, Iowa, Kentucky, Louisiana, Maine, Maryland, Massachusetts, Mississippi, Nebraska, Nevada, New Hampshire, New Jersey, New York, Ohio, Oregon, Pennsylvania, Rhode Island, South Dakota, Tennessee, Utah, Vermont, Virginia, Washington, West Virginia, Wyoming, Alaska, District of Columbia, Oklahoma.—Total, 32.

NAYS—Alabama, Arkansas, California, Colorado, Delaware, Georgia, Kansas, Michigan, Missouri, Montana, North Carolina, North Dakota, South Carolina, Texas, Wyoming, Arizona, New Mexico, Indian Territory.—Total, 18.

Recapitulation—Yeas, 32; Nays, 18. Necessary to a choice, 26.

NOTE.—Minnesota, not being represented by member or proxy, did not vote.

THE CHAIR: The Secretary will please announce the vote as recorded.

THE SECRETARY: The vote is: Yeas, 32; nays, 18.

THE CHAIR: The Chair understands it that July 7, 1896, is the date fixed by this Committee for holding the next Democratic National Convention.

MR. NIBLACK, of Oklahoma: Mr. Chairman, I beg leave to present the following resolution, which I hope will be adopted by this Committee:

WHEREAS, By resolution duly adopted by the Democratic National Convention of 1892, the Territories of New Mexico and Arizona were allowed six delegates each on the floor of said Convention; and,

WHEREAS, Oklahoma and Indian Territories have each an estimated population of 300,000, or a voting strength of 50,000 each; and,

WHEREAS, It is desirable to avoid a discrimination that would seem un-Democratic in the representation allowed these Territories; therefore be it

Resolved, That it is recommended that in the next Democratic National Convention, the Democrats of Oklahoma and Indian Territories shall be entitled to like representation with Arizona and New Mexico, of six delegates each.

THE CHAIR: What is the pleasure of the Committee with regard to the resolution just read?

MR. NORRIS, of the District of Columbia: I move that they include the District of Columbia, also.

(This motion was duly seconded.)

THE CHAIR: The gentleman from the District of Columbia moves to amend by adding the District of Columbia and the motion as made has been duly seconded.

SENATOR MORGAN, of Alabama: That resolution, as I understand it, is addressed as a petition to the next Convention, is it not?

THE CHAIR: The Chair so understands it.

SENATOR MORGAN, of Alabama: This Committee would have no jurisdiction to change the representation?

THE CHAIR: That is the view the Chair would take of it.

SENATOR GORMAN, of Maryland: The Convention itself fixes the representation, and that has been fixed.

SENATOR MORGAN, of Alabama: Did the last Convention fix the representation for the next one?

SENATOR GORMAN, of Maryland: Yes, sir; that has been the rule from the beginning. Each Convention itself fixes the representation. It has been done and each State should have double the number of——

SENATOR MORGAN, of Alabama: If that is so, then the resolution is out of order, because if the last Convention fixed the basis of representation, we cannot alter it.

SENATOR GORMAN, of Maryland: I think we cannot; with all due deference to the proposer of the resolution, I do not think this is the time for this resolution. At the last Convention, when we met at Chicago, the question regarding New Mexico and Arizona came up. They wanted increased representation. Bills having been passed by the lower House of Congress to admit New Mexico and Arizona, only two days before the Senate passed upon the bill to bring them as states into the Union, they claimed that it was only fair, that as they were practically already states in the Union, they ought to have representation according to the population, and the convention itself acted upon that matter in respect to New Mexico and Arizona, allowing New Mexico and Arizona six votes each, and the Convention itself said it. It is a matter with which the Committee has nothing to do. It is true that just before the action of the Convention, the matter was brought up in the Committee, and in the hurry the resolution was passed. This Committee has nothing whatever to do with it and could not take any action that would be binding at all.

SENATOR BRICE, of Ohio: Let me call the attention of the members of the Committee to something which occurred in a meeting corresponding to this one of the National Committee preceding the Convention of 1892. The meeting was held here, in this room, and the following resolution was offered: (Resolution read.)

When the Committee on Credentials of the National Committee met, after giving their decision of the contested seats, they proceeded, "In the District of Columbia Messrs. James L. Norris and Henry E. Davis are given seats and votes upon this floor. In the Territories of New Mexico and Arizona, it was recommended by the National Committee that each be given six seats upon the floor of this Convention."

MR. THOMAS, of Colorado: The recommendation was made at Chicago.

SENATOR BRICE, of Ohio: Whether it was made there or not the Committee recommended that each be given six delegates on the floor of the Convention. That was the Convention of 1892. After their resolution had been adopted I offered the following resolution to the National Convention:

(Resolution read.)

I want to amend the motion made, so that there will be no distinction in any recommendation to the Convention, but that these territories will be treated all alike.

Mr. Prather, of Missouri: It is an indisputable fact that every Convention has the right to determine the election and qualifications of its members, and that the next Convention will pass upon the delegates from Oklahoma and the District of Columbia, but I believe it to be proper in every way that we at least recommend that these two territories be accorded the same representation that has already been given to the other territories. I see no objection in recommending what has already been given; they should all be placed upon the same footing.

The Chair: It will go before the Convention as the recommendation of this Committee.

Mr. Owen, of Indian Territory: I would like to call the attention of the Committee to the phraseology of the resolution itself. It distinctly states that it is a recommendation. It is not proposed that this Committee shall pass finally upon the apportionment for Indian Territory and Oklahoma, but only the Convention shall make them equal with the territories already cited. Certainly the limitation of this body cannot be so great that the right to recommendation shall be denied them. That is all the Democrats of Indian Territory and Oklahoma ask for, and I would like to make this further suggestion. I am informed from responsible sources that the action already taken by the Republican Committee is to allow that character of representation to the territories, six each, and I hope that the Indian Territory and Oklahoma Democracy will not be confronted with a difference in treatment, not only contrasting them with the territories cited but also the contrast would be drawn between the Democratic organization and the Republican.

Mr. Thomas, of Colorado: Mr. Chairman, I want to say what the delegate from Indian Territory has already said. I think we have a right to recommend whatever we please. When we consider that the District of Columbia, Indian Territory and Oklahoma have a population far in excess of at least two States in the Union, and when we further consider the fact that they have no voice in public affairs, or in the choice of their rulers, it is no more than right and just that in the selection of candidates that they have at least as much representation as the gentleman suggests.

The Chair: The question is first on the amendment offered by the gentleman from the District of Columbia.

Mr. Norris, of the District of Columbia: I understood that to be accepted.

The Chair: The Chair did not so understand it. Did the gentleman from Oklahoma accept the amendment offered by the last gentleman, from the District of Columbia?

Mr. Niblack, of Oklahoma: Yes sir; all amendments are accepted.

The Chair: The vote then will be on the resolution as amended so as to include all the territories. Shall the roll be called?

Several members of the Committee: A viva voce vote. (Which motion to adopt the resolution as amended was put and carried.)

Mr. Howell, of Georgia: So as to expedite matters this afternoon as much as possible, I move that the cities which are to be heard from, that are applicants for the location of the Convention, be requested this afternoon to submit in writing a definite statement of their proposals. I do not wish to preclude by that the verbal statement of the representatives of these cities, but I am informed by persons well acquainted with matters of this kind, that there has been in times past considerable trouble and a good deal of difference between the accommodations actually furnished by the cities where the Convention met and the promises which were made to those Conventions. In order that there may be no misunderstanding about the matter, and so that the Secretary may notify the representatives of these cities during recess, I move that the representatives of these cities be requested to submit with their verbal addresses a definite statement of the proposals of each one, in writing, to be filed with the Secretary.

(This motion was duly seconded and carried.)

Mr. Gorman, of Maryland: I move that the Chair appoint a committee of seven (I think that is the usual number), of which the chairman of this Committee shall be chairman, to have exclusive control of the management of the next Convention, and to issue the usual call for that Convention.

Mr. THOMAS, of Colorado: I would suggest as an amendment that the committee of seven include not only the Chairman, but the Secretary as well.

SENATOR GORMAN, of Maryland: I accept the amendment.

(Which motion was duly seconded and carried.)

Mr. SHERLEY, of Kentucky: It occurs to me that if this matter is left to the sub-committee, this Committee ought to inform the cities before they make their proposition what will be expected. I allude to one particular thing, and that is the hall in which the Convention is to be held. It ought to be understood distinctly that this committee suggested by Mr. Gorman shall have exclusive control over that hall, and the city which secures this Convention must consult with this sub-committee not only as to the hall, but as to the location of your telegraph department, and every detail connected with the proper management and conduct of the Convention. These gentlemen must understand in advance that this Committee must have exclusive control over all these matters.

SENATOR GORMAN, of Maryland: I agree to that also.

THE CHAIR: The question is on the motion offered by the gentleman from Maryland.

(The motion was duly seconded, put and carried.)

Mr. SMALLEY, of Vermont: Would not the appointment of the committee be in order?

THE CHAIR: The Chair will appoint hereafter, at a convenient time, the members of the sub-committee.

Mr. HOWELL, of Georgia: Hadn't we better fix the time we are going to allow each city to present its case? I would suggest that when we adjourn, we adjourn to meet at 3 P. M., and that each city be limited to thirty minutes in which to present its claim.

THE CHAIR: Does the gentleman offer that as a motion—that when we adjourn we adjourn to meet at 3 o'clock this afternoon; and that we will invite the cities to present their respective claims at that time, and that each city is to be limited to thirty minutes?

Mr. HOWELL, of Georgia : Yes sir.

THE CHAIR : The motion practically is, that we take a recess until three o'clock this afternoon; and that the cities, in presenting their respective claims, shall be limited to thirty minutes each.

(This motion was duly seconded, put to a vote and carried.)

MR. CABLE, of Illinois : I move that there be roll call this afternoon of the States to disclose what States have cities desiring the Convention ; and that the delegates of the various cities be heard in the alphabetical order. That is the rule adopted last year, and I believe each city is to be allowed one half hour to present its claim.

THE CHAIR : The motion of the gentleman from Illinois is that at the afternoon session the roll of States shall be called, in order to ascertain what States have cities desiring the Convention ; and that when it has been ascertained definitely what cities in the various States desire it, then that those cities be called alphabetically, and that a half hour each be accorded to such cities as want the Convention.

MR. PASCO, of Florida : I ask in reference to the suggestion made by the gentleman from Georgia, that written propositions be submitted. Is that to be done before or after these addresses are made ? It seems to me that it would be appropriate that these propositions be the basis of the speeches made. I should think we ought to base the right of any city to be heard before this Committee by its presentation of its written promises first.

THE CHAIR : There is a motion before the Committee. In order that there may be no doubt about it, the Chair will repeat the motion offered by the gentleman from Illinois, namely : that the roll of States be called to ascertain what States have cities desiring the Convention, and that the cities be then called alphabetically, giving one-half hour to each city for the presentation of its claims.

(Which motion, duly seconded, was put and carried.)

Motion to adjourn until 3 P. M. duly seconded, was put and carried.

(Recess until 3 o'clock P. M.)

AFTERNOON SESSION, 3 P. M.

OPEN SESSION.

The Chair: The meeting will be in order, please. The Sergeant-at-Arms will see that the doors are closed so that we may have quiet.

Ladies and Gentlemen: In pursuance of the order of business established by this Committee, the roll of States will be called for the purpose of definitely ascertaining the States that desire the Convention, to be held within their borders. After the call of the roll, and after it has been definitely and finally ascertained what cities desire the Convention, the cities themselves will be called in alphabetical order, and each city will be given one-half hour in which to present reasons why the Convention should be held in that city. After that, and after the gentlemen have been heard in support of their claims of their respective cities, the Committee will go into executive session, in order to determine in which city the Convention shall be held. The suggestion of the Chair is that when that stage shall have been reached that the speaking is to begin, the Chairman of the delegation representing each city shall indicate the number of gentlemen who are to speak, and the order in which they are to speak, always bearing in mind that each city is limited to thirty minutes.

The Secretary will kindly call the roll of States, and the member of each State having a city desiring the Convention, will indicate to the Secretary the name of the city.

The Secretary called the roll of States to Illinois.

The Secretary then called the State of Illinois.

Mr. Cable, of Illinois: Mr. Chairman, the State of Illinois will offer to the Committee the City of Chicago, and desires that that place be named for the holding of the Convention.

The Chair: The City of Chicago is named by Illinois.

(The Secretary continued the call of the roll of States to Missouri.)

The Secretary then called the State of Missouri.

COL. PRATHER, of Missouri: Missouri names St. Louis.

THE CHAIR: St. Louis is named by Missouri.

(The Secretary continued the call of the roll of States to New York.)

The Secretary called the State of New York.

GOV. SHEEHAN, of New York: New York names the City of New York.

THE CHAIR: Gov. Sheehan of New York names the city of New York.

(The Secretary continued the call of the roll of States to Ohio.)

The Secretary called the State of Ohio.

SENATOR BRICE, of Ohio: Mr. Chairman, the State of Ohio names the City of Cincinnati.

THE CHAIR: The City of Cincinnati is named by the State of Ohio.

(The Secretary concluded the call of the roll of the States.)

THE CHAIR: Under the order of the Committee, the cities named will be heard in alphabetical order, namely, Chicago, Cincinnati, New York and St. Louis.

The Chair will be glad to hear from the gentleman from Illinois, as to the order of speaking by the representatives of Chicago.

MR. CABLE, of Illinois: The claims of Chicago will be presented by one speaker, Judge Goodrich.

THE CHAIR: The ladies and gentlemen and the Committee will be glad to hear from Judge Goodrich.

ADDRESS OF JUDGE ADAMS A. GOODRICH

ON BEHALF OF THE CITY OF CHICAGO.

Mr. Chairman, and Gentlemen of the Democratic National Committee: I am delegated by the citizens of Chicago, without respect to party, to extend to the Democratic National Committee and through it to the National Democratic party a cordial and hearty invitation to hold the next National Democratic Convention within the borders of that city. It will not take, gentlemen of the Committee, a half hour for me to state the reasons why you should hold that convention in Chicago. Most of you have heard the reasons given before, and the reasons exist to-day, as they have for years, only to a greater extent. We invite you, gentlemen of the Committee, upon the terms and conditions and with all the guarantees required by the Democratic National Committee. It is needless for me to say that Chicago, as she has always done, will fulfill every guaranty that she makes. With none but the kindest feelings for every other city entered in this contest, with a feeling only of generous rivalry, yet with a feeling of modesty which always becomes Chicago (laughter) we claim to be the best convention city in the United States. We claim that we have better facilities than any other city for entertaining the vast crowds that will assemble at that time. I mean not only the delegates and the alternates who will compose that convention, but the vast crowd of Democrats who will come there for the purpose of seeing that the work of the convention is well done. The transportation facilities of Chicago, it is needless for me to say, are unsurpassed. It is the great inland city of this continent. All railroads run to Chicago. Since the last Democratic convention was held in Chicago that city has entertained the world. At the great World's Fair we entertained more people than were ever entertained in a similar length of time in any other city. I leave it to you to say whether or not we did it well. This convention is invited to Chicago, as I said, without any feeling of partisanship, but on behalf of all the people. The Democracy of Chicago, the Democracy of Illinois, do not need the stimulus of this convention to do their duty. Whether it be held in Chicago or elsewhere the Democracy of that great State will be found in the campaign of 1896 doing its duty as it always has done. (Applause.)

Gentlemen, if you want to win, come to Chicago. You have never elected and seated a Democratic President who was not nominated in that city since 1856. (Applause.) Come this year to Chicago and I believe the people of this country will again ratify your action and elect a Democratic President in November next. We have agreed on the part of the hotel-keepers in that city that the rates shall be the usual ordinary rates. We will furnish you a hall of such size as the sub-committee of the Democratic National Committee may see fit to call upon us to provide. We will give you every facility of every kind. We will receive you with a generous hospitality. On behalf of that peerless city resting upon the shores of a great inland sea, I heartily and cordially invite you to come to Chicago. (Applause.)

THE CHAIR: Cincinnati will now have an opportunity to show cause why the Convention should be held there.

SENATOR BRICE, of Ohio: The claims of the city of Cincinnati will be presented by Mr. M. E. Ingalls and Judge John F. Follett. Mr. Ingalls, I now introduce.

THE CHAIR: Ladies and gentlemen and members of the committee, Mr. M. E. Ingalls of Ohio.

ADDRESS OF MR. M. E. INGALLS, OF CINCINNATI.

Gentlemen of the Democratic National Committee: I have faced a good many Democratic audiences, but this is the first time I ever appeared before the National Committee. We have among the members of our delegation men celebrated for their learning, for their eloquence and for their Democracy, but, after due consideration they thought as this was more a business question than anything else that it should be presented by a business man and not by an orator or a statesman. This is my apology for coming before you. If I fail in my duty to-day it will be, perhaps, because I am not familiar with your ways, and it may be due to the intense interest which I have for my own city of Cincinnati and my love for Democracy. I hope to have the merit of the gentleman who just preceded me of being brief. I will try to present the claims of our city with malice toward none and charity for all. As I understand it, there are two questions involved in this proceeding: one is a business question, whether the city of Cincinnati shall be chosen as the city in which to hold the Democratic National Convention, and the other is a political question, whether or not it is advisable for the Democrats to hold their convention in that city. I will endeavor to confine myself to both questions so as to present the matter before you in a manner that they may be considered and fairly decided by you.

Cincinnati has had no National Convention since 1880. In the meantime a new city has grown up on the banks of the Ohio and her people, without regard to political creed, age, sex or condition, decided they would invite the Democratic National Committee to hold the National Convention there. They wanted to have the Republican Convention there, too, but the price was a little too high. (Laughter.) Furthermore, we thought we would be generous to St. Louis.

We have, in the first place, the best hall in the world for a political convention. We have not a hall twice as large as the prairies around Chicago or the levees around St. Louis, but it is a hall that will hold ten thousand Democrats, and that is as many as ever will go to any convention. It will seat comfortably—every man having as good a seat as each of you here to-day—a trifle over 6,000, 4,354 in the auditorium and over 1,500 on the stage. We are spending now $100,000 to improve its acoustic properties, and there is not one nook or corner in the hall where any speaker with a reasonable voice can not be heard. It has large aisles, large areas where standing room can be used to enlarge its seating capacity, and that is where we can accommodate the other four thousand people, if you wish. But we will take care of 6,000 people and make them as comfortable as you are in this room. This hall is lighted by electricity. It has reception rooms and committee rooms; connected with it are two other buildings under the same roof. We will arrange for a restaurant to be located adjoining your committee rooms, where you can get your refreshments without going outside of the building, and if it is like any former Democratic Convention we will take care of some of you after the convention is over. (Laughter.) We have as good railroad facilities as there are in the world. We have leading to the South the great trunk lines that traverse every part of that country. We have going to the east and the west the largest trunk lines of America, and there is no city on earth that can be reached by so many Democrats, so comfortably, so easily and in such a short space of time, as the city of Cincinnati. People will tell you how hot a city Cincinnati is in summer and the representatives of New York will doubtless talk to you about the sea breezes. Ohio is a hot country in the summer time. I do not know of any place in July, when you propose to hold this convention, that is not liable to be hot; but I will guarantee, if you have ever struck a hot day in Chicago or New York, that you will never find anything like it in Cincinnati. We do not keep that kind of weather.

We have the transportation facilities and the facilities to accommodate you all. Speaking of the facilities for accommodation I am reminded of the story of a man in Cincinnati who keeps a hotel. When asked how many people he could accommodate, he said: "Well, if they come from New York about one hundred; if they come from Kentucky, if the bar is large enough, I can take care of a thousand." If, gentlemen, you are real good Democrats, when night comes you wont care much about any bed. (Laughter.) You would just waste the hours in sleep; you would rather wait until you get home. I have had a hotel man from Cincinnati figure up for me the hotel capacity of our city. In the first place, I want to say to those of you who were there in 1880 that since then the Grand Hotel, the Burnett and the Gibson have all been enlarged. Since then the new hotels erected inside the city limits make the number fifteen. Outside of the city on the hills we have a large and beautiful hotel. The St. Nicholas has trebled its size. The capacity of the hotels of Cincinnati at a conservative estimate is 11,400 guests. If you bring 10,000 Democrats to Cincinnati it will be enough for any convention.

We have in the month of July one of the handsomest cities on earth. We will show you the best paved, the best cleaned city in America, the best public buildings of any city in America. We will show you more than 400 miles of the finest street railroad system on earth. We will show you suburbs such as no other city outside of Boston can boast of.

I hope that gentlemen from the other cities will pardon me if I criticise them slightly. In the first place, regarding St. Louis there is an insuperable objection, and that is we never want to fish in water that has been muddled by the Republicans.

Chicago has had the convention for the last two or three times. We have heard the same old argument that it was a convention city, but down in your hearts do your feelings respond to that claim? Does the recollection of your experiences there justify you in accepting that statement? As to New York, that city is one of the finest in the world (applause from New York delegates), but last summer I had occasion to hold a railroad meeting down at Coney Island. It was a pleasant place, but when I came to pay the hotel proprietor I parted with him with tears in my eyes, because I knew I would never have money enough to go there again.

The great question overshadowing every other now, is the financial question. Do you suppose that there is any power, human or divine, that can write a platform in New York which will be accepted in the West? It will be rung on you that the money changers have written your platform. It will be a false cry, a demagogical cry, but why should you take such a risk as that? Recently a gentleman said to me that he was for free silver and for that reason you must go to St. Louis. My friends, that question has got to be decided upon neutral ground where you will all have fair play. You want time to consider that question. Let the free silver people from the West and the gold bugs from the East meet with us and have it out.

Gentlemen, don't make the mistake of going to a place where you will be criticised, where you will find that your convention is overshadowed by a howling mob (as it was in Chicago), but hold your convention in Cincinnati, where you can have entire control over your convention, and deliberate without fear of outside influence of any kind. At Cincinnati you will be on neutral ground. Our invitation comes not from Democrats alone, but from every citizen of the Queen City of the West. We want to show you that we have not been idle for fifteen years; we want to show you that we have the finest city for a convention in this country. Our hearts will go out warm to you. Our hospitality will be so generous, we will take such good care of you, that your stay will be long and pleasantly remembered. You will be sorry to go, and wish to return. (Applause.)

SENATOR BRICE, of Ohio: I announce Judge John F. Follett, of Cincinnati.

THE CHAIR: Judge Follett of Ohio.

ADDRESS OF JUDGE JOHN F. FOLLETT

ON BEHALF OF THE CITY OF CINCINNATI.

Gentlemen of the National Committee: It is a pleasure to a Democrat to invite the National Convention of his party to be held in the community where he lives, and more especially at this time in view of the importance of the convention which is to be held this year, not because I expect the holding of the convention in Cincinnati will make any difference in the vote, but because I know that in Cincinnati your deliberations will not be interfered with and you will have an opportunity to hold your councils together and reach your conclusions without any attempt at outside interference. What Democracy wants is, we believe, that calm, deliberate consideration and judgment that shall commend itself to the people of the United States. We are right on the border between what was once the North and the South. We are right at the center of population of the United States. We have all the facilities for taking care of the convention that any city in the United States has. I do not mean as ample, but ample enough. If you come to Cincinnati you will not be lost in the swim; you will not be overlooked; you will not be in a city where the people will not know whether there is anything going on or not. It will be the pride of every citizen to make your stay there not only pleasant, but as cheerful as it is possible to be. (Applause.)

It has been said that Cincinnati is a hot city. There are hot days there and if any gentleman of this committee has been in the summer time in any of the cities designated and has not found a hot day he has been more fortunate than I have. I think the only time in my life that I was ever apprehensive of sunstroke was in New York in 1876. I know that our sister cities in the West share with us the discomforts of heat when the weather is hot; but we have a number of resorts in the immediate vicinity where we can cool you off if it becomes necessary by reason of heated discussions arising while the convention is in session.

I have heard it charged many times that the Democratic party is simply a follower of the Republicans. I do not want to be fed on the crumbs that fall from their table. I do not think for success this year it is necessary for the Democratic party to be fed on those crumbs. I expect after the election is over in November to see the Democratic party resting in the bosom of the people and looking down to hear the wail of the Republican party calling for a drop of water. (Applause.) I am not a Democrat who ever gets discouraged. I am an Ohio Democrat. (Applause.) I am one who has got accustomed to being beaten. We are as ready after defeat as we ever were before to engage in the contest again, and that is because we believe that we represent the party of the people and the party that will live while the government lasts and the rights of the people are preserved.

Come to Cincinnati. Let us help you to deliberate calmly and without any interference whatsoever. Come to the point that stands midway between the east and the west. Adopt your platform and again put afloat the grand old ship of state properly mastered and then we will all join in the grand ovation, "Sail on, O ship of state; sail on, O Union strong and great," etc.

Gentlemen, we ask for this convention because we want it. We are here because we want it. If we do not satisfy you that of all the other cities in the Union Cincinnati is triumphantly a convention city, we will not be here again to trouble you. (Applause.)

THE CHAIR: From the announcement made by Mr. Ingalls of the failure of Cincinnati to invite the Republican Convention to be held within its borders, it is apparent that he and his associates consider and treat political Conventions in about the same way they do their business matters. If it were suggested that he and his friends should buy a railroad he would promptly inquire into its bonded and floating indebtedness, etc., and not being satisfied as to its financial condition, the proposition would be declined with thanks. They probably inquired as to the financial condition of the Republican National Committee, only to learn that that committee was looking for a city that would make up a very considerable deficiency. It is quite likely that they also made some inquiries with reference to the condition of the affairs of the Democratic National Committee. If they did they found that organization without any liabilities whatever. (Applause.) They likewise found it without any assets, except its political principles and the fidelity and loyalty of its people.

Gentlemen of the Committee, it is quite likely that New York has some reasons why the Convention should be held there, and the gentlemen representing New York will now be accorded an opportunity of presenting her claims.

GOV. SHEEHAN, of New York: The claims of New York will be presented by Mr. G. Waldo Smith, President of the National Wholesale Grocers Association; by Mr. Simeon D. Ford, representing the hotels; by Mr. Crane and by Col. John R. Fellows, and in that order.

THE CHAIR: The ladies and gentlemen who are present and the committee will be glad to hear the gentlemen in the order named. Please, gentlemen, remember the limitation of time.

ADDRESS OF G. WALDO SMITH, OF NEW YORK.

Gentlemen of the National Democratic Committee: I appear before you in behalf of the New York Board of Trade and Transportation and other commercial bodies of the City of New York. I wish that I had the wisdom of Solomon and the eloquence of Demosthenes, in order that I might know just what to say, and just how to say such words as would impress you with the importance of my theme. But as I have not, I can only say a few plain things in a few plain and simple words.

New York is not only the greatest American city, but it is also the greatest commercial city on earth. This fact has always been so well known, not only to New Yorkers, but to all the world, that New York people have rarely thought it worth while to even mention the fact. Hence, unlike other cities, she has never told of her greatness, nor vaunted herself.

The population of New York City proper has not quite reached the two million point, but take the population of the six cities that make up the greater New York, all contiguous to each other, not a vacant lot intervening, and we have a compact city of four million inhabitants in all except the name. New York has such capacity for entertainment that I once heard Mr. Depew say that a million people came to New York to attend the great Centennial celebration, and no one was crowded, and a million people went away, and no one missed them. Many people are exceptionally afraid of a crowd, but there never has been a crowd in New

York City, there never can be, there never will be; there is room enough for all.

The New York newspaper is the greatest press on earth, and with its enormous dailies, its numerous pictorial weeklies and monthlies, it reaches not only every city, but every town and village in America, and indeed every place on earth where English speaking people can be found; this would be worth as much to any political party as large sums of money spent in circulating campaign documents.

New York has more large and magnificent stores, and on exhibition a greater variety of all the products of the earth, the loom, the factory, and the laboratory, than any other city in the country. It is not only the Paris of America, but it is the Paradise of ladies as well, and nearly all the beautiful and wonderful things that were exhibited at the World's Fair, in Chicago, can be found in New York City. In fact New York is a world's fair exhibition such as cannot be found in any other place in the world. Even the celebrated "Midway Plaisance" of Chicago is found in fact at our Coney Island, only thirty minutes away from our City Hall. Large numbers of delegates and others who will attend the Convention are merchants who make regular trips to New York for business purposes, and who could thus combine public business, private business and pleasure at greatly reduced expense.

New York harbor is the grandest harbor in the world, and the numerous vessels continually arriving and departing make it the grandest sight that human eyes can behold. A few days since I stood where I had a range of vision covering but a small portion of the harbor, and yet I counted one hundred and eleven moving vessels, including ocean greyhounds and four-masted ships. It is a sight worth coming from the foot hills of the Sierra Nevadas to see. The real ocean greyhound, of which only a model was exhibited at Chicago, may be found at any one of sixty piers on our North River front. The real "White Squadron," of which only a model was exhibited at Chicago, to the wonderment of those who saw it, can be found across our East River at our Brooklyn Navy Yard, an enduring testimony of the efficiency, patriotism and foresight of our esteemed fellow citizen, William C. Whitney, late Secretary of the Navy.

We have the most numerous and the most elegant places of amusement of any city on earth, and all the world's best artists can always be seen and heard. Our Park roads are crowded with the most elegant equipages that can be seen at any place on earth, affording a sight that will delight the eye of the wives and daughters of the delegates. We have finer seaside resorts, and more of them, and we have a thousand miles of seashore within three hours of New York, with elegant hotels that will accommodate hundreds of thousands of people, and the greatest charm of all is found in the fact that the Atlantic Ocean washes the shore at our very feet.

A week spent in New York and intelligently spent, seeing the best it has to show, and learning the best it has to teach, is a university course and a liberal education. New York is but five hours from the capital at Washington, and I take it for granted that every patriotic

American citizen desires not only to see the metropolis of America, but also the capital of the nation, with its magnificent public buildings, its broad avenues and its palatial residences. If the convention is held in a western city, this privilege can only be enjoyed at greatly increased expense, because delegates will not have the advantage of reduced rates to these cities as they will from their homes to the place where the convention is held. New York is one of the cleanest, also one of the healthiest of cities. It is entirely surrounded by deep, swift-running saltwater, and is swept by ocean breezes, and I know of no city that will compare with it for average summer coolness, especially when we remember that we can leave the city and in one hour be sporting with Neptune in the cooling waters of the sea.

New York has the best telegraphic facilities on earth, as it is the centre of the entire system, and the point from which the telegraphic business radiates to all points of the compass.

Only one national convention has ever been held in New York City, and all the delegates from Eastern and Middle States have been compelled to travel West and South in order to attend these quadrennial gatherings. Hence it would seem, in common justice, as if it were New York's turn. It will be urged that Western cities are more central, and while this is true geographically, yet I believe that if a careful estimate were made it would show that all the delegates could reach New York with an aggregate of less miles of travel than they could reach any place in the Mississippi Valley.

I engaged an expert accountant to make an estimate of what proportion of our population lived within twenty-five hours, or less, of New York, with the following result: Taking the census of 1890, which gives a population of 62,968,448, there are living in New York, 3,394,000; within two hours or less of New York, 5,510,000; within six hours, or less, of New York, 10,531,000; within twelve hours of New York, 18,712,000; within twenty-five hours of New York, 34,653,000. Living beyond the twenty-five hour limit, 27,968,000, showing also that about 35,000,000 of our population occupy about one-seventh of our entire territory, while only 28,000,000 occupy the remaining six-sevenths of our territory. It is about time that the 28,000,000 visited the homes of the 34,000,000, and return the numerous visits which they have received from the people of the East.

Madison Square Garden will seat more people than any other fireproof building on earth. It has separate convention headquarters for every State and Territory in the United States. It is situated in the very heart of the city, on a fine park, within from one to twenty minutes of enough hotels to accommodate all visitors without putting two in a bed, or even two in a room. New York receives the finest and freshest food products of the earth, both from land and sea, and the cuisine of our hotels is the best that the markets of the world can provide, and skill prepare.

In conclusion, gentlemen, I beg to extend to you, on behalf of the merchants and the citizens of New York generally, without regard to party affiliations, a most earnest invitation to hold your National Convention in our city. We will give you a right royal welcome, worthy of the metropolis. We will provide you with accommodations and facilities that cannot be approached in any other city, and if you come to New York, you will be so thoroughly satisfied that, I venture to predict, the question of where the Democratic National Convention shall meet will be settled for all time, and that no other place than the great metropolis of America will ever be thought of thereafter.

ADDRESS OF SIMEON FORD,

Proprietor Of The Grand Union Hotel, New York City.

Mr. Chairman and Gentlemen of the Committee: Mr. Straus suggested that your committee should be addressed by what he was pleased to term a "plain up-and-down New York hotel-keeper;" and as I am undoubtedly the "plainest" facially and the most "up-and-down" architecturally of all the landlords, I have been selected.

Fortunately for me, landlords are not expected to be intellectual. (Laughter.) Brains are not required in our business. All we have to do is to open our hotels and the boarders will tell us how to run 'em. (Great applause and laughter.) We landlords hope to have this convention held in New York first, because we believe it is the best place for it; second, for the honor of our metropolis, of which we are loyal citizens; third, because it is to be held at a time of year when our great hotels are well-nigh empty and it will give us a chance to make an *honest* dollar—with the accent on the *honest*—and likewise give us an opportunity to entertain and care for the delegates and visitors in a way novel in the history of National political conventions, and which would redound to the credit of New York and her hotel keepers.

I will not attempt to recite the glories of New York. That has already been done by a tongue of silver and by a lung of brass. (Laughter.) Besides, you have all been there before, many a time, and probably know more about the city than we do.

You have already heard and have still to hear the most dazzling accounts of the beauties and glories of other cities. But of what avail are all these beauties and glories to the weary delegate if he must spend his nights fitfully slumbering upon a billiard table, or uneasily tossing within the narrow confines of a hotel bath-tub? (Laughter.)

I admit that there may be some delegates who would not be seriously injured by spending a night or two in a bath-tub. I understand that the Honorable Chauncey M. Depew slept in one at Minneapolis, and I presume it was of benefit to him; but the ordinary delegate naturally prefers to "wrap the drapery of his couch about him and lie down to pleasant dreams;" and you can't blame him.

To such I would say that New York is the only city in the land that can give every visitor to a National Convention a comfortable bed—at night. Our motto is "Excelsior," but we don't force our motto into our hair mattresses.

> "Sleep sweetly in this quiet room
> O thou, whoe'er thou art,
> And let no mournful yesterday
> Disturb thy peaceful heart."

This sentiment doubtless sounds strained to delegates who have been accustomed to sleeping four in a bed and two in a bureau at conventions, but New York is a big town and has big hotels and lots of 'em.

New York has more hotel accommodations than the cities of Chicago, Cincinnati and St. Louis combined. Lest I be accused of boasting, I will not dwell upon their merits, but content myself with the modest assertion that they are the best and finest in the world.

We have fine hotels for fine people; good hotels for good people, plain hotels for plain people and a few bum hotels for bums; but we do not expect the latter to be patronized or to come into requisition during the convention.

We have heard some very glowing descriptions of western cities from gentlemen here and in the lobbies, and especially the most entrancing tales of the beauties of the Union Depot of St. Louis. I spent two days at St. Louis once, during one of those crisp, frosty spells which they describe as being so prevalent there in the month of July (laughter), and when I got to the Union Depot bound for New York, I admit that it was the most beautiful and welcome sight that ever gladdened my eyes. Now we have a number of depots in New York (most of which are located in Hoboken, New Jersey); but were they as fair as Alladin's palace you would not enjoy seeing them, for your heart would be heavy at the thought of leaving our beautiful City by the Sea.

Chicago has a sign in front of her headquarters which reads, "Most of the delegates pass through Chicago on their way here." Can you blame 'em? (Laughter.)

We have to 'pass through' lots of uncomfortable things in life—teething, measles and mumps—but why remind us of them? While it is true that most of the delegates have gone through Chicago, Chicago, it is equally true, has gone through most of the delegates. (Laughter.)

Gentlemen of the Committee, come down to salt water and hold the next Democratic National Convention, and the hotel-keepers of our city pledge themselves, through me, to treat you and all who come with you with absolute justice and fairness. We agree not to increase our prices one iota. We are accustomed to handling large gatherings and we have yet to hear a complaint of extortion against a New York landlord. You will find us hail fellows, men of fair dealing, to be relied upon. We make you this pledge and we will live up to it to the letter, and when you are ready to return to your homes, which you will do with regret, you will sigh with the poet Shenstone:

> "Who 'er has traveled life's dull round,
> Where'er his stages may have been,
> May sigh to think he still has found,
> The warmest welcome at an inn."

MEETING, JANUARY 16, 1896.

ADDRESS OF T. C. T. CRAIN

ON BEHALF OF NEW YORK.

Mr. Chairman and Gentlemen of the Committee: It seems to me that a very plain and a very direct question is presented to us for our consideration and for your determination, and it is really this: In which city would it be best for the Democratic party—considering it from the standpoint of party expediency, considering it from the standpoint of our party's success—to hold the next Democratic Convention?

We are here not so much to discuss the beauties of different cities, not even so much to discuss the question of the comforts and the conveniences to be had in the different cities as we are to determine the plain and practical question, in which city would it be best from the standpoint of the success of our party to hold the next Democratic Convention? Now, it is possible that some member of the committee may say, or some member of the committee may think, that it does not make very much difference in what city the convention shall be held so far as the success of the Democratic party is concerned in the coming campaign. I regard the very fact, Mr. Chairman, that this question is up for consideration at this time; the very fact that it is receiving the thoughtful consideration of earnest men; the very fact that it is being presented by the representatives of different cities; the very fact that it has always in the past history of our party received careful consideration, as a conclusive demonstration that it is of importance in its relation to our party's welfare whether we shall hold our convention in one city rather than in another. The reasons which make this question important are easily stated. They will readily occur to you all. To demonstrate the fact that it is important requires merely a statement of the difference between choosing the most expedient, the most convenient and the most accessible place on the one hand, or, on the other hand, of choosing a place confessedly inconvenient, confessedly remote and confessedly inexpedient. I shall, therefore, at the very threshold present this question in the light of political expediency and it is along this line rather than any other that I intend to submit a few considerations to the gentlemen of the committee.

We have heard from the gentlemen representing Cincinnati of the intention to improve their auditorium. Very likely it requires improvement. We have heard the fact mentioned in somewhat mixed phrase that the delegates will be there "*taken in*," whatever that may mean; but in a discussion of the question of the political advantages to accrue from the holding of the convention in Cincinnati rather than in any other city we have heard only this singular, this strange, this anomalous, this unreasonable argument advanced that it must be held there because it should be held upon neutral ground upon the financial question.

I have heard it stated, and it has been a matter of current rumor in the lobbies of the hotel here, that certain gentlemen were urging that the silver question entered into the consideration of a selection of the place, and that the members of this very committee were going to be influenced one way or another along the very lines of the argument laid down in the speech of one of the speakers representing the City of Cincinnati. I can hardly credit it. It seems too astounding. It seems to me to be like an affront, if I may use that word, to the intelligence and the judgment of those sterling Democrats and men of political experience who have been selected in every State and Territory as the representatives of our party in the National Committee.

Then I have heard the charge about Wall street dominating a convention held in the City of New York. Why, if that influence is so great, if that influence is so harmful, should it not be rather harmful to the democracy of the city in which the street is located? St. Louis sometimes has gone other than Democratic. In Chicago they have fought many a desperate struggle to hold aloft the banner of our party; but in the City of New York, where they tell us that the money influence militates against the strength of the party, we find it triumphant in the hour of national defeat, and when in other portions of the country it is in despair. We are always the band of Democrats upon whom the whole party from east to west relies in the hour of emergency. (Applause.)

The gold influence of New York detrimental to the Democratic party? Mr. Chairman, ask the treasurer of the Democratic National Committee during the hours of a trying campaign if it is not out of the doors of the offices on Wall street and out of the doors of its banking institutions that the gold rolls and the money is poured into the coffers of the party to enable us to preach Democratic doctrine in the west? What, the wealth of New York and the gold of New York against Democratic doctrine? I hardly think that argument will receive serious consideration.

Some of these gentlemen tell us that New York City does not require a Democratic convention because the people of the City of New York have been tried and found so true and so steadfast in their Democracy. There have been times in our political history when men have seemed to think it wise to put a slight upon those sections of the country the political principles of whose people were firmly grounded, and have seemed to think it wise to pacify those sections where the people seem most doubtful. I confess that it has always seemed to me to be of the very essence of political wisdom to encourage and build up the party in its strongholds, but I will meet the gentlemen on their own ground. Suppose you are right. Suppose the convention ought to go to some State that is trembling in the balance. What of the State of New York? I venture to predict that the next Republican candidate for the presidency will be selected from the State of New York. Every influence that the Republican party can bring to bear will be brought to bear to swing that State from the Democratic column into the Republican column. This is the time above every other time when, if the political parties in the State of New York are evenly matched, we should hold the Democratic Convention in the City of New York. Consider the influence of it. Consider the influence of it upon the surrounding States; the influence of it upon the State of New Jersey and upon the State of Connecticut, which are debatable grounds.

Let me tell you another thing: the newspapers of the City of New

York, and I say it advisedly, to a greater extent than perhaps any other city circulate in every section of the country. They will contain fuller and ampler accounts necessarily of the proceedings of the convention if held in the very city in which they are published. This of itself is an argument in favor of the City of New York.

Gentlemen, you who come from the South, members of this committee from Southern States, remember what the City of New York has done for the South. We stood by you in Congress on the question of the Force Bill, and time and time again the press of the State of New York has been found faithful on all issues which are purely Southern. I appeal to you by the bond of that memory. I appeal to one and all of you in the interest of the Democratic party to consider whether your party's success is not a greater question than the question of the free coinage of silver or any other subsidiary question. Let us ask ourselves the single question, in what manner can we best promote the success of our party? If there is some one who is hesitating between two opinions, I ask him to lay local pride aside and, independent of local feeling, to act solely for the preservation of Democratic principles.

ADDRESS OF HON. JOHN R. FELLOWS

ON BEHALF OF THE CITY OF NEW YORK.

Mr. Chairman and Gentlemen of the Committee: A citizen's committee of the City of New York have desired me to express their wish that the next Democratic Convention shall be held in that city. My politics are fairly well known to many of these gentlemen and I do not deem it essential that, in the very brief remarks I shall make, I should enter the domain of political discussion in the least. All that has been admirably done by those who have preceded me. I speak solely in the name of the citizens of New York, irrespective of party. These gentlemen, with most commendable spirit and liberality, have raised such a fund as will be necessary in any place where the convention may be located to furnish the requisite accommodations to the Committee and to make comfortable those who shall be present as the representatives of the party throughout the nation. In this contribution all alike have joined, Republicans and Democrats. It has not been in the slightest a party movement. It is a spontaneous request; the wish and desire of our entire population. New York has been generously treated in regard to the time allowed for the discussion of its merits and to present its claims for your consideration. Therefore I should be a trespasser if I traveled over the ground which has already been so well covered by those who have spoken before me. I will not speak at any length of the perfect character of the accommodations that can be extended to delegates in the City of New York. Nearly every one knows them. Every person in this hall has at one time or another visited that city, and they know well that in this respect there is no place upon this continent which for one moment can present a claim of that kind in comparison with the City of New York.

I have listened to what has been stated with regard to the other cities and I believe that the gentlemen who represent those cities will, to the best extent of which they are capable, see that everybody is made as comfortable as possible. But their capacities are inadequate. Every gentleman here knows that we have been attending conventions for the past twenty years of our history in which we have been crowded to the point of extreme and almost insufferable inconvenience. Everyone knows that in the great city of the interior, the only rival in population and in extent of the City of New York, the hotel accommodations are utterly and absolutely inadequate to the wants of the convention in so far as preserving the comfort of the individual man goes.

In the city of New York you have already received the assurance of a body of gentlemen who have never yet failed to keep their promises, that there shall be no advancement of hotel rates, no extortion or increase whatsoever. In the name of our hotel proprietors and in behalf of our citizens, and in behalf of the Citizens' Committee who all desire this convention, we promise that each delegate shall have the accommodation of a separate room, a place alone by himself, if he desires it, with no increase whatsoever in the hotel rates. There is no other city in the Union in which that is possible. Cincinnati has told you that she has hotel accommodations for 10,000. Within five minutes walk of Madison Square Garden, the hall in which the convention will be held if the convention shall come to our city, there is hotel accommodation for more than 20,000 people upon just such terms as I have suggested. In that immediate neighborhood I will mention the Imperial Hotel, the Grand Hotel, the Hoffman House, the Brunswick, the Fifth Avenue, the Union Square, and, but a short distance away, the Grand Union Hotel, worthily represented by the gentleman who, with inimitable humor, has presented the cause of the hotel-men. In the hotels I have mentioned and others the names of which for the moment I do not recall, more than 20,000 guests can be accommodated upon the terms I have mentioned. The whole City of New York at any time can provide for 100,000 visitors in its midst with separate rooms, separate beds and with all the accommodations of hotels unequaled in their character.

Now, whatever may be the merits of other cities, one claim is at least our own, and that is that in the summer during the heated term, all of you know our opportunity for going within thirty minutes from the crowded city to the numerous seaside resorts which have accommodations for from 250,000 to 300,000 people. That number of people can in thirty minutes go from their places of business to their hotels and cottages upon the sea shore, which is a benefit which no other city in this country can extend to its visitors.

More than that, we have a hall which is simply unequalled in this country. It has been told you that it will seat 15,000 people—16,000, to be accurate, is its seating capacity—and 10,000 more can easily be accommodated. Its acoustic properties are magnificent. It was originally prepared for concerts and it has been tested by the voices of our most distinguished singers and speakers. It is one of the best halls for convention purposes that exists. It is not a structure to be erected; it is not a temporary building to be torn down after the convention is over with all the inadequate accommodations that such a structure affords; but it is a permanent building and one of the grandest specimens of architecture that the country possesses. It is in the very heart of the city within a stone's throw of Madison Square, resting, indeed, upon the northern extremity of the park and exceedingly convenient to every important location. We can give you in that hall a separate committee room of ample size for each of the forty-five states and the territories. There is no other hall in the country that can do that or that can do anything in comparison with it. So that if it is requisite that a delegation should meet for consultation at various periods during the sitting of the convention they may go into these reception rooms without going from under the roof in which the convention itself is held. We will decorate that room in any manner the committee may prescribe in order to make it attractive to our visitors. We will supply—what all cities will supply so far as that goes—the music, the telegraph accommodations, ample resources for the press; and all these will be at the expense not of the Democratic party but of the citizens of New York. We are here to extend an invitation, not to bid at an auction. It matters not what those expenses are; they will be fully met. You have heard from the political part of New York; you have heard from the hotel-men; you have heard from its great trade organizations, but on behalf of the Citizen's Committee I undertake now to pledge to this committee that, if the question of railroad expenditures is a hindrance in the way of securing us this convention, we are prepared now to make the railroad rates from the extremest point of this country to the City of New York as low as they would be to any central city in our country. It shall cost the delegate from Washington, Oregon, California and the extremest part of the South no more to come to the city of New York than it would cost him to go to the central city nearest to his residence. This we are prepared to do because it is only proper that the people of a great city, desiring the honor of an assemblage like this, should do as much for their visitors. New York's hospitality and liberality are too well known to need me to advert to it in your presence. You have never called upon her in any hour or situation of calamity or disaster that any portion of our country has experienced when she has not responded with a limitless generosity. (Applause.) She is prepared to extend and she pledges herself to extend to you a welcome that no other city in this Union is capable of, conceding to them the most earnest desire to do their best. New York is better equipped for the convention than other city but we are deserving of some inspiration at your hands. Why, gentlemen, in your hour of defeat, when the heart of the Democracy all over this Union was bowed down, you have received encouragement from the city of New York. You talk of Democratic faith. Where has it ever been kept so completely and left as vigorous and active as in the City of New York? One after another of the States have been prostrated under the blows of our enemy. One after another of our cities to which we are accustomed to look for large majorities have gone down in the dust, but New York City stands to-day, as she is prepared to stand through all the future, never having given her vote to any but a Democratic candidate; and I pledge now for the next Democratic candidate a majority in that city which will carry him safely through the Empire State. (Applause.)

Where is the locality that has shown as much recuperative power to lift itself up above adverse influences? A year ago we almost fell under the stroke of our enemy. A year passed and by 25,000 majority we regained the city. Give us that touch of elbow and that response of heart to heart with the Democracy of the three States which, joined to the south, we must have to give success, and we will be invincible against any assaults which can be made by our enemies. (Applause.)

You fear Wall Street. You, gentlemen, who are afraid of the influences of Wall Street hold your virtue, it seems to me, by too slight a tenure. Are you going to New York to fall easy victims to the blandishments of Wall Street, or are your delegates to this convention going to be men with convictions which no locality can change, which no surroundings can influence—convictions which impel you to endeavor to assure the success and the welfare of the party? If such is indeed the spirit that animates you, then I apprehend that, seductive as New York is and as lavish as may be the blandishments of Wall Street upon you, you will not surrender yourselves easy victims to those seductions any more than we will yield our principles or surrender our views when we shall be called to go as delegates to some western city. (Applause.) This fight is not to be determined by the locality in which the convention is held; but very much influence may be exerted by the locality. This is especially true if you speak of the pivotal states which must range themselves in the Democratic column if there is to be any hope of success. I apprehend that neither Ohio nor Illinois can be counted upon to give its electoral vote next fall to the Democratic candidate. I imagine that, so far as Missouri is concerned, if Missouri is to return by virtue of the inflexible integrity of her Democrats to the Democratic legions she will do it as well without the convention as with it. Besides, if a convention exercises such influence over the localities where they are held it seems to me that the best we could do in St. Louis would be to occupy the three or four days we would be there dispelling the contagion breathed by the preceding convention assembled there, because if our convention is important to St. Louis it must be that the Republican Convention will have an influence when it assembles there. No, gentlemen, the States that need encouragement are those where all the history of the past has demonstrated to you that there is a majority of Democrats and whose electoral votes can be obtained if there are no disturbing local influences to prevent that majority from asserting itself.

Now one little bit of sentiment and I have finished. You will pardon me if I indulge in it. Here I see before me gentlemen who are representatives of that State in which I passed my whole boyhood and my young manhood. I loved the State as I love all these gentlemen who represent the States of the South, by whose side I stood and with whom I suffered in that eventful past from 1861 to 1865. I went to New York and I have learned to love that city, with a love that shall never die, for the generous treatment it has extended to me, a treatment typical and illustrative of the treatment which it extends to all who go there and seek in that active competition honor and remuneration. With what a thrill I remember how, when you were in peril, when troops were overrunning your legislatures, when armed forces were dragging representatives of the people from their high stations, when the South sent up a piteous cry for simple justice to the nation, that it was the voice of New York, uttered through Cooper Union, rolling like thunder over this broad land, which gave to you the rights which no hand since has dared to wrest from you. (Applause.)

New York, with a heart as great as her enterprise, knows no enemies; she recognizes all as friends and will treat all as such. Come to New York, come to a Democratic city, come to the welcome which its citizens will extend to you irrespective of party. Having come and experienced once the courtesy and generosity of our citizens, I am sure that each delegate will thank this committee for a duty most carefully and graciously performed. (Applause.)

THE CHAIR: With becoming modesty, St. Louis will be heard last. Col. John G. Prather, of Missouri, will indicate the order in which the speakers are to be heard.

COL. PRATHER, of Missouri: Governor Francis will speak first in the interest of the city; then our Mayor, Mayor Walbridge; then Gov. Stone will say a few words; and Senator Vest will do the wind-up.

THE CHAIR: I am sure you will all be charmed to hear the speakers in the order named.

ADDRESS OF EX-GOVERNOR DAVID R. FRANCIS

ON BEHALF OF THE CITY OF ST. LOUIS.

Mr. Chairman and Gentlemen of the Democratic National Committee: St. Louis salutes you as the worthy representatives of the greatest political party the world has ever seen, a party whose organization was contemporaneous with the birth of the Republic; a party whose principles will endure as long as our Republican institutions survive. We recognize that it is your duty and your desire to act for the best interests of the Democratic party. I am here as a Democrat, but, proud as I am of St. Louis, devoted as I am to Missouri, I would not ask you to locate the National Democratic Convention in my city or my state if I did not sincerely feel that it would be promotive of the best interests of the Democratic party. (Applause.) This is a business proposition, it has been said. There is also politics in your action. This is a critical period in the history of the Democratic party. There are serious differences in our party, as none can deny. We ask you to come to a city, frame your platform and nominate your candidates in a place where you will not be influenced by any local sentiment whatever. We propose to give you entire and exclusive control of the convention hall and all the tickets of admission. Our citizens have generously contributed ample means to defray the entire expenses of the convention and the members of the National Committee. We ask nothing in return except the honor of your presence. A National Democratic Convention is a big event in the history of St. Louis. Gentlemen from New York have told you of the greatness of that city, that a million people may come and a million people may go and their presence never be felt and their exit never be known. We want you to come to a place where a National Democratic Convention is a very important event. We shall look forward to your coming. We shall remember your presence there. Not only will our hotels be open and their rates not advanced but we will extend to you that generous hospitality which opens to you the doors of our residences and our hearts as well. The Democratic Convention was held in St. Louis in 1888. I happen to have here, handed to me but a few moments ago, the report of the committee which had in charge the arrangements of that convention and, with your permission, I will read to you six lines of that report.

"It is difficult to speak of the recent convention at St. Louis and of the hospitality of that city without seeming to exaggerate. When her delegates appeared before the National Committee in Washington in February, 1888, to urge St. Louis' claims as the city in which the convention should be held, so many promises were made in the way of attractions that it did not seem possible that all of them could be fulfilled. The result, however, proved the contrary. Not only was every promise redeemed in full but many steps were taken to insure the comfort and happiness of the thousands of guests not contemplated at the outset, etc."

We have a hall with a seating capacity of 12,000 persons. It is not a temporary structure; it is a substantial brick building of modern architecture containing an area of 434 by 330 feet. Within the walls of that building are more than forty-five committee rooms. Under one roof every State and every committee can have a separate room assigned to it.

So far as the location is concerned, as you all know, St. Louis is, of all the cities competing for this convention, the nearest to the center of population. It is the center of the productive power of this country; in that section of the country which has built up these great cities of which the gentlemen have spoken so eloquently. We want you to come to our midst. We want an opportunity to show you how we can appreciate your presence. A gentleman from New York stated that within twenty-five hours' ride of New York were 34,000,000 of people. Within 500 miles of St. Louis, or within twelve hours' ride, are 32,500,000, or, within a distance which can be traversed in one-half the time, there are as many people as there are within twenty-five hours ride of New York. The gentleman has told you of the greatness of New York. We are not here to advertise St. Louis, but there are a few very potent facts in connection with that city which I cannot forbear stating upon this occasion. St. Louis has the largest railroad station in the world—not in the United States, but in the world. It has the largest hardware house in the world. It has the largest drug house in the world. It has the largest woodenware house in the world. It has the largest tobacco factory in the world. It has the largest lead works, the largest brick yards and the largest stove and range factory in the world. We are small in population compared with New York but we have western enterprise and push, and now we have the largest brewery in the United States. Time will not admit of my recounting all the advantages of St. Louis. I only want to remind you, members of the committee, if you are civil service reformers, that St. Louis has been tried as a convention city and has proven equal to the task. Therefore, if you believe in civil service reform, give us another convention. If you do not believe in civil service reform, then we appeal to you as the followers of the immortal Jackson. What has Missouri done for the Democratic party? For twenty-four years, with unwavering fidelity, her electoral vote has been cast for the Democratic nominee. What other State can say as much? In 1896, just as surely will that vote be cast for the Democratic candidate. If, therefore, you want to reward party service and act in a way in which the party can be held together, give St. Louis this convention. It has been charged that the Republican party has already given its convention to St. Louis. It is true the Republican convention will be held in that city on June 16, and about the middle of June is the only hot weather we ever have in St. Louis. July is always cool with us and I think the bureau of statistics will bear out that statement. Are you going to allow us to return and say to the Democrats of our city and State that you have refused to us what the Republican Committee gave to the Republican party of Missouri? They are claiming that State. We do not despair of carrying it. We did not despair of carrying the State in 1894. We never believed that they had carried it until the returns were in and counted the second time. We do not believe that they will carry that State in 1896. For all that we cannot see how you can resist the appeal we make to you to bring your convention to our gates and thereby inspire the Democrats of Missouri with that enthusiasm which will carry the State by a majority of 40,000. The Republicans are going to have the largest convention that they have ever held, but if you bring the Democratic convention there the attendance at it will be larger than at the Republican Convention if we have to go to the States of Texas and Arkansas to bring in Democrats to help it out. St. Louis is not only the geographical center of this country but it is accessible by twenty trunk lines of railroad to say nothing of the mighty Mississippi and its tributaries which flow by our doors. We are nearer the center or nearer the meeting line of the different sentiments that are said to prevail in the Democratic party on the important issue that is now before us, than any other city. In the citizenship of St. Louis are combined the characteristics of the Puritan and the cavalier, and there, we flatter ourselves, is the true type of American citizenship. We want you to come to that kind of a community and we say to you — I believe it sincerely — that the platform you will there adopt and the nominations you will make will meet with more enthusiastic support than the platform adopted or candidates chosen in any other city in this country.

We are the largest commercial city west of the eastern border of the country and the largest commercial city south of the northern boundary of the country. So, for every reason, we think ourselves entitled to this convention. We are here in force, we are in earnest and we appeal to you as Democrats to come to St. Louis knowing that, as you did not regret it in 1888, you will not regret it in 1896. (Applause.)

ADDRESS OF MAYOR CYRUS P. WALBRIDGE

ON BEHALF OF ST. LOUIS.

Mr. Chairman and Gentlemen of the Committee: It would be a matter of considerable surprise if the managers of the great Democratic party were to give much weight to the political advice of a Republican mayor, and for that reason I shall refrain from offering any such advice. There are, however, gentlemen upon our delegation from whom you will hear or have heard, whose political experience, whose standing in your party, whose records in the history of their state and the nation entitle their political views to your careful and respectful consideration. (Applause.)

I shall take only enough of your time to officially extend the courtesy of St. Louis to this committee; not as a mere perfunctory duty, but as the glad mouthpiece of a united people, who, without regard to party, honestly and earnestly desire to entertain the Democratic Convention of 1896. (Applause.) As the official head of that city I promise that every pledge made upon this platform by representatives of St. Louis shall be honestly and carefully executed. I ask you to remember that this tender and these promises come from the financial Gibraltar of 1893 — from a city whose finances and financial methods are always safe. I ask you to remember that they come from the metropolis of a State that stands above all other states except four, and which is now awakening to a period of prosperity that is likely in the near future to place her at the head of the column. I ask you to remember that these pledges come from that focal point which Governor Francis has so well described where are merged waves of sentiment from every part of the Union, from the only city of which it can be truly said she knows no section except the broad domain of the Union, a city that is controlled by no "ism" except Americanism. We are aware of the difficulty and the responsibility resting upon this committee, but we believe also if you select St. Louis as a place for holding your convention that every St. Louis Republican and St. Louis Democrat will vie with each other to so entertain the delegates to that convention that, when they return to their homes, all will say as the result of your action to-day, "you acted wisely and well."

ADDRESS OF GOV. WILLIAM J. STONE, OF MISSOURI,

ON BEHALF OF THE CITY OF ST. LOUIS.

Mr. Chairman and Gentlemen of the Committee: In view of what has been already said and of the further fact that Senator Vest is to follow me, it is really unnecessary that I should occupy your time at all, and I would not do so except to oblige my colleagues who have requested it. It seems to me that in selecting a place to hold the next national convention three things should be considered: the accessibility of the place, its capacity to accommodate delegates and visitors, and the political aims and effects of the convention. With reference to the first two, I will not add anything to what has been already said. I will not take time in comparing the merits of the several cities competing for this distinction at your hands. I haven't any doubt that either can take care of a convention, and that those who attend the same in any city will be satisfied. I have the greatest respect for all these cities. I am proud of their greatness because I share in their glory. The convention which is about to assemble under your authority, will be, in my judgment, the most important party convention held in recent history. It is of the first importance that it should be a deliberative body. The best, the wisest, the purest, the most patriotic, the most faithful and devoted Democrats from all the states should be sent to that convention to represent their constituencies, and when assembled, now more than ever in our history, these men should deliberate with one principal purpose in view, the welfare of the Democratic party. (Applause.)

St. Louis has added 300,000 people to its population within the last ten years. These have come from every section of the Union in almost equal numbers. East, north and south have contributed to this growth and to-day St. Louis is the most typical and thoroughly American city in America. It more thoroughly than any other represents all the social, industrial and political conditions which characterize our National life. Delegates attending a convention in St. Louis, no matter from what section or State they come, will find instantly large numbers of St. Louisians with whom they will be immediately at home. St. Louis and Missouri, as Governor Francis remarked, are equidistant between the two extremes of the country and the sentiments of the people there upon all great political questions are conservative. You cannot find a city on the continent where this convention can assemble under auspices that will leave it so entirely free from extraneous influences calculated to dominate it, as will prevail in St. Louis. True, upon the important issues of the day, upon the currency and other questions which have engaged the attention of our party and all parties, we have pronounced convictions, but we respect each other's views and are conservative in our treatment of them. (Applause.)

We want this convention at St. Louis. We want it in Missouri; not because without it we cannot carry Missouri, for we will carry Missouri anyhow. (Applause.) I have not a shadow of doubt as to that. But, gentlemen of the committee, the Western States, the trans-Mississippi States, have asked very little at the hands of the Democratic party of the nation. For twenty odd years we have voted with uncomplaining and with enthusiastic regularity for New York, Ohio, Indiana and Illinois candidates for the presidency and vice-presidency. We have on two occasions only in this generation had a national convention west of the Mississippi, and, on one occasion we had a candidate for the vice-presidency on a Democratic ticket and one on the Greely ticket. That is all we have had in this way from the Democratic party of the United States. It is about all we have asked.

When the battle is on upon whom do you most surely rely, to whom do you most confidently look to rally 'round the flags, upon whom do you most surely depend? The hosts that gather on the bosoms of the great States tributary to St. Louis—States that were lifted up out of the imperial domain which Thomas Jefferson gave to the Republic to shine as stars in the galaxy of the Union.

We ask you now, gentlemen of the committee, to give us this convention. We will entertain you as well as any other city, and we will afford you and afford the convention an opportunity to deliberate and reach conclusions absolutely free from outside pressure from those influences that are likely to make its results unfavorable to success. We will go as far as any when the battle is on to carry the flag to victory. We want success, and to attain success unity of the party should be the main purpose of our assembling together. I thank you for your attention.

ADDRESS OF SENATOR GEORGE G. VEST, OF MISSOURI,

On Behalf of The City of St. Louis.

Mr. Chairman and Gentlemen of the Committee. After the eloquence, wit and humor which have preceded me, even with an exaggerated opinion of my own abilities as a speaker, I should hesitate to detain you beyond a reasonable time. My associates, who have presented the claims of St. Louis for the next convention, have so thoroughly and fairly established the ability of that city to entertain the delegates if they assemble there that I shall spend no time in discussing that branch of the subject, nor will I indulge in any unjust criticisms of the three great cities which are rivals with St. Louis in the contest for this convention.

Of all men living, I am the last who would say one word that had the suspicion of criticism of that splendid New York Democracy that has always stood firm. As I had occasion to say before at a similar meeting and time, I have no criticism to make against Tammany Hall because, whatever may have been its sins of omission or commission, the claws of the Tammany tiger are always red with the blood of the Republican party. (Applause.)

It would be an absolute contradiction of the views of one of the eloquent gentlemen who preceded me if I should for one instant insinuate that the presence of our convention would add to the commercial prosperity of New York or to our political chances in the Empire State and Empire City of the Union.

As to the City of Cincinnati, bound to St. Louis by so many commercial and social ties, I should be false to my people and myself if I expressed anything but the kindest feeling for her. (Applause.)

This, however, is an occasion when we must speak plainly, as a gentleman from New York expressed it, in considering this question. It is said that the place where the Democratic Convention assembles is of no special importance and exerts no political influence. No soldier in actual war or in a political contest who ignores the slightest advantage in the fight is worthy of his commission or fit even to be a private in the ranks. It has been said that a farm house in the battle of Waterloo decided that contest and to this day to the tourist is pointed out the ruins of the chateau where the flowing and ebbing tide of battle rolled for hours and for the possession of which the French met the English and the Prussians in deadly conflict. A fence, a stone, an elevation of the ground, has often decided the fate of armies and it is so in political battles. A campaign song, the sobriquet given to a candidate, a chance shot of some partisan in the midst of the canvass, has often carried the day and decided the battle one way or the other. Blaine was beaten for the presidency by the foolish speech of a preacher as all the world knows, and but for that imprudent utterance, he would have been President of the United States.

When we are engaged in battle we must not disregard any single circumstance that helps to win. Men may laugh at sentiment, but the world is controlled by it; in politics, in religion, in state craft, in every department of business. Men have died for women, for a flower, and for a sweet smile have poured out their blood willingly and freely as the torrents that leap the mountain sides. We are told that the place of holding the convention may not effect the result of the canvass. You must not ignore the fact that in all the incidents and affairs of life "trifles light as air" may decide the fate of nations and of mankind.

The City of Chicago, that splendid city upon the lakes, has derived world-wide reputation, as has been stated here, from the Columbian Exposition. It has been often honored in the past by both parties holding their conventions there. Chicago would not be made greater by this convention. Chicago, like Cincinnati, as was stated by Col. Fellows, is in a hopelessly Republican State, if there is anything in the past by which to judge of in the future. But once since the war has Illinois ever given its electoral vote to a Democratic candidate and that was in the tidal wave of 1892. Ohio is hopelessly Republican. If the talent and resources of my friend, Calvin S. Brice, added to the aggressiveness of James E.

Campbell (with Ike Hill to manage the details of the canvass), could not succeed, if that combination could not win, what chance will there ever be for us to carry that State?

Two things are urged against the city of St. Louis. I will consider them briefly: We are told in the first place, that climatic conditions are against this city. It has been described in the corridors and in this hall as the "Black hole of Calcutta," where we are parched, burned, fried and fricasseed. I have lived in Missouri more than forty years and I am only a reasonably fair specimen of the baked democrat. We are told that the water is bad there. Why bother any Democratic Convention Committee by complaining about water? (Laughter.) One would suppose from the attacks made upon the climatic conditions of St. Louis that delegates to the next convention are to be made out of either ice or wax and that they must not go to St. Louis lest they melt. I had supposed they were heroes, with iron in their blood and nerves of steel, willing to fight against the heat in summer and the cold in winter, and to carry the flag in all latitudes and in all dangers.

We are told that the Democratic party should not live upon the crumbs which fall from the Republican table. Gentlemen, the Democracy of Missouri ask at your hands nothing but the equality that should always exist between men belonging to the same political faith. We do not ask you to camp where the Republicans camped the year before. We are simply taking up the gauge of battle thrown down by Chauncey I. Filley, the great leader of the Republican party, who, in aggressive attitude stood where I stand now and shouted to the Republican Committee three weeks ago: "We've got them; we've got them." If you give us the convention I will be personally responsible for 20,000 Democratic majority in Missouri. Yes, he has got them. He has got them like the boy got the hornet when he screamed to his mother to come and take the infernal thing away.

We do not ask any undue advantage or any special privileges in the way of partisan warfare from even the committee of our party. We ask to be put on an equality only. We do not desire to go back to our friends in Missouri and say in an apologetic way: "The Republican party gave the convention to St. Louis to help the Republican organization, but we were unable to obtain the same thing from our brethren in our own organization." We are Democrats, Democrats who have never faltered in the hour of peril and in the hour of battle. Missouri came into the Union in a state of revolution which threatened civil war. We were for long years engaged in a factional fight but always true to the flag of national Democracy. That internal conflict ended with the defeat of Col. Benton for Governor in 1856. Then came that terrible border warfare of 1859 that bathed the people in blood and lit with fire the whole of that Western country. Then on top of that came the Civil war. Then five long years of dark proscription and persecution at the hands of the Republican party when they held us down with their bayonets. In 1870 we broke the manacles, and from that day to this the State flag of the Missouri Democracy has stood side by side with the great oriflamme of the National party to which we belong. *These* are the Democrats who are accused of coming here to pick up the crumbs from the Republican table. There is no fiercer animal on the face of the earth, not even excepting the Tammany tiger, than the Missouri Democrat. We are ready to fight and we are not here imploring for anything. As Governor Stone said, we will win this fight. But is it wrong to ask our own brethren to put us on an equality with the Republicans when the legislature has a majority of twenty-one against us on joint ballot? Do you know what it means to lose Missouri? You expect to lose Illinois, you expect to lose Ohio, you may lose New York. When you lose Missouri you break that solid phalanx of Democratic States that have stood like a granite wall before the advance of the Republican cohorts. If you lose Missouri you break the center stone in the great Democratic arch, and you are in the hands of the Republican enemy for an indefinite time to come. We ask simply to be put on equality with the enemy, not on the vantage ground. If we claim the same influence with our committee which the Republicans had with theirs, is that picking up crumbs that fall from the Republican table?

Allusion has been made to the silver and gold question. We have in Missouri the two factions, but we have but one State Committee, one organization, and we will make together one fight. Governor Francis believes in the single gold standard, I believe in the free coinage of silver. But when the fight commences we will stand together like brothers, for we are all Democrats, if nothing else. What more can I say than this? What delegate here is willing to put personal interest in a time like this above the behest of our party? We are not here to beg; we are here to state facts. In conclusion I can simply say, as my immediate predecessor, Governor Stone, said, the Democracy of Missouri will do their duty; they will fight and they will win as they have won in the past. We will scatter Filley and his gang as a cyclone scatters the dust.

THE CHAIR: A recess of five minutes will now be taken, immediately after which the committee will meet again in executive session. Those who are not members of the committee will kindly retire. Members of the Committee are requested to remain.

(Five minutes recess.)

THE CHAIR: The meeting will be in order. The Secretary will proceed to call the roll, and as each State is called, the member, or proxy therefor, will announce the name of the city of his choice. The Secretary and the tellers are to keep a careful record of the vote.

SENATOR BRICE, of Ohio: I do not know what assurances

have been received from the city of New York or the city of St. Louis, or the city of Chicago, as to what would be done if this Convention should be located at any of these places. If the chairman, or any member of the Committee has made sufficient examination to see that the propositions made will be entirely satisfactory to the Committee, I do not care to have them read. I do not know what propositions have been made by these cities. I speak with some experience in the matter, because in previous conventions we have had differences as to what the local committee has agreed to do. In one or two cases it has been necessary for the chairman of the National Committee to seriously consider the question whether he would not be obliged to recall the National Committee to consider the differences between the sub-committee appointed by the National Committee to manage the Convention, and the local committee in the Convention city.

Representing one of the cities which desires to have this Convention I am prepared to make, on its behalf, certain well understood engagements, and I am prepared to obligate myself to the other members of this Committee that these engagements will be carried out in good faith, and that we will obey to the letter what is understood between the parties; but I am a little in doubt whether we ought to go into ballot, until it is understood what these cities agree respectively to do. I would not ask that the time of the Committee be taken up by a full reading, but if some gentleman would state in brief what is understood will be done in each case I think we would all be better prepared to vote.

THE CHAIR: Perhaps to submit the written communications would be the best way to answer the inquiry. It is proper to say that the representatives of each city have signed and sent in similar communications, signed by gentlemen who are reputed to be quite able to fill their engagements and obligations. The names will all be furnished, if desired. The Secretary will kindly read the communication from the gentlemen representing the city of Chicago, as indicating what they are ready to do.

The Secretary at this point read the communication from Chicago, which was in words and figures following:

THE ARLINGTON.
WASHINGTON, D. C., January 16, 1896.

HON. W. F. HARRITY,
    Chairman, Democratic National Committee.

DEAR SIR: Desiring that the Democratic National Convention of 1896 shall be held in the city of Chicago, in the State of Illinois, we do hereby agree and guarantee that in the event of said city of Chicago being selected for the meeting of said Convention, that to that end we will be responsible for the expenses of said Convention, to the extent of forty thousand dollars, and that there will, on or before March 1, 1896, be deposited to the credit of such sub-committee of the Democratic National Committee as may be appointed to make arrangements for said Convention the sum of forty thousand ($40,000) dollars for the purpose of defraying all of the expenses that it may be necessary or proper to incur in the judgment of said sub-committee, in connection with the usual and necessary arrangements for the meeting of the said convention, including the proper and usual expenses of the Democratic National Committee.

It is understood and agreed that said sub-committee will furnish to the undersigned or to those duly authorized to act for them, sufficient and satisfactory vouchers for all expenditures made in connection with the meeting of the said Convention, and the attendance and meeting of the Democratic National Committee, etc., and will return to the undersigned the unexpended balance of the amount so deposited with such sub-committee.

It is also understood and agreed that the arrangements for the meeting of said Convention and all matters properly incident thereto shall be made under the direct control and supervision of the sub-committee of the Democratic National Committee, it being understood and agreed that, if desired by the undersigned, ten per cent. of the spectators' tickets that may be issued for admission to the Convention Hall shall be given to the undersigned for distribution.

It is further agreed that the undersigned will arrange with the proprietors of the leading hotels of the said city of Chicago that no allotment of headquarters, committee rooms, guest rooms, etc., shall be made until after the selection of rooms for the headquarters, committee rooms, etc., of the Democratic National Committee, shall have been made by the said sub-Committee of the Democratic National Committee, such selection to be made not later than, say, thirty days from date hereof. It is likewise understood that the rates of charges to be made by hotels of the said city of Chicago shall be reasonable and moderate and not above the usual and regular rates of such hotels. Respectfully,

    L. Z. LEITER,
    ERSKINE M. PHELPS,
    JOSEPH DONNERSBERGER,
    MARTIN J. RUSSELL,
    ADAMS A. GOODRICH,
    BEN. T. CABLE.
    ALBERT S. GAGE,
    BENJAMIN J. ROSENTHAL

MEETING, JANUARY 16, 1896.   55

THE CHAIR: The communications from the other cities are of the same character.

MR. BRICE, of Ohio: I had the impression the amount was different, in that it was $50.000. That had been my impression, as the way we made it.

THE SECRETARY: It was $50,000 originally, but was reduced to $40,000.

MR. BLAIR, of Kansas· Did I understand the Chair to say that the promises all were the same? In their speeches they were different.

THE CHAIR: In what particular? Different in what particular?

MR. BLAIR, of Kansas: Railroad fare. One or two of the gentlemen made the statement very different—and that they would claim none of the National Convention tickets.

THE CHAIR: It is parenthetically stated in each communication that a percentage of the tickets would be given "if desired."

The Secretary will read the signatures to the communications from the cities of Cincinnati, New York and St. Louis.

Which signatures were read to the Committee as follows:

From Cincinnati·
    M. E. INGALLS,
    THOS. B. SAXON,
    H. D. PECK.
    JOHN F. FOLLETT,
    S. HOWARD HINKLE.

From New York:
    ISIDOR STRAUSS,
    JOHN D. CRIMMINS,
    SIMEON FORD.

From St. Louis:
    D. R. FRANCIS,
    SAMUEL M. KENNARD,
    C. C. MAFFITT,
    CHARLES D. MCLURE,
    C. C. RAINWATER,
    W. H. THOMPSON,
    CHAS. N. KNAPP,
    L. M. RUMSEY.

Senator Brice, of Ohio: Of course I had no doubt in any case as to the signatures; I had no reference to that. In the case of the proposition from the State of Ohio, however, I would like to ask for three minutes' delay while I consult with the local committee of the city of Cincinnati. I would not like to have any difficulty arise. I do not dispute the authority of the Secretary to reduce this proposition, but I understand the people in our city of Cincinnati raised a fund of $50,000 and made a tender of it to this Committee. If the city of Cincinnati has seen fit to reduce it to $40,000 I have nothing to say about it, but I would not wish that reduction to be made unless it is clearly understood by the Committee that they have withdrawn the extra $10,000 which they had offered. I do not say it would have any influence upon the deliberations of this body, but it may have some influence upon our own people. If I am not taxing the Committee too much, I would like to ask permission to consult with that Committee. I would not detain you more than three or four minutes.

The Secretary: I would like to say, for the information of Mr. Brice and the Committee, when the other parties put their proposition down to $40,000, in order that they might all be uniform, I made known the fact to Mr. Ingalls, or rather suggested that they reduce theirs, to make it uniform, and he authorized me to make the reduction.

Senator Brice, of Ohio: If you take the responsibility of that statement, I withdraw my request.

Mr. Cable, of Illinois: That was put to Mr. Ingalls. There were three others—the matter was put to Mr. Ingalls and he concurred. I would say as I was personally concerned, representing one of the cities, and being one of the Committee, I was endeavoring to get as large an appropriation made as possible and not endeavoring to get them to reduce the amount. That would be my own feeling as a member of the Committee. The Convention of 1884, the amount expended was about $24,000; that of 1892 about the same amount of money. * * * They thought the sum might be reduced to $40,000. If you desire to see Mr. Ingalls, if they change it, if a change is going to be made in any place, we want——

THE SECRETARY: I would like to say further that the original propositions were for the expenses of the Convention up to $50,000; they had agreed to pay the expenses up to $50,000, if that sum should be required, but in no event more than the actual expenses of the Convention.

MR. BLAIR, of Kansas: Who is to determine what are the expenses in all these cases?

THE CHAIR: The sub-Committee. Has the gentleman from Ohio withdrawn his request?

SENATOR BRICE, of Ohio: Yes, sir; with that understanding.

MR. SHERLEY, of Kentucky: I would like to inquire if there is any guarantee about the building?

THE CHAIR: The Chair understands it is to be paid for out of the fund subscribed or guaranteed.

GOV. SHEEHAN, of New York: I desire to have, with the consent of the other gentlemen, Mr. Strauss, Mr. Crimmins, who is here, and Mr. Ford, it added to the New York proposition, that if this Committee selects New York as the place, that we will guarantee to carry the delegates and alternates to New York from their respective homes as cheaply as they could reach the nearest city to that locality that is an aspirant for the Convention. I desire to have that added to the proposition.

THE CHAIR: In justice to New York, as well as to the other cities named, I think it ought to be said, that this statement made by the representative of that city will not be considered as an additional offer.

GOV. SHEEHAN: I do not desire to change the proposition we have made because we have all gone in on the same proposition, but I make it as an addition; I simply give that guarantee, and I wish it so understood.

THE CHAIR: The Secretary will proceed to call the roll.

The Secretary then proceeded to call the roll for the selection of the city in which the Convention should be held.

Meeting, January 16, 1896.

FIRST BALLOT.

Chicago.. 6
Cincinnati..11
New York...14
St. Louis...19

Whole number of votes cast..............................50

SECOND BALLOT.

Chicago.. 5
Cincinnati.. 9
New York...17
St. Louis...19

Whole number of votes cast..............................50

THIRD BALLOT.

Chicago.. 5
Cincinnati..10
New York...16
St. Louis...19

Whole number of votes cast..............................50

FOURTH BALLOT.

Chicago.. 4
Cincinnati..10
New York...16
St. Louis...20

Whole number of votes cast..............................50

FIFTH BALLOT.

Chicago.. 5
Cincinnati..11
New York...16
St. Louis...18

Whole number of votes cast..............................50

A motion was made to take a recess until 9 o'clock P. M. An amendment to motion making the hour 8:30 o'clock P. M. was offered.

The amendment was accepted.

A further motion to amend, naming 8 o'clock P. M., was offered and seconded.

This amendment was lost.

The motion to adjourn until 8:30 o'clock P. M. was put to a vote and carried.

Recess until 8:30 P. M.

EVENING SESSION, 8:30 P. M.

EXECUTIVE SESSION.

THE CHAIR: Order, gentlemen. The Secretary will proceed to call the roll. The sixth ballot is about to be taken.

SIXTH BALLOT.

Chicago	5
Cincinnati	11
New York	16
St. Louis	18
Whole number of votes cast	50

SEVENTH BALLOT.

Chicago	4
Cincinnati	11
New York	16
St. Louis	20
Whole number of votes cast	51

On the sixth ballot, the Chair (W. F. Harrity) presented the proxy of Michael Doran and voted then and thereafter for Minnesota.

Meeting, January 16, 1896.

EIGHTH BALLOT.

Chicago... 5
Cincinnati..12
New York...16
St. Louis...18

Whole number of votes cast.............................51

NINTH BALLOT.

Chicago... 5
Cincinnati..11
New York...15
St. Louis...20

Whole number of votes cast.............................51

TENTH BALLOT.

Chicago... 6
Cincinnati..12
New York...14
St. Louis...19

Whole number of votes cast.............................51

ELEVENTH BALLOT.

Chicago... 7
Cincinnati..10
New York...14
St. Louis...20

Whole number of votes cast.............................51

TWELFTH BALLOT.

Chicago... 6
Cincinnati..12
New York...14
St. Louis...19

Whole number of votes cast.............................51

THIRTEENTH BALLOT.

Chicago 8
Cincinnati 10
New York 15
St. Louis 17

Whole number of votes cast 50

FOURTEENTH BALLOT.

Chicago 10
Cincinnati 9
New York 13
St. Louis 17

Whole number of votes cast 49

FIFTEENTH BALLLOT.

Chicago 10
Cincinnati 10
New York 13
St. Louis 18

Whole number of votes cast 51

SIXTEENTH BALLOT.

Chicago 10
Cincinnati 10
New York 13
St. Louis 18

Whole number of votes cast 51

SEVENTEENTH BALLOT.

Chicago 11
Cincinnati 10
New York 13
St. Louis 17

Whole number of votes cast 51

Meeting, January 16, 1896.

EIGHTEENTH BALLOT.

Chicago 11
Cincinnati 9
New York 12
St. Louis 19

Whole number of votes cast 51

Motion made to take a recess for one-half hour. This was followed by a motion to amend that after three more ballots shall have been taken, the city receiving the smallest number of votes shall be dropped from the roll. The amendment was not accepted, nor seconded. The question was put on the original motion to take a recess for half an hour and lost.

NINETEENTH BALLOT.

Chicago 11
Cincinnati 9
New York 12
St. Louis 19

Whole number of votes cast 51

TWENTIETH BALLOT.

Chicago 13
Cincinnati 9
New York 11
St. Louis 18

Whole number of votes cast 51

TWENTY-FIRST BALLOT.

Chicago 15
Cincinnati 9
New York 8
St. Louis 19

Whole number votes cast 51

Meeting, January 16, 1896.

TWENTY-SECOND BALLOT.

Chicago	14
Cincinnati	9
Columbus	1
New York	9
St. Louis	18
Whole number of votes cast	51

TWENTY-THIRD BALLOT.

Chicago	13
Cincinnati	10
New York	9
St. Louis	18
Whole number of votes cast	50

TWENTY-FOURTH BALLOT.

Chicago	15
Cincinnati	10
New York	7
St. Louis	19
Whole number of votes cast	51

TWENTY-FIFTH BALLOT.

Chicago	15
Cincinnati	11
New York	6
St. Louis	19
Whole number of votes cast	51

TWENTY-SIXTH BALLOT.

Chicago	16
Cincinnati	9
New York	6
St. Louis	20
Whole number of votes cast	51

MEETING, JANUARY 16, 1896.

TWENTY-SEVENTH BALLOT.

Chicago...20
Cincinnati.. 6
New York 3
St. Louis...21

Whole number of votes cast............................50

TWENTY-EIGHTH BALLOT.

Chicago...21
Cincinnati.. 4
New York.. 4
St. Louis...22

Whole number of votes cast............................51

TWENTY-NINTH BALLOT.

Chicago...26
Cincinnati.. 1
St. Louis...24

Whole number of votes cast............................ 51

Mr. Ross, of New Jersey, changed his vote from New York to St. Louis.

Mr. Cummings, of Rhode Island, changed his vote from New York to Chicago.

Mr. Donaldson, of South Carolina, changed his vote from Chicago to St. Louis.

Mr. Terry, of Arkansas: I would like to have the tally verified; there has been some confusion.

The Chair: The Secretary will verify the vote.

The Secretary read aloud the vote of each State and Territory as recorded on the tally sheet, and the result as previously announced was verified.

The Chair: Chicago having received a majority of all the votes cast, I declare it to be the choice of this Committee for holding the next Democratic National Convention.

Mr. THOMAS: I desire that the following Official Call be adopted—it is similar to the Call which was issued in 1892, namely:

CALL FOR THE DEMOCRATIC NATIONAL CONVENTION, 1896.

The Democratic National Committee, at a meeting held this day in the City of Washington, D. C., has appointed Tuesday July 7, 1896, as the time, and chosen the City of Chicago, Illinois, as the place for holding the Democratic National Convention. Each State is entitled to representation therein equal to double the representation to which it is entitled in the next Electoral College, and each Territory and the District of Columbia shall have two delegates. All Democratic conservative citizens of the United States, irrespective of past associations and differences, who can unite with us in the effort for pure, economical and constitutional government, are cordially invited to join in sending delegates to the Convention."

I move that it be adopted as the Official Call for the Convention.

This motion was duly seconded.

THE CHAIR: In view of the resolution adopted this morning, the Chair will regard the motion just made as a direction or request to the officers of the Committee, inasmuch as a request to prepare the Official Call was incorporated in the resolution offered this morning by the gentleman from Maryland, which resolution was adopted.

MR. OWEN, of Indian Territory: At the last meeting of the Democratic National Convention, the declaration was made on behalf of Arizona and New Mexico that they should have a representation of six. The Convention adopted that before, and we think it should be embodied in this call. The motion was passed at the previous Convention declaring that the same representation should be given at the succeeding Convention as obtained during the last.

The motion of Mr. Thomas, of Colorado, adopting the Official Call, having been duly seconded, was put to a vote and carried.

Mr. Donaldson, of South Carolina : I think it is a very opportune time for this Committee to set a good example to its constituency, and perhaps to show that, although we have had a little fight amongst ourselves, we are ready to present a united front against a common enemy, I therefore move that we make the decision for Chicago unanimous.

Which motion was warmly seconded by Mr. Prather, of Missouri, put to a vote and carried.

Mr. Wallace, of Washington : I move that the thanks of this Committee be tendered to the proprietor of the Arlington Hotel for the courtesies extended during our stay here.

Which motion, duly seconded, was put to a vote and carried.

Mr. Sherley, of Kentucky : It occurs to me that as our Convention will be later than usual, it would not be out of place that our Committee suggest and recommend to our successors that instead of wasting two weeks and traveling to New York for the purpose of electing a Chairman and Secretary that they do that the day after the Convention meets. This is just simply a recommendation. Is it not customary for the Committee to meet the day before the meeting of the Democratic National Convention?

The Chair : The Chair will take the responsibility of calling the National Committee to meet on the day before the Convention at Chicago ; but will of course be governed by the wishes of the Committee.

Mr. Sherley : I move that when we adjourn we adjourn to meet at 12 o'clock, noon, on the day before the assembling of the Democratic National Convention, at such place in Chicago as may be designated by the Chairman.

Which motion, duly seconded, was put and carried.

Mr. Thomas, of Colorado: I move that a copy of the resolution of recommendation that was adopted this morning,

recommending six delegates from the territories, be furnished by the Secretary to each of the members of the National Committee from the Territories.

Which motion was duly seconded, put to a vote and carried.

The chair announced the appointment of the following members of the sub-Committee, authorized under the resolution offered by Senator Gorman, of Maryland, to make arrangements for the meeting of the Democratic National Convention in Chicago, Illinois, on Tuesday, July 7, 1896, viz: William F. Harrity, of Pennsylvania, Simon P. Sheerin, of Indiana, Arthur P. Gorman, of Maryland, Ben T. Cable, of Illinois, Edward C. Wall, of Wisconsin, John G. Prather, of Missouri, and Thomas H. Sherley, of Kentucky.

Senator Gorman, of Maryland, asked to be excused from service upon the Committee and Hon. Hugh C. Wallace, of Washington, was appointed in his place.

ADJOURNMENT.

Meeting, July 6, 1896.   68a

DEMOCRATIC NATIONAL COMMITTEE MEETING.

Parlors Palmer House, Chicago, Ill., July 6, 1896.

The National Committee met in the parlors of the Palmer House, Chicago, Ill., pursuant to adjournment, at 12 o'clock M., July 6, 1896. Hon. WILLIAM F. HARRITY, of Pennsylvania, Chairman, presiding, and Hon. SIMON P. SHEERIN, of Indiana, Secretary, recording.

The following is a roll of the members and proxies present:

Alabama—HENRY D. CLAYTON.
Arkansas—T. V. MCREA.
  (Proxy for U. M. ROSE.)
California—M. F. TARPEY.
Colorado—CHARLES S. THOMAS.
Connecticut—CARLOS FRENCH.
Delaware—L. C. VANDEGRIFT.
Florida—SAMUEL PASCO.
Georgia—CLARK HOWELL, JR.
Idaho—D. B. HILLIARD.
  (Proxy for F. W. BEANE.)
Illinois—BEN. T. CABLE.
Indiana—SIMON P. SHEERIN.
Iowa—J. J. RICHARDSON.
Kansas—C. W. BLAIR.
Kentucky—THOS. H. SHERLEY.
Maine—ARTHUR SEWALL.
Maryland—L. V. BAUGHMAN.
  (Proxy for A. P. GORMAN.)
Massachusetts—JOSIAH QUINCY.
Michigan—DANIEL J. CAMPAU.
Minnesota—D. W. LAWLER.
  (Proxy for MICHAEL DORAN.)
Mississippi—C. B. HOWRY.
Missouri—JOHN G. PRATHER.
Montana—A. J. DAVIDSON.
Nebraska—TOBIAS CASTOR.
Nevada—R. P. KEATING.
New Hampshire—A. W. SULLOWAY.
New Jersey—JAMES SMITH, JR.
  (Proxy for MILES ROSS.)

New York—W. F. SHEEHAN.
North Carolina—F. H. BUSBEE.
  (Proxy for M. W. RANSOM.)
North Dakota—W. C. LEISTIKOW.
Ohio—GEORGE B. GILLILAND.
  (Proxy for C. S. BRICE.)
Oregon—FRED V. HOLMAN.
  (Proxy for E. D. MCKEE.)
Pennsylvania—WILLIAM F. HARRITY.
Rhode Island—R. B. COMSTOCK.
  (Proxy for SAMUEL R. HONEY.)
South Carolina—M. L. DONALDSON.
South Dakota—JAMES M. WOODS.
Tennessee—HOLMES CUMMINS.
Texas—O. T. HOLT.
Utah—S. A. MERRITT.
Vermont—BRADLEY B. SMALLEY.
Virginia—PETER J. OTEY.
Washington—HUGH C. WALLACE.
West Virginia—JOHN SHERIDAN.
Wisconsin—W. F. VILAS.
  (Proxy for E. C. WALL.)
Wyoming—W. L. KUYKENDALL.
Alaska—A. L. DELANEY.
Arizona—C. M. SHANNON.
District of Columbia—J. L. NORRIS.
New Mexico—H. B. FERGUSON.
Oklahoma—T. M. RICHARDSON.
Indian Territory—ROB'T L. OWEN.

Senator JONES, of Arkansas, Senator TURPIE, of Indiana, Governor ALTGELD, of Illinois, Governor STONE, of Missouri, and Senator DANIEL, of Virginia, appeared before the committee, stating through Senator JONES, their spokesman, that they were authorized by the delegates to the Convention, in favor of the free and unlimited coinage of silver, at the ratio of 16 to 1, to request the National Committee, in its selection of a Temporary Chairman, to regard the wishes of what they believed to be a majority of the delegates to compose the

Convention, and select for Temporary Chairman some gentleman of well known silver views, whose name would be presented by a member of the National Committee in sympathy with the free silver movement.

On motion of Mr. PRATHER, of Missouri, seconded by Mr. BLAIR, of Kansas, the committee proceeded to the work of making up the temporary roll of the Convention.

Upon motion of Mr. CABLE. of Illinois, seconded by Mr. SMALLEY, of Vermont, it was ordered that where but one set of delegates were reported from a State, that the same should be placed on the roll without further action.

The roll was called without interruption until Indiana was reached, when the Secretary reported that there was a contest in the 7th Congressional District, the contestants being JOHN P. FRENZEL and CHARLES M. COOPER. Both parties appeared in person and by attorneys, and after argument and full consideration the Secretary was instructed by unanimous vote to put the name of CHARLES M. COOPER upon the roll.

When Michigan was reached, Hon. DANIEL J. CAMPAU, member from Michigan, moved that the delegates from the State of Michigan, headed by Hon. ELLIOTT G. STEVENSON, be stricken from the roll, and that the determination of who were the regular delegates from that State be left entirely to the Committee on Credentials. In answer to an inquiry as to whether any other list of delegates had been filed, the Secretary replied that no other list had been filed with him, and that he knew of no delegation from Michigan, except the one headed by Hon. ELLIOTT G. STEVENSON, the credentials of which delegation were now upon his desk. Mr. CAMPAU's motion was lost. Mr. SHERIDAN, of West Virginia, moved that the delegation headed by Hon. ELLIOTT G. STEVENSON, be placed on the temporary roll, which motion was seconded by Mr. SULLOWAY, of New Hampshire. Hon. DANIEL J. CAMPAU, member from Michigan, asked that the roll be called on said motion, which was done, and said roll-call resulted in every member present, except Mr. CAMPAU, voting aye; Mr. CAMPAU voted no. The motion was carried.

When Nebraska was reached, the Secretary reported two delegations—one headed by Hon. TOBIAS CASTOR and the other by Hon. WM. J. BRYAN. Representatives of each delegation, and attorneys for each, were admitted. After long and exhaustive argument, the committee, by majority vote, instructed the Secretary to place upon the temporary roll the delegation headed by Hon. TOBIAS CASTOR.

When Nevada was reached, the Secretary reported two delegations—one headed by Gen. R. P. KEATING and the other by THEODORE WINTERS. After argument and full consideration, the Secretary was directed by unanimous vote to place upon the temporary roll the delegation headed by Gen. R. P. KEATING.

When Ohio was reached, the Secretary reported two sets of delegates, for the 18th Congressional district, to-wit: No. 1, JOHN H. CLARK and EDWARD S. RAFF; No. 2, WILSON S. POTTS and CONRAD SCWEITZER. The parties were present in person and by attorney, and after argument and full consideration the roll was called and by a majority vote the Secretary was instructed to place the names of WILSON S. POTTS and CONRAD SCWEITZER upon the temporary roll.

When the State of South Dakota was reached, the Secretary reported two delegations—one headed by V. SEBLAKIN-ROSS, and the other by F. M. STOVER. Members of the respective delegations were present in person, and represented by attorneys. After argument and full consideration the Secretary was instructed by unanimous vote to place upon the temporary roll the delegation headed by F. M. STOVER.

When Texas was reached, the Secretary reported two delegations—one headed by Hon. J. W. BAILEY, and the other by Hon. GEORGE CLARK. Before any action was taken by the Committee, the delegation headed by Mr. CLARK was withdrawn and the contest abandoned. The Secretary was directed by unanimous vote to place the delegation headed by Hon. J. W. BAILEY on the temporary roll.

There were no further contests and the Secretary was instructed to make up the temporary roll of the Convention in accordance with the above action of the Committee.

The Chair then declared the next thing in order to be the selection of Temporary Officers for the Convention.

Hon. WILLIAM F. SHEEHAN, of New York, presented the name of Senator DAVID B. HILL, of New York, and Hon. HENRY D. CLAYTON, of Alabama, presented the name of Senator JOHN W. DANIEL, of Virginia. The roll being called the members voted as follows:

Alabama—HENRY D. CLAYTON............................ DANIEL
Arkansas—T. V. MCREA (Proxy for U. M. ROSE.)...... DANIEL
California—M. F. TARPEY................................ DANIEL
Colorado—CHARLES S. THOMAS........................... DANIEL
Connecticut—CARLOS FRENCH......................HILL
Delaware—L. C. VANDEGRIFT........................HILL
Florida—SAMUEL PASCO................................. DANIEL
Georgia—CLARK HOWELL, JR............................. DANIEL
Idaho—B. N. HILLIARD (Proxy for F. W. BEANE.)...... DANIEL
Illinois—BEN. T. CABLE..............................HILL
Indiana—SIMON P. SHEERIN..........................HILL
Iowa—J. J. RICHARDSON.............................HILL
Kansas—C. W. BLAIR.................................... DANIEL
Kentucky—THOMAS H. SHERLEY........................HILL
Louisiana—JAMES JEFFRIES..................Absent
Maine—ARTHUR SEWALL .... DANIEL

Maryland—L. V. Baughman (Proxy for A. P. Gorman).Hill
Massachusetts—Josiah Quincy........................Hill
Michigan—Daniel J. Campau......................   Daniel
Minnesota—D. W. Lawler (Proxy for Michael Doran).Hill
Mississippi—C. B. Howry...........................Hill
Missouri—John G. Prather..........................Hill
Montana—A. J. Davidson...........................   Daniel
Nebraska—Tobias Castor...........................Hill
Nevada—R. P. Keating.............................   Daniel
New Hampshire—A. W. Sulloway....................Hill
New Jersey—James Smith, Jr. (Proxy for Miles Ross).Hill
New York—William F. Sheehan.....................Hill
North Carolina—F. H. Busbee (Proxy for M. W. Ransom),   Daniel
North Dakota—W. C. Leistikow.....................   Daniel
Ohio—George B. Gilliland (Proxy for C. S. Brice)..Hill
Oregon—Fred V. Holman (Proxy for E. D. McKee)..Hill
Pennsylvania—Wm. F. Harrity......................Hill
Rhode Island—R. B. Comstock (Proxy for Samuel R.
  Honey)..Hill
South Carolina—M. L. Donaldson....................   Daniel
South Dakota—James M. Woods.....................Hill
Tennessee—Holmes Cummins.......................Hill
Texas—O. T. Holt.................................Hill
Utah—S. A. Merritt...............................   Daniel
Vermont—Bradley B. Smalley......................Hill
Virginia—Peter J. Otey............................   Daniel
Washington—Hugh C. Wallace.....................Hill
West Virginia—John Sheridan......................Hill
Wisconsin—W. F. Vilas (Proxy for E. C. Wall)......Hill
Wyoming—W. L. Kuykendall.......................   Daniel
Alaska—A. L. Delaney.............................Hill
Arizona—C. M. Shannon...........................   Daniel
District of Columbia—J. L. Norris..................   Daniel
New Mexico—H. B. Ferguson.......................   Daniel
Oklahoma—T. M. Richardson......................   Daniel
Indian Territory—Robert L. Owen..................   Daniel

Recapitulation.—Hill, 27; Daniel, 23; total, 50. Necessary to a choice, 26.

The Chairman declared that Senator Hill, having received the majority of the votes, was the choice of the Committee for Temporary Chairman of the Convention.

On motion of Hon. Charles S. Thomas, of Colorado, seconded by A. W. Sulloway, of New Hampshire, Hon. Simon P. Sheerin, of Indiana, was unanimously selected as Temporary Secretary of the Convention.

On motion of Col. John G. Prather, of Missouri, seconded by Hon. T. H. Sherley, of Kentucky, Col. John I. Martin, of Missouri, was unanimously elected Temporary Sergeant-at-Arms of the Convention.

On motion of Hugh C. Wallace, of Washington, seconded by Hon. Clark Howell, of Georgia, the Temporary Secretary was empowered to select such Assistant Secretaries and Reading Clerks as he might require.

There being no further business the meeting adjourned.

DEMOCRATIC NATIONAL CONVENTION.

FIRST DAY.

CHICAGO, July 7, 1896.

The Democratic National Convention, to nominate candidates for the offices of President and Vice-President of the United States, assembled in the Coliseum Building in the city of Chicago this day at 12 o'clock noon, pursuant to the call of the Democratic National Committee.

Hon. WILLIAM F. HARRITY, of Pennsylvania, the Chairman of the Democratic National Committee, called the Convention to order at 12:30 P. M., in the following words:

THE CHAIR: The Convention will be in order. The Sergeant-at-Arms will see that the aisles are cleared and that everyone shall take his seat. The aisles must be cleared. The delegates will kindly take their seats as promptly as possible. There must be order, especially in the neighborhood of the platform. (Pause, while the aisles are being cleared.)

THE CHAIR: Gentlemen of the Convention, Ladies and Gentlemen: The proceedings of the Convention will be opened with prayer. Prayer will be offered by Rev. ERNEST M. STIRES, Rector of Grace Episcopal Church, Chicago. Delegates, ladies, gentlemen and all in the Convention will please rise while prayer is being offered.

PRAYER.

Almighty God, the hearts of Thy people are lifted in gratitude to Thee for the manifold blessings Thou hast vouchsafed to our country from the dawn of independence unto this day. We thank Thee for the wisdom and courage which enabled our fathers to build better than they knew, for deliverance from all dangers within and without our borders, and for our unparalelled progress in times of prosperity and peace.

O God of our fathers, continue to guide and sustain Thy children. In fear and distress we cry unto Thee for help. Grant us wisdom to know along all the perplexing problems of this time where lies the path of honor and safety. Help us consider the vital questions which must be answered, with thoroughness, patience and tolerance. Give us strength and courage to do what an enlightened conscience shall declare to be our duty. Inspire us with a patriotism above expediency. Remind us that honesty is not only the best, but the only policy worthy the consideration of a great people. May the hearts of all be filled with profound respect and sympathy for our toiling multitudes, oppressed with burdens too heavy for them to bear—heavier than we should allow them to bear. Teach us how to give them relief without doing violence to the rights of any.

While we plead for ourselves we are mindful of the sorrows of others. May the day soon come when no power shall be permitted to inflict upon a brave people indefensibl slaughter and unspeakable shame; when no cloud of despotism shall overhang those who sigh for liberty. May we ever feel the deepest sympathy for the distressed in the great brotherhood of mankind and yet be able to maintain an honorable peace with all.

Upon the great Convention now assembled in Thy presence send Thy gracious blessing. May its members be inspired with the most exalted patriotism, seeking no private or sectional advantage, but only the National good; so that our united and prosperous land may continue to be in all that is truest and best, an inspiration to the nations of the earth. And to Thee, our God, shall we ascribe all the honor and glory, forever and ever. Amen.

THE CHAIR: Gentlemen of the Convention: By direction of the Democratic National Committee, I desire to report the following as the temporary organization of the Convention:

For Temporary Chairman—Hon. DAVID B. HILL, of New York.

For Temporary Secretary—Hon. SIMON P. SHEERIN, of Indiana.

For Sergeant-at-Arms—Col. JOHN I. MARTIN, of Missouri.

For Official Stenographer—EDWARD B. DICKINSON, of New York.

For Assistant Secretaries—WILLIAM D. EDWARDS, of New Jersey; HENRY G. WILLIAMS, of North Carolina; LEOPOLD STRAUSS, of Alabama; A. M. HOLDING, of Pennsylvania; T. O. TOWLES, of Washington, D. C.; J. A. HUDSON, of Missouri; EUSTACE B. GRIMES, of Pennsylvania; THOMAS P. CURLEY, of New Jersey; ALFRED J. MURPHY, of Michigan; GEORGE J. BRENNAN, of Pennsylvania; J. M. CLANCY, of ———.

For Principal Reading Clerk—Hon. JOHN C. NELSON, of Indiana.

For Assistant Reading Clerks—CHARLES P. DONNELLY, of Pennsylvania; VIRGIL RULE, of Missouri; J. H. GILLESPIE, of Iowa; JOSEPH DEUTSCH, of Illinois; WILLIAM J. KOUNTZ, JR., of Pennsylvania; WILLIAM E. THOMPSON, of Michigan; JOHN MINOR, of ———; Hon. JOHN E. CRAIG, of Iowa; CHARLES T. ARNETT, of Arkansas; J. F. POLLARD, of Missouri.

THE CHAIR: What is the pleasure of the Convention as to the report made from the Democratic National Committee? Hon. HENRY D. CLAYTON, of Alabama, has the floor.

Mr. CLAYTON: Mr. Chairman and Gentlemen of the National Democratic Convention: In behalf of twenty-three members of your National Committee, as opposed by twenty-seven, and, as I believe, in accordance with the wish of the great majority of this Convention, I am authorized to present to this Convention a minority report that I shall move as a substitute for a part of the report made by the Chairman of our National Committee, as follows:

July 7, 1896.

To the Democratic National Convention: The undersigned members of the Democratic National Committee, respectfully recommend that the name of the Hon. JOHN W. DANIEL, of Virginia, be substituted in the Committee report for that of the Hon. DAVID B. HILL, of New York, and that the HON. JOHN W. DANIEL be chosen Temporary Chairman of this Convention.

HENRY D. CLAYTON, Ala.
THOMAS C. MCRAE, Ark.
MICHAEL F. TARPEY, Cal.
C. S. THOMAS, Colorado.
SAMUEL PASCO, Florida.
CLARK HOWELL, Georgia.
BARRY N. HILLARD, Idaho.
C. W. BLAIR, Kansas.
ARTHUR SEWALL, Maine.
D. J. CAMPAU, Michigan.
A. J. DAVIDSON, Montana.
R. P. KEATING, Nevada.
F. H. BUSBEE, North Carolina.
WM. C. LEISTIKOW, N.Dakota.
M. L. DONALDSON, South Car.
P. J. OTEY, Virginia.
J. M. BURTON, Utah.
W. L. KUYKENDALL, Wyo.
C. M. SHANNON, Arizona.
J. L. NORRIS, Dist. Columbia.
H. B. FERGUSON, New Mex.
F. M. RICHARDSON, Oklahoma.
ROBERT L. OWEN, Indian Ter.

I therefore move that the minority recommendation of the Committee be adopted; and that the Hon. JOHN W. DANIEL, of Virginia, be chosen Temporary Chairman of this Convention. Upon that proposition, I demand a vote by States and ask for a roll call.

Hon. CHAS. S. THOMAS, of Colorado: I desire to second the minority substitute.

THE CHAIR: The Chair will state the question. The gentleman from Alabama moves to substitute the name of Hon. JOHN W. DANIEL, of Virginia, in place of Hon. DAVID B. HILL, of New York, for Temporary Chairman of the Convention. (Prolonged applause and temporary confusion.) It may as well be understood that so long as the present incumbent is in the chair these proceedings will be conducted in a regular and orderly manner. The Chair recognizes the gentleman from Connecticut, Hon. THOMAS M. WALLER.

Hon. THOMAS M. WALLER: Mr. Chairman: I will give way for the gentleman from New Jersey, who desires to make a statement.

THE CHAIR: The chair recognizes Hon. ALLEN L. MC-DERMOTT, of New Jersey.

Mr. MCDERMOTT: Mr. Chairman and Democrats: Representing the Democracy of a Union in which we hope, after the work of this convention shall have been completed, there will be but one banner and that the one under which every Democrat in the nation can march, head up, proudly on to victory, I rise to pay a tribute from the only State north of the Mason and Dixon line that has never failed to record its electoral vote for the candidates of the National Democratic Convention. A representative of the sentiment of that State I desire to pay the tribute of love and respect of the State of New Jersey to the Hon. JOHN W. DANIEL, of Virginia, but to ask that this Convention give its support to the majority resolutions of the National Committee, placing in the temporary chairmanship that man who gave us the legend under which in the days of trouble in our Eastern Democracy we sailed; that man who electrified this nation by giving us a legend which every Democrat can put upon the banner he followed; who echoed the sentiment that had no East, no South, no North, no West in it, but simply a declaration of faith, "I am a Democrat."

Standing beneath the portrait of the grandest man who ever wrote the word liberty (alluding to Jefferson) I would be false to the spirit of that liberty if I did not believe that on all occasions a Democratic body had the right, by its majority, to select any one whom it chooses to preside over it. But we are here in response to precedent; we are here because it is our custom every four years to meet and deliberate. If it shall be that when we have adjourned from this convention there be in its declaration of principles a plank novel within Democratic declarations, will not that be sufficient introduction of novelty in the campaign?

We understand that the duties of a temporary chairman have for the entire existence of the Democratic party been imposed upon the one selected by the National Committee. Why, then, if the one selected by the National Committee comes from a section of the country not entirely in sympathy with some proposed declaration of principles, should there be a violation of tradition? Why send it out—you will have the majority in this Convention, you whose right to rule the Convention is recognized by a minority—why send it out that this Convention started in its advocacy of a principle that you propose to put in your platform, in the mere matter of selecting a Temporary Chairman, departed from the principles that have governed every Democratic Convention since Democracy assembled in Convention to represent the Democratic party of the country? Let me appeal to your reason. I want, as does every Democrat in the North, to support the actions of this Convention, every one. We of the North are maligned if it is alleged that the Democracy of the North does not desire the substantial prosperity and happiness of every quarter of the Union; for whenever there has been assault upon that prosperity, none has so quickly jumped to the rescue and protection of that section as the Democracy of the North.

Don't begin your Convention by violating a tradition. Don't begin your Convention by violating a rule. If you have the strength of giants use it, not as giants do, but reserve that strength and all the spirit that is in it for the battle that will come in November. You have not, even in the moment of exultation, because of a majority in this assembly, any reasonable right to attack the minority by setting aside traditional rule. We pay the tribute of respect to the candidate selected by the minority of the committee, but we say that tradition is in favor in a Democratic convention of abiding by the rule of the majority; for that is what the majority of this Convention is going to ask the Democrats of this country to do at the election.

Now, Mr. Chairman, we ask of those who represent that sentiment which will undoubtedly be incorporated in the platform, that they do not make the avenue of incorporation offensive to those Democrats of this nation who disagree with them, and we ask the majority to meet the minority in the spirit of reverence for Democratic precedent. Do this and thy gentleness shall make thee great.

The Chairman recognized Hon. THOMAS M. WALLER,

of Connecticut, who took the platform and addressed the Convention as follows:

Mr. WALLER: Mr. Chairman and Fellow Democrats: It will be no fault of mine if I detain you with the remarks I propose to submit for your consideration for more than five minutes; and we all start agreeing, I think, in the first remark I have to make. There are no abler men, there are no braver Democrats than the two whose names are involved in this preliminary discussion. They may be named together and they should be cheered together, and they should be called together in a Democratic Convention: DAVID B. HILL, of New York; and JOHN W. DANIEL, of Virginia. Fellow Democrats, one is a candidate according to the immemorial usage of your party for this position, and the other is a candidate by the exercise of a power never before invoked, and as a substitute candidate.

What ought the Convention to do about it? (A voice "Elect DANIEL.") I agree with the gentleman who squeaked out that honored name, you ought to elect him. Now, hear my suggestion. You ought to elect DAVID B. HILL as your temporary chairman, and every man in this audience, 16 to 1, or 1 to 16, ought to vote for him, and then you ought to elect Senator DANIEL the permanent chairman. (A voice from the Michigan delegation: "We have got another man for that.") I will vouch for it that every man in this Convention whom I assume especially to represent will vote for DANIEL and cheer for DANIEL so that the reverberation of that cheer will be heard in Virginia.

Gentlemen, what is there to prevent it? Are there some other arrangements made? Wipe them out; be equal to the emergency. Have your DANIEL of the South; have your HILL of the East. Disappoint your enemies by doing the courteous, the chivalrous, the judicious thing at the very opening of your Convention. Fellow Democrats, when I came from Connecticut the Republicans told me that we were going to a Convention where we would receive no courtesy, where we would receive no consideration, where we would be trampled upon sixteen men to one, and we should be the underneath ones. I told them, and I believe it to-day, we shall receive no such treatment. We may be disappointed in the platform that they will adopt; we may be disappointed in the candidate they put in nomination, but we will return to the East with the story that while we were beaten, because they had more votes than we had, still we received every courtesy from Democrats. We received the hospitality of the West from the Western Democrats, and we received the chivalrous action of the South from the Southern Democrats.

Fellow Democrats, we can stand your beating us with votes; we can stand any candidate that you will nominate, for you will nominate an honest man. We are in this Convention to stay. I am going to be here, and if every Eastern man bolts I will stay here with the janitor and cheer the last one out. You cannot drive us out of this Convention by the exercise of power. I will tell you what you can do, and I will tell you in a minute. In the name of common sense, fellow Democrats who differ with me on the issue of issues, let me ask you, if you have got two to one in this Convention against us, as I suppose you have, what are you afraid of? Are there any two men down there afraid of me? I am just as good a fighter as there is in the gold section of this place; I will fight as hard and fight as long. Now, if you are not afraid of me, why are you afraid of my associates? What will the Republican party say if you violate your traditions at the very opening of your Convention? One of two things they will say— that you did it because you were afraid of us; and the other thing they will say will be still worse; they will say you did it not because you were afraid of us, but because you glory in heaping upon the East personal indignites. (Cries of "No, no, no.") You say no, but you are asked to do it.

Fellow Democrats, whom are you supposed to turn down in vindicating DANIEL? Who is he? Who is he? He is a man who has voted for the Democracy and never against the interests of the people since he first voted. More than that, he has fought for the Democracy since he has first voted; and more than that, he has fought *successfully*. More than that, he has fought against criticism and the insults of Republicans; he has fought without the approval of Mugwumps, and without the aid of patronage or power. He has fought alone. Turn him down in a Democratic convention? In

God's name, if you turn him down, for what? Afraid of him? Do you think you will stop any Democrat, from North, South or East, from making a speech in this Convention, expressing his views? Do you think you will stop DAVID B. HILL from making a speech? Never, never. The speech he will make to you upon the platform will be, as you can all prophesy, a quiet, conservative and statesmanlike speech that becomes the position. He will know the position, and that he is the organ and officer of both sides as your Temporary Chairman. Let that speech go to the public, and, gentlemen, stop his doing it—stop his doing it, and that speech that he makes from the floor and that goes to the people, with what enthusiasm will it be received. The indignity you put upon him will add to his honor. In God's name, think of this with reason, and with sense, before you impose on the East this indignity.

Gentlemen, you are going to do it, you will do it, will you? (Cries of "Yes, yes," and "No, no.") You will do it, will you? Listen a minute. I want to say one word to you about the Eastern Democrats. We will stand everything from a Democrat—very little from a Republican—but we are not worms. My Southern and Western friends, some of you know it. We are not worms, and if we were, worms sometimes turn against you. Treat us badly, as you mean to do, but as you ought not to do; insult us by breaking the traditions of your party; turn down DAVID B. HILL, as indiscreet men would advise you, and I will tell you just what we will do. There is no threat about it. We will do this: We will fight you for your indignities and insults. In Southern phrase, we will fight you here and elsewhere, and we will fight you until you are sorry for your indiscretion of this day. (Confusion, cries, noise, etc.)

Gentlemen, I will finish what I have to say—if I have the right to do so—if I stay here all summer. And all I have to say in leaving you is this: This is the grand old party of my life; I love it as I love my family, and I regret an unwise action that may harm the party, almost as badly, I believe, as one that might bring disaster to the country. Now, this is the feeling of at least one-third of this Convention in the minority. I ask you to consider that feeling. Let us act together in the preliminary proceedings, and let us stand together in the Democratic party, that party that has stood by the people and fought for them since the birth of the Republic, and I trust in God that nothing will be done here to prevent its continuing to do so while the Republic lasts.

The Chairman recognized the gentleman from Colorado, Hon. CHARLES S. THOMAS.

Mr. THOMAS: Mr. Chairman and Gentlemen of the Democratic National Convention: I shall not detain you long in saying something on behalf of the minority of the Democratic National Convention, and I would say nothing but for the speech of the distinguished gentleman who has just taken his seat. You are told that the majority of this Convention, over-riding precedent and disturbing tradition, proposes by revolutionary methods to force upon this Convention an unheard of procedure. I desire to call your attention to the fact that although in the past history of the Democratic National Conventions there have been no minority reports, nevertheless it is a fact that that which the Committee does is simply a recommendation to be adopted or rejected, as the Convention may decide to do.

And a convention which has the power to adopt, necessarily, if it sees fit to exercise it, has the power to reject. We have no desire whatever to extinguish discussion or to suppress debate; but I will say to my friend from Connecticut that when he left his home in connection with other distinguished Easterners, the papers, through the Associated Press, declared that their purpose was to come to this Convention and capture it without yielding an inch to any one; we felt that a duty was consequently imposed upon the members of the National Committee to carry out, as far as possible, what we conceived to be the wish of the assembled majority of the delegates of the Democracy of the Union. We knew that the Committee, if constituted to represent that sentiment, would have reported in favor of JOHN W. DANIEL, of Virginia.

My friend asks what the Republicans will say of our action. Democrats who have fought in the West, as I have for twenty-five years, have long ago become indifferent to what Republicans say. But we do know that if precedents were necessary, they furnished us one by their own action in this magnificent city in 1880, and those who are so fearful of Republican public opinion ought to pay some deference to Republican precedents.

My friends, I desire to repel the charge that the Democrats of the United States desire to inflict indignity and disgrace upon the senior senator of New York. Nothing can be further from our intention. I recall that four years ago I stood in the Convention as his friend, while his new found friends declared him to be unworthy of the respect of a Democratic Convention. I stood here with others asking a hearing for his advocates, which hearing was denied by the very men who say to-day that he should preside over this Convention. I say with my whole heart God bless him. (Cries of "Amen.") I hope to see him in this campaign with us. If we are to judge his future by his past, his utterances upon the great question which now confronts us will warm the hearts of the free coinage men of the West.

Now, my fellow citizens, every speaker who has preceded me upon this platform has declared, one of them pointing to the portrait of the immortal Washington, which looks down in benediction upon us. (At this point the speaker was interrupted by laughter and was informed that the picture he referred to was Jefferson and not Washington.) Well, Washington is a good name in a Democratic convention, anyhow. They are both immortal Democratic names. They have said, and they have said truly, that it is a matter for the majority to determine.

Now, my fellow citizens, why did we take this action? One word more and I am through. We took this action because we have been told in the public prints of this and other cities where we have no voice, and through which we cannot be heard, where everything we do seems to be misrepresented, for the purpose, I presume, of creating improper impressions, we were told that your purpose was to assume control of this Convention, if possible, and we made up our minds that if the battle must come the sooner it came the better. And, if, as a matter of fact, we are acting within the line of Democratic precedent, so far as majorities are concerned, then I submit to the calm and deliberate judgment of this Convention whether they, and they alone, are not to determine who shall be their presiding officer. I appeal to you, fellow delegates, to stand by the minority report. Let it not be said that in the first skirmish the pickets which you yourselves threw out were driven back into the lines. I ask you to adopt the mainrity substitute upon this question.

The Chair recognized Hon. C. E. WALLER, of Alabama.

Mr. WALLER: Gentlemen of the Convention: I come from a state where a Democrat casts his first vote without a scratch from top to bottom, and his proudest legacy as he passes away is that that was his whole life's work. Twenty-five years ago I began my career as a Democrat by honoring these, our Eastern brother Democrats, and I come here now to say to them that we do not propose to take any action which would look like casting a reflection upon them.

It is a misconstruction of our purpose. We have given the great state of New York every Democratic candidate for the last twenty-five years. I came here four years ago to this great city fighting as hard as I could for the gentleman that is now proposed for Temporary Chairman of this Convention, and I did not take very pleasant medicine when another of New York's honored sons was nominated over him.

I stand here now to say to you we have nothing but the highest regard and respect for him. We have the highest regard and respect for all of the Eastern Democrats of our party. We have given them every important nomination for the last twenty-five years. Haven't the Western and Southern Democrats stood squarely by you? Now, then, I want to know why the creature of the Democratic party—not the party itself, nothing but the Executive Committee—I want to know why that Executive Committee, recognizing the great voice of the majority of the people, did not recognize it in its report? I want to understand how the creature became above the master. I want to know why you gentlemen did not do like we do in my country when we find we have lost a battle—let the majority have all the management of the campaign, its platform and its officers? And I want to say to our Eastern friends that, if I read his story aright, in 1812 the whole of Europe marched with Napoleon, and in 1813 they marched against him. We have been your friends for twenty-five years, voted for every candidate you put up, and when called upon to do it again we will. I say this to show we have no want of courtesy in this matter, and to tell you we think we are entitled to this nomination and the Committee ought to have given it to us.

The Chairman presented Hon. M. F. TARPEY, of California.

Mr. TARPEY: Gentlemen of the Convention: I do not intend to detain you at the outside over three minutes. There is one point that has not been discussed by any gentleman who has been on his feet. I want to explain to this Convention why a minority of the National Committee took the action that they did. The financial question has become and is the only question that the Democratic party feels an all-absorbing interest in to-day.

The Democratic party has been losing its adherents because the Democratic party has failed through its candidates to keep faith which it made with the voter by the platform it adopted. Knowing this fact, and desiring to see the Democratic banner in the ascendancy in November—which I have every hope to see—feeling and knowing that every delegation sent here pledged for silver has a constituency at home looking to this Convention, and if this Convention places as its Temporary Chairman, or Permanent Chairman, in this chair a man who represents the other side, there will be a lukewarmness and a coldness in the campaign that we cannot afford to hazard. It was because the temporary officer of this Convention would sound the keynote which would go all over this country, and which would be the basis of the battle in November. We want the keynote to be sounded by a silver representative. That is the reason, gentlemen, the minority of your committee makes this recommendation, and I submit to you that I think it is right that the majority of this Convention should select its candidate for Temporary Chairman.

THE CHAIR: The Convention will be in order. The Chair will now recognize the gentleman from New York, Hon. JOHN R. FELLOWS.

Mr. FELLOWS. Mr. Chairman and Gentlemen of the Convention: Ordinarily it would be a comparatively immaterial question as to which of these two distinguished, capable and deserving Democrats occupied the position at this table as Temporary Chairman during your deliberations; but the fact of rejection may be pregnant with a good deal of significance. I recognize here and everywhere, and my voice will have ceased its power of utterance when I fail to recognize the splendid ability and the almost unparalelled eloquence, the long devotion to the Democracy which characterize the senator from Virginia, and had he been named for a position in this Convention, or upon our ticket, New York would gladly have responded to the expression and given to him an enthusiastic Democratic support.

But a great deal more than that is involved in this question to-day. I have yet to hear upon the part of these gentlemen who have addressed you an expression or argument, any logical statement as to why you should trample under foot the immemorial usages of your party, why you should violate all of its precedents and adopt a hitherto unheard of mode of procedure. What is the reason for it? What is concealed behind it? What purposes undeveloped in the fact itself are to be accomplished by its consummation?

Is it that you dare not trust the gentleman whom the majority of your National Committee has presented for your temporary officer? No: you repel with becoming and indignant scorn that imputation; his whole life behind him exposed to the glare of the public gaze, always in the light of public observation, repels an insinuation of that character. No right of the majority of this Convention would be assailed, no restrictions placed in the way of the completion of the purpose they have in view.

Now, what is your attitude here to-day? Let us think it over for a moment, at least, before we proceed to this unheard of, this unnecessary act. The National Committee is the only organization existing through four years of interregnum that represents the entire body of the party. When each four years your Convention assembles it then takes matters in its own hands so far as the formulation of its policy and the selection of its candidate is concerned. But there is no power authorized to call this body together, and there is no power authorized to assert the presence of a Convention save this National Committee; and hitherto, for a longer period than is covered by the lives of any of the delegates who sit before me, the National Committee has presented, for purposes of organization alone, and not with reference to deciding the policy of the party—it has presented officers temporarily to fill the chair.

The gentleman from Colorado was unfortunate in his political reminiscence. It would have been better had he left unsaid that which he said, because for the first time in all the history of our Democratic party you are going back of its old traditions; you are violating its time-honored usages, and you are accepting a thing that was done for the first time in the history of parties in this Republic by a Republican Convention.

The gentleman from Colorado told us with powerful force of expression that they of the West who had been fighting the battles of Democracy so long had learned to be somewhat indifferent to the views or wishes of the Republican party. And yet you begin the proceedings of this Convention by accepting a Republican precedent—disowned, denounced, flouted and spit upon by every Democratic body that has ever met.

And against whom have you done it? Ah, gentleman, you will neither question the Democracy, the fealty or the fairness of the gentleman whom the National Committee, in accordance with precedent, has presented here. But go further. Go further and see what precedent you ask us to establish, and see what the significance of your action is. You tell me this is not a personal affront; this is not a thrust at an individual or a section. Then, if this Convention desires to follow the policy suggested by the gentleman from Colorado, and from the first take charge of it in the name of the majority, why is it you propose to accept all the rest of the report of the majority and select for your temporary officers all the persons that they have named other than the illustrious citizen of New York?

I stated that it was the fact of your rejection that would be pregnant with significance and importance. Think, now that you propose to take all the rest that the National Committee offered you. You are willing they should be opposed in sentiment to you, but you decline the gentleman from New York. You cannot evade the consequences of the suspicion that will be aroused.

I trust that it will create no permanent breach, but I cannot understand why it is you strike down a temporary officer, singling him out from the entire list for the rude effects of your blows. I cannot understand it, unless there be some latent and undisclosed reason for it.

Now, gentlemen of the majority, for we perfectly well understand that there is a majority of this Convention, large, pronounced, honest in conviction and decided in purpose, that stands opposed to some of us from the eastern part of the country. We recognize your right to control. You will go on, whoever is chairman here, and through your appropriate medium you will formulate and present to the country your policy. It cannot be changed by the selection of a temporary presiding officer. It will not be effected by anything that may be done during the temporary organization. It is the work of the permanent convention, after it is ascertained, and through its committees.

Now, I want to tell you there is a precedent, and a powerful one, for your accepting here to-day the action of the National Committee, although it is not in accord with the majority sentiment of this Convention. Four years ago we met here, on the part of New York and some other portions of the country, to oppose the candidacy of the present President of the United States whom we all knew had an exceedingly large majority of the delegates elected, but whom we did not believe at the time, perhaps, had the requisite two-thirds.

But the sentiment of the majority was overwhelmingly in favor of the nomination of Mr. CLEVELAND, and we all knew it. And yet, gentlemen, and yet think of it for a moment, when in the National Committee it was suggested that a person known to be friendly to Mr. CLEVELAND's nomination and in sympathy with the majority was named for Temporary Officer it was voted down, and Mr. OWENS, of Kentucky, who was an opponent of Mr. CLEVELAND's and voted against him in the Convention, was selected as Temporary Officer, and every member of the Convention accepted the action of the Committee.

Then when the majority came to its own, it put in the chair a Permanent Officer of its choice. It made up its committees in accordance with this sentiment and had its rightful way in the rest of the Convention.

Gentlemen, do not do this thing. Do not do this thing. It rudely shatters old customs and ancient usages. There is much of sentiment that clings around the past; there is much that appeals to those who have grown wrinkled and gray in the service of the party, that appeals for perpetuation. We may walk after hitherto unknown leaders; we may accept hitherto, as we believe, unknown promulgation of Democratic faith; we may do all you ask of us for the sake of the perpetuation of the party; but at least do it along the paths over which the fathers walked and in accordance with the usages that have grown sacred by years of custom to all of us.

I do not know why you should do this thing. The gentleman has told us that for twenty-five years, the eloquent gentleman from Alabama, that for twenty-five years they have been giving candidates to New York. Very well, it is true that we have been more than honored and favored beyond our deserts. We are grateful in the name of the common Democracy for your generous action, but remember this, Alabama, remember it, Colorado, let it ring like the notes of the Coronation hymn through your hearts and brains, that although you gave us the candidate, New York gave you the only Democratic President you have had for years. Do not strike this blow at your loved son. Indiana has been named for a place upon your temporary organization. Indiana has been accepted. Other States have been named by the choice of gentlemen who will participate in this temporary organization.

You consent to accept them, but you turn against New York and would strike the Democrat whom every Democrat loves, I believe. You single him out for humiliation and sacrifice, and you present in his stead a gentleman we love, revere and honor, and yet who fought four years ago upon the platform of a Democratic National Convention, and who fought by the utterance of one of the most eloquent speeches to which I ever listened for DAVID B. HILL as the rightful candidate; who seconded the nomination of DAVID B. HILL for President of these United States, who now seems to believe that he is unworthy to occupy this position. (Cries of "No, no, no," and cheers.) Ah, gentlemen, gentlemen. "Methinks you do protest too much or not enough;" not far enough if you do not desire to leave the expression of action to the National Committee, then reject all this report and name other officers—the Secretaries, the Sergeant-at-Arms and other officers who are upon that list. The significance of this is that you abandon all precedent, you trample under foot all past laws, and you do it against one man whom you select from this entire list. I make no threats; I shall regret any such action by this Convention. It is not a question of what we will do. We are Democrats, desiring to march with our party, to do what we can toward making its perpetuity and its ascendancy successful, but do not humiliate us; do not seek to inflict what seems to be a mark of punishment upon us, and, especially, if you must select a victim to drag to the altar and throw away the creed of your fathers, the customs you have followed from youth up, at least select a victim not so hallowed to the people, not so beloved by the Democracy, and not so necessary to its success as the one you have selected to-day.

Upon the conclusion of Mr. FELLOWS' speech the Chairman recognized Hon. B. W. MARSTON, of Louisiana, who spoke as follows:

Mr. MARSTON: Mr. Chairman and Gentlemen of the Convention: It is not that we love DAVID B. HILL less, but we love Democracy more. We would not cast any aspersion upon our eastern friends. The best blood of Massachusetts courses through my veins, and I assure you, coming as I do from Louisiana, that we would not cast any aspersions upon you. But, gentlemen, you have got hold of the wrong end of the dilemma. It is us that you would trample upon two-thirds of this Convention; we ask you in the name of two-thirds of this Convention to give us the temporary chairmanship. We state to the Democracy of the United States now that we are on top and mean to assert our rights. If you had given us the temporary chairmanship we would never have protested. (Temporary confusion here resulted growing out of the applause, cheers and laughter that occurred because of an incident in the proceedings.)

THE CHAIR: I want to repeat, and you may depend upon it that I mean it, that no progress will be made with the proceedings of this Convention except in the usual, regular and orderly manner, and the Chair will not be hastened in his action or otherwise influenced by calls from or demonstrations in the galleries.

Mr. MARSTON then continued as follows: Gentlemen of the Convention: Be quiet; listen that ye may hear. If DAVID B. HILL, of New York, had stood by his speech of four years ago he would be the nominee of this Convention. Mr. HILL is now considered by two-thirds of this Convention as representing the other side of this question. It is not against HILL, no; it is not against anybody that we have proceeded in this manner, but it is in favor of the grand labor of America. We know as politicians that there is a wheel within a wheel. We knew that you intended to capture the chairmanship of this Convention, and we were to be held up to scorn and ridicule throughout the length and breadth of this land; we are forcing the issue, we are meeting the enemy in their own den; we are killing them. And now the rule of the majority will be as fair by you as you have been by us and we will make this glorious country of ours blossom like a rose.

The chair recognized Hon. JOHN M. DUNCAN, of Texas, who spoke as follows:

Hon. JOHN M. DUNCAN: Mr. Chairman and Gentlemen of the Convention: It has been urged that to vote against DAVID B. HILL in this Convention is to turn him down. (Cheers and hisses.)

(A DELEGATE: There is some disorder in the galleries. We want the speaker's name and we want order in the galleries.)

THE CHAIR: The Sergeant-at-Arms will see that perfect quiet is preserved. The delegates will kindly co-operate to that end. (Pause.) The name of the Speaker is Hon. JOHN M. DUNCAN, of Texas.

Mr. DUNCAN: Now, I will begin again. It has been said that DAVID B. HILL is to be slaughtered in this Convention. I want to ask you men who is least guilty of the slaughter; those who slaughter, or those who lead to the slaughtering? His name was not cast before this Convention by the silver Democrats. On the contrary, I am informed through the public prints that the National Committee realized that there was a silver majority and it should have arranged a temporary organization of this Convention, so that it might be in consonance with the views of a majority.

We love the name of DAVID B. HILL down in Texas; in proportion as it has decreased for every other Democrat, has it waxed for DAVID B. HILL; and we would that it were in our power to take his name out of this Convention. But we silver men are terribly in earnest, and outside of this Convention, throughout this United States, are thousands on thousands who are as earnest as we are.

Therefore, I say, let no message of things done in this Convention go out to these people who are to do the voting, from which disloyalty to silver might be implied, and no message which would exaggerate in their minds the strength and influence of gold in this convention. Talk of Democratic precedent! I want to know if the first violation of precedent was not when a majority of the Committee whose views were not in consonance with the views of the majority of this Convention, and over the protest of that majority, named a man, knowing that his views were diametrically opposed to the views of a majority of this Convention.

They have forced the issue. We have not. We have got to meet it, and we might as well meet it now as at any time. I want to tell you that I do not believe that there is a single utterance from this platform on the part of Mr. HILL's supporters which would imply a threat against the Democratic party that is indorsed by Mr. HILL. He said, " I am a Democrat." He is a Democrat now, and he is the sort of a Democrat that when his party speaks in Conventions by a majority he will yield obedience to its will. Those who are speaking for him on this platform had best marshal themselves in behind him. What we want is success in November, and as I said we do not want it to go out to the people any exaggeration of the strength of gold in this Convention where they admit that we have almost, if not quite, a two-thirds majority. I thank you for your attention.

THE CHAIR: The Chair recognizes Hon. C. K. LADD, of Illinois.

Mr. LADD: Mr. Chairman and Gentleman of the Convention: I will not take up your time to make a speech. I wish to say as a member of the Democratic party and of the Democratic family, that there is no family quarrel, and I want the neighbors to understand it. I wish to say that the gentlemen from New York and Connecticut cannot say words in praise that shall go beyond the approval of the West, of the Senator of New York, neither can they of the Senator from Nevada or Virginia, or any other place; we know no difference; all Democrats are good and some are better.

There is no antagonism to Senator HILL; a great man, an able man, an honest man. It is not our wish to turn down Mr. HILL as has been said, but it is to be recognized as a majority of the Democratic party of the United States, and that is all. The little giant from Connecticut pleaded with us to stand by traditions of our fathers: we will oblige him, we will do that. The tradition of our fathers is to honor your father and mother, and we cannot honor them any better than by correcting their mistakes. If it was a mistake to allow the Committee to make a Chairman then let us correct it.

The issue is this: By a majority of four the National Committee presents a candidate for Chairman here that is not in accord with the wishes of a majority of the Democrats of the United States. He would preside fairly; no man doubts it. He would make a speech; no man doubts it. It would be an able speech; no man doubts that. It would be a New York speech, and no man doubts that; and the Democratic party —the majority of it—would have to explain that speech to our Republican enemies during the whole campaign. They would say to us "you are divided amongst yourselves."

I say to you that a house divided against itself shall not

succeed in November. The gentleman who says he would fight any other nomination or any other candidate meant to say that this minority report must be disposed of. I say let it be disposed of; let it be done as friends. Why should four men present a candidate that was to them preferable to another, when two-thirds of the party are opposed to his sentiment? And why should we question the integrity of these men?

These men on the National Committee were selected four years ago. No one questions their Democracy. Our state, that we are so proud of, selected her candidate then to represent her—not fully in accord with us on the money issue, yet he is in accord with us as a Democrat, and that is enough. We will not quarrel if you will let us alone. I say to the gentleman from Connecticut that when he made the statement that he would fight us, his tongue slipped; he meant to talk to Republicans; he meant that he would fight them, for no New England Democrat was ever known to desert the ranks.

Let us cease to call hard names; let us cease to be bitter. Let us be all one family. Let us exchange our views and ideas good naturedly and in a candid way and bow to the will of the majority. Why is a motion submitted to an audience if it is not to be passed upon; if it is to be passed upon, it must be by the majority; and may we not vote?

If the Committee has made a recommendation that we do not like, may we not vote against it? And when we do it, exercise the greatest Democratic privilege in the world, of voting as we please. Now, Senator HILL nor his friends can justly take offense. It is not a fight against New York, against Senator HILL, but a recognition of the time-honored Democratic proposition that the majority shall rule. And so let it be.

THE CHAIR: The Chair presents Hon. J. W. ST. CLAIRE, of West Virginia.

Mr. ST. CLAIRE: Mr. Chairman and Gentlemen of the Convention: I came here as warmly in favor of the free and unlimited coinage of silver, and in favor of the nomination of a rock-ribbed silver Democrat as any man in this body, but I feel, my silver friends, that you are about to make a mistake. It is not to honor your platform that you give it to the people; it is not honor for the candidate of your choice that you like to have, but it is his election that you must have, in November. I shall vote, I say, for the adoption of a silver platform and a silver candidate, but we are all here as Democrats; let us adopt silver and a silver candidate according to Democratic methods.

This is a Democratic Convention, and whatever you do, do it as Democrats. If you do otherwise I fear, my friends, as I have said, you will make a serious mistake. I shall vote against JOHN W. DANIEL. Born in his own community and in his own State—it is the regret of my life to have to do it—but my judgment is that it is wrong for the Democratic party, and it will make a mistake should we elect him to preside here now.

Why, gentlemen, what can DAVID B. HILL do in this Chair as your Temporary Chairman? He can do nothing more than make a speech, and if you cannot afford to discuss the money question in your own family how can you better afford to discuss it in the country?

I am too good a silver man to be influenced by a speech from DAVID B. HILL or anybody else; but DAVID B. HILL and every other man in the minority of this Convention is entitled to be heard, heard fairly, heard justly. Again, gentlemen, above everything what we must have, if we would carry our standards to success at the polls, is a united Democracy. What, I repeat, can he do? The great majority of this Convention have selected every committee that is to be appointed by this body. Your platform, your credentials, your permanent organization, every committee has been selected by the silver people in this Convention. He can do nothing more than did WILLIAM OWENS in 1892, an anti-Cleveland man, who presided as its Temporary Chairman. I came here four years ago, and with my friend from Colorado fought hand in hand in favor of DAVID B. HILL for President and against GROVER CLEVELAND. My friends, I believe some of you have lived to see the mistake that you did not follow the wisdom of that minority at that time. Don't make any mistake. Let us be Democrats, let us be silver Democrats.

Throw out the olive branch; you can afford to do it: you can afford to be liberal. Above all, gentlemen, I appeal to you to be just.

The Chair: Gentlemen of the Convention: Unless a clear majority of the delegates to the Convention shall seem to determine or indicate to the contrary, the Chair will direct a call of the roll immediately after the recognition of the next gentleman. It is for the delegates to determine whether the Chair is unduly hasty in thus directing the calling of the roll. (Applause and cries of "Roll, roll.") Then, as the Chair understands the sentiment of the delegates, he will present the last gentleman to be heard upon this question, namely, Hon. Henry D. Clayton, of Alabama.

Mr. Clayton: Mr. Chairman and Gentlemen of the Convention: I promise you that I will not offend the majority with threats. But, gentlemen, what objections have been presented for your consideration against the adoption of the report or recommendation of the minority of the National Committee? First, they say that it is personal to Senator Hill. That we deny. Four years ago, when the anti-snappers, who now praise him, were dominant, I was his friend and champion. There is nothing personal in it.

Again, it is said that it is sectional. We have gone, as the speakers have said, to New York, time after time, for our candidate. We have honored New York. We will honor her again, and let David B. Hill, as I know he will, support the nominee of this Convention—reiterate his declaration for independent free coinage of silver, in line with that great Elmira speech—and we will make him President. I love, honor and respect him, for at his feet I have learned Democracy. He helped to indoctrinate you and me with the faith that is in us in respect to this great and burning issue that we must settle.

Now, then, it is said that we violate tradition. What tradition? Read the writings of the fathers, search them in vain and tell me what law you would bring to bear upon this case. What declaration would you quote as here and now applicable? That is, that the majority of Democrats are entitled to rule in a Democratic Convention.

And it is said again, the fourth objection, that the Republicans will criticise us. Great God, my fellow citizens, has it come to that, that a Democrat is driven to the extremity for an argument to look to Republican approval for what we shall do in our Convention? If there were no other reason than the fact, if it be a fact, that the Republicans will condemn us for it, that in God's name would be enough to make me support the minority.

Now, gentlemen, and you, Mr. CHAIRMAN, I ask you that this debate be closed. We hope that we will have just as free and unlimited coinage of silver as we have had free and unlimited speech. (Applause.)

THE CHAIR: The vote is now to be taken upon the motion offered by the gentlemen from Alabama that the name of Hon. JOHN W. DANIEL, of Virginia, be substituted for that of Hon. DAVID B. HILL, of New York, for the position of Temporary Chairman of this Convention. The Secretary will call the roll of States, and the chairmen of delegations will announce the votes of their respective States.

The Secretary called the roll with the following result:

	Yea.	Nay.
Alabama	22	
Arkansas	16	
California	18	
Colorado	8	
Connecticut		12
Delaware		6
Florida	4	4
Georgia	26	
Idaho	6	
Illinois	48	
Indiana	30	
Iowa	26	

Hon. W. H. STACKHOUSE, of Iowa: I protest against the vote of Iowa as reported.

THE CHAIR: The vote of Iowa is challenged, as I understand it?

Mr. STACKHOUSE: Yes, sir.

THE CHAIR: The Secretary will call the roll of delegates from the State of Iowa.

Hon. WILLIAM J. STONE, of Missouri: Mr. Chairman: I understand the Democracy of the State of Iowa in convention assembled adopted the unit rule; and I desire to know whether a majority of the delegates cannot cast the entire vote of the State?

THE CHAIR: The Chair holds that the proposition, as stated by the gentleman from Missouri, is entirely correct. The Chair further holds that if a delegate from any given State challenges the accuracy or integrity of the vote of the State as announced that then the list of delegates from that State shall be called for the purpose of verifying the vote as reported. The Secretary will proceed with the call of the roll of delegates from the State of Iowa.

The result having been counted by the Secretary, the Chairman made the announcement that the vote had resulted in yeas 19, nays 7, and then said:

THE CHAIR: The Iowa delegation having been instructed to vote as a unit, the vote of that State will be recorded as 26 votes yea.

The Secretary proceeded with the roll-call as follows: Kansas, yeas 20; Kentucky, yeas 26. When Kentucky was reached Hon. W. B. HALDEMAN, of Louisville, challenged the vote cast by Chairman JAMES. Thereupon the Secretary was directed to call the roll.

The Chairman announced the vote as follows: Kentucky casts 24 yeas, 2 nays. Kentucky being under instructions to vote as a unit, the vote will be recorded as 26 yeas.

The roll-call was then continued with the following result: Louisiana 16 yeas; Maine, yeas 2, nays 10; Maryland, yeas 4, nays 12; Massachusetts, nays 30; Michigan, nays 28.

Hon. W. F. McKnight, of Michigan, challenged the announcement made by the Chairman of the Michigan delegation and asked that the delegation be polled.

The Chair announced the result as follows: The vote within the Michigan delegation resulted in 12 yeas and 16 nays. Under the usual practice the 28 votes of Michigan will be cast "nay."

The Secretary continued the call of the roll as follows: Minnesota, yeas 7, nays 11; Mississippi, yeas 18; Missouri, yeas 34; Montana, yeas 6; Nebraska, nays 16; Nevada, yeas 6; New Hampshire, nays 8; New Jersey, nays 20; New Mexico, yeas 2.

When New York was called the Chairman of the New York delegation (Hon. Roswell P. Flower) arose and said that one delegate, Hon. David B. Hill, did not vote. The vote stood 71 nays.

The Chair: As the Chair understands the Chairman of the New York delegation, Senator Hill did not vote on this question, and New York, therefore, cast but 71 nays. Is that correct?

The Chairman of the New York delegation: That is correct. (Loud applause.)

The roll call was continued as follows: North Carolina, yeas 22; North Dakota, yeas 6.

When the State of Ohio was called, the Chairman of the delegation arose and said: "On the poll of the State there were 8 votes nay; but by the operation of the unit rule Ohio casts 46 votes yea."

Hon. S. A. Holding, of Ohio, challenged the vote and the roll of the State was called.

The Chair announced the result as 38 yeas and 8 nays, and stated that, under the unit rule, the vote would be cast as 46 yeas.

The call of the roll was then resumed as follows: Oregon, yeas 8; Pennsylvania, nays 64; Rhode Island, nays 8;

South Carolina, yeas 18; South Dakota, nays 8; Tennessee, yeas 24; Texas, yeas 30; Utah, yeas 6; Vermont, nays 8.

When Virginia was called the Chairman of the delegation said: "Virginia casts 23 votes yea and 1 vote—that of Hon. JOHN W. DANIEL—nay." (Loud applause.) Washington, 5 yeas, 3 nays; West Virginia, 9 yeas, 3 nays.

When Wisconsin was called, the Chairman of the delegation announced that the State cast 24 votes nay. The vote was challenged by Hon. E. J. DOCKERY, and the roll was directed to be called.

THE CHAIR: The Chair desires to know whether the unit rule was adopted by the State of Wisconsin? Will the Chairman of the delegation be kind enough to inform him?

Gen. EDWARD S. BRAGG: I desire to inform the Chair that Wisconsin votes as a unit on all questions, as the majority shall direct.

THE CHAIR: The vote of Wisconsin is 4 yeas and 20 nays; but under the unit rule she casts 24 nays.

Upon the Territories being called, the Chair said:

THE CHAIR: The Chair holds that each of the Territories and the District of Columbia is entitled to but two votes. The vote of New Mexico, as announced, was received inadvertently; but the roll will be corrected, and the attention of the Convention is now called to the mistake. The Secretary will be kind enough to correct the roll by crediting New Mexico with 2 votes instead of 6 votes.

The District of Columbia, Oklahoma and Indian Territory each cast 2 yeas.

The total vote was counted and verified.

THE CHAIR: The tellers agree in their tally and report the vote as follows: Yeas, 556; nays, 349; not voting, 1. The motion offered by the gentleman from Alabama substituting the name of Senator DANIEL for that of Senator HILL for the Temporary Chairmanship of this Convention is adopted.

DEMOCRATIC NATIONAL CONVENTION.

(Although Alabama voted as a unit, it was announced that the following in that delegation would have voted for Senator HILL but for the adoption of the unit rule: D. R. BURGESS, J. P. KNOW, S. J. CARPENTER, J. H. MINGE and H. B. FOSTER.)

The ballot by States was as follows:

States	Total Vote	Yeas	Nays	States	Total Vote	Yeas	Nays
Alabama	22	22	..	New York	72	..	71
Arkansas	16	16	..	North Carolina	22	22	..
California	18	18	..	North Dakota	6	6	..
Colorado	8	8	..	Ohio	46	46	..
Connecticut	12	..	12	Oregon	8	8	..
Delaware	6	..	6	Pennsylvania	64	..	64
Florida	8	4	4	Rhode Island	8	..	8
Georgia	26	26	..	South Carolina	18	18	..
Idaho	6	6	..	South Dakota	8	..	8
Illinois	48	48	..	Tennessee	24	24	..
Indiana	30	30	..	Texas	30	30	..
Iowa	26	26	..	Utah	6	6	..
Kansas	20	20	.	Vermont	8	..	8
Kentucky	26	26	..	Virginia	24	23	1
Louisiana	16	16	..	Washington	8	5	3
Maine	12	2	10	West Virginia	12	9	3
Maryland	16	4	12	Wisconsin	24	..	24
Massachusetts	30	..	30	Wyoming	6	6	..
Michigan	28	..	28	Alaska	2	..	2
Minnesota	18	7	11	Arizona	2	2	..
Mississippi	18	18	..	Dist. Columbia	2	2	..
Missouri	34	34	..	New Mexico	2	2	..
Montana	6	6	..	Oklahoma	2	2	..
Nebraska	16	..	16	Indian Territory	2	2	..
Nevada	6	6	..				
New Hampshire	8	..	8	Totals	906	556	349
New Jersey	20	..	20				

(When the result of this vote was announced there was a period of nearly twenty minutes during which no business could be transacted, on account of the applause, cheers, noise and confusion. The Sergeant-at-Arms directed every delegate to take his seat. He also ordered his assistants to clear the aisles. When order had been restored the Chairman said:)

The Chair: Unless objection be made by the Convention, the Chair will regard the vote which has just been announced as a practical rejection of the report of the Democratic National Committee, and he will not consider it necessary to put the questions involved to formal votes. (Pause.) There being no objection to this suggestion the Chair will appoint Hon. J. K. Jones, of Arkansas, Hon. R. P. Keating, of Nevada, and Hon. Stephen M. White of California, as a committee of three to escort Senator Daniel to the Chair.

Escorted by the committee, the Temporary Chairman, Hon. John W. Daniel, of Virginia, passed up to the platform. When order was restored, Mr. Harrity said:

The Chair: Gentlemen of the Convention. I have the honor of introducing as your Temporary Chairman, Hon. John W. Daniel, of Virginia.

The Chair (Hon. W. F. Harrity) then surrendered the gavel to Senator Daniel, who accepted it and spoke as follows:

Hon. John W. Daniel: Mr. Chairman of the Democratic National Committee: In receiving from your hands this gavel as the temporary presiding officer of this Convention, I beg leave to express a sentiment, which I am sure is unanimous, that no national convention was ever presided over with more ability or with more fairness or with more dignity than by yourself. I can express no better wish for myself than that I may be able in some feeble fashion to mould my conduct by your model and to profit by your example. (Applause and cheers with cries of "Harrity, Harrity.")

Mr. Chairman, the high position to which this Convention has chosen me is accepted with profound gratitude for the honor which it confers and with a keen sense of the responsibility which it entails upon me.

That responsibility I would be wholly inadequate to bear did I depend upon myself, but your gracious aid can make its yoke easy and its burden light. That aid I confidently invoke for the sake of the great cause under whose banner we have fought so many battles and which now demands our stanch devotion and loyal service.

I regret that my name should have been brought in even the most courteous competition with that of my distinguished friend, the great Senator from New York; but no one of dispassionate and candid judgment will misinterpret your meaning, but he will readily recognize the fact as I do, that there is no personality in the preferment given us. He must know as we all do that it is solely due to the principle that this great majority of Democrats stands for and that I stand for with them; and that it is given, too, in the spirit of the instructions received by these representatives of the people, from the people, whom all Democrats bow to as the original and purest fountain of all power.

The birth of the Democratic party was coeval with the birth of the sovereignty of the people. It can never die until the Declaration of American Independence is forgotten, and that sovereignty is dethroned and extinguished.

As the majority of the Convention is not personal in its aims, neither is it sectional. It blends the palmetto and the pine. It begins with the sunrise in Maryland, and spreads into a sunburst in Louisiana and Texas. It stretches in unbroken line across the continent from Virginia and Georgia to California. It sends forth its pioneers from Plymouth Rock and waves over the wheat fields of Dakota. It has its strongholds in Alabama and Mississippi and its outposts in Minnesota, Florida and Oregon. It sticks like a tar-heel in the old North State, and writes sixteen-to-one on the saddlebags of the Arkansas traveler. It pours down its rivulets from the mountains of West Virginia and makes a great lake in New Mexico, Arizona, Wyoming and Idaho, Nevada, Montana and Colorado. It stands guard around the National Capitol, in the District of Columbia, and camps on the frontiers of Oklahoma. It sweeps like a prairie fire over Iowa and Kansas, and lights up the horizon in Nebraska. It marshals its massive battalions in Ohio, Indiana, Illinois and Missouri.

Last, but not least—when I see this grand army and think of the British Gold Standard that recently was unfurled over the ruins of Republican promises in St. Louis. I think, too, of the battle of New Orleans, of which 'tis said:

> "There stood John Bull in marshal pomp,
> But there was Old Kentucky."

Brethren of the East, there is no North, South, East or West in this uprising of the people for American emancipation from the conspiracy of European Kings led by Great Britain, which seeks to destroy one-half of the money of the world, and to make American manufacturers, merchants, farmers and mechanics hewers of wood and drawers of water.

And there is one thing golden that let me commend to you. It is the Golden Rule, to do unto others as you would have them do unto you. Remember the creed of JEFFERSON, that absolute acquiescence in the will of the majority is the vital principle of the Republic, and Democrats as you have been, Democrats that you should be, acquiesce now in the will of this great majority of your fellow Democrats, who only ask you to go with them as they have often times gone with you.

Do not forget that for thirty years we have supported the men that you named for President—SEYMOUR, GREELEY, TILDEN, HANCOCK and CLEVELAND. Do not forget that we have submitted cheerfully to your compromise platforms and to your repeated pledges for bimetallism, and have patiently borne repeated disappointments as to their fulfillment.

Do not forget that even in the last National Convention of 1892, you proclaimed yourself to be in favor of the use of both gold and silver as the standard money of the country and for the coinage of both gold and silver without discrimination against either metal or charge for mintage, and that the only question left open was the ratio between the two metals.

Do not forget that just four years ago in that same Convention the New York delegation stood here solid and immovable for a candidate committed to the free and unlimited coinage of silver and gold at the ratio of sixteen to one; and that if we are for it still it is in some measure from your teachings.

That we owe you much is readily acknowledged and gratefully acknowledged, but are not our debts mutual, and not one sided to each other?

The Force Bill, the McKINLEY Bill and the SHERMAN Law

were the triplet progeny of the Republican party. The first was aimed not more at the South than at the great cities of the East, and chief among them at the great Democratic city of New York, with its munificent patronage. It got its death blow in the Senate where there was not a single Democratic vote from New York and all New England. If you helped to save the South it also helped to save you, and neither the East nor the South could have saved itself had not these great American Republican Senators from the West, TELLER and WOLCOTT, STEWART, JONES, and SANFORD sunk partisanry in patriotism and come to the rescue of American institutions. No man can revive Force Bills now in this glorious reconciled and reunited republic. Our opponents themselves have abandoned them; there is none that can stand between the union of hearts and hands that GRANT in his dying vision saw was coming on angels' wings to all the sons of our common country.

When Chicago dressed with flowers the Southern graves she buried sectionalism under a mountain of fragrance; and when the Southern soldiers cheered but yesterday the wounded hero of the North in Richmond, she answered back "let us have peace, peace and union and liberty forever."

As this majority of Democrats is not sectional neither is it for any privilege or class or for class legislation. The active business men of this country, its manufacturers, its merchants, its farmers, its sons of toil in counting room, factory, field and mine, know that a contraction of currency sweeps away with the silent and relentless force of the gravitation the annual profits of their enterprise and investment, and they know, too, that the gold standard means contraction and the organization of disaster.

What hope is there for the country, what hope for Democracy unless the views of the majority here be adopted?

Do not the people know that it was not silver legislation but the legislation dictated by the advocates of the gold standard that has caused and now continues the financial depression? Do they not know that when their demands upon Democracy were complied with in 1893 and the SHERMAN Law repealed without a substitute,—that the very States of the East that demanded it turned against the Democrats who granted it and swept away their majorities in a torrent of ballots. Had the silver men had their way instead of the gold monometallists,—what storms of abuse would now burst here upon their heads.

But the people are now applying the power of memory and analysis to discover the causes of their arrested prosperity and they need not go far to find them.

They do not forget that when Democracy came to power in 1893 it inherited from its Republican predecessors a tax system and a currency system of which the McKINLEY Law and the SHERMAN Law were the culminating atrocities. It came amidst the panic which quickly followed their enactment, amongst decreased wages, strikes, lock-outs, riots and civic commotions, while the scenes of peaceful industry in Pennsylvania had been turned into military camps. Besides manifold oppressive features the McKINLEY Law had thrown away $50,000,000 of revenue tax derived from sugar under the spectral plea of a free breakfast table, and had substituted bounties to sugar planters, thus decreasing revenue and increasing expenditure, burning the candle at both ends, and making the people pay at last for the alleged free breakfast. From the joint operations of the McKINLEY Law and SHERMAN Law an adverse balance of trade had been forced against us in 1893, a surplus of $100,000,000 in the Treasury had been converted into a deficit of seventy million in 1894 before a Democratic statute had yet come into operation, and engraved bonds prepared by a Republican Secretary to borrow money to support the Government were the ill omens of the preorganized ruin which awaited incoming Democracy at a depleted treasury.

More significant still, the very authors of the ill starred and ill-connected SHERMAN makeshift were already at confessional and upon the stool of penitence and were begging help from Democrats to put out this conflagration of disaster which they themselves had invited.

So far as revenue to support the Government is concerned the Democratic party with but a slender majority in the Senate was not long in providing it, and had not the Supreme Court of the United States reversed its settled doctrines of a hundred years the income tax incorporated in their tariff bill would long since have supplied the deficit.

Respecting finance, the Republicans, Populists and Democratic parties, while differing upon other subjects, had alike declared for the restoration of our American system of bimetallism.

By Republican and Democratic votes alike the SHERMAN Law was swept from the statute books. The eagerness to rid the country of that Republican incubus being so great that no pause was made to provide its substitute. But in the very act of its repeal it was solemnly declared to be the policy of the United States to continue the use of both gold and silver as standard money and to coin them into dollars of equal intrinsic and exchangeable value.

The Republican party has now renounced the creed of its platforms and of our statutes. It has presented to the country the issue of higher taxes, more bonds and less money. It has proclaimed for the British gold standard.

We can only expect, should they succeed, new spasms of panic and a long protracted period of depression. Do not ask us then to join them on any of these propositions. Least of all, ask us not to join them upon the money question to fight a sham battle over the settled tariff, for the money question is the one paramount issue before the people and it involves true Americanism more than any economic issue ever presented to the people at a Presidential election.

Existing Gold standard ? Whence comes the idea that we are upon it. Not from the Democratic platform of 1892, which promised to hold us to the double one. Not from the last enactment of Congress on the subject in repealing the SHERMAN Law, which pledges us to the continuance of the double one. Not from any statute of the United States now in force. No, we are not upon any gold standard, but we have a disordered and miscellaneous currency, of nine varieties, three of metal and six of paper, the product for the most part of Republican legislation, rendered worse by Treasury practices begun by Republican Secretaries and unfortunately copied.

And consider these facts. The federal, state and municipal taxes are assessed and paid by the standard of the whole mass of money in circulation. No authority has ever been conferred by Congress for the issue of bonds payable in gold, but distinctly refused. The Specie Resumption Act of 1875 made the surplus revenue in the Treasury, not gold only, the redemption fund. Before the period for the operation of that act arrived provision was made by the BLAND-ALLISON Act which has added to our circulation some three hundred and fifty millions of standard silver money or paper based upon it and they are sustained at parity with gold by nothing on earth but the metal in them and their legal tender functions. We have no outstanding obligations payable in gold except the small sum of forty-four million of gold certificates which of course should be so paid. All of our specie obligations are payable in coin, which means silver or gold at Government option, or in silver only. There is more silver or paper based upon it in circulation than there is in gold or paper based on gold. And that gold dollars are not the sole units of value is demonstrated by the fact that no gold dollar pieces whatever are now minted.

If we should go upon the gold standard it is evident that we must change the existing bimetallic standard of payment of all public debts, taxes and appropriations, save these specifically payable in gold only. And as we have twenty billions of public and private debt it would take more than three times all the gold in the country to pay one year's interest in that medium.

We should be compelled hereafter to contract the currency by paying the five hundred millions of greenbacks and SHERMAN notes in gold, which would nearly exhaust the entire American stock in and out of the Treasury, and the same policy would require that the three hundred and forty-four millions of silver certificates should be paid in gold as foreshadowed by the present Director of the Mint in his recommendation.

This means the increase of the public debt by five hundred millions of interest bearing bonds with the prospect of three hundred and forty-four millions to follow.

The disastrous consequences of such a policy are appalling to contemplate, and the only alternative suggested is the free coinage of silver as well as gold and the complete restoration of our American system of bimetallism.

Bring us we pray you no more makeshifts and straddles. Vex the country with no more prophesies of smooth things to come from the British republican gold propaganda.

The fact that European nations are going to the gold standard renders it all the more impracticable for us to do so, for the limited stock of gold would have longer division and a smaller share for each nation.

Remember how punctually predictions made when the unconditional repeal of the SHERMAN Law out of silver have been refuted.

Instead of protecting the treasury reserve, as was proclaimed it would do, an unprecedented raid was promptly made upon it, and two hundred and sixty-two millions of borrowed gold have been insufficient to guarantee its security.

Instead of causing foreign capital to float to us, it has stimulated the flow of gold to Europe, and the greenback notes and the SHERMAN notes, which are just as much payable in silver as in gold, have been used to dip the gold out of the Treasury and pour it into the strong boxes of the war lords of Europe.

Instead of reviving business, this policy has further depressed it. Instead of increasing wages, this policy has further decreased them. Instead of multiplying opportunities for employment, this policy has multiplied idlers who cannot get it.

Instead of increasing the prices of our produce, this policy has lowered them, as is estimated, about fifteen per cent. in three years. Instead of restoring confidence, this policy has banished confidence. Instead of bringing relief, it has brought years of misery, and for obvious reasons; it has contracted the currency four dollars a head for every woman, man and child in the United States since November 1, 1893. And with this vast aggregate of contraction the prices of land and manufactured goods and of all kinds of agricultural and mechanical produce have fallen; the public revenue has fallen, the wages of labor have fallen, and everything has fallen but taxes and debts, which have grown in burden. While on the other hand, the means of payment have diminished in value. Meantime, commercial failures have progressed. The dividends of banks have shrunken.

Three-fourths of our railway mileage have gone into the

hands of receivers, and the country has received a shock from which it will take many years to recover. In this condition the new-fledged monometallists ask us to declare for a gold standard and wait for relief upon some ghostly dream of International Agreement.

But the people well know now that the conspiracy of European monarchs led by Great Britain has purposes of aggrandizement to subserve in the war upon American silver money, and stand in the way of such agreement. They are creditor nations and seek to enhance the purchasing power of the thousands of millions of debt owed to them all over the world and much of which we owe. They draw upon us for much of their food supplies and raw materials, for meat, wheat, corn, oil, cotton, wool, iron, lead and the like staples, and seek to get them for the least money. Besides this Great Britain has large gold mines in South America, Australia and South Africa, and by closing our silver mines has greatly enhanced their value and their products. Recent British aggressions against Venezuela and the settlements in South Africa were moved by the desire to add to the possession of gold mines and by monopolizing that metal as far as possible to assert the commercial supremacy of the world.

No nation can call itself independent that cannot establish a financial system of its own. We abhor the pretense that this the foremost, richest, and most powerful nation of the world, cannot coin its own money, without suing for International Agreement at the courts of European autocrats, who having that primary interest to subserve, have for many years held out to us the idea before every Presidential election that they would enter upon such an agreement and foiled every effort to obtain it afterwards.

We have never had an international agreement about our money system with foreign nations, and none of the founders of the Republic ever dreamed that such an agreement was essential. We have had three international conferences with European powers in order to obtain it and to wait longer upon them is to ignore the people's interest, to degrade our national dignity and to advertise our impotence and folly.

The concession that the scientific thought is for the double standard as the only solution of financial difficulty is concession that wisdom far and wide cheers us on. The declaration that the English Commons, the Prussian Diet and French Minister of Finance have recently expressed themselves in its favor shows that it would succeed if not suppressed by the sinister influences of autocratic power.

The concession that international agreement could restore the metals to equality and that such restoration would be a boon to mankind, is a concession that law regulates the value of money and that the bimetallists are right in their theories of a double standard.

The framers of our Constitution knew this when they gave power to Congress to coin money and regulate the value thereof and of foreign coins, and when they prohibited the States from making any thing but gold and silver legal tender. HAMILTON knew this when he framed the first mint act in 1792 and based the unit of our currency upon both metals for the double reason assigned by him that to exclude one would reduce it to a mere merchandise and involve the difference between a full and a scanty circulation. JEFFERSON knew this when he indorsed the work of HAMILTON, and WASHINGTON when he approved it. DANIEL WEBSTER knew this when he declared that gold and silver were our legal standard and that neither Congress nor any State had the right to establish any other standard or displace this standard.

Gen. GRANT knew this when he looked to silver as a resource of payment and found to his astonishment that a Republican Congress had demonetized it and that he as President had unwillingly signed the bill. The people of the United States know this now and know also that "they who would be free themselves must strike the blow."

We maintain that this great Nation with a natural base, as GLADSTONE said, of the greatest continuous empire ever established by man, with far more territory and more productive energy than Great Britain, France and Germany combined, without dependence upon Europe for anything that it produces and with European dependence upon us for much that we produce, is fully capable of restoring its constitutional money system of gold and silver at equality with each other, and as our Fathers in 1776 declared our National Independence, so now has the party founded by THOMAS JEFFERSON, the author of that declaration, met here to declare our financial independence of all other nations and to invoke all true Americans to assert it by their votes and place their country where it of right belongs as the freest and foremost nation of the earth.

Gentlemen of the Convention, I now announce that the National Democratic Convention is in session and is ready to proceed to the business of permanent organization.

(There was so much confusion in the hall when Chairman DANIEL finished his speech that he requested the Sergeant-at-Arms to restore order. The Sergeant-at-Arms thereupon directed the Assistant Sergeants-at-Arms to see that all were seated, and the police were directed to remove everybody from the hall who were not seated.)

The Chair then recognized Senator J. K. JONES, of Arkansas, who said:

Senator JONES: On behalf of the silver members of this Convention and at the personal request of a number of them, I offer the following resolution and move its adoption:

(The resolution was sent to the platform, and read as follows:)

Resolved, That the thanks of this Convention are due to Hon. WILLIAM F. HARRITY, Chairman of the Democratic National Committee, for the able and impartial manner in which he has discharged his duty while presiding over the deliberations of this Convention. (Cheers and applause.)

The resolution was unanimously adopted.

The Chair recognized Senator STEPHEN M. WHITE, of California, who offered the following resolution and moved its adoption:

Resolved, That the rules of the last National Democratic Convention, including the rules of the House of Representatives of the Fifty-third Congress, so far as applicable, govern this body until otherwise ordered.

The resolution was unanimously adopted.

Hon. J. S. HOGG, of Texas, introduced the following resolution, and moved its adoption:

Resolved, That the roll of the States and Territories be now called, and that each delegation name one member to act as a member of the Committee on Credentials; one member as a member of the Committee on Permanent Organization; one member as a member of the Committee on Rules and Order of Business; one member as a member of the Committee on Platform, and that all resolutions relating to the platform and all communications addressed to the Convention, be referred, without reading or debate, to the Committee on Platform, and that the credentials of each delegation be delivered to the member of the Committee on Credentials from such delegation.

The Secretary called the roll of States and Territories for the appointment of these several Committees.

The following are the Committees as thus selected:

COMMITTEE ON CREDENTIALS.

Alabama—R. T. GOODWIN.
Arkansas—S. M. TAYLOR.
California—WILLIAM R. BOURKE.
Colorado—T. J. O'DONNELL.
Connecticut—E. D. COOGAN.
Delaware—WILLIAM H. BOYCE.
Florida—E. D. LUKENBILL.
Georgia—H. T. LEWIS.
Idaho—T. REGAN.
Illinois—A. W. HOPE.
Indiana—ELI MARVIN.
Iowa—WILL A. WELLS.
Kansas—J. H. ATWOOD.
Kentucky—DAVID R. MURRAY.
Louisiana—H. W. OGDEN.
Maine—L. B. DEASY.
Maryland—EDWIN WARFIELD.
Massachusetts—JOHN C. CROSBY.
Michigan—A. R. TRIPP.
Minnesota—C. L. BAXTER.
Mississippi—A. J. MCLAURIN.
Missouri—M. E. BENTON.
Montana—W. G. DOWNING.
Nebraska—C. HOLLENBECK.
Nevada—R. P. KEATING.
New Hampshire—C. A. SINCLAIR.
New Jersey—E. P. MEANY.
New York—SMITH M. WEED.
North Carolina—W. D. TURNER.
North Dakota—J. H. HOLT.
Ohio—ULRIC SLOAN.
Oregon—W. F. BUTCHER.
Pennsylvania—J. H. COCHRAN.
Rhode Island—JOHN E. CONLEY.
South Carolina—W. H. ELLERBE.
South Dakota—S. A. RAMSEY.
Tennessee—T. M. MCCONNELL.
Texas—J. W. BLAKE.
Utah—DAVID EVANS.
Vermont—S. C. SHURTLIFF.
Virginia—C. A. SWANSON.
Washington—THOMAS MALONEY.
West Virginia—W. E. R. BYRNE.
Wisconsin—JOHN H. BRENNAN.
Wyoming—J. W. SAMMON.
Alaska—LEWIS L. WILLIAMS.
Arizona—J. F. WILSON.
Dist. of Columbia—JOHN BOYLE.
Indian Ter.—Z. JAMES WOODS.
New Mexico—JOHN Y. HEWITT.
Oklahoma—W. S. DENTON.

110   OFFICIAL PROCEEDINGS OF THE

COMMITTEE ON PERMANENT ORGANIZATION.

Alabama—R. E. Spraggins.
Arkansas—J. G. Wallace.
California—J. V. Colman.
Colorado—B. O. Sweeney.
Connecticut—James Aldis.
Delaware—B. L. Lewis.
Florida—T. J. Appleyard.
Georgia—G. Pope Brown.
Idaho—J. C. Rich.
Illinois—William Prentiss.
Indiana—John Overmeyer.
Iowa—Richard F. Jordan.
Kansas—J. Mack Love.
Kentucky—G. G. Gilbert.
Louisiana—O. O. Provosty.
Maine—Charles L. Snow.
Maryland—Spencer C. Jones.
Massachusetts—G. F. Maxwell.
Michigan—L. H. Salisbury.
Minnesota—John F. McGovern.
Mississippi—H. Cassidy.
Missouri—C. F. Cochran.
Montana—Paul Fusz.
Nebraska—J. C. Luikart.
Nevada—P. J. Dunne.
New Hampshire—G. Woodbury.

New Jersey—George A. Helme.
New York—Fred'k R. Coudert.
North Carolina—E. B. Jones.
North Dakota—H. R. Hartman.
Ohio—E. B. Finley.
Oregon—J. Welch.
Pennsylvania—C. H. Noyes.
Rhode Island—Jas. J. Van Alen.
South Carolina—D. J. Bradham.
South Dakota—Geo. H. Culver.
Tennessee—E. W. Carmack.
Texas—J. M. Duncan.
Utah—Samuel R. Thurman.
Vermont—Wells Valentine.
Virginia—H. S. K. Morrison.
Washington—James E. Fenton.
West Virginia—E. D. Talbott.
Wisconsin—James G. Flanders.
Wyoming—T. Dyer.
Alaska—Richard F. Lewis.
Arizona—W. H. Burbage.
Dist. of Columbia—F. P. Morgan.
Indian Ter.—Wm. P. Thompson.
New Mexico—W. S. Hopewell.
Oklahoma—H. C. Brunt.

COMMITTEE ON RULES.

Alabama—A. O. Lane.
Arkansas—Charles Coffin.
California—J. G. McGuire.
Colorado—H. H. Seldomridge.
Connecticut—Lyman T. Tangier.
Delaware—John F. Saulsbury.
Florida—F. B. Carter.
Georgia—C. T. Zachry.
Idaho—George V. Bryan.
Illinois—George W. Fithian.
Indiana—E. Henderson.
Iowa—F. D. Bayless.
Kansas—S. A. Riggs.
Kentucky—W. T. Ellis.
Louisiana—S. T. Baird.
Maine—John Scott.
Maryland—James W. McElroy.
Massachusetts—S. K. Hamilton.

Michigan—John B. Shipman.
Minnesota—C. W. Schultz.
Mississippi—H. D. Money.
Missouri—David A. DeArmond.
Montana—J. M. Fox.
Nebraska—W. D. Oldham.
Nevada—J. W. Petty.
New Hampshire—A. M. Blondin.
New Jersey—Henry D. Winton.
New York—Francis N. Scott.
North Carolina—A. M. Waddell.
North Dakota—J. B. Eaton.
Ohio—Frank Harper.
Oregon—J. D. McKennon.
Pennsylvania—Chas. A. Fagan.
Rhode Island—John S. Tucker.
South Carolina—W. D. Evans.
South Dakota—Edward Cook.

Tennessee—J. D. RICHARDSON.
Texas—W. W. GATEWOOD.
Utah—R. C. CHAMBERS.
Vermont—WELLS VALENTINE.
Virginia—THOMAS E. BLAKEY.
Washington—J. L. SHARPSTEIN.
West Virginia—J. W. ST. CLAIR.
Wisconsin—JOHN J. WOOD.

Wyoming—T. DYER.
Alaska—GEO. R. TINGLE.
Arizona—HUGH E. CAMPBELL.
Dist. of Columbia—E. L. JORDAN.
Indian Ter.—E. POE HARRIS.
New Mexico—M. M. SALAZAR.
Oklahoma—E. F. MITCHELL.

COMMITTEE ON RESOLUTIONS.

Alabama—JOHN H. BANKHEAD.
Arkansas—J. K. JONES.
California—STEPHEN M. WHITE.
Colorado—C. S. THOMAS.
Connecticut—LYNDE HARRISON.
Delaware—GEORGE GRAY.
Florida—R. A. DAVIS.
Georgia—ENAN P. HOWELL.
Idaho—B. N. HILLERD.
Illinois—N. E. WORTHINGTON.
Indiana—JAMES MCCABE.
Iowa—J. S. MURPHY.
Kansas—J. D. MCCLEVERTY.
Kentucky—P. W. HARDIN.
Louisiana—S. M. ROBERTSON.
Maine—C. V. HOLMAN.
Maryland—JOHN PRENTISS POE.
Massachusetts—J. E. RUSSELL.
Michigan—GEORGE P. HUMMER.
Minnesota—JAMES E. O'BRIEN.
Mississippi—J. Z. GEORGE.
Missouri—F. M. COCKRELL.
Montana—E. D. MATTS.
Nebraska—W. J. BRYAN.
Nevada—T. W. HEALY.
New Hampshire—IRVING W. DREW.

New Jersey—A. H. MCDERMOTT.
New York—DAVID B. HILL.
North Carolina—E. J. HALE.
North Dakota—W. N. ROACH.
Ohio—ALLEN W. THURMAN.
Oregon—M. A. MILLER.
Pennsylvania—R. E. WRIGHT.
Rhode Island—DAVID S. BAKER.
South Carolina—B. R. TILLMAN.
South Dakota—W. R. STEELE.
Tennessee—A. T. MCNEIL.
Texas—JOHN H. REAGAN.
Utah—J. L. RAWLINS.
Vermont—P. J. FARRELL.
Virginia—CARTER GLASS.
Washington—R. C. MCCROSKEY.
West Virginia—W. M. KINCAID.
Wisconsin—WILLIAM F. VILAS.
Wyoming—C. W. BRAMEL.
Alaska—CHAS. D. ROGERS.
Arizona—W. H. BARNES.
Dis. Columbia—R. E. MATTINGLY.
Indian Territory—R. L. OWEN.
New Mexico—A. A. JONES.
Oklahoma—M. L. BIXLER.

Hon. E. B. FINLEY, of Ohio: The delegation from Ohio desires to enter its protest on behalf of the contesting delegates from South Dakota. They desire to enter their protest against any of the members now upon the roll being assigned to any committee until the contest is settled.

THE CHAIR: Any protest that is desired to be filed by the contesting delegation of South Dakota will be received and referred to the Committee on Credentials unless the Convention desires otherwise.

General FINLEY: The point I make is that they protest against those other delegates serving upon the respective committees pending the contest.

THE CHAIR: The Chair desires to say to the delegates from Ohio that the temporary organization of the Convention must recognize the temporary roll as furnished to it and accept it as *prima facie* correct. It cannot undertake to do anything about it except to refer it to the Committee on Credentials, which is according to the custom of Democratic conventions heretofore.

Hon. WM. SULZER, of New York: I offer the following resolution and ask to have it referred to the Committee on Resolutions.

THE CHAIRMAN: The resolution of the gentleman from New York can only be considered by unanimous consent while other business is pending, but if there be no objection the resolution of the gentleman will be received and read. (Cries of "No, no, no.") Objection is made to the reception of the resolution and it will not be read.

Hon. S. M. WHITE, of California: At the request of the Sergeant-at-Arms, I will announce that immediately upon a recess of the Convention the several Committees appointed will meet in the rooms to my right, in the direction to which I now point. All of the members of such Committees are requested to be prompt.

On motion of Senator J. K. JONES, of Arkansas, the Convention adjourned until Wednesday, July 8th, 1896, at 9 o'clock A. M.

SECOND DAY.

MORNING SESSION.

CHICAGO, July 8, 1896.

The Convention was called to order at 10:47 A. M. by the Chairman, Hon. JOHN W. DANIEL, in the following words:

THE CHAIR: The Convention will be in order. The proceedings of the Convention will be opened with prayer by Rev. THOMAS EDWARD GREEN, of Grace Episcopal Church, Cedar Rapids, Iowa.

PRAYER.

We praise Thee, oh Lord. We acknowledge Thee to be the Lord. All the earth doth worship Thee, Father everlasting. We adore Thee as the King of nations, for by Thee they are and have their being. We worship Thee as the God of wisdom and truth, for of Thee cometh every good and perfect thing. We adore Thee as the great all-Father, for of one blood Thou hast made all peoples of the earth. Reveal Thyself to us, we beseech Thee, alike as Creator, as Father and as Guide. Rule Thou over us, for Thou art mighty. Teach us, for Thou alone doth know the secret things of eternity. Still the voices of our contention, for Thou alone art infinite good.

Especially grant Thy blessing, we beseech Thee, to this great convention, gathered together from all parts of our fair land. In the days that are gone Thou didst guide our fathers; teach us, we pray Thee, their children. Oh, Thou, who alone canst rule the unruly wills and affections of sinful men, dominate our minds for good, for humanity and for God. And as these, Thy servants, meet for the high concerns of state, grant them wisdom, we beseech Thee, that that which they do may tell in the years to come for the advancement and the lifting up of our human kind. Save them from error, cleanse them from prejudice and passion, and may righteousness by their action triumph over wrong; may liberty ever drive away oppression; may virtue ever dominate darksome vice, and may Thy kingdom come and Thy will be done on earth, and so may the great true democracy, good of all people, the sublime philosophy of the Commoner of Nazareth everywhere prevail. May Thy blessing be upon us and upon our children, now and forever more, Amen.

Secretary SHEERIN announced that F. F. STOLL, the Postmaster of the Convention, desired to say to the delegates that if they wished to have their mail addressed to the Convention hall it will be delivered to them on the floor. There is a good deal of mail already in his hands addressed to persons in care of delegates, which could be obtained by calling at the Convention postoffice at the southeast end of the building.

THE CHAIR: The first business in order to-day is the reports of the committees. Are any of the committees ready to report? No business can be conducted except by unanimous consent until they report. The Committee on Credentials.

The Sergeant-at-Arms MARTIN reported that the Committee on Credentials would meet at once in its room.

Hon. JOHN MARTIN, of Kansas: I move that a recess of five minutes be declared and that ex-Governor HOGG, of Texas, be requested to address the Convention.

The motion was adopted.

THE CHAIR: Gentlemen of the Convention, I have the honor to present to you ex-Governor J. S. HOGG, of Texas.

Mr. HOGG: Mr. Chairman and Gentlemen of the Convention: This should be a proud occasion to every American citizen. The Democrats, not the voters, but the Democrats of the United States, have gathered here upon a mission of importance to the great American people. We should conduct our meeting, our Convention, in a spirit of friendliness, as brethren of the same family, with a full, fixed intent of winning the victory next November. The Democracy is a party of majorities. Unless the majority can rule then we must have the minority in control of our government, which in time will lead to centralism. We have more before us than a fight against our brethren who differ with us. We have a common enemy to contend with this fall, and every Democrat in the United States should lay aside his personal feelings, his personal preferences, and march lockarmed with his rival brother in the common cause of American liberty against Republicanism.

The Republican party to-day is again arraying itself in robes of glittering generalities, pleading for supremacy again in these United States. It is dealing in glittering generalities; it is treating the people with a pledge of better behavior if it is trusted again. With one common refrain the great American people next fall will reply to this great dissembler, this great deceiver: "We will not try you again. Your train of iniquities has marked a black spot of shame across the American escutcheon, and we, the people, will eradicate it if it takes fifty years of hard work. When we overthrew you four years ago we only clipped part of the top growth. We thought we were getting it all, but made a mistake which shall not be repeated. Now, we propose to dig you up, root and branch, and lay you out upon the hillside of despair, there to wither and rot and dry up and blow away forever."

The American people cannot in self-respect tolerate this great class-courtier; this masked coquetter, this great classmaker and mass smasher, this great bounty giver and poorhouse maker, called the Republican party. Upon three grounds alone, to say nothing of other good and potent reasons, the people cannot and will not tolerate the return of the Republican party to power in this government. Our fight now, my brethren, is not to be waged with one another, but with the common foe. If we will unite, we can carry consternation, disaster and defeat into the Republican ranks. The three grounds upon which we cannot tolerate the Republican party, to say nothing of others, are these:

First: It proposes to filter through the fingers of the rich men to the wageworker, under the pretext of taxation for revenue, the paltry stipends which they receive.

Second: It proposes to give bounties from the public treasury to wealthy planters under the pretense of giving sugar to the poor.

Third: It proposes to belittle Americanism and to assert the inability of the people of this government to control themselves by yielding to the will of the crowned heads of other countries the regulation of our Federal finances.

These are the basic principles upon which our government is to rest if this Republican party is returned to power. They forebode the usurpation of the rights of the masses, the constitutional rights of the great masses of people, to make way for their beloved and favored few, who may have the time and the means of reorganizing our government into a centralism. These men to-day are aiming at the liberties of the great masses of people by suppressing their constitutional rights.

For over thirty years this party of promises has been telling the wage worker that the way for him to get rich and independent is for the government to first make the manufacturer rich; that by the process of protection wealth would flow into the corporate treasuries and be paid out in high wages. These people have to a great extent believed those promises, until they have found them to be shams, frauds and farces. The quintescence of that farcical practice has been governmental protection of the wealthy, with the laborer left to protect himself. He has done this through labor organizations in part, without which his condition to-day would be that condition to which a man is reduced whenever he depends upon protection from any other source than himself, that condition of penury, of pauperism and of pity.

This protected class of Republicans proposes now to destroy labor organizations. To that end it has organized syndicates, pools and trusts and proposes through Federal courts, in the exercise of their unconstitutional powers by the issuance of extraordinary, unconstitutional writs, to strike down, to suppress and to overawe those organizations, backed by the Federal bayonet. My friends, when that day comes you will see the last bulwark of labor gone. You will see the exposure of this system of protection in all its criminal phases. You will see when that day comes this pampered pet of protectionism, standing like a colossal giant, with one hand in the Federal treasury, with the other upon the throat of the producer, proclaiming to the world the beauty of the bounty system called protection.

You understand here what protection means as applied in its general form. Down South we know what it means applied to its special form, in its undisguised, its realistic, its true form, in the nature of a bounty, applied in the way of bounties upon sugar, bounties to those who are able themselves to protect themselves and to support themselves independent of any government. Under the Federal law passed by the Republican party under Republican rule the planter of the South who raised over five hundred pounds of sugar got from the public treasury two cents a pound, paid by the government in cash. You see the point? These men who run those plantations and got the bounty are the wealthiest planters in the Southland, and they are among our richest men. Many of them got from $10,000 to $100,000 a year in bounty, in addition to immense profits upon their great crops. Contrast those wealthy men, rolling in wealth, backed by the government under the sugar bounty system, with those farmers who work day by day, from sunrise to sundown, and pay their taxes out of four cent cotton, fifteen cent corn and thirty cent wheat.

My friends, in addition to the payment of that bounty then to a rich class of Democrats, the Republican party by that insidious method reduced and prostituted many of those poor creatures from Democracy into Republicanism. Do you catch the point? When the Democratic party took that sugar teat out of the mouths of these agricultural tax-eating government wards they bleated around like lost calves in a storm. They claimed they were bound to starve. Men who lived there in their mansions and rolled in luxury were the only ones to get the benefit of this Republican bounty called protection.

My friends, in 1893, to illustrate by giving you some facts and figures, the State of Texas owned and operated a sugar plantation of 2,100 acres by convict labor. In that year the aggregate amount of yield from the crop in money was $70,000. She was out in expenses $44,000. She received by way of net profit $26,000 upon that one sugar crop. Had she received the twenty odd thousand dollars tendered by the Federal government by way of sugar bounty her yield net would have been about double. She would not accept it; she would not accept it because she would not stoop to such a crime against the American people. In her sovereign capacity she spurned the poisonous bait, hurled it back, and set the example of Democracy by the sovereign action of a sovereign State, in condemnation of the Republican poisonous bait aimed at the prostitution of the people.

My friends, that sugar bounty is but a practical illustration of the protective system. Down there we have it thoroughly illustrated. We have seen it in all of its criminal phases; we have seen it in its natural form; we saw it before it got its clothes on; we saw it as it came from the womb of Republicanism; we saw its deformities. We know its iniquities; we know the slimy breath that hovers around its iniquitous form. My friends, these men who received the bounty from the Federal treasury are rampant Republicans, intending in this campaign to contribute to the campaign corruption fund for the purpose of endeavoring to carry Illinois, Ohio, Indiana, Iowa and Michigan, together with other agricultural states of the West, and thus to fasten upon the liberty-loving people of this country the festering, the putrid, the nauseating ulcer of the sugar bounty in the name of protection.

If you people could see that thing in its pure, natural form you would say that it is the bastard mongrel of protection and crime, the very existence of which, the natural conception of which, and the corrupt existence of it here is a menace to the rights and liberties of a free people. With one fell swoop, by the terrible power of your ballots next fall, you will strike down the hideous monster and the whole corrupt family to which it belongs.

This bounty protective system of Republicanism has lost that great party its moorings, has forced it to surrender its independence and to confess the inability of the American people to govern themselves. It has caused them to bow down before foreign powers, to confess that the people of the United States are incapable of self-government. It is the quintescence of Republicanism, it is the capstone of their crime, leading them on to confess the inability of the American people to manage their own affairs.

My friends, when I say that, I wish to call your attention to the proof. Read what they said in their St. Louis platform, and if what I charged is not supported by the proof I will confess myself an ignoramus, unable to understand plain English. Here is what they said upon the money question at St. Louis: "We are opposed to the free coinage of silver, except by international agreement with the leading commercial nations of the world, and until such agreement the existing gold standard must be continued." Perforce therefore this Republican party admits that the gold standard is not the best, but that it cannot change it, except by the consent of the foreign powers.

Why did not that Republican party come out like men and say that the gold standard is the best for the American people? Why say that until they can have an international agreement, the present gold standard must be maintained? Why say in terms that they would agree to free silver coinage on an equality with gold provided they could get the consent of foreign powers? My friends, are you Americans, or are you truckling sycophants, winning smiles from foreign crowned heads?

Yes, we will agree to free silver, provided the foreign nations enter into the agreement with us. That "if," so mountain high, is the obstruction which makes the American people, according to the Republican doctrine, dependent upon the consent of foreign powers. Why should that great party confess what political philosophers have for many years contended, that the American people were incapable of self-government—that this republic is a failure? Why humiliate the proud American spirit of our fathers by this false, this useless, this criminal confession, that our people are not able to run their own financial system without the consent of crowned heads?

My friends, look and turn back four annual leaves in the history of our country and see what this Republican party then stated as its principles and demands upon the money question. I will read to you the platform adopted at Minneapolis by the Republican party June 10, 1892. Read it, boys; it is mighty good. "The American people from tradition and interest favor bimetallism; and the Republican party demands the use of both gold and silver as the standard money, with such restrictions and under such provisions, to be determined by legislation, as will secure the maintenance of the parity of values of the two metals so that the purchasing or paying power of a dollar, whether of silver or gold or paper, shall be at all times equal."

Then those protection-promising, bounty-paying Republicans declared that it was the interest of the American people, that it was their tradition and their right to have a standard money, consisting of gold and silver, upon equal terms. Then they wanted a bimetallic system, consisting of gold and silver; but now they want a single standard consisting of gold alone. Then they declared that every tradition and every interest of the American people, through the Republican party, demanded both gold and silver. This year they do not declare what is to the interest of the American people, but they pin the United States to the destinies of foreign powers controlled and operated by kings and princes, and propose to pledge this people, body and soul, purse and pride, to their will, to their edict, to their commands and to their laws.

My friends, the Republican party of to-day stands forth the first time in the history of the American government as a confessor of the weakness of the American people, of the inability of the people to manage their own affairs, and before the civilized world they carried humiliation into the heart of every liberty-loving, tory-hating American on this continent. It is the quintescence of Republicanism; it is the work of those men who have gone abroad too rich to remain Americans as the titled lords in the role of haunting and fawning, bending their nimble forms obsequiously before crowned heads, and returning here to the American people in their convention for the purpose of teaching them how to construct their platforms upon which the independent foreign-hating—

I take that word back—crown-hating, American people shall stand and conduct their affairs. Then, my friends, take the three planks of the Republican party platform as a declaration that the American people cannot attend to their own affairs, but we, as a united Democracy, whatever the will of the Convention may be and whatever ticket may be placed upon the platform, will march on and throw into their faces the defiance of a people, who, when contending for their liberty a hundred years ago, were able even in their swaddling clothes to withstand the onset of every foreign power, and to assert our ability to run our own affairs, according to our own will, without the interference of foreign influences and foreign powers.

I thank you for your kind attention and will not detain you any longer, and when this Convention is through, let us go home and heal the sores that have been inflicted, and join hands and march on with the grand army of independence of the American people under the common flag, followed by our fathers, to the victory that I am sure awaits us; and without the interference of foreign influences from any quarter; and we will say to all such, "Hands off."

THE CHAIR: I desire to announce that any member of the Committee on Credentials now on the floor will please step to the Committee room at the right, his presence there being requested. We are now in recess, but whenever the Convention desires to proceed with its business, of course it may do so; but it can only do so when the Credentials Committee has reported. The Chair will declare the Convention in session and recognize the gentleman from Mississippi, Mr. MONEY.

Hon. H. D. MONEY, of Mississippi: I move that Senator BLACKBURN, of Kentucky, be invited to address the Convention during the period of waiting.

This motion was adopted.

THE CHAIR: Gentlemen of the Convention, I present Senator J. C. S. BLACKBURN, of Kentucky.

Senator BLACKBURN: Mr. Chairman and Fellow Democrats: The Democratic party of America is gathered here to do an important work. The Democratic party of the country is to-day in session charged with a grave duty. The American people, by a vast majority, believe that they are needlessly suffering to-day. The majority of the American people look to this Convention to correct its grievances and to right its wrongs. You have opened this campaign in splendid style. State by State you have swept over the skirmish line. You have come here instructed by an overwhelming majority of your party, of your people. There can be no doubt as to where your duty lies. You are here to meet the reasonable expectations of your people. They did not need to be told, because they know that they are to-day the victims of vicious, deliberate, unjust legislation. They know, and they have instructed you to declare, that they will no longer tamely submit to the class legislation under which they have groaned for the last twenty years.

They have not sent you here to quarrel among yourselves. We, those who think as we do, have already proved that the people are at our backs. Let us take no action that is not tempered with the full measure of fairness. Let us declare to the world what it is that we approve and what we disapprove. Let us promulgate a platform that neither human nor devilish ingenuity can subject to but one construction. Let us declare that we are here to promulgate a platform which shall be in line and in consonance with the oft-repeated declarations of our party, and a platform that shall not obscure nor deflect public attention from the one main issue upon which this contest is to turn.

Let us declare what we approve and what we disapprove, that we want to unlock the doors of the American mint; that we mean to put silver back where it was in 1873, that we mean the unrestricted, the unlimited free coinage of both gold and silver on even terms without discrimination, and without the slightest regard to action of any other power on this earth. Let us declare further, my countrymen, that the Democratic party does not approve of the issuance of coin bonds in times of profound peace. Let us declare, further, that we do not approve of giving the right of option to the man who holds the obligation, but reserve it to the man who has to pay the debt. Let us declare, further, that we do not approve, but we denounce and we condemn the proposition to retire the non-interest bearing legal tender greenbacks and treasury note paper of this country. Let us declare, further, that we are not in favor of perpetuating either a national debt or a national banking system.

My countrymen, you cannot persuade the American people to believe that the depressed condition of their industries is not the result of vicious legislation. You cannot make them believe that the fires have gone out in their furnaces, that the spindle has ceased to hum in the factory, that the farmer is no longer able to get the cost of production for the products of his sweat and toil. You cannot make them believe that while an army of more than a million of unemployed laborers is to-day tramping the highways of your country, and yet make them believe that the laws under which they live have been equitable and fair. They know better. The American people know, and you had as well voice the knowledge, they know that Christ with a lash drove from the temple a better set of men than those who for twenty years have shaped the financial policy of this country.

These, my countrymen, it seems to me, are the duties that devolve upon this great Democratic gathering. The eyes of the country, the eyes of the world, rest fixed and centered upon this hall of assembled Democrats. If fair dealing is to be restored, if prosperity it to be brought back to take the place of poverty, if happiness is to be given to the American people, if free institutions are to feel safe, protected and anchored in the hearts of our people, it will only be when the banner under which you gather here once more floats out in proud triumph from the dome of our country's capitol. It is in your hands to give this boon to the American people. Be temperate, be conservative, but be manly and be brave. Do not fail to gather the fruits of the splendid victory that you have already so splendidly inaugurated. You have carried the skirmish line, but the inner citadel is to be contested for in November. Let us do nothing except with an honest effort to voice the sentiment of the people behind us. Appeal to every Democrat, whether he be with the majority or the minority, whether he is for a single standard or for a double standard, in God's name let him remember that he is a Democrat still.

My countrymen, I can but express this hope, coupled with the firm conviction, for, next to the revealed truths of the Christian religion, I pin my faith to the principles and the loyalty of my party. Remember, my countrymen, for twenty years we have waged this fight, unawed by power, stubbornly contesting every inch of ground, and now we are on the eve of the fruition of our hopes. A brighter day is dawning, and through its effulgence as it breaks upon us we read, without doubt or uncertainty, the restoration of Democracy to power. By all the splendid traditions that gather about that party, by the hopes that nerve us for the future, appealing to your courage, and to your love of country, I beg you, my fellow Democrats, make a platform that shall tell the truth, and rally as one man to vindicate its utterance.

THE CHAIR: No business will be transacted in the midst of noise and confusion. Nothing can be done in this Convention if this immense audience insists upon obstructing its proceedings.

Hon. J. D. RICHARDSON, of Tennessee: I move that the Convention take a recess for thirty minutes.

This motion was lost.

Mr. R. H. HENRY, of Mississippi: I move that Hon. W. J. BRYAN, of Nebraska, be invited to address the Convention.

This motion was adopted; but it was ascertained that Mr. BRYAN was not present.

Hon. A. W. HOPE, of Illinois: I move that Gov. ALTGELD be invited to address the Convention.

This motion was adopted; but Gov. ALTGELD, standing upon his chair, declined to speak, and asked that Gov. HILL be given an opportunity to address the Convention.

Hon. N. M. BELL, of Missouri: I move that DAVID OVERMEYER, of Kansas, be invited to address the Convention.

This motion was adopted.

The Chair: The Chair desires to state that the distinguished gentleman from New York, who has been called for so often, is upon the Committee on Resolutions, and is not here. I present Mr. Overmeyer.

Mr. Overmeyer: Mr. President and Gentlemen of the Convention: This is not the time at which I desire to say anything to this vast audience. The duties which may devolve upon me later may require me to say something to you. All I care to say now is that yesterday the seat of empire was transferred from the Atlantic States to the great Mississippi Valley. That the day of the common people has dawned. The State of Kansas, the great State of Kansas, on whose shining crest is written liberty, on whose fair escutcheon is graven the words, "*ad astra per aspera*," stands here to welcome its friends from the South and from the Northern States to redeem this good land and turn it back to the way of prosperity and greatness, and to begin the good work by restoring the dollar of the daddies, 16 to 1.

Hon. L. T. Genung, of Iowa: I move that Gov. Altgeld be requested to address this Convention.

This motion was adopted.

The Chair: I present Governor Altgeld, of Illinois.

Governor Altgeld: Mr. Chairman, and Gentlemen of this Convention: I did not come here to make speeches, I came here to assist in nominating the next President of these United States, I came here to assist in formulating a declaration of principles that shall again offer hope to our people.

Rarely in the history of government has an assembly of free men been confronted with the far-reaching questions, with questions that are fraught with so much of weal or woe to human kind, as those questions with which this Convention must deal. For a number of years there has existed in Europe and this country stagnation in trade, paralysis in industry and a suspension of enterprise. We have seen the streets of our cities filled with idle men, with hungry women and with ragged children. The country to-day looks to the deliberations of this Convention to promise some form of relief. In order to deal intelligently with these unhappy conditions, it is necessary to glance for a moment at the cause which produced them.

During the decade which followed the civil war we became the great debtor people of the earth. Everything from the government down to the sewing machine of the seamtress, was mortgaged. There was the great national, state, city, county and other municipal debts. There were the great railroad and other corporation debts. There were the farm and city mortgages, the great private indebtedness, all amounting to thousands of millions of dollars, and nearly all held by English money lenders. The interest on this great indebtedness had to be paid every year out of the toil of our people, but under the conditions as they then existed we met those payments and our people had a surplus. They were able to, in addition, supply themselves with the necessaries and comforts and even the luxuries of life. As a consequence the farmer prospered, the manufacturer prospered and labor was employed. But unhappily for the world the large security-holding classes conceived the idea that it would be to their interest to make money dear and property and labor cheap. It being an immutable law of finance that when you increase the volume of money in the world you increase the selling price of property and things, so, on the other hand, when you reduce the volume of money in the world you reduce the selling price of property and of labor.

These gentlemen then determined to destroy one-half of the money of the world, and between 1873 and 1890 they got our government and the governments of Europe to strike down silver. They demonetized it, they stopped its coinage, they took away its legal tender functions, they reduced it to the position of token money, where it was used at all. The effect of this was to double the burden that was put upon gold. Formerly, the two metals together did the work of the business world. After that time, the one metal alone had to do all the business of the world. Consequently, the number of people who had to have it was doubled. It was doubled in importance, and its purchasing power was doubled, so that thereafter the gold dollar bought twice as much labor, twice as much property, twice as much of the bread and sweat of mankind as it did before. Not only this but they reduced by one-half the annual addition to the stock of money of the world. Formerly there was added every year all of the gold to the world's stock of primary or redemption money. Since that time there is added every year only the gold of the world, so that we have a constantly shrinking standard of value with a constantly increasing population, which means a constantly decreasing scale of prices.

Now, when these great debts were created the world's standard and the world's measure of values consisted practically as one. They formed the standard of prices. To-day the standard of prices consists of only one metal and it is only half as high as it was when it consisted of the two, and as a consequence prices to-day are only half as high as they were when we had two metals. What has been the result? Why, my fellow citizens, to-day it takes all that the farmer, all that the producer can scrape together to pay these fixed charges; all that he can get to pay interest, taxes and other fixed charges; for, mind you, this great debt was not reduced, interest was not reduced, taxes were not reduced. On the contrary, they are higher than they were, and as a result our American market has been destroyed. The farmer now cannot buy as much at the store as he formerly could. The result is that the farmer is prostrated, the merchant does less business, the railroads do less business, the manufacturer cannot sell his product and the laborer finds that there is nobody to buy the things that he makes and he is out of employment.

Now, the question is, shall we continue this system or shall we go back to where we were? Gentlemen, we are suggesting nothing new, we are suggesting no experiments; we are simply declaring that when you pay a creditor in the same kind of money which he gave you, you are doing everything that God or man could demand at your hand. Now, gentlemen, those foreign people, those English money lenders, they gave us gold and silver, and we propose to pay them back in the same money which they gave us. Let me say to you that the statement that silver has fallen is not sustained by the facts. A pound of silver to-day buys as much wheat, buys as much cotton, buys as much property of every kind, and buys as much as it did when we got that money. It is gold, the gold dollar, that has gone up to where it buys twice as much as it then did. Now, these debts, my fellow citizens, cannot be paid for centuries, and shall we now declare that our people must go on paying interest, paying principal, with 200-cent dollars, or shall we go back and say we will pay in 100-cent dollars? That is the great question before this Convention.

But these English money lenders and their American agents and representatives do not intend to give up the advantage they have gained. They are making a determined fight. Two weeks ago they went to St. Louis and they took charge of the Republican Convention, an assembly that will go into history as Mr. Hanna's trust. At that Convention Mr. Hanna nominated a candidate for President, a candidate with one idea, and that idea wrong. That Convention declared in favor of the present single standard of English gold, a standard which the London newspapers have complimented. They are delighted with it. An Englishman always feels good when he sees a prospect of getting more sweat and more blood out of the American people. To be sure, they said something about a tariff in that platform; but the moneyed people cared nothing about that; they knew that was simply a little dough intended to hide the hook.

Then, after they had harnessed the Republican party to the English cart, the other members of the firm are here trying to put the same English halter upon this Convention. Are you going to allow them to do it?

What are the arguments that you have heard around your hotels and headquarters? You noticed some weeks ago these Eastern people declared they would have nothing on earth but a single gold standard; but when they found that the people were against them, when they found that the Democracy of this country would not tolerate it, then they were willing to modify their demands. They have come on here and are talking compromise. "Get together and agree upon something that we can all accede to and indorse." We are to do as we have done in the past; we are to adopt a declaration of principles which will not mean one thing to one man and another thing to another man; which will not mean one thing in one section of the country and another thing in another section, but which will mean exactly what we say it shall be. We will not adopt a platform which will enable these people to maintain a single gold standard.

These forces are powerful. They, the large banks in the East control nearly all the banks through the country, so that a few bankers in London and New York control the whole banking system in this country now. They control all of the newspapers, all of the agencies that formulate thought, and we have recently had something like a money terrorism. Anyone who did not subscribe to their wishes was threatened with social, financial and political death. Catch phrases are invented. There was a time in the history of the world when men and women were slaughtered in the name of liberty. We have seen a time when a great nation can be robbed in the name of an honest dollar. There are men who otherwise are intelligent and seem patriotic, who claim that they love their country, and yet who are doing all they can to fasten this English system upon our people. Now, my fellow citizens, shall we in this Convention stand squarely for principles, or shall we straddle? Shall we dodge? Shall we put ourselves in the position of the steer which had jumped part way over the fence and could neither hook before nor kick behind?

Now, gentlemen, there is a prime principle involved here that rises above vote-getting, that rises above office-getting, a principle that affects the welfare of a great nation. In 1776 the question was, shall republican institutions be established in America? In 1896 the question is, shall republican institutions be perpetuated in America? Or shall we make the great toilers and producers of this country mere vassals, mere tribute-paying serfs to English capitalists? That is the question, my fellow citizens. England devours the substance of Ireland. She gathers the harvest in the valley of the Nile; she has carried away the riches of India; she has ravished the islands of the sea; she has drawn the life-blood out of every people that have ever come under her domination. Shall this mighty nation, after we have triumphed over British armies upon land, after we have destroyed English fleets upon the waters, after we have triumphed upon every field of honor and field of glory, shall we now supinely surrender to English greed, English cunning and corruption?

My fellow citizens, we must make no mistakes. Our people are in earnest. They will have neither straddling on platform nor straddling on candidate, and those prudent, cautious, wise gentlemen who have to consult the tin roosters every morning to see what their opinion should be during the day shall have no show in this Convention. We must have a declaration of principles which will admit of no quibbles.

We must have a declaration of principles that will mean the same thing on the mountain, in the valley and at the seashores. We must have a declaration of principles that we can hold up before all Israel and the sun.

Gentlemen, it is not the time of compromise. It is a time to be serious, because the question is serious. It involves the future of our country. If the present standard of values, the present standard of prices, is to be maintained, then the great producing classes of this country will be devoured by the fixed charges. They will have no money to buy the comforts of life. They will have no money to educate their families. We must return to, we must resurrect the standard that existed when these debts were created. It is not a question that can be compromised. Compromise is proper when it involves only personal interest, but not when the interests of a great nation are at stake.

Gentlemen, just see how history repeats itself. In 1776 the money classes of the East in our country were opposed to the Declaration of Independence. They represented foreign interests, and they talked compromise. In 1861 the money classes of the East were opposed to making great sacrifices to maintain the Union. They talked compromise. In 1896 the same interests are again represented, and they talk compromise.

My fellow citizens, the hand of compromise never yet ran up the flag of freedom. The spirit of compromise never yet laid the foundations of republican institutions. No compromise army ever fought the battles of liberty. Go search the hundred thousand graves found on hilltop, found in forests and in fields, where sleep the men who died to uphold this flag, and you will not find the bones of a single man who talked compromise. They stood erect and said to the Almighty, "Here are our lives."

Gentlemen, the time has come when the Democratic party must announce to the world that we stand for great principles—that we stand for those principles that offer hope to humanity, and here are our lives to defend them. And if this Convention will rise to the occasion, as I believe it will—if this Convention will rise to meet the needs of a great people, then, gentlemen, our morning will be wrapped in splendor. If we do that, then the ides of November will usher in a new century of prosperity, of industry, of enterprise and of happiness. It will usher in a century which in grandeur and in glory will surpass any of those that have gone before.

Gentlemen, I thank you very much.

Hon. W. A. JONES: I move that Hon. GEORGE F. WILLIAMS, of Massachusetts, be invited to address this Convention.

THE CHAIR: The Committee on Credentials will meet in the committee room at once.

I present Hon. GEORGE F. WILLIAMS.

Mr. WILLIAMS: Fellow Democrats of the Union of the United States: This is not a sectional Convention. The battle which is now opened is a battle for the restoration of the union of the States. There has been no transfer of the seat of empire from the Atlantic to the Mississippi. The seat of empire is where it always has been, and I pray that it may always be in the logging camp of Maine, in the tobacco fields of Virginia, the orange groves of Florida, the plantations of Louisiana, the wheat fields of the West and the mining camps of California. I believe, fellow Democrats, that the interests of New England are represented here as well as the interests of the South and West.

The contest in this cause that I wish to make is in behalf of the honest capital of New England and in behalf of the five million spindles that are now silent. We have seen the process going on which has created the talk of sectionalism, against which I protest. Under the existing system which this Convention will condemn, first, our customers have been ruined;—the farmers of the West and the South. Then the railroads into which we put our honest earnings have been ruined, and we have finally come down on our knees to you. It is to rescue the honest investments of every man in the United States that we are here to-day.

I beg you, gentlemen, not to utter another word of sectionalism in this campaign. Let me assume that I am somewhat a representative of the real capitalist of New England—the man who leads a life of honest toil to make what money he can to support himself and those upon whom he is dependent. (Laughter.)

Of course I suppose I should have said those who are dependent upon him, but I think I may be able to show that my proposition is not exactly absurd. I have been aware that my capital, my honest earnings, have been dependent upon the railway manager and the corporation organizer, and I have seen my earnings go out with the earnings of the people of the West into the hands of dishonest capital. The watered stock of the corporation has done as much harm to the East as anything else. This, gentlemen, is not sectional, and I trust before this campaign is over that New England will join in this great movement not to transfer the seat of empire from one section to the other but to transfer the control of the United States Treasury and the money of everyman here from the magnates of Lombard street in London to the honest people of the United States.

THE CHAIR: We now have before us the report of the Committee on Credentials; not complete. I am told, but nevertheless as far as it has been prepared it will be presented to the Convention.

I present Hon. J. H. ATWOOD, of Kansas, the Chairman of the Committee.

Mr. ATWOOD: Mr. Chairman and Gentlemen of the Convention: Your Committee upon Credentials begs leave to present the following partial report:

1. It is respectfully recommended that the National Democratic Convention take action to the end of granting to each of the Territories and to the District of Columbia six votes as representation in this body. This conclusion was arrived at after considerable discussion, but the great majority of your

Committee deem it proper to embody this recommendation in this, their partial report.

2. After a careful and painstaking comparison of the original and official credentials with the list of delegates and alternates as prepared by the secretary of the National Executive Committee, your Committee begs leave to report that it finds its roster or roll of names correct with the exception of those names appearing thereon as delegates and alternates from the States of Nebraska and Michigan.

Relative to the contest from Nebraska, your Committee begs leave to report that after a careful examination of the testimony presented to your Committee and after a full hearing from the respective parties, a careful consideration of their several arguments, your Committee finds and begs leave to report that the delegates and alternates headed by WILLIAM J. BRYAN, of Nebraska, are entitled to seats in this Convention as delegates and alternates. With your leave, Mr. Chairman, I will refrain from reading the complete list. It is in the hands of the Committee.

In regard to the contest from the State of Michigan, your Committee is not ready to report and asks further time for the consideration of the same.

And now, Mr. Chairman, before I move the adoption of this partial report, I desire to present, by the direction of the committee of which I am the official head, this request: The tickets assigned to the State of Nebraska have been received by those gentlemen who now occupy seats in this Convention as the representatives of that state, and your Committee desires, if this Convention will do so, to have the Sergeant-at-Arms directed to supply the newly seated delegates and alternates with their full quota of tickets, and in the event of this being impossible, that some substitute therefor that will assure them admission into the assemblage here shall be provided. With this explanation and suggestion, I move the adoption of the report.

THE CHAIR: I present Hon. T. J. MAHONEY, of Nebraska.

Mr. MAHONEY: Mr. Chairman, in view of the fact that prior to the reception of the Committee's partial report the sitting delegation from Nebraska has received a notice from the officers of this Convention that seats have been provided for them in the rear, we will save the Convention the time of taking a roll upon this report, and those who are to occupy our seats can have our tickets if they desire them. We will proceed to occupy the seats so kindly provided in advance of the report by the officers of the Convention.

The Chairman thereupon put the question upon the adoption of the partial report, and declared it adopted.

Hon. JOHN E. RUSSELL, of Massachusetts: We respectfully doubt the vote, and ask for a call of the roll of the states.

Hon. T. W. BLAKE, of Texas: I make the point of order that he cannot call for a division after the result of the vote had been announced.

THE CHAIR: The Chair did declare the result, but it is the opinion of the Chair that the point of order ought not to be made, and that a roll call, if demanded, as this has been, by a considerable number of this Convention, should be accorded and the Chair will so rule. Unless the house reverses his decision the roll will be called.

Mr. ATWOOD: I wish to state for the information of the Convention, that the report upon the matter from Nebraska was unanimous; New York, Massachusetts and everyone voted for it.

Mr. RUSSELL: I withdraw my motion.

THE CHAIR: Mr. RUSSELL withdraws his motion for a call of the roll. The result as announced will stand. The Chair has been informed that there are alternates who are occupying the seats of delegates, and the Chair is also notified that the delegates are too modest to ask the alternates to step aside. The Chair has no such scruples, and the alternates are requested to permit the delegates to take their seats.

Mr. MARSTON, of Louisiana: I move that Senator TILLMAN, of South Carolina, be requested to address the Convention.

This motion was adopted; but Mr. TILLMAN was not present.

Gov. ALTGELD: I move, Mr. Chairman, that this Convention take a recess until 5 o'clock P. M. in order to enable the Committee on Credentials to make its report.

THE CHAIR: The Chair will state that upon consulting with the Committee on Credentials it has become manifest that no report will be presented for some time. This motion is the result of an examination into that condition.

Mr. E. B. FINLEY, of Ohio: I move, Mr. Chairman, as a substitute for that motion, that the Committee on Permanent Organization be now allowed to make its report, and that this Convention proceed to permanently organize and proceed in the transaction of its business, and that we dispose of the report of the Committee on Credentials later on.

THE CHAIR: The Chair will rule that, as there is no recognized roll showing who are members of this Convention, there can be no permanent organization or declaration of party principles until the membership of the Convention is first settled. The question now is upon the motion of the gentleman from Illinois to adjourn.

The motion was adopted and the convention took a recess until 5 o'clock P. M.

SECOND DAY.

EVENING SESSION.

CHICAGO, ILL., July 8, 1896.

The Chairman (Senator WHITE) called the Convention to order at 5:45 P. M. in the following words:

THE CHAIR: The Convention will please come to order, the gentlemen will take their seats. The Committee on Credentials is now ready to report. I present Hon. J. H. ATWOOD, of Nebraska.

Mr. ATWOOD: A majority of your Committee on Credentials beg leave to complete the report of the Committee made heretofore and respectfully submit and report that after a careful examination and consideration of the record and evidence submitted to it, respectively by the contestants and contestees it has concluded and recommends:

1. That the contesting delegates from the Fourth Congresional district of Michigan be seated and recognized as delegates to this Convention. Said delegates are HENRY CHAMBERLAIN and HANNIBAL HART.

2. That the contesting delegates from the Ninth Congressional district of Michigan, to wit: H. J. HOYT and J. S. WHITE, be seated and recognized as delegates from said district.

3. That the remaining delegates as they appear on the temporary roll of the Convention remain seated as delegates.

Hon. JOHN C. CROSBY, of Massachusetts: Mr. Chairman and Gentlemen of the Convention: Representing eighteen States in this Convention, I desire to move an amendment to the report of the Committee, which has just been submitted to the Convention. I move, sir, that the delegations from the Fourth district and the Ninth district of Michigan be entitled to keep the seats which they now occupy. The matter of this discussion has lasted through yesterday, nearly all night and most of the day, and after a careful consideration of the merits of this Michigan case, we of the minority feel that if this report is accepted and adopted, it means one of the greatest injustices that could be perpetrated upon any Convention.

Mr. Chairman, the Convention which met in the State of Michigan in April last consisted of about 800 delegates. There was not a single contest as to a single delegate to that Convention. There was a unanimous report, and after that report had been made these delegates were elected. They were elected in accordance with the law of the State of Michigan, and there was not the slightest question made, or contest or challenge made as to the legality or the validity of the election of those delegates. I may say further there is not, whatever may be said to the contrary, there is not the slightest evidence that there was any fraud on the part of anybody.

Now, Mr. Chairman, all we want—all those of us who represent the minority want—is fair and decent treatment at your hands. We do not attempt or desire to overrule the majority here, but we do wish to have a fair and just discussion and consideration of this matter, and so, Mr. Chairman, I move that this amendment may be adopted, and I trust that the honest sentiment of the Convention will give to these sitting delegates the seats which they now occupy.

The Chair then recognized Hon. JOHN L. BRENNAN, of Wisconsin.

Mr. BRENNAN: Mr. Chairman and Gentlemen of the Convention: I do not desire to submit to this Convention an argument on this question; but so that you may vote intelligently, I would like to state for you the exact question that was submitted. The Committee on Credentials has reported to this Convention that they will seat the present delegates-at-large from Michigan, headed by Mr. STEVENSON. They also have reported to this Convention that they will seat the contestants from the Fourth and Ninth districts—four to be seated that have their seats in the Convention now, and four contestants from the districts to be seated. This is the majority report. The minority submits a report that the four delegates from the districts remain, and the contests with reference to the districts be disallowed. The question recurs upon the amendment and will be submitted in that form.

The Committee on Credentials has had a long session, and has gone over all the facts in the case very carefully. We of the minority, believing and relying upon the future of this country, as embraced in the principles of the Democratic party, fear the result of the action of the majority of the Committee on Credentials. The State of Michigan elects its delegates from the districts, the districts recommending to the State Convention the names only.

With reference to the Ninth district two names were proposed and were voted upon in that Convention, and there is no record submitted by the secretary of that Convention that there was any protest entered there, and it was there that they should have had their fight, and not here. There is no precedent for National conventions except each recurring convention every four years, and we are making precedents every minute of our time to-day, and this will establish a precedent that a majority in the first flush of enthusiasm may go into a sovereign state and overturn the will of its people in order that their friends may have a seat in this Convention.

Gentlemen of the Convention, in my judgment, after listening to the evidence submitted to the Committee on Credentials, it rests upon glittering generalities and conclusions. Facts are what you want. There was a convention in Detroit of 900 Democrats. It was a big, large, unwieldy gathering. There is no record in the newspapers that any exception was taken at the time. None was submitted to me as a member of the Committee on Credentials. I have concluded from the evidence that this contest originated three or four weeks ago, when it was ascertained that this Convention would be ruled by a certain majority, and I have become acquainted with that majority, and I appeal to its honesty and fairness not to let it pass.

The Chair then recognized Hon. S. M. TAYLOR, a delegate from Arkansas.

Mr. TAYLOR: Mr. Chairman and Gentlemen of the Convention: According to my judgment, as a member of the Committee on Credentials of this great National Democratic Convention sitting on the trial of this controversy as a jury, intending to do and vote as I believe for the right, I derive from the testimony in the case that in the State of Michigan one of the greatest wrongs was perpetrated by the selection of the delegation as recognized by the National Committee I ever saw; the defense as interposed to the prosecution of this matter set on foot by the contesting delegates if it amounted to anything, according to the evidence was nothing more than a plea of "confession and avoidance."

The gentleman who has just spoken on the minority report said that what you wanted was facts. You have received no facts. This case was left in the hands of the Committee and we have been in earnest, solemn session over this question ever since we have been appointed. All night long we heard testimony. Statement after statement that was made by the contestees was deliberately denounced as being untrue by the contestants present and supported by affidavits of citizens.

Fellow citizens, it is a question for you to decide whether Democrats in the great State of Michigan, who are honestly and fairly here representing the majority of the Democracy of that State, shall be stifled and throttled and driven from this Convention, or whether you will recognize them as the legal and lawful representatives of that constituency. Now, gentlemen of the Convention, we want no wrong done; we want that done here which will be just and which will be right. As a representative of one-half of the financial question, representing the minority report, we have voted to retain and seat only two contestants from the Fourth, and two from the Ninth districts, the others to remain seated, as was recommended by the National Committee. We intend to be fair and to do what is right and what is just and what is honest with the Democracy of that State.

Now, gentlemen of the Convention, I do not desire to take up your time, but I would say that if you had heard the sworn testimony as we had it, the undisputed facts, on many points as we had them, you would come to the same conclusion that the majority has come to, and that the majority report should be adopted by this Convention. I thank you.

The Chair: I have the honor to present Gov. A. J. McLaurin, of Mississippi.

Gov. McLaurin: Mr. Chairman and Gentlemen of the Convention: I have not come to make a speech, but to state the facts as we found them by an investigation of this contest, and I will beg of the audience to remain quiet and give me their attention, because I think the delegates to this Convention want to act intelligently and want to act upon conclusions. It has been said that we have no right to go into the State of Michigan and overturn the will of the majority of the Democrats of that State. I agree to that.

I have been endeavoring, to the best of my humble ability, ever since you adjourned yesterday evening, to ascertain what are the facts and who have the majority in this contest. Right here let me say to you that the undisputed evidence, the unquestioned fact, so far as the evidence has been presented to your Committee on Credentials, is that there were 783 delegates in that Convention. There was a great question of national importance that was submitted to the Democracy of the State, as was submitted to the Democracy of every State in the Union, and in the determination of that question there were 424 men instructed as delegates to the Convention at Detroit to vote for silver. There were 127 of those delegates instructed to vote for gold. There were 232 of the delegates who were uninstructed—leaving a clear majority in favor of the cause of silver over those who were instructed. Therefore, you see that there is no effort here to throttle the will or stifle the purpose of the majority of the Democrats of Michigan. But there is an effort here to put upon the floor men who represent a majority of these delegates, and that without reference to any technicalities.

Now, sir, there was a great issue to be submitted to the people of this country. There are two parties: two great national parties. One of those parties has taken its stand, and the other was looking out for the stand that it was to take on this question. All other questions had been subordinated, and in the State of Michigan, as in every other State in this Union, this question was being discussed and debated as the leading one to put to the front in the November election.

There was a man went from that State to the city of Washington, and the question was propounded to him, so far as this evidence goes, and I am stating to you sworn testimony of one of the delegates who I believe sits upon this floor, that this man who had gone to Washington, when he came back, told him, " I have made up my judgment upon it." I give the evidence to you and you can act for yourselves. This man told him when he came back that he had stated in Washington that it was impossible to carry the State of Michigan for the gold standard, that he was told that at all hazards he must carry it for the gold standard and for the Administration.

Now, I want to give you, gentlemen of the Convention and Mr. President, some of the methods adopted to carry it for the gold standard. I have already shown you, my fellow citizens, gentlemen of the Convention, that of the 783 delegates who constituted the Convention at Detroit a clear majority, a handsome working majority, had been instructed to vote against the commands that had been given to carry this State at all hazards for the Administration and for gold.

In the Fourth district—and I want to say right here that I am one of those twenty-two who voted against retaining the four men who occupy seats here from the State at large—the vote was 22 to 24 to retain them and to unseat the delegates from the Fourth district and from the Ninth district, and I am one of the twenty-two who voted against retaining the delegates who are now upon the floor from the State at large. When the Convention met from the Fourth district the executive committeeman, RODGERS, called the Convention of the Fourth district to order, and named one KIPLER, I believe his name was, for Temporary Chairman. The Convention asked the privilege of doing what we did here yesterday, of naming their own chairman. That proposition was refused, and after some considerable discussion KIPLER was permitted to take the stand as Temporary Chairman and did take it. Presently there came up a question of appeal from the ruling of the Chair. I do not recall now exactly on what that was, but the vote of those who were opposed to KIPLER and opposed to the delegates who occupy seats on this floor from the State at large was 22 against 20, and two of that twenty were not entitled to seats on that floor. There was a motion made then to adjourn. Twenty-three men voted against twenty for adjournment. The Convention was adjourned.

After these twenty-three had left that Convention and gone into the hall the other twenty elected the two men who occupy seats now on the floor from the Fourth district of Michigan.

A gentleman by the name of O'HARA, who was a brother, I believe, of some man who has gone across the waters with a commission from this Administration, went into the Convention and made the announcement that these two gentlemen were elected. It was stated that this Convention, the District Convention from the Fourth district, had adjourned, and that after the adjournment twenty members had made the election. The Convention, taken in charge as it was, for the purpose of running it at all hazards, did do the decent thing to refer it back to the delegates from the Fourth district and said that they should elect their man. What then? No chairman called it to order, nobody called the Convention of the Fourth district to order, but a majority of them met and elected the contesting delegates here and made Mr. KIPLER the Chairman of the Convention, and asked them to report it to the State Convention, and he did so. When he went to report it to the Convention he found that this gentleman, Mr. O'HARA, had reported to the Convention that another set of delegates—those occupying seats here—had been elected, and the Chairman of the Convention refused to recognize Mr. KIPLER and refused to give him any hearing. Now, that is the state of the case from the Fourth district. These are the facts from the Fourth district, as found by the Committee.

Gentlemen, I want to call your attention to another fact, because I am telling you the facts—I am not making a speech; I cannot make a speech. I do not know how, but I am giving you the facts here.

The facts of that Convention are that when they went in

there they did not elect them by the State, but merely recorded them as the action of that District Convention. It was not the District Convention; and I will call your attention to another fact. The Committee on Credentials being unwieldy, appointed seven delegates as a sub-committee to take evidence and compare it carefully. The chairman of the Committee on Credentials was the chairman. I had the honor to be a member of that sub-committee, and we took up this evidence. The gentleman who made his speech here and charged that we intended to take away the right of representation from the people of Michigan, had not the opportunity, has not given it the investigation that the Committee has done—the committee of eight—and these are the facts in it.

That is the way, then, that the Fourth District Convention was run; "at all hazards we had to have it, and at all hazards we had to get it, in any way. We were willing to take twenty men after the Convention adjourned, and by a majority of three make this election of two delegates, and get the State at all hazards by a vote of a majority of three." Now, let us see about the Ninth district. In the Ninth district there were twenty-four men voting for silver and twenty-six for gold. Two of these men who were for gold were representing the County of Lake, where there had been no Democratic Convention held, according to the sworn testimony, and they were men who were not residents of the County of Lake. According to the laws of the State of Michigan a man cannot be a delegate of a State Convention who is not a resident of the county that he undertakes to represent. Now, then, these two men were in there. Take those two men from twenty-six, and that leaves you twenty-four. Now, then, they come before our committee with a report signed by somebody who purports to be the Chairman of a Convention and somebody else who purports to be the Secretary of a Convention, in which they say that these two men were elected. There is no denial of the proposition.

Hon. W. P. Murray, of Tennessee: There is so much confusion in the galleries that nothing can be heard by the delegation of which I am a member, and I move that the Sergeant-at-Arms be directed to clear the galleries.

THE CHAIR: The gentleman from Tennessee moves that the galleries be cleared unless quiet is maintained. The galleries must be quiet.

Mr. McLAURIN (continuing): Now, this is the sworn testimony of witnesses, who have testified to the fact that no Convention was held in the county which these two men claimed to represent. They testified to the further fact, under oath, that these two men purporting to represent the County of Lake were not residents of that county. The statute book says that they are not authorized to represent any county unless they are residents of the county. So much for that. Those were the men who voted for and were instructed for silver.—

The speaker not being able to proceed, Sergeant-at-Arms MARTIN said:

The Chair has requested the Sergeant-at-Arms to instruct the Assistant Sergeant-at-Arms and the Police Department to remove anyone in the galleries who may disturb this meeting, and I will carry out that order.

When quiet was restored Governor McLAURIN continued as follows:

Now, there was another county in that Convention entitled to thirteen votes. They were instructed to vote as a unit. There were seven men in that county who were elected because they were for silver. Their places were taken by the seven men who cast the thirteen votes of the county. That is the sworn testimony. That was the Ninth district.

Now for the State at large. I say that I voted against seating anybody that was sent here by that Convention. As I said before, there was a great question before the American people. I am not here for the purpose of arguing that. I might, if I so desired, call attention to the fact that in 1812 Great Britain was in the throes of a great struggle that taxed her power and resources. I might call attention to the fact that during that time they had to obtain money, the sinews of war, to carry on their fights and to maintain their armies. I might call attention to the fact that during that time government securities were issued, and government obligations were incurred, and just after the war, in 1816, when these men who held these securities and these government obligations wanted to double the price that they had put upon their merchandise, put upon their money that had been loaned to the government, secured the demonetization of silver in Great Britain. I might call attention to the fact that, if I were disposed to discuss this question, in 1861 and 1865 there was a great struggle in this country that taxed the power of the country and the resources of the country, and it became necessary to obtain money to carry on the war, and that securities were issued, and that after the war the men who held these securities and these obligations against the government were desirous of doing the very thing that Britain did in 1816, and I might say that they are the very men, as a rule, who in Great Britain, or descendants of the very men who had obtained the demonetization of silver, for the purpose of doubling their contracts and their obligations, in 1816. I might call attention—

Hon. ALLEN L. McDERMOTT, of New Jersey: I rise to a point of order. My point is that no question of seventy years ago can affect the election of delegates to a Convention held in 1896.

Governor McLAURIN: You want to put a coal of fire on a terrapin's back if you want to see him move.

THE CHAIR: The gentleman is not in order.

Gov. McLAURIN: Gentlemen of the Convention: You have facts so far as I have been able to gather them. You have facts that the State of Michigan is not represented here by men who are in accord with the majority of the Democrats of that State, and I have not heard it asserted by any man who contends for a seat on this floor because he was sent from that State Convention that he does represent a majority of the Democrats of the State of Michigan.

The Chair then recognized Hon. E. G. STEVENSON, of Michigan. Hon. JOHN F. SAULSBURY, of Delaware, asked permission to be heard, and Mr. STEVENSON yielded the platform to him.

Hon. JOHN F. SAULSBURY: Gentlemen of the Convention: I was elected to this Convention as a free silver man, to vote for free silver at 16 to 1. I expect to do it, but I cannot believe that this Convention will do an injustice to any State by unseating men legally elected, and I shall not vote for it. If Michigan men elected to their State Convention, men that would sell out and vote against their instructions, to send delegates here, this is not the place to wash their dirty linen. That is all I have to say.

Hon. E. G. STEVENSON, of Michigan: Gentlemen of the Convention: I am the man they say who stole Michigan. I desire, gentlemen of the Convention, not to discuss the financial issue which will be settled by the platform of this Convention, but to discuss the right of the delegates elected by a sovereign Convention.

The Democrats of the State of Michigan are represented in myself as the chairman of its committee, who carried on the only silver campaign that Michigan ever had—a man who is a Democrat now, and who hopes that his State will be so treated that he can be a Democrat when this Convention concludes its labors. The Convention of the State of Michigan is organized by law, not merely by usage. The delegates elected get their certificates of election from our city clerk, and no man who desires to sit can sit in a convention in our city without such credentials. When the County Conventions are organized the officers, Chairman and Secretary, have to take a solemn oath to discharge their duties faithfully, and so as to the State Convention. The State Convention of Michigan convened, and this contest was on. They organized in the regular manner. Their officers were duly sworn. A Committee on Credentials was appointed, one from each district, seven so-called sound money men and five free silver men, and they passed upon the credentials and reported them unanimously. All agreed. There was not a single contest in the entire State. When the Convention organized the gentlemen who are here contesting stood by, voted in our Convention and never uttered a protest.

A VOICE: "You didn't give us a chance."

Every delegate selected to this Convention was elected on

a roll-call of counties, where each county openly announced its vote, and the vote of not one single delegate was challenged; not one. When the Convention concluded its labors the district delegates were elected by the State Convention, not by districts. The district merely recommended to the State Convention, and the report of the district delegates whose seats are here contested were reported to the Convention and adopted and ratified by the unanimous vote of the Convention.

And, gentlemen, the officers of that Convention have sent their credentials here under oath. These men who contest have no credentials from any convention; not even a rump convention. If there was any unfairness, if there was any one whose vote should have been challenged, there was the place to do it. This Convention has no right to sit as a Committee on Credentials on our State Convention. It may suit the purpose of some of the gentlemen in this Convention to pursue this course to-day, but, gentlemen, you are making a precedent that will damn you some day. The only safe Democratic doctrine is to stand by precedent and stand by the delegates who got the only credentials to this Convention.

By what right does this Convention investigate who had the right to a seat in this Convention, when we had a Committee appointed that did that work in our Convention and settled that question by a unanimous vote? Now, my friends, this is not a question of gold and silver; it is a question of honesty and right. This is a question of whether the Credentials Committee with South Dakota, that has only eight votes, will resolve that they cannot go behind the returns—the credentials—but in Michigan, to get twenty-eight votes, they will go behind the returns.

We ask you, gentlemen, simply to vote to sustain the regular organization of your party. Only Monday night of this last week in this great city was I elected to conduct the coming campaign. I want to go home to the discharge of my duty in that capacity feeling that my State associates have received justice. I thank you for your attention.

THE CHAIR: The Hon. WILLIAM F. SHEEHAN, of New York.

Mr. SHEEHAN: Mr. Chairman and Gentlemen of the Convention: I will be fortunate, indeed, if my voice will be strong enough to reach the remotest part of the section of the hall devoted to the delegates elected to this Convention. I will make no effort whatever to throw my voice beyond that distance, because it is impossible.

I was a member representing the State of New York, and am now its member of the National Committee. It became the duty of that National Committee to make up the preliminary roll of delegates to the Convention. We heard, patiently, all contests submitted to that Committee, including this Michigan contest. We heard first the contest from the State of Indiana. That was a case—and it will be the only one that I will cite, except this particular case—that was a case the reverse of this. That was a case where a district, a Congressional district in Indiana, elected, according to precedent, in a district Congressional Convention, two delegates to this Convention, but the State Convention when it met saw fit to recognize a time-honored Democratic principle, that within the sovereign State itself the State Convention is the sole and only judge of Democracy. And that Democratic National Committee by a unanimous vote, although twenty-seven men in that Committee believe not in 16 to 1, although we had views not in accord with the views of the majority of this Convention, we decided to seat the silver men from Indiana, and to throw out the gold men from Indiana.

We came along to this contest and we heard the contest, and, Mr. Chairman, after we had listened to that contest a call of the States was made, and, by a vote of 49 to 1, the delegation headed by Mr. STEVENSON was declared the choice of that Committee for preliminary purposes. We heard the contest and my friend THOMAS, from Colorado; my friend TARPEY, from California, and the distinguished gentleman from Alabama, who yesterday moved to override the will of that majority, all on the roll call declared that Michigan in its sovereign Democracy was the sole and only judge of the qualifications of the delegates from that State.

Now what are the facts with reference to this particular case, with reference to the chief points of interest in it? It is well known that the Michigan delegation is here under the unit rule. It is well known that a poll of the delegates from that State shows that fifteen of them are for gold, or rather against 16 to 1, and thirteen are for silver, 16 to 1. My friend, the distinguished governor from Mississippi, has said that the prevailing sentiment of Michigan was in favor of silver, and that that sentiment should be recognized by giving them representation in this Convention on the delegation. Why, sir, if that were true, why not give that sentiment all the delegation from Michigan? Why, sir, it was but last night when this Committee whose report is now under consideration even had the hardihood to decide in favor of throwing out STEVENSON and the other three delegates-at-large from that State, but when the wise men of the majority here got together this morning they saw how impolitic such a course as that was, and orders were given not to put STEVENSON and the other delegates-at-large out, but simply content themselves by putting two silver men from a congressional district in.

What is its purpose? The purpose is plainly this: If this majority report is adopted, there will be fifteen 16 to 1 men in the delegation and thirteen gold men. They will vote the delegation as a unit, and in that way some gentlemen here are foolish enough to believe that you will indirectly succeed in violating the old, time-honored Democratic doctrine of a two-thirds rule in this Convention. The only subject and purpose of the adoption of this report necessarily must be so that you can vote Michigan so that you can override indirectly, when you dare not directly, the two-thirds rule.

One word more: I warn my friends from the South, I warn those men who fought with me and with whom I fought four years ago, to hesitate before you commit this second unprecedented and un-Democratic act. I ask you, gentlemen of this Convention—there are many people who believe in this country that the proceedings of this Convention were begun in revolution—in God's name do not end them in revolution.

THE CHAIR: The Chair recognizes Hon. T. W. BLAKE, of Texas.

Mr. BLAKE: Gentlemen of the Convention: This is too important a matter to act in haste about. I am both tired and sleepy. (A voice " What State ?") I am from the Lone Star State, sir, of Texas. I am both tired and sleepy by reason of the fact that I have been at work upon this case since 8 o'clock last night. I want to tell you that what I say with reference to my course upon it will be borne out by the gentlemen on that Committee who are gold men, I believe, when I say that I acted conservatively and with the end only in view to do what was right. I want to tell you that I am on general principles opposed to going behind the returns of a State convention, and there is but one ground that will justify it, in my judgment, by a National convention; and that ground is fraud, and it was on this ground that we did go behind the returns of the State Convention of Michigan. It was because the evidence was so abundant that that Convention has been manipulated and the will of the people of Michigan had been disregarded.

Democracy means the will of the people, and these gentlemen who are here upon this floor know that the reports in all of the papers of this country told you that a majority of the counties of Michigan before that Convention had assembled had declared for the free coinage of silver. The evidence before us showed that to be the case and that the judgment of the people was overturned by federal office holders manipulating the delegates, getting proxies and voting them contrary to law.

I want to tell you right now that, in my judgment, this whole infernal delegation from Michigan ought to be turned out, if half the facts are true that were proved and stated before that Convention. You are told that no protests were made and that these whole proceedings were regular. I hold in my hand and in the hands of the Secretary of our Committee can be found abundant evidence that that statement is not true. I will tell you why they did not do anything. After trying all they could, by getting up a protest, the Chairman overruled everything and ran that Convention by revolutionary tactics himself and when they failed to get recognition what on God's earth could they do but sit down and keep quiet? And they come to you at this Convention and ask that you give them their rights. Now, listen; I believe that the four delegates-at-large from that State are not entitled to seats upon this floor, but in a spirit of compromising the matter. I do not want to do that which is wrong, and I want to state here and now that if we cannot nominate a President upon a silver platform by votes that are honest and fair, I do not want it. I do not expect to cast my vote to rob any State in this Union of any vote to which it is justly entitled. I am not doing it. That Committee acted wisely, in my judgment, when it voted to unseat the delegates from the Fourth district and from the Ninth. I cannot go into the details of this evidence.

We have spent the whole time since 8 o'clock last night until now, and after mature deliberation we have come to the conclusion that the delegates from the Fourth district should be unseated, and the men who are contesting should be put in their places; that the delegates from the Ninth district should be unseated, and those that are contesting should be put in their places. And I say furthermore, to every silver man upon this floor, that I believe it is your duty to do it; you ought to do it if you want to correct a wrong, and if you want to repudiate fraud; and you are going to do it, too.

Mr. SHEEHAN told you that the National Committee had investigated this matter; but they did not go into the details of this evidence, as I am informed, as we did, because they acted upon all these contests in one-fourth of the time that we spent on this particular case. Now, that doesn't look like they had given the consideration to it that we had. We appointed a special committee of seven, of which I was one, and we went into the details of this question, and took up every single particle of evidence that we had and we did it just as judges do in considering a case. I have talked myself down and I am tired; you understand the question, and if you vote for the majority report you will do what is right. I thank you.

THE CHAIR: Hon. W. F. McKNIGHT, of Michigan.

Mr. McKNIGHT: Mr. Chairman and Gentlemen of the Convention: In addition to the request of the last gentleman who preceded me, I will ask that not only the silver delegates of this Convention but the entire delegations from the various states vote to support this report of the majority. But in the few moments which I have to occupy I hope to be able to present you such facts that every delegation here will vote to maintain and pass this majority report. I am somewhat surprised by the position taken by the gentleman from New York. He has made up his mind, I presume, as some other gentlemen from that State have done, who made up their minds three or four days before this matter was presented either to the Committee on Credentials or to this Convention. The gentlemen on that Committee have given this matter careful and candid consideration, and they are here to-day to testify from this platform to some—only some of the outrages perpetrated upon the Democracy of Michigan.

The several county Conventions in the State of Michigan at an early date, and long before the State Convention was held, selected from the various counties a majority of over two hundred in favor of silver—and when the administration at Washington learned of this fact, Mr. STEVENSON, who has appeared upon this platform, was called to Washington by the great chief and after he was told that Michigan was solidly in the silver column——

Hon. ELLIOTT G. STEVENSON, of Michigan: There is not a word of truth in that.

Mr. McKNIGHT (Resuming): After he was told that Michigan was solid in the silver column, he was requested to get possession of the State of Michigan, and how far they had succeeded you are the judges. Let me illustrate to you some of the things that took place. Men holding federal positions were sent up and down the State, interviewing delegates and working with them for the purpose of distorting the will of the people who elected them. We found that when the Convention met, even up to that time there was a great majority in favor of silver, but federal forces of the State of Michigan to the extent of over 300 were in attendance at the Convention, and they practically took hold of and managed and ran and conducted it in favor of gold. That is the condition of affairs.

Hon. THOMAS A. E. WEADOCK, of Michigan: It is not true.

Mr. McKNIGHT: Now, then, by a bare majority of one, after that Convention assembled, they selected a gentleman for Chairman who was with them upon every proposition that came before that Convention. He ruled with them against the will of the majority. To illustrate in one instance how they managed and manipulated this Convention: one county, Berrien, was entitled to nineteen delegates. There were present in that Convention from that county three silver men and two gold men. Those were all representing the entire delegation of nineteen. What did they do? Two men favorable to gold were telegraphed for the night before the Convention to come on, and the next morning, under the protest of the three silver men on the delegation, these two men were placed upon that delegation and given rights in the Convention, and these four men controlled the other three and distorted the will of the people from the county whom they represented. And what did these men do, and what did the Chairman of that Convention recognize? He allowed and permitted those four gold men in that Convention to cast 16 votes, solidly every time; and the other three men to cast but three. These were some of the practices, these were some of the methods pursued in that State Convention.

Now, gentlemen, you have heard here detailed by the majority of this Committee, or members representing the majority, the facts in the case. Governor McLaurin, of Mississippi, has gone over it carefully. He has presented the matter to you, and he has presented it fairly, and he has represented not even the facts as strong as they are, and the matters which occurred in the Fourth district are not even put as strong by the Governor as they might and could be from the sworn testimony in this case.

I am somewhat surprised to learn of the recent conversion of the gentleman from Michigan known as Mr. Stevenson. When, under God's heaven, did he become a convert to silver? Gentlemen, we ask you in all fairness, in all justice, that you support here to-day the majority report, which is approved by over two to one, and by so doing you will carry Michigan next November by at least 25,000 majority.

The Chair: I present Judge Ferdinand Brucker, of Michigan.

Mr. BRUCKER: Mr. Chairman and Gentlemen of the Convention:

> When all of us poor Democrats, weary of breath,
> Seek relief from these political trials in death;
> When we have all had enough of contentions and strife,
>   And, longing for peace,
>   We sign a release
> Of the bodies whereof we've been tenants for life;
> Whereupon it is said, without further delay,
> The boat of old Charon will take us away;
> And when a good Democrat loses his place,
>   With a wild ghostly cheer
>   We will quit this sphere
> And sail through the star-sprinkled regions of space.

But at length we emerge from the regions of night and splendors celestial will burst full upon the sight of every Democrat. I am from Michigan—from the city that raises more sawdust and salt and free-silver Democrats than any other city in the Union. I was one of the Michigan Democrats who, when the vote was challenged on the election of a Temporary Chairman of this Convention, voted for the free-silver candidate. I have always been a free-silver man, and I was a member of the Committee on Resolutions in the State Convention two years ago that nominated that honest man, Hon. SPENCER O. FISHER, on a free-silver platform.

But I want to say this to you, my friends and fellow delegates, we have got votes enough in this Convention to nominate a free-silver candidate by a two-thirds majority without committing highway robbery. You may take my head for a foot ball if the twenty-eight votes from Michigan are not voted for a free and unlimited coinage silver man for President and Vice-President, regardless of what your vote may be here to-day. I thank you for your attention.

THE CHAIR: I present Hon. C. S. THOMAS, of Colorado.

Mr. THOMAS: Gentlemen of the Convention: It would be a great misfortune, in my opinion, for this Convention to do otherwise than nominate a candidate representing the wishes of the majority; it would be a greater one to secure such nomination by overturning the officially expressed wish of one of the sovereign States of this Union. We were charged, on yesterday, with a violation of a Democratic precedent, and the charge, in my opinion, was not well founded. If this majority report shall receive the official sanction of this Convention, then those who made the charge on yesterday will repeat it with truth to-morrow.

Four years ago practically the same question was presented from the State of New York, and before the Committee on Credentials could determine it, it was declared that the expressed sentiment of the Convention itself must determine the official character of the candidate. Now, I understand from the testimony here that at the time of the recommendations of certain names to the State Convention, that Convention adopted the recommendation without any protest whatever being made. There was the time and there was the place in which to make it. It seems to me that when a number of weeks is necessary for an individual to find out the fact that his virtue has been debauched, then such virtue should be received at least with some suspicion by a National Convention.

If I understand the testimony correctly, from what has been detailed and presented here—and I have not yet heard it contradicted—so far as the action of that Convention is concerned, it set the seal of its approval without objection and without protest, upon the forehead of every one of these Michigan delegates that were recognized by the National Committee. If that be so, gentlemen of the Convention, it does seem to me in all candor that we should regard the precedents of parties and recognize the sovereignty of the States thus casting their vote under the unit rule. We cannot under any circumstances transform ourselves into a returning board, and by going behind these returns, seat anyone here except those who have these credentials. If these four delegates who are said to be not entitled to seats in this Convention are, by reason of the manner in which they have been chosen not so entitled, then it follows that every one of the twenty-eight delegates similarly commissioned in this Convention are not entitled to recognition. It was said by one of the speakers that we should only go behind the returns because of fraud. It has been my teaching that fraud vitiates everything; and I put it to your sense of consistency, how it is possible that this fraud, of which complaint is made, affects but four of these delegates, while the others remain untainted.

Now, my fellow citizens, I shall not detain you longer. I was a member of the National Committee that passed upon this question, without receiving, I admit, a great deal of testimony. But I warn you, fellow delegates of the South and West, that we cannot afford to strike the sovereignty of the State of Michigan squarely in the forehead simply for the purpose of obtaining a two-thirds majority for our candidate.

Gentlemen, I hope, therefore, that this report of the minority Committee will be sustained by the vote which you shall take.

THE CHAIR: Judge O. W. POWERS, of Utah.

Judge POWERS: Mr. Chairman and Gentlemen: The question that it seems to me is presented for the consideration of those who are to do the voting at this Convention is as to whether the report of a duly and regularly constituted committee of this Convention, representing a majority of all the States of the Union, shall be sustained, or whether we shall take the word of gentlemen upon this platform as to whether the facts are this way or that way, we being unable to tell whether they are fully acquainted with the facts or not.

Our Committee has carefully investigated this matter and it has made its report to this Convention. It has said to you that it has found in the case of Michigan, fraud—fraud which vitiates all things.

The party that had the Presidency of the United States wrested from it after Tilden had been elected, ought to abhor fraud even though it be committed in organized Michigan or any other State.

What are the facts, gentlemen, as known to the people of this Union? The political history of this country informs us that Michigan has been and is a State in favor of free and unlimited coinage of silver at a ratio of 16 to 1, independent of any nation upon the face of the earth, or what it may care. Nevertheless, we find seated in this Convention a delegation bound to the gold idol, proposing now, by way of compromise, to cast its votes for a free silver candidate. If their cause was

DEMOCRATIC NATIONAL CONVENTION.   157

just, why should it be stated here by the delegates from Michigan that they propose now to abandon their golden standard and vote for a free silver candidate. It has been stated that free silver is dishonest. If it is dishonest, honest men cannot sustain it, and honest men cannot vote for its candidates.

We have been made aware by the public press that this is a free silver State. We were informed that the majority to the Convention were elected as silver delegates. The result of that Convention surprised the whole land. The people have been made acquainted with these facts, and I, for one, believing in the right of States to elect their own delegates, but believing also that no delegation should sit in this Convention whose title is tainted with fraud, am in favor of sustaining the report made by the majority of the States after patient deliberation; not that we may have a two-thirds vote for a free silver candidate, because we have that already; but because it is right, and right wrongs no man; because it is just and justice is what we seek for. The 650 delegates sitting upon the floor have no reason to seat these men to gain more strength and they should be seated if the report of the Credentials Committee is correct. Having faith in those men who have investigated it, I submit to you that the only question is, shall we sustain the majority of the States?

THE CHAIR: Senator THOMAS F. GRADY, of New York.

Senator GRADY: Gentlemen of the Convention: The question submitted to you for determination is one that goes far beyond and reaches far above the simple question as to whether twenty-four or more men, constituting a committee, shall be sustained, because you are to determine whether a Democratic principle and precedent as old as the party itself is to be violated, and that under the most suspicious circumstances. Let us not be deceived. The delegates are not deceived and the people cannot be deceived as to just what this means. It was the very height of generosity in the calm, judicial member from Texas that they are willing to leave the delegates-at large remain. Adopt the majority report, and under the unit rule you have every vote from Michigan, so that the generosity was more in name than in fact.

Answering the gentleman from Utah, who has placed his

judicial determination upon what he read in the newspapers, let me remind him that some of us since coming to Chicago have read in the newspapers that right or wrong some of the Michigan delegation were to be unseated, and were to be unseated for the purpose of making the abrogation of the two-thirds rule unnecessary. If the newspapers are to be relied upon for the gossip and the rumors and the statements that they have published regarding the Michigan contest, be sure before you vote that the people of the United States do not believe that your action in unseating regularly elected delegates is not misunderstood as an attempt to pack the Convention.

Mr. Grady was interrupted at this point by some disturbance at the entrance to the floor; the band played, and for a few moments he could not continue. Order being restored, he resumed as follows:

Mr. Grady: It is a most unfortunate circumstance that it would seem as if I never can make a speech in a National Convention without creating some kind of a row. My purpose in speaking was to avoid a row, yet there must be a row, if not here, in some place else, if we are to overturn a precedent that is a part of the party discipline itself.

What have we here? We have under the seal of the State of Michigan, through the only officers of any Democratic State Convention held in that State this year, a certificate that certain men had been duly elected at a Convention, uncontested in its parts and uncontested as to its actions. As against that some four men have come to the City of Chicago and have written out their own credentials, because there are but two sources from which credentials could emanate:—the State Convention for the regularly elected delegates, and the claimants themselves for the contestants. They have written out their own credentials, and they have presented them to you, and you are asked upon affidavits, rumors, newspaper reports, anything and everything, that you cannot see, that you cannot judge, that you cannot weigh, you are asked to overturn the action of a sovereign State and grab four votes.

They say the four votes thus to be grabbed are not necessary for any practical purpose. Then the less excuse for grabbing them. One of the gentlemen complains that it was a Convention that was manipulated. Well, what does he call manipulation? Some of us thought there was manipulation at the Convention of the great State of Missouri. There a district voted for two gold standard men. You could go through that delegation and you would not find them there. The silver sentiment of the Missouri Convention turned them down. They were hostile to the prevailing sentiment of the Convention, and the recommendation of the district was ignored and a solid silver delegation was sent. Suppose the two men thus turned down had held a convention in some hotel, as the Michigan claimants did, and wrote out their own credentials, and came here and told you that the Convention of the State of Missouri had been manipulated, how you would have laughed them out of the Convention.

Now, the other member of the committee did not complain about the Convention being manipulated. With him it was the delegates who were manipulated. They had been selected to do something. They went to the Convention and they did not do it, or they did not do it in the way that the majority of your Committee on Credentials would like that they should have done it, and because they disagree with the way in which they carried out the wishes of their constituents, then there is fraud, fraud that vitiates all things. There was fraud introduced into our national politics in 1876. There was a fraud by which Democracy was robbed of the President legally elected, and how was the fraud triumphant? By the action of the returning board, which threw out the votes legally cast; but they did not go so far as the returning board of the compromise on credentials. They not only threw out the votes that were cast but they counted votes never cast, and they undertook to say who was the individual who would best represent the prevailing sentiment in the State of Michigan.

Now, gentlemen, this question goes further than Michigan. This question in its determination affects every sovereign state. This question is to be passed upon not only by you here, but is to be passed upon by your constituency when you return to them. It is against the Democratic precedent, and let me call your attention to the fact that it is not well to violate Democratic precedent, particularly when we are assured that the violation of it is unnecessary.

Speaking for the State of New York, we have in times past claimed that there was no power in this Convention to override the will of our sovereign state, and having claimed that for ourselves, we are willing to yield it to our fellows.

THE CHAIR: The Chair will state to the Convention that there are two more speeches to be made, the one by Delegate-at-large T. A. E. WEADOCK; and the other by Mr. O'DONNELL on behalf of the Committee. I now present Mr. WEADOCK.

Mr. WEADOCK: Mr. Chairman and Gentlemen of the Convention: I desire to be heard for a very few moments for the honor of my party and the honor of my State. I want to say that there has been no contest in reference to the delegation from Michigan; but on the last day, in the afternoon, when the Convention was about to open, somebody came in here without notice, and with false affidavits which they knew there was no opportunity to meet and stated that they wanted an opportunity to be heard. That is what they called a contest. There were not three hundred Federal officeholders in that Convention; there were not twenty Federal officeholders; and half of those at least were voting for silver. Neither was the delegation instructed for gold. That Convention approved the platform of the last National Convention and voted to remit to the coming National Convention the question as to the platform.

We are here not to remove the delegates from that State, but to abide by the will of this Convention both in its platform and its candidate; but we insist that the sovereign will of the people in all good faith and fairness should be obeyed in this Convention, but on the other hand we are not to be influenced by some weak and cozening knave who wishes to give this Convention some advice and who is ready with his slander. I thank you for your attention.

THE CHAIR: The last speech on this subject is now about to be made and the debate closed by the gentleman from Colorado, Mr. T. J. O'DONNELL.

Mr. O'Donnell: Mr. Chairman and Gentlemen of the Convention: I will say a few words upon this question by the direction of the Committee on Credentials. We sat up until 4 o'clock this morning. We resumed the consideration of this question at 10 o'clock to-day. We referred it to a subcommittee upon which there was a gentleman from New York, and one from Maryland. Neither of those gentlemen has appeared upon this platform to dispute the honesty of the report of the Committee. But other men from the State of New York have come with threats against the majority of this Convention. I thank God that I have lived to see the time in a Democratic Convention when no threat of the gentleman from New York can drive it from doing its duty.

Gentlemen, the cause of the four men represented by the majority report is as honest as the silver dollar. As to the cause of the four sitting delegates whom this Committee proposes to unseat by the vote of members of the Committee on Credentials representing gold states, so apparent was the fraud that men representing gold states voted for a part of this report. I give you facts. No gentleman has been here on the other side who heard a word or line of this testimony. We have here affidavits by the hundred; documents of all kinds supporting this contest. It shows that the gentlemen from Michigan who have spoken to you and whom the representatives of twenty-two sovereign states voted ought to be dispossessed of their seats because of the fraud they had committed, or that has been committed. It shows, gentlemen, that these other men, represented by the majority report, were elected in the Michigan State Convention.

You talk about upsetting the will of a sovereign state. The purpose of the Committee is that the will of the sovereign State may and will be heard. We are not here to suppress it. We are here that truth, crushed to the earth in Michigan, may rise again and soar aloft; that the expression and voice of the people of that State may not be stifled. That a delegation may not speak a lie on behalf of that State. We are here with this report to compel the truth to be spoken for the State of Michigan.

Now, gentlemen, I ask you to sustain the report adopted in the Committee—twenty-five votes in the affirmative to nine in the negative. I move the previous question, Mr. Chairman.

The Chair then put the question whether the previous question should be ordered, and it was adopted.

The Chair: I will now state the question in order that it may be clearly understood. The majority of the Committee have reported in favor of the Fourth and Ninth Congressional districts of Michigan. A minority of the Committee have offered an amendment in favor of the sitting delegates of Michigan. A vote of aye upon the amendment, which will be submitted first, continues in their seats the sitting members. A vote of no is to the contrary of that proposition, and, should it carry, the question would then arise upon the report of the majority of the Committee. The question now is, gentlemen, upon the amendment offered by the minority of the Committee.

Mr. Stevenson, of Michigan: I demand the roll call upon the question.

The Chair: A roll call being demanded, the Chair will order that the roll of States be now called.

The Secretary then called the roll. Alabama cast 22 nays. John B. Knox, of Alabama, challenged the vote and the delegation was polled.

The Chair: The tally is 7 yeas, 14 nays, one absent. Under the unit rule, Alabama's twenty-two votes must be recorded No.

Arkansas cast sixteen negative votes. The Chairman of the California delegation announced the vote of that State as 11 yeas, 6 nays, one absent.

Hon. Thomas Dozier: I challenge the vote of California.

The Chair: Whoever challenges the vote must state his grounds; the vote of California will be recorded as amended by the Chairman of the delegation.

Mr. Dozier. I challenge the accuracy of the vote.

THE CHAIR: The State will be polled.

The roll of the California delegation was called.

The vote as recorded was 11 yeas, 6 nays and one absent. The Clerk then continued the call with the result:

	Yeas.	Nays
Colorado	4	4
Connecticut	12	..
Delaware	6	..
Florida	8	..
Georgia	..	26
Idaho	..	6
Illinois	..	48
Indiana	8	22
Iowa	..	26
Kansas	..	20
Kentucky	..	26

Mr. JAMES, of Kentucky: Mr. Chairman, under the unit rule, Kentucky votes 24 votes nay and 2 votes yea, which makes the 26 votes of Kentucky, nay, under the unit rule.

Mr. HALDEMAN, of Kentucky: I challenge the vote.

The Clerk then called the roll of Kentucky.

THE CHAIRMAN: 24 nays; and 2 ayes; the 26 votes of Kentucky under the unit rule will be counted no.

The Secretary then continued the calling of the roll of States, as follows:

	Yeas.	Nays.	Not voting.
Louisiana	..	16	..
Maine	10	..	2
Maryland	15	1	..
Massachusetts	27	3	..
Michigan	28	..	1
Minnesota	13	4	1
Mississippi	..	18	..
Missouri	..	34	..
Montana	..	6	..

	Yeas.	Nays.	Not voting
Nebraska		16	
Nevada		6	
New Hampshire	8		
New Jersey	20		
New York	72		

Upon the announcement of the vote of the State of New York a prolonged and loud demonstration of approval took place. When it subsided the Clerk continued to call the roll, calling the State of North Carolina. The Chairman of that delegation declined to announce the vote until order had been fully restored; this having been accomplished, the vote of North Carolina was recorded 21 nays, 1 aye. North Dakota vote 6 nays.

Gov. ALTGELD: I arise to a point of order and in that connection desire to challenge the vote of Michigan. We are proceeding here under the rules of the House of Representatives. Under the rules of the House of Representatives no member can vote upon any matter in which he is personally interested. Consequently, no member of this Convention can vote upon a question in which he is personally interested. I will sit down, and the Chair can pass upon it.

THE CHAIRMAN: The Chair will state to the delegate from Illinois that pending the roll call no debate or interruption can be entertained except when upon the call of the name of a State its vote is challenged. At the end of the roll call the Chair will consider whether or not it be then in order to entertain the suggestion of the delegate from Illinois.

Governor ALTGELD: Then I ask that at the conclusion of the roll call I be recognized to renew the point of order.

When order was restored the secretary proceeded with the roll call. Ohio announced forty-six nays, and the vote was challenged. The poll of the State showed the following result: 39 nays, 7 yeas.

Mr. SLOANE, of Ohio: Ohio has the unit rule and I state that her 46 votes are recorded no.

The roll call then proceeded thus:

	Yeas.	Nays.
Oregon	..	8
Pennsylvania	64	..
Rhode Island	8	..
South Carolina	..	18
South Dakota	8	..
Tennessee	..	24
Texas	..	30
Utah	..	6
Vermont	8	..

When Virginia was called, the Chairman of the delegation announced the vote as twenty-four nays; but the statement was challenged by Hon. MICHAEL GLENNAN, and the Chairman ordered the Secretary of the Convention to call the roll of the delegates, which was done. The roll call having been completed, the Chair announced the result as 6 yeas and 18 nays, and stated that under the unit rule, Virginia would cast her twenty-four votes nay. The roll call was then concluded as follows:

	Yeas.	Nays.
Washington	4	4
West Virginia	2	10
Wisconsin	24	..
Wyoming	..	6
Alaska	6	..
District of Columbia	1	5
Oklahoma	..	6
New Mexico	..	6
Indian Territory	..	6

After the Secretary had computed the ballot, the Chairman announced the result of the vote as follows: Yeas, 368; nays, 558; absent or not voting, 4. The detailed vote was as follows:

STATES.	TOTALS.	YEAS.	NAYS.	ABSENT.	NOT VOTING.
Alabama	22		22		
Arkansas	16		16		
California	18	11	6	1	
Colorado	8	4	4		
Connecticut	12	12			
Delaware	6	6			
Florida	8	8			
Georgia	26		26		
Idaho	6		6		
Illinois	48		48		
Indiana	30	8	22		
Iowa	26		26		
Kansas	20		20		
Kentucky	26		26		
Louisiana	16		16		
Maine	12	10			2
Maryland	16	15	1		
Massachusetts	30	27	3		
Michigan	28	28			
Minnesota	18	13	4	1	
Mississippi	18		18		
Missouri	34		34		
Montana	6		6		
Nebraska	16		16		
Nevada	6		6		
New Hampshire	8	8			
New Jersey	20	20			
New Mexico	6		6		
New York	72	72			
North Carolina	22	1	21		
North Dakota	6		6		
Ohio	46		46		
Oregon	8		8		
Pennsylvania	64	64			
Rhode Island	8	8			
South Carolina	18		18		
South Dakota	8	8			
Tennessee	24		24		
Texas	30		30		
Utah	6		6		
Vermont	8	8			
Virginia	24		24		
Washington	8	4	4		
West Virginia	12	2	10		
Wisconsin	24	24			
Wyoming	6		6		
Alaska	6	6			
Arizona	6		6		
District of Columbia	6	1	5		
Oklahoma	6		6		
Indian Territory	6		6		
Totals	930	368	558	2	2

For thirty minutes there was noise, confusion, cheers, etc.; when order was restored the Chairman said:

THE CHAIR: The question now recurs upon the adoption of the report of the majority.

The question of the adoption of the majority report was then put.

THE CHAIR: By the sound, the ayes seem to have it. The ayes have it, the majority report is adopted.

THE CHAIR: Is the Committee on Permanent Organization ready to report? I present Gen. E. B. FINLEY, of Ohio, the Chairman of the Committee on Permanent Organization.

Gen. FINLEY: Gentlemen of the Convention: I am directed by your Committee on Permanent Organization to report to you for your consideration the following names as your permanent officers:

For Permanent President of the Convention, Senator STEPHEN M. WHITE, of California.

For Permanent Secretary, THOMAS J. COGAN, of Ohio.

For Reading Clerk, E. B. WADE, of Tennessee.

For Sergeant-at-Arms, JOHN I. MARTIN, of Missouri.

For Assistant Secretary, LOUIS D. HIRSHHEIMER, of Illinois.

For Assistant Reading Clerks, N. R. WALKER, of Florida; F. JEFF POLLARD, of Missouri; LINCOLN DIXON, of Louisiana; WILLIAM E. THOMPSON, of Michigan, and CHAS. NICKELL, of Oregon.

The Committee ratifies and suggests to this Convention for honorary Vice-Presidents and honorary Secretaries and the members of the Notification Committee and National Democratic Committee, the gentlemen severally named by States and Territories. Mr. Chairman, I move the adoption of the report of the Committee.

THE CHAIR: It is moved and seconded that the report of the Committee on Permanent Organization be adopted.

Mr. McKNIGHT of Michigan: May I inquire whether or

not the National Committeeman of Michigan is included in that report, and also the various other Convention officers.

Mr. FINLEY: The report embraces the National Committeemen.

Mr. McKNIGHT: I desire to ask at this time that the Michigan delegation be allowed time to confer together before they can make a report. If there is any report for that Committee, we ask that it be withdrawn.

THE CHAIR: The gentleman rises to a parliamentary inquiry and desires to know from the Chairman of the Committee on Permanent Organization whether or not his report embraces the names of the members of the National Committee suggested by the States, and, if so, whether or not the State of Michigan is included.

Mr. FINLEY: I answer that, Mr. Chairman, the report of the Committee does embrace the several National Committeemen reported by the several States and Territories, and embraces one also from Michigan.

THE CHAIR: The Chair suggests to the gentleman from Michigan, that he can ask for the reading of the entire report.

A MICHIGAN DELEGATE: What are the names from Michigan?

Mr. McKNIGHT: That is a report made by members who are, a part of them, unseated, and we ask that the part in reference to Michigan be passed for the present, and I will make a motion that the names of the National Committeemen and the officers and members of this Convention that have been sent in be withdrawn and omitted from the report until we have an opportunity to caucus and report these various names of officers.

THE CHAIR: The Chairman will state to the delegate from Michigan that he can request that the whole report be read and he will be recognized; or to offer an amendment if it be done upon demand of the delegation from Michigan.

Mr. HUMMER, of Michigan: The delegation from

Michigan is not ready to vote on that question. I therefore move you that the report be adopted excepting as to Michigan.

General FINLEY: On yesterday in behalf of the contesting delegates from South Dakota I raised the objection to the several contesting delegates being reported to the several committees, but the Chairman ruled as a point of order that until the Committee on Credentials had disposed of it that the several delegates on the rolls could be recognized. Consequently, when your Committee on Organization met, we had to consider the several Committeemen and the several Vice-Presidents that had been reported to this Convention. It has been requested by the Chair that I again read the report of the Committee on Permanent Organization. The language of the report in regard to that is as follows:

"The names of honorary Vice-President, honorary Secretary, Notification Committee, and member of National Democratic Committee are ratified as sent in by the Chairmen of the respective State delegations."

The Chair recognized Mr. C. J. SMYTHE, of Nebraska.

Mr. SMYTHE: I desire, sir, in behalf of the Nebraska delegation, which has been seated this morning, to hand up the correct list of the officers which we desire placed upon the list. The National Committeeman is W. H. THOMPSON, and not the one handed in yesterday.

THE CHAIR: The delegate from Nebraska asks that the following names be substituted for the names reported by the Committee on Permanent Organization as the names of the persons chosen by the delegates from the State of Nebraska for the positions named. Is that correct?

Mr. SMYTHE, of Nebraska: That is correct, Mr. Chairman.

The list handed up by Mr. SMYTHE was read by the Clerk as follows:

Chairman of the Delegation—C. J. SMYTHE.
Committee on Credentials—C. HOLLENBECK.

Committee on Permanent Organization—J. C. Luikhary.

Committee on Rules and Order of Business—W. D. Oldham.

Committee on Resolutions—W. J. Bryan.

Honorary Vice-President—Charles H. Brown.

Honorary Secretary—F. A. Thompson.

Notification Committee—John A. Creighton.

Member of Democratic National Committee—William H. Thompson.

The Chairman: Gentlemen, the question is on the adoption of the amendment offered by the delegate from Nebraska to the report of the Committee on Permanent Organization.

The Chair recognized Mr. G. Gilbert, of Kentucky.

Mr. Gilbert: I want to say, as a member of that Committee on Permanent Organization, that blanks have been filled up by each State and Territory similar in form and substance to the one submitted by the delegate from Nebraska, and I suggest to the Convention that the Committee on Permanent Organization considered that all of those forms and all of those officers were reported upon and acted upon by the Committee on Permanent Organization and that the time of this Convention ought not to be consumed by reading the forty-eight reports of substantially the same character, of the stereotyped form, that are embodied in the report as presented by the Chairman of the Committee.

The Chair put the question on the amendment offered by Mr. Smythe, of Nebraska, and declared the amendments carried.

The Chair: Is there any other amendment?

Mr. Stevenson: I move that so much of the report submitted by the Committee on Permanent Organization as concerns the persons elected by the delegation of Michigan be recommitted to the Committee on Permanent Organization.

The question on the amendment was put and carried.

THE CHAIR: The question now recurs upon the adoption of the report of the Committee on Permanent Organization.

The report was thereupon adopted as amended.

THE CHAIR: The delegate from Michigan moves that so much of the report submitted by the Committee on Permanent Organization as concerns the persons selected by the delegation from Michigan be recommitted to that Committee.

Mr. STEVENSON: On that we demand a call of the roll. (Cries of No! No!)

The motion was adopted, *viva voce*.

THE CHAIR: It is moved that a committee of three be appointed to wait upon the Permanent President of this organization and escort him to the chair.

This motion was adopted.

THE CHAIR: The Chair appoints Gen. FINLEY, of Ohio, Judge MCCONNELL, of Illinois, and Senator GEORGE VEST, of Missouri, as such committee.

When this committee had escorted the new Chairman to the platform, Temporary Chairman DANIEL turned to the Convention and said:

Mr. DANIEL: Gentlemen of the Convention: In retiring from the Chair, which I have had the honor to occupy by your partial suffrage, I beg to extend to each and all of the membership of this Convention my cordial acknowledgment and thanks for the courtesy and consideration they have shown me. And I am happy now to present to you your Permanent Chairman in the person of the distinguished Democratic Senator from California, STEPHEN M. WHITE, into whose hands I am proud and happy to deliver this gavel.

Upon receiving the gavel, Chairman WHITE said:

Mr. WHITE: Gentlemen of the Convention: I will detain you with no extended speech. (Applause.) I see I am getting popular already. The Democratic party is here represented by delegates who have come from the Atlantic and Pacific shores. Every State has its full quota; every State, so far as I can bring about such a result, shall have full, equal, absolute and impartial treatment from this stand. Every State is entitled to such treatment; every question should be considered carefully and deliberately, and when the voice of this Convention is crystallized into a judgment it should be binding upon all true Democratic members of this Convention.

We differ, perhaps, to-day upon certain vital issues, and we might express some feelings of bitterness in these discussions, but we submit to the voice and the candid judgment of our brethren, and upon that judgment we will certainly rely. Time passes as we stand here; it leaves many with unsatisfied ambition. It leaves numerous aspirations and hopes unrealized. Men now prominent will pass away—some to oblivion while they live—and others, because they have been summoned to another shore; but the Democratic party will not die, even when we all have ceased to live.

When the differences which challenge consideration to-night have passed into history, when the asperities of this hour no longer obtain, the Democratic party, the guardian of the people's rights and the representative of the sentiments of the United States in support of constitutional right, will endure to bless mankind.

My ambition or yours is of but little moment. Whether I succeed, or you, in impressing sentiments upon this Convention is not of supreme importance. In this council chamber the Democratic party looks for an indication of its existence. The people seek here the righting of their wrongs, and the constitution—the great charter of our liberties—here must find its best, its truest and its most loyal defenders. No sectionalism whatever; equal, impartial justice to all in this land; the triumph of the people's cause, as here exemplified and expressed, is the object for which we have assembled, and to carry out that object I will consecrate my best exertions.

Hon. W. A. CLARKE, of Montana, obtained the floor, and, holding aloft a solid silver gavel, the product of the silver mines of Montana, addressed the Chair as follows:

Mr. W. A. CLARKE: I desire, in behalf of the people of Butte City, the greatest mining camp on the face of this globe, to present this gavel to you as Chairman of this Democratic National Convention.

Chairman WHITE received it, and said:

THE CHAIR: In the absence of objections, the Chair considers that he is authorized to accept this elegant donation made by the delegation from Montana.

Senator JONES, of Arkansas, received recognition by the Chair, and said:

Senator J. K. JONES: Before putting the motion to adjourn, I wish to announce that there will be a meeting of the Committee on Platform and Resolutions at the room of that Committee, to the right of the President, to-morrow morning at 9:30 o'clock.

Chairman WHITE recognized Hon. C. K. SMYTHE, of Nebraska, who said:

Mr. SMYTHE: I have a resolution here which I desire to have submitted, with reference to tickets for the Nebraska delegation, which has been seated. I wish to have it read, and move its adoption.

THE CHAIR: I presume that there is no objection to the resolution enforcing their desire; in the absence of objection, it is so ordered.

Mr. TRISTRAM GOLDTHWAITE, of Maine: I move that the Convention do now adjourn until to-morrow at 10 o'clock

This motion was adopted and the Convention adjourned to Thursday, July 9, 1896, at 10 o'clock A. M.

The following list of delegates from the different States and Territories are entitled to seats in this Convention as delegates as reported by the Committee on Credentials:

LIST OF DELEGATES.

ALABAMA.

AT LARGE.

A. H. Keller.
A. O. Lane.

John H. Bankhead.
John B. Knox.

District.
1st ......D. R. Burgess.
J. H. Minge.
2nd. .....Tennent Lomax.
W. L. Parks.
3rd........W. R. Painter.
T. P. Hudmon.
4th........R. T. Goodwyn.
C. W. Hooper.
5th........A. J. Driver.
W. D. McCurdy.

District.
6th........H. B. Foster.
Sam Carpenter.
7th........L. L. Cochran.
G. C. Almon.
8th........R. E. Spraggins.
J. E. Brown.
9th........C. E. Waller.
J. W. Tomlinson.

ARKANSAS.

AT LARGE.

James K. Jones.
James H. Berry.

Carroll Armstrong.
T. T. W. Tillar.

District.
1st........Charles Coffin.
John B. Driver.
2nd.......S. M. Taylor.
John J. Sumpter.
3rd........Paul Jones.
W. K. Ramsey.

District.
4th........J. G. Wallace.
George A. Mansfield.
5th........B. R. Davidson.
Philip D. Scott.
6th........J. W. Crockett.
A. S. Layton.

CALIFORNIA.

AT LARGE.

Stephen M. White.
W. W. Foote.

J. V. Coleman.
James G. Maguire.

District.
1st........Henry E. Wise.
Thos. B. Dozier.
2nd.......Thos. T. Lane.
A. Caminetti.
3rd........R. M. Fitzgerald.
E. E. Leake.
4th........J. J. Dwyer.
Louis F. Metzger.

District.
5th........Dr. W. F. Ragan.
Augustus Lion.
6th........T. F. Darmody.
William R. Bourke.
7th........Oscar A. Trippet.
George E. Church.

COLORADO.

AT LARGE.

Charles S. Thomas.   Thomas J. O'Donnell.
Adair Wilson.   B. O. Sweeney.

District.   District.
1st........Robert W. Speer.   2nd........Harry H. Seldomridge.
            Edward J. McCarty.   Samuel I. Hallett.

CONNECTICUT.

AT LARGE.

Miles B. Preston.   Thomas M. Waller.
Lynde Harrison.   James Aldis.

District.   District.
1st........E. D. Coogan.   3rd........W. H. Shields.
            Lyman T. Tingier.   Frederick T. Morrell.
2nd........William Kennedy.   4th........Charles P. Lyman.
            Horace B. Butler.   M. J. Houlihan.

DELAWARE.

AT LARGE.

Hon. George Gray.   Willard Saulsbury.
Dr. B. L. Lewis.   John F. Saulsbury.

FIRST DISTRICT.

William H. Boyce.   Harry C. Penington.

FLORIDA.

AT LARGE.

Robert W. Davis.   T. J. Appleyard.
Francis B. Carter.   D. D. Lukenbill.

District.   District.
1st........J. Ed. O'Brien.   2nd........G. B. Sparkman.
            C. B. Rogers.   Nat. R. Walker.

GEORGIA.

AT LARGE.

Evan P. Howell.   Patrick Walsh.
H. T. Lewis.   J. Pope Brown.

District.   District.
1st........John C. Dell.   4th........R. O. Howard.
            J. A. Brannen.   J. S. Anderson.
2nd........E. L. Wright.   5th........R. D. Spalding.
            Jno. E. Donalson.   J. A. Morrow.
3rd........J. T. Hill.   6th........C. T. Zachry.
            F. C. Houser.   Buford M. Davis.

District.
7th........W. M. Gammon.
           J. M. McBride.
8th........W. B. Burnett.
           W. P. McWhorter.
9th........Tyler M. Peoples.
           Howard Thompson.

District.
10th.......Ira E. Farmer.
           George W. Warren.
11th.......C. R. Pendleton.
           W. H. Clements.

IDAHO.

AT LARGE.

H. C. Shafer.
W. H. Watt.

G. V. Bryan.
Barry N. Hillard.

FIRST DISTRICT.

Timothy Regan.

J. C. Rich.

ILLINOIS.

AT LARGE.

John P. Altgeld.
W. H. Hinrichsen.

Samuel P. McConnell.
George W. Fithian.

District.
1st........A. S. Trude.
           Jesse Sherwood.
2nd.......Edward Tilden.
           Thos. Byrne.
3rd........Charles Martin.
           Jno. C. Schubert.
4th........Jno. Powers.
           Wm. Loeffler.
5th........John J. Brennan.
           M. C. McDonald.
6th........Henry F. Donovan.
           Jos. S. Martin.
7th........Wm. Prentiss.
           Jas. Burke.
8th........Mark W. Dunham.
           J. D. Donovan.
9th........Frank M. Barron.
           Samuel Ray.
10th.......C. K. Ladd.
           Jas. T. Wasson.
11th.......G. W. Stipp.
           E. M. Johnson.

District.
12th.......Dr. M. Cushing.
           Free P. Morris.
13th.......Wm. E. Krebs.
           J. T. Heffernan.
14th.......N. E. Worthington.
           W. H. Masters.
15th.......Felix Regnier.
           B. P. Preston.
16th.......Frank Robinson.
           A. M. Bell.
17th.......T. T. Beach.
           H. W. Clendenin.
18th.......A. W. Hope.
           C. W. Bliss.
19th.......R. N. Stotler.
           H. S. Tanner.
20th.......Wm. H. Green.
           J. R. Williams.
21st.......J. N. Perrin.
           W. A. J. Sparks.
22nd.......L. O. Whitnel.
           Wm. W. Clemens.

INDIANA.

AT LARGE.

Daniel W. Voorhees.
G. V. Menzies.
David Turpie.
James McCabe.

District.		District.	
1st	James R. Goodwin.	8th	Ralph S. Gregory.
	C. B. McCormack.		W. A. Humphries.
2nd	W. A. Cullop.	9th	Daniel Sims.
	John H. O'Neall.		Eli Marvin.
3rd	George H. Voigt.	10th	James Murdock.
	A. P. Fenn.		J. A. Lautmann.
4th	John Overmeyer.	11th	S. E. Cook.
	Joseph Matlock.		John T. Strange.
5th	Eb. Henderson.	12th	Henry Colerick.
	S. M. McGregor.		Joseph Washburn.
6th	U. S. Jackson.	13th	John B. Stoll.
	D. W. Andre.		Preston F. Miles.
7th	Wm. E. English.		
	Charles M. Cooper.		

IOWA.

AT LARGE.

Horace Boies.
Will A. Wells.
S. B. Evans.
Louis T. Genung.

District.		District.	
1st	W. H. Stackhouse.	7th	M. H. King.
	W. R. Wherry.		J. S. Cunningham.
2nd	May Mayer.	8th	S. A. Brewster.
	T. M. Gobble.		Charles Thomas.
3rd	J. S. Murphy.	9th	F. D. Allen.
	D. C. Filkins.		W. H. Ware.
4th	T. Donovan.	10th	R. F. Jordan.
	F. D. Bayless.		C. C. Colclo.
5th	T. F. Bradford.	11th	T. P. Murphy.
	T. M. Terry.		C. L. Soister.
6th	H. C. Taylor.		
	W. A. McIntyre.		

KANSAS.

AT LARGE.

John Martin.
J. D. McCleverty.
J. H. Atwood.
David Overmyer.
Frank Bacon.
James McKinstry.

District.
1st........Moses Saurback.
J. B. Taylor.
2nd. .... S. A. Riggs.
L. C. Stine.
3rd........J. H. Cushingberry.
J. Mack Love.
4th........J. G. Johnson.
Charles Stackhouse.

District.
5th........C. W. Brandenburg.
C. P. Carstenson.
6th........John B. Rea.
E. G. Collins.
7th........J. H. Haymaker.
C. F. Diffenbacher.

KENTUCKY.
AT LARGE.

J. C. S. Blackburn.
W. T. Ellis.

P. Wat. Hardin.
John S. Rhea.

District.
1st........Ollie M. James.
J. D. Mocquot.
2nd. .....J. F. Dempsey.
E. P. Millett.
3rd........J. M. Richardson.
Ben T. Perkins.
4th........David R. Murray.
Robert Lancaster.
5th........Zach Phelps.
W. B. Haldeman.
6th........N. S. Walton.
J. T. Scott.

District.
7th....... T. E. Moore.
R. F. Peake.
8th........G. G. Gilbert.
Robert F. Thompson.
9th........George R. Vincent.
G. W. Bramlett.
10th.......John S. Garner.
George B. Clay.
11th..... .C. M. Sales.
Ben V. Smith.

LOUISIANA.
AT LARGE.

S. D. McEnery.
S. M. Robertson.

N. C. Blanchard.
John Fitzpatrick.

District.
1st ....Thomas Duffy.
Victor Manberret.
2nd.......Peter Farrell.
L. H. Marrero.
3rd........Edmund C. McCollam.
Jos. St. Amant.

District.
4th........H. W. Ogden.
B. W. Marston.
5th........R. H. Snyder.
S. T. Baird.
6th........T. S. Fontenot.
T. J. Kernan.

MAINE.
AT LARGE.

Seth C. Gordon.
Frederic W. Plaisted.

John Scott.
Charles L. Snow.

District.
1st....... E. B. Winslow.
Tristram Goldthwaite.
2nd.......C. Vey Holman.
J. H. Sherman.

District.
3rd........Fred Emery Beane.
L. B. Deasy.
4th........Richard W. Sawyer.
Ara Warren.

MARYLAND.

AT LARGE.

John E. Hurst.
Chas. C. Homer.
John P. Poe.
*Charles C. Crothers.

Richard M. Venable.
John Gill.
Edwin Warfield.
Marion DeKalb Smith

District.
1st........Henry R. Lewis.
  John R. Patterson.
2nd.......Frederick von Kapff.
  Thos. H. Robinson.
3rd........John Hannibal.
  Louis M. Duvall.
  *By Murray Vandiver.

District.
4th........James W. McElroy.
  Wm. T. Biedler.
5th........Wm. B. Clagett.
  Dr. Geo. H. Jones.
6th........Spencer Watkins.
  Henry F. Wingert.

MASSACHUSETTS.

AT LARGE.

John W. Corcoran.
George Fred Williams.

John E. Russell.
James Donovan.

District.
1st....... John C. Crosby.
  Michael Connors.
2nd.......Selig Manilla.
  Ralph L. Atherton.
3rd........Andrew Athy.
  John O'Gara.
4th........Robert M. Burnett.
  Herbert H. Lyons.
5th........Jeremiah T. O'Sullivan.
  Peter H. Donohue.
6th........Thomas A. Devin.
  Edward J. Donahue.
7th........Joseph J. Corbett.
  Samuel K. Hamilton.

District.
8th........John F. O'Brien.
  Frank X. Fitzpatrick.
9th........Patrick J. Kennedy.
  Martin M. Lomasney.
10th.......John J. Nawn.
  F. S. Gore.
11th.......Patrick Maguire.
  George F. Maxwell.
12th.......William L. Douglass.
  Joseph L. Sweet.
13th.......Henry C. Thatcher.
  James T. Cummings.

MICHIGAN.

AT LARGE.

Elliott G. Stevenson.
R. R. Blacker.

Thos. A. E. Weadock.
Peter White.

District.
1st........W. V. Moore.
  W. A. Dwyer.
2nd.......Elmer Kirkby.
  Lester H. Salsbury.
3rd........James M. Powers.
  John B. Shipman.

District.
4th........Hannibal Hart.
  Henry Chamberlain.
5th........W. F. McKnight.
  George P. Hummer.
6th........S. L. Bignall.
  Arthur R. Tripp.

District.
7th........F. W. Hubbard.
M. Crocker.
8th........Mayor Baum.
Ferdinand Brucker.
9th........J. S. White.
H. J. Hoyt.

District.
10th.......F. A. McDonald.
J. F. Moloney.
11th.......C. H. Sutherland.
T. J. Potter.
12th.......E. F. Brown.
M. J. McGee.

MINNESOTA.

AT LARGE.

Daniel W. Lawler.
Chauncey L. Baxter.

Philip D. Winston.
Logan Breckenridge.

District.
1st........John Noonan.
J. F. McGovern.
2nd.......B. F. Voreis.
C. W. Schultz.
3rd........Albert Schalier.
John Sheehy.
4th........Wm. H. Harris.
George J. Mitsch.

District.
5th........A. D. Smith.
W. H. Dunahue.
6th........Thos. R. Foley.
Wm. R. Remer.
7th........M. F. Noonan.
J. E. O'Brien.

MISSISSIPPI.

AT LARGE.

J. Z. George.
H. D. Money.
R. H. Henry.

E. C. Walthall.
A. J. McLaurin.

District.
1st........W. J. Lamb.
C. M. Johnson.
2nd.......J. R. Stowers.
R. W. Bailey.
3rd........William T. Yerger.
Patrick Henry.
4th........W. S. Hill.
Walter Price.

District.
5th........*W. P. Tackett.
R. F. Cochran.
6th........†D. M. Watkins.
‡M. Quinn.
7th........H. Cassidy.
Ben H. Wells.

MISSOURI.

AT LARGE.

G. G. Vest.
W. J. Stone.

F. M. Cockrill.
George W. Allen.

*Represented by T. F. Pettus.
†Represented by W. A. Taylor.
‡Represented by Geo. M. Govan.

DEMOCRATIC NATIONAL CONVENTION.

District.
1st........Dr. R. Gillespie.
　　　　　John A. Knott.
2nd.......William M. Eads.
　　　　　C. B. Crawley, Jr.
3rd........W. W. Mosby.
　　　　　John A. Cross.
4th........C. F. Cochran.
　　　　　Wm. E. Ellison.
5th........J. D. Shewalter.
　　　　　J. W. Mercer.
6th........D. A. DeArmond.
　　　　　Wm. S. Byram.
7th........E. W. Stephens.
　　　　　E. A. Barbour.
8th........L. V. Stephens.
　　　　　James F. Bradshaw.

District.
9th........Thomas R. Gibson.
　　　　　William L. Gupton.
10th.......John W. Booth.
　　　　　John T. Gibson.
11th.......Hugh J. Brady.
　　　　　Nicholas M. Bell.
12th.......M. C. Wetmore.
　　　　　Charles R. Gregory.
13th.......E. C. Lysle.
　　　　　James F. Green.
14th.......Marshall Arnold.
　　　　　W. N. Evans.
15th.......M. E. Benton.
　　　　　J. W. Halliburton.

MONTANA.

AT LARGE.

W. A. Clark.
E. D. Matts.

S. T. Houser.
W. G. Downing.

FIRST DISTRICT.

Paul A. Fusz.

Dr. J. M. Fox.

NEBRASKA.

AT LARGE.

W. J. Bryan.
W. H. Thompson.

C. J. Smythe.
W. D. Oldham.

District.
1st........Frank J. Morgan.
　　　　　Chas. S. Stone.
2nd.......Jno. A. Creighton.
　　　　　Chas. H. Brown.
3rd........C. Hollenbeck.
　　　　　J. C. Luikart.

District.
4th........C. J. Bowlby.
　　　　　Ed. Biggs.
5th........P. Walsh.
　　　　　F. A. Thompson.
6th........Dr. A. T. Blackburn.
　　　　　J. C. Dahlman.

NEVADA.

AT LARGE.

R. P. Keating.
John Sparks.

Jacob Klein.
Dr. J. W. Petty.

FIRST DISTRICT.

J. C. Hagerman.

Jos. Raycraft.

NEW HAMPSHIRE.

AT LARGE

Frank Jones.
Irving W. Drew.

Alvah H. Sulloway.
Chas. A. Sinclair.

District.
1st........Gordon Woodbury.
Herbert J. Jones.

District.
2nd ......Amos N. Blondin.
Jeremiah J. Doyle.

NEW JERSEY.

AT LARGE.

James Smith, Jr.
Albert Tallman.

Rufus Blodgett.
Allen McDermont.

District.
1st........Henry M. Harley.
Geo. M. Betchner.
2nd.......James W. Lanning.
B. Frank Budd.
3rd........Geo. A. Helne.
James J. Bergen.
4th........Lewis J. Martin.
Elias C. Drake.

District.
5th........Henry D. Winson.
Munson Force.
6th........Gottfried Krueger.
Edward P. Meany.
7th........Wm. D. Daly.
Wm. D. Edwards.
8th........Fred C. Marsh.
Thos. F. Noonan.

NEW YORK.

AT LARGE.

David B. Hill.
Edward Murphy.

Roswell P. Flower.
Frederic C. Coudert.

District.
1st........Perry Belmont.
W. A. Hazard.
2nd.......William C. DeWitt.
P. J. Carlin.
3rd........John Delmar.
Bird S. Coler.
4th........Daniel Ryan.
John J. O'Keefe.
5th........James D. Bell.
James Moffett.
6th........Bernard Gallagher.
Rudolph C. Bacher.
7th........Franklin Bartlett.
John R. Fellows.
8th........Amos J. Cummings.
Thomas F. Grady.

District.
9th........John F. Ahern.
Henry M. Goldfogle.
10th.......James W. Boyle.
John C. Sheehan.
11th.......C. C. Baldwin.
William Sulzer.
12th.......Francis M. Scott.
George B. McClellan.
13th.......James O'Gorman.
De Lancey Nicol.
14th.......Hugh J. Grant.
John D. Crimmins.
15th.......Thomas F. Gilroy.
Ashbel P. Fitch.
16th.......Henry D. Purroy.
Francis Larkin.

DEMOCRATIC NATIONAL CONVENTION. 183

District
- 17th.......Arthur McLean.
  Frank Comesky.
- 18th.......James W. Hinckley.
  John G. Van Etten.
- 19th.......Francis J. Molloy.
  *James Purcell.
- 20th.......Erastus Corning.
  Charles Tracy.
- 21st.......Geradus Smith.
  James H. Brown.
- 22nd.......Thomas Spratt.
  Robert A. Anibal.
- 23rd.......Thomas F. Conway.
  Edward T. Stokes.
- 24th.......Fred C. Schraub.
  James R. O'Gorman.
- 25th.......Henry W. Bently.
  Clinton Beckwith.

District.
- 26th.......James C. Truman.
  Elliott F. Danforth.
- 27th.......William M. Kirk.
  D. Monroe Hill.
- 28th.......Thomas Osborn.
  Henry V. L. Jones.
- 29th.......Dr. Barnes.
  F. G. Babcock.
- 30th.......James A. Hanlon.
  E. A. Dodgson.
- 31st.......A. E. Rickson Perkins.
  James L. Whalen.
- 32nd......Daniel N. Lockwood.
  Norman E. Mack.
- 33rd.......Wilson S. Bissell.
  Joseph Mayer.
- 34th.......Thomas Troy.
  Thomas O'Connor.

NORTH CAROLINA.

AT LARGE.

John R. Webster.
E. J. Hale.

Thomas J. Jarvis.
Alfred M. Waddell.

District.
- 1st........Charles F. Warren.
  B. B. Winborne.
- 2nd.......Jesse W. Grainger.
  T. L. Emry.
- 3rd........P. M. Pearsell.
  J. H. Currie.
- 4th........M. W. Page.
  Wm. C. Hammer.
- 5th........N. B. Cannady.
  Dr. E. Fulp.

District.
- 6th........W. C. Dowd.
  Joseph A. Brown.
- 7th........Theo. F. Kluttz.
  W. D. Turner.
- 8th........E. B. Jones.
  Dr. B. F. Dixon.
- 9th........W. E. Moore.
  G. S. Powell.

NORTH DAKOTA.

AT LARGE.

Wm. N. Roach.
J. B. Eaton.

M. F. Williams.
H. R. Hartman.

FIRST DISTRICT.

James H. Holt.

F. A. Wilson.

*Represented by J. Van Ness Phillips.

OHIO.

AT LARGE.

John R. McLean.
A. W. Thurman.
E. B. Finley.
L. E. Holden.

District.
- 1st........Lewis G. Bernard.
  Thos. T. Mulvihill.
- 2nd........L. J. Dolle.
  Thos. J. Cogan.
- 3rd........Peter Schwab.
  John C. Patterson.
- 4th.........John C. Clarke.
  Robert B. Gordon, Jr.
- 5th........J. K. Kaunneke.
  Levi X. Jacobs.
- 6th........Ulric Sloan.
  M. R. Denver.
- 7th........A. L. Claypool.
  G. S. Long.
- 8th........F. M. Marriott.
  Phil M. Crow.
- 9th........Barton Smith.
  William Gordon.
- 10th.......Thomas B. H. Jones.
  C. E. Crawford.
- 11th. .....John H. Blacker.
  Virgil C. Lowry.

District.
- 12th.......James Kilbourne.
  M. A. Daugherty.
- 13th.......Reuben Turner.
  Frank Hollbrook.
- 14th.......Cyrant D. Holliday.
  Frank Harper.
- 15th.......Charles A. Richardson.
  A. J. Andrews.
- 16th.......D. McConville.
  R. W. McCommon.
- 17th.......A. W. Patrick.
  John W. Cassingham.
- 18th.......Wilson S. Potts.
  Conrad Schweitzer.
- 19th.......C. A. Corbin.
  I. T. Siddall.
- 20th.......Horace Alford.
  John B. Foster.
- 21st.......Tom L. Johnson.
  S. A. Holding.

OREGON.

AT LARGE.

M. A. Miller.
J. W. Howard.
J. H. Townsend.
Dr. J. Welch.

District.
- 1st........J. D. McKennon.
  Charles Nickell.

District.
- 2nd.......Dr. Mullinix.
  W. F. Butcher.

PENNSYLVANIA.

AT LARGE.

William F. Harrity.
J. Henry Cochran.
John Todd, M. D.
John S. Rilling.
Robert E. Wright.
Charles A. Fagan.
Benjamin F. Meyers.
John T. Lenanan.

DEMOCRATIC NATIONAL CONVENTION.

District.
- 1st........George W. Gibbons.
  Henry C. Loughlin.
- 2nd.......Charles E. Ingersoll.
  Louis J. McGrath.
- 3rd........Thomas J. Ryan.
  Matthew Dittmann.
- 4th........Thomas Delahunty.
  Gustavus A. Muller.
- 5th........John Taylor.
  Edward F. Bennis.
- 6th........Frank B. Rhodes.
  J. Frank E. Hause.
- 7th........Paul H. Applebach.
  Edward F. Kane.
- 8th........Frank P. Sharkey.
  Howard Mutchler.
- 9th........W. Oscar Miller.
  F. F. Bressler.
- 10th.......Richard M. Reilly.
  H. E. Haldeman.
- 11th.......C. G. Boland.
  Joseph O'Brien.
- 12th.......Elliott P. Kisner.
  John M. Garman.
- 13th.......James Ellis.
  William A. Marr.
- 14th.......John A. Magee.
  S. P. Light.

District.
- 15th.......Miller S. Allen.
  John M. Rahm.
- 16th.......John J. Reardon.
  William Dent.
- 17th.......D. Clinger.
  Grant Herring.
- 18th.......Jay G. Weiser.
  Thomas C. Barber.
- 19th.......H. N. Gitt.
  F. E. Beltzhoover.
- 20th.......Joseph A. Gray.
  Americus Enfield.
- 21st ......W. A. McCullough.
  John B. Keenan.
- 22nd......George S. Fleming.
  E. J. Frauenheim.
- 23rd.......Samuel W. Black.
  Hay Walker, Jr.
- 24th.......Frank Thompson.
  A. F. Silveus.
- 25th.......Robert Ritchie.
  Stephen Markham.
- 26th.......William H. Gaskill.
  Frank E. McLean.
- 27th.......Charles H. Noyes.
  Charles O. Laymon.
- 28th.......James Knox Polk Hall.
  Matt Savage.

RHODE ISLAND.

AT LARGE.

Richard B. Comstock.
Miles A. McNamee

George W. Greene.
Jesse H. Metcalf.

District.
- 1st........James J. Van Alen.
  David S. Baker.

District.
- 2d.........John H. Tucker.
  John E. Conley.

SOUTH CAROLINA.

AT LARGE.

B. R. Tillman.
D. J. Bradham.

John G. Evans.
W. H. Ellerbe.

District.
- 1st........M. R. Cooper.
  Thomas Martin.
- 2nd........M. B. McSweeny.
  B. L. Caughman.

District
- 3rd........J. H. McCalla.
  J. B. Watson.
- 4th. ......J. C. Walling.
  J. D. M. Shaw.

District.   District.
5th........W. F. Strait.   7th........Oscar R. Lowman.
          T. Y. Williams.   H. T. Abbott.
6th........W. D. Evans.
          A. H. Williams.

SOUTH DAKOTA.

AT LARGE.

F. M. Stover.   J. E. Carland.
Edmund Cook.   S. A. Ramsey.

District.   District.
1st........George H. Culver.   2nd.......James M. Woods.
          S. V. Arnold.   W. R. Steele.

TENNESSEE.

AT LARGE.

Isham G. Harris.   Wm. B. Bate.
E. W. Carmack.   T. M. McConnell.

District.   District.
1st ....John K. Shields.   6th........C. W. Parker.
          H. H. Gouchenour.   Thos. Claibourne.
2nd.......John M. Davis.   7th........N. B. Chiers.
          Wm. F. Park.   Frank Boyd.
3rd.......H. C. Snodgrass.   8th........J. W. Lewis.
          W. P. Murray.   J. W. N. Burkett.
4th.......W. C. Dismukes.   9th. ......J. B. Phillips.
          L. D. Smith.   C. M. Hall.
5th.......James D. Richardson.   10th.......A. T. McNeil.
          C. A. Armstrong.   H. C. Moorman.

TEXAS.

AT LARGE.

J. W. Bailey.   J. M. Duncan.
J. S. Hogg.   C. A. Culbertson.

District.   District.
1st........John H. Reagan.   5th........H. B. Marsh.
          Horace Chilton.   B. F. Looney.
2d ....E. G. Center.   6th........John L. Sheppard.
          J. W. Blake.   Jake Hodges.
3d ....L. T. Dashiel.   7th....... C. P. Randell.
          O. T. Holt.   W. T. Beverly.
4th.......T. M. Campbell.   8th........O. W. Odell.
          M. R. Gear.   W. I. Hooks.

DEMOCRATIC NATIONAL COMMITTEE. 187

District.		District.	
9th	Huling P. Robertson.	13th	J. B. Dibbrell.
	Chas. H. Coffield.		R. A. Pleasants.
10th	James M. Richards.	14th	T. M. Paschall.
	Eugene Moore.		W. W. Gatewood.
11th	Jefferson Johnson.	15th	Fred Cockrell.
	Heber Stone.		J. A. Templeton.
12th	W. S. Robson.		
	John Lovejoy.		

UTAH.
AT LARGE.

Moses Thatcher. O. W. Powers.
J. L. Rawlins. Robert C. Chambers.

FIRST DISTRICT.

Samuel R. Thurman. David Evans.

VERMONT.
AT LARGE.

T. W. Maloney Wells Valentine.
P. J. Farrell. S. C. Shurtliff.

District.		District.	
1st	Michael Magiff.	2d	W. H. Cramer.
	John W. McGarry.		W. H. Miner.

VIRGINIA.
AT LARGE.

John W. Daniel. W. A. Jones.
Claude A. Swanson. H. S. K. Morrison.

District.		District.	
1st	J. W. G. Blackstone.	6th	Carter Glass.
	Thomas E. Blakey.		W. P. Barksdale.
2nd	M. Glennan.	7th	J. R. Wingfield.
	J. E. West.		N. W. Waller.
3rd	Thomas B. Murphy.	8th	S. R. Donohoe.
	A. J. Bradley.		Charles M. Waite.
4th	R. G. Southall.	9th	Walter E. Addison.
	Robert Turnbull.		T. A. Lynch.
5th	B. L. Belt.	10th	Frank T. Glasgow.
	E. G. Sutherland.		Camm Patterson.

WASHINGTON.
AT LARGE.

R. C. McCroskey. J. E. Fenton.
Hugh C. Wallace. W. H. White.

District.		District.	
1st	Thos. Malony	2nd	John L. Sharpstein.
	Charles A. Darling.		J. F. Girton.

WEST VIRGINIA.

AT LARGE.

W. M. Kincaid.
J. W. St. Claire.

John T. McGraw.
B. B. Harding.

District.
1st......W. E. R. Byrne.
John A. Howard.
2nd......John J. Cornwell.
E. D. Talbott.

District.
3rd......James H. Miller.
Lawrence E. Tierney.
4th......H. S. Wilson.
J. R. Wilson.

WISCONSIN.

AT LARGE.

Edward S. Bragg.
James G. Flanders.

Wm. F. Vilas.
James J. Hogan.

District.
1st......George M. McKee.
Thos. M. Kearney.
2nd......James E. Malone.
Wm. H. Rogers.
3rd......Dr. Hermann Gasser.
Dr. W. A. Synon.
4th......Henry Hase.
Wm. Bergenthal.
5th......M. C. Mead.
Dr. Henry Blank.

District.
6th......H. P. Hamilton.
John J. Wood, Jr.
7th......Robert Lees.
A. C. Larson.
8th......John H. Brennan.
John Wattawa.
9th......E. J. Dockery.
Amos Holgate.
10th......R. J. Shields.
W. F. McNally.

WYOMING.

AT LARGE.

C. W. Brumel.
Tim Dyer.

Robert Foote.
M. L. Blake.

FIRST DISTRICT.

John E. Osborne.

J. W. Samman.

ALASKA.

AT LARGE.

Louis L. Williams.
Richard F. Lewis.
R. D. Crittenden.

Charles D. Rogers.
James Carroll.
George R. Tingle.

ARIZONA.

AT LARGE.

W. H. Burbage.
Wiley E. Jones.
J. F. Wilson.

H. E. Campbell.
Jos. L. B. Alexander.
W. H. Barnes.

DISTRICT OF COLUMBIA.

AT LARGE.

John Boyle.
Edward L. Jordan.
Robert E. Mattingly.

William Holmead.
George Killeen.
Frank P. Morgan.

NEW MEXICO.

AT LARGE.

Demetrio Chaves.
Antonio Joseph.
John Y. Hewitt.

W. S. Hopewell.
M. M. Salazar.
A. A. Jones.

OKLAHOMA TERRITORY.

AT LARGE.

A. J. Beale.
Temple Houston.
W. S. Denton.

Mort L. Bixler.
E. F. Mitchell.
H. C. Brunt.

INDIAN TERRITORY.

AT LARGE.

Robt. L. Owen,
William P. Thompson.
Harry Campbell.

Joseph M. Lahay.
E. Poe Harris.
Fol. J. Woods.

THIRD DAY.

MORNING SESSION.

CHICAGO, July 9, 1896.

The Convention was called to order by the Chairman, Senator WHITE, at 10:50 A. M. Senator WHITE being so hoarse as to render the use of his voice very painful, called Hon. JAMES D. RICHARDSON, a delegate from Tennessee, to the Chair.

THE CHAIR: The Convention will be in order; the gentlemen in the aisles will take their seats. The Convention will be opened with prayer by the Rev. THOMAS EDWARD GREEN, rector of Grace Episcopal Church, of Cedar Rapids, Iowa. The gentlemen of the Convention will rise; and also all others in the audience.

PRAYER.

We thank, Thee, Almighty God, for the blessing of another day that Thou hast given us. At its beginning we pray that we may be true to its responsibilities and brave for its duties. Especially grant Thy blessing to these, thy servants, who face this day the great responsibilities and duties of this Convention. As they shall make their declaration of principles, may they set forth these truths that shall be founded upon the eternal principles of truth and justice, and that may redound for the benefit of all the people and the uplifting of humanity. And as they shall designate him who shall be their candidate for the chief magistracy of this great nation, guide Thou their minds and their voices. May they choose a man of clean hands and pure heart, whose aims shall be his country and his God, and who may so live that mankind, by his virtues, may be lifted nearer to heaven, and so may the angels of peace and prosperity bless this land, and may Thy kingdom come in all our hearts through the blessed gospel of Jesus Christ, to whom, with the Father and Holy Ghost, be ascribed all glory now and forever more. Amen.

THE CHAIR: The Committee on Platform is now ready to report. I recognize Hon. JAMES K. JONES, of Arkansas, the Chairman of this Committee.

Senator JONES: Mr. Chairman: I am directed by the Committee on Resolutions and Platform to report the following platform and to move its adoption:

We, the Democrats of the United States in National Convention assembled, do reaffirm our allegiance to those great essential principles of justice and liberty, upon which our institutions are founded, and which the Democratic Party has advocated from Jefferson's time to our own—freedom of speech, freedom of the press, freedom of conscience, the preservation of personal rights, the equality of all citizens before the law, and the faithful observance of constitutional limitations.

During all these years the Democratic Party has resisted the tendency of selfish interests to the centralization of government power, and steadfastly maintained the integrity of the dual scheme of government established by the founders of this Republic of republics. Under its guidance and teaching the great principle of local self-government has found its best expression in the maintenance of the rights of the States and its assertion of the necessity of confining the general government to the exercise of the powers granted by the Constitution of the United States.

The Constitution of the United States guarantees to every citizen the rights of civil and religious liberty. The Democratic Party has always been the exponent of political liberty and religious freedom, and it renews its obligations and reaffirms its devotion to these fundamental principles of the Constitution.

Recognizing that the money question is paramount to all others at this time, we invite attention to the fact that the Federal Constitution names silver and gold together as the money metals of the United States, and that the first coinage law passed by Congress under the Constitution made the silver dollar the monetary unit and admitted gold to free coinage at a ratio based upon the silver-dollar unit.

We declare that the act of 1873 demonetizing silver without the knowledge or approval of the American people has resulted in the appreciation of gold and a corresponding fall in the prices of commodities produced by the people; a heavy increase in the burden of taxation and of all debts, public and private; the enrichment of the money-lending class at home and abroad; the prostration of industry and impoverishment of the people.

We are unalterably opposed to monometallism which has locked fast the prosperity of an industrial people in the paralysis of hard times. Gold monometallism is a British policy, and its adoption has brought other nations into financial servitude to London. It is not only un-American, but anti-American, and it can be fastened on the United States only by the stifling of that spirit and love of liberty which proclaimed our political independence in 1776 and won it in the War of the Revolution.

We demand the free and unlimited coinage of both silver and gold at the present legal ratio of 16 to 1 without waiting for the aid or consent of any other nation.

(The speaker was here interrupted by demands all over the hall that he read this paragraph again.)

Senator JONES: If the Convention will be quiet I will read it as many times as they want to hear it. But I am hoarse, and I must appeal for order, because my voice is in bad condition, and I cannot hope to be heard unless the gentlemen of the Convention will be quiet. I will read it again:

"We demand the free and unlimited coinage of both silver and gold at the present legal ratio of 16 to 1 without waiting for the aid or consent of any other nation."

We demand that the standard silver dollar shall be a full legal tender, equally with gold, for all debts, public and private, and we favor such legislation as will prevent for the future the demonetization of any kind of legal-tender money by private contract.

We are opposed to the policy and practice of surrendering to the holders of the obligations of the United States the option reserved by law to the Government of redeeming such obligations in either silver coin or gold coin.

We are opposed to the issuing of interest-bearing bonds of the United States in time of peace and condemn the trafficking with banking syndicates, which, in exchange for bonds and at enormous profits to themselves, supply the Federal Treasury with gold to maintain the policy of gold monometallism.

Congress alone has the power to coin and issue money, and President Jackson declared that this power could not be delegated to corporations or individuals. We therefore denounce the issuance of notes intended to circulate as money by National banks as in derogation of the Constitution, and we demand that all paper which is made legal tender for public and private debts, or which is receivable for dues to the United States, shall be issued by the Government of the United States and shall be redeemable in coin.

We hold that tariff duties should be levied for purposes of revenue, such duties to be so adjusted as to operate equally throughout the country, and not discriminate between class or section, and that taxation should be limited by the needs of the Government, honestly and economically administered. We denounce as disturbing to business the Republican threat to restore the McKinley law, which has been twice condemned by the people in National elections, and which, enacted under the false plea of protection to home industry, proved a prolific breeder of trusts and monopolies, enriched the few at the expense of the many, restricted trade and deprived the producers of the great American staples of access to their natural markets.

Until the money question is settled we are opposed to any agitation for further changes in our tariff laws, except such as are necessary to meet the deficit in revenue caused by the adverse decision of the Supreme Court on the income tax. But for this decision by the Supreme Court, there would be no deficit in the revenue. Under the law passed by a Democratic Congress in strict pursuance of the uniform decisions of that court for nearly 100 years, that court having in that decision sustained Constitutional objections to its enactment which had previously been overruled by the ablest Judges who have ever sat on the bench. We declare that it is the duty of Congress to use all the Constitutional power which remains after that decision, or which may come from its reversal by the court as it may hereafter be constituted, so that the burden of taxation may be equally and impartially laid, to the end that wealth may bear its due proportion of the expense of the Government.

We hold that the most efficient way of protecting American labor is to prevent the importation of foreign pauper labor to compete with it in the home market, and that the value of the home market to our American farmers and artisans is greatly reduced by a vicious monetary system which depresses the prices of their product below the cost of production, and thus deprives them of the means of purchasing the products of our home manufactories; and as labor creates the wealth of the country, we demand the passage of such laws as may be necessary to protect it in all its rights.

We are in favor of the arbitration of differences between employers engaged in interstate commerce and their employes, and recommend such legislation as is necessary to carry out this principle.

The absorption of wealth by the few, the consolidation of our leading railway systems, and the formation of trusts and pools require a stricter control by the Federal Government of those arteries of commerce. We demand the enlargement of the powers of the Interstate Commerce Commission and such restrictions and guarantees in the control of railroads as will protect the people from robbery and oppression.

We denounce the profligate waste of the money wrung from the people by oppressive taxation and lavish appropriations of recent Republican Congresses, which have kept taxes high, while the labor that pays them is unemployed and the products of the people's toil are depressed in price till they no longer repay the cost of production. We demand a return to that simplicity and economy which befits a Democratic Government and a reduction in the number of useless offices the salaries of which drain the substance of the people.

We denounce arbitrary interference by Federal authorities in local affairs as a violation of the Constitution of the United States and a crime against free institutions, and we especially object to government by injunction as a new and highly dangerous form of oppression by which Federal Judges, in contempt of the laws of the States and rights of citizens, become at once legislators, judges and executioners; and we approve the bill passed by the last session of the United States Senate, and now pending in the House of Representatives, relative to contempt in Federal courts and providing for trials by jury in certain cases of contempt.

No discrimination should be indulged in by the Government of the United States in favor of any of its debtors. We approve of the refusal of the Fifty-third Congress to pass the Pacific Railroad Funding bill and denounce the effort of the present Republican Congress to enact a similar measure.

Recognizing the just claims of deserving Union soldiers, we heartily indorse the rule of the present Commissioner of Pensions, that no names shall be arbitrarily dropped from the pension roll; and the fact of enlistment and service should be deemed conclusive evidence against disease or disability before enlistment.

We favor the admission of the Territories of New Mexico, Arizona and Oklahoma into the Union as States, and we favor the early admission of all the Territories, having the necessary population and resources to entitle them to Statehood, and, while they remain Territories, we hold that the officials appointed to administer the government of any Territory, together with the District of Columbia and Alaska, should be bona fide residents of the Territory or District in which their duties are to be performed. The Democratic party believes in home rule and that all public lands of the United States should be appropriated to the establishment of free homes for American citizens.

We recommend that the Territory of Alaska be granted a delegate in Congress and that the general land and timber laws of the United States be extended to said Territory.

The Monroe doctrine, as originally declared, and as interpreted by succeeding Presidents, is a permanent part of the foreign policy of the United States, and must at all times be maintained.

We extend our sympathy to the people of Cuba in their heroic struggle for liberty and independence.

We are opposed to life tenure in the public service, except as provided in the Constitution. We favor appointments based upon merit, fixed terms of office, and such an administration of the civil service laws as will afford equal opportunities to all citizens of ascertained fitness.

We declare it to be the unwritten law of the Republic, established by custom and usage of 100 years and sanctioned by the examples of the greatest and wisest of those who founded and have maintained our Government that no man should be eligible for a third term of the Presidential office.

The Federal Government should care for and improve the Mississippi river and other great waterways of the Republic, so as to secure for the interior States easy and cheap transportation to tide water. Whenever any waterway of the Republic is of sufficient importance to demand aid from the Government such aid should be extended upon a definite plan of continuous work until permanent improvement is secured.

Confiding in the justice of our cause and the necessity of its success at the polls, we submit the foregoing declaration of principles and purposes to the considerate judgment of the American people. We invite the support of all citizens who approve them and who desire to have them made effective through legislation, for the relief of the people and the restoration of the country's prosperity.

Senator JONES: At the request of the minority of the Committee I now present an amendment which is to be proposed by the minority, and also two amendments which will be proposed by Governor HILL. All of these will be read for the information of the Convention, after which, by agreement, there are to be two hours and forty minutes' debate, one hour and twenty minutes on each side. I hope the Convention will listen patiently to what is to be said.

The amendment offered by the minority of the Committee was read by the Reading Clerk as follows:

To the Democratic National Convention: Sixteen delegates, constituting the minority of the Committee on Resolutions, find many declarations in the report of the majority to which they cannot give their assent. Some of these are wholly unnecessary. Some are ill considered and ambiguously phrased, while others are extreme and revolutionary of the well recognized principles of the party. The minority content themselves with this general expression of their dissent, without going into a specific statement of these objectionable features of the report of the majority; but upon the financial question, which engages at this time the chief share of public attention, the views of the majority differ so fundamentally from what the minority regard as vital Democratic doctrine as to demand a distinct statement of what they hold to as the only just and true expression of Democratic faith upon this paramount issue, as follows, which is offered as a substitute for the financial plank in the majority report.

We declare our belief that the experiment on the part of the United States alone of free silver coinage and a change of the existing standard of value independently of the action of other great nations would not only imperil our finances, but would retard or entirely prevent the establishment of international bimetallism, to which the efforts of the government should be steadily directed. It would place this country at once upon a silver basis, impair contracts, disturb business, diminish the purchasing power of the wages of labor and inflict irreparable evils upon our nation's commerce and industry.

Until international co-operation among leading nations for the coinage of silver can be secured we favor the rigid maintenance of the existing gold standard as essential to the preservation of our national credit, the redemption of our public pledges and the keeping inviolate of our country's honor. We insist that all our paper and silver currency shall be kept absolutely at a parity with gold. The Democratic party is the party of hard money and is opposed to legal tender paper money as a part of our permanent financial system, and we therefore favor the gradual retirement and cancellation of all United States notes and treasury notes, under such legislative provisions as will prevent undue contraction. We demand that the national credit shall be resolutely maintained at all times and under all circumstances.

The minority also feel that the report of the majority is defective in failing to make any recognition of the honesty, economy, courage and fidelity of the present Democratic administration. And they therefore offer the following declaration as an amendment to the majority report.

"We commend the honesty, economy, courage and fidelity of the present Democratic National Administration."

(Signed) : DAVID B. HILL, New York ; WILLIAM F. VILAS, Wisconsin ; GEORGE GRAY, Delaware ; JOHN PRENTISS POE, Maryland ; IRVING W. DREW, New Hampshire ; C. VEY HOLMAN, Maine ; P. J. FARRELL, Vermont ; WILLIAM R. STEELE, South Dakota ; ALLEN MCDERMONT, New Jersey ; LYNDE HARRISON, Connecticut ; DAVID S. BAKER, Rhode Island ; THOMAS A. E. WEADOCK, Michigan ; JAMES E. O'BRIEN, Minnesota ; JOHN E. RUSSELL, Massachusetts ; ROBERT E. WRIGHT, Pennsylvania ; CHARLES D. ROGERS, Alaska.

THE CHAIR : The Chair is informed that the gentleman from New York, Mr. Hill, will offer the following amendments also :

The Clerk read the amendments as follows:

"But it should be carefully provided by law at the same time that any change in the monetary standard should not apply to existing contracts."

"Our advocacy of the independent free coinage of silver being based on belief that such coinage will effect and maintain a parity between gold and silver at the ratio of 16 to 1, we declare a pledge of our sincerity that if such free coinage shall fail to effect such parity within one year from its enactment by law, such coinage shall thereupon be suspended."

THE CHAIR : If the Convention will be in order the Chair will make an announcement. The Chair is informed that under the agreement Senator TILLMAN will proceed for fifty minutes ; after which the debate will proceed as announced by the Chairman of the Committee on Resolutions.

I present to you the gentleman from South Carolina, Senator TILLMAN.

Mr. TILLMAN : Mr. Chairman, it will hardly be expected that in the brief space of fifty minutes I can do more than make passing allusion to even the most important planks in this platform. I never was good at running against time anyhow, and when conscious that at a certain time I may be called from the floor while my heart and brain are surging with thoughts and feelings I am always at a disadvantage as to what to say and what to leave unsaid.

I will begin by introducing myself to the representatives of the Democracy of the United States as I am, and not as the lying newspapers have taught you to think me. It is said that the truth never overtakes a lie, but I hope that when this vast assembly shall have dispersed to its home the many thousands of my fellow-citizens who are here will carry hence a different opinion of the pitchfork man from South Carolina to that which they now hold. I come to you from the South—from the home of secession—from that State where the leaders of —(the balance of the sentence of the speaker was drowned by hisses.)

Mr. TILLMAN (resuming): There are only three things in the world that can hiss—a goose, a serpent, and a man. And the man who hisses the name of South Carolina in this audience, if he knew anything of the history of his country, must be reminded of the fact that in the darkest days of the Revolutionary War, when it seemed that the cause of liberty was hopeless, the indomitable courage of the men of that State kept alive the fires of liberty and there were more battles fought upon the soil of that State than upon all the other thirteen. Get your history and read it, then. I say I come here from South Carolina. I come at an opportune time. South Carolina in 1860 led the fight in the Democratic party which resulted in its disruption. That disruption of that party brought about the war. The war emancipated the black slaves. We are here now heading a fight to emancipate the white slaves. And if need be, with the conditions reversed, we are willing to see the Democratic party disrupt again to accomplish that result. I do not know whether I can truly say I am a representative of the entire South or not. (Cries of "No, no; I should hope not." "No, never.") I have been in fourteen States since April, making the announcement of a new declaration of independence, that "16 to 1 or bust" is the slogan, and all of them have endorsed it. And I say while there is the danger of the Democratic party surrendering its time-honored principle, a return to the faith of the fathers is best; and then there is no danger of it as an entity disappearing from our politics. That if those who hold the contrary opinion, in their purse-proud blindness, choose to imitate the old slaveholders and go out, we say let them go. The South since the war has been Democratic. Until a year ago, or rather until last election, it was solidly Democratic.

When the war closed we were vassals, and the only party which offered us a helping hand or any sympathy was the Democracy. We had in necessity, therefore, been in subserviency to that wing or that end of the Democratic party in the North which controlled the electoral vote, and therefore New York has been the one predominant factor and dictator in National politics.

I see it is utterly useless for me to make a speech or attempt to make any speech here that can pretend to represent or to fill out the outline even of this struggle. I must hasten away from the logical and proper opening of the subject and present some thoughts in vindication and justification of the existing attitude of our people.

While we look back and thank the Democracy of New York and Connecticut and New Jersey for their assistance and co-operation in the past, for the protecting aegis which they have extended over us, we have realized long since that we were but mere hewers of wood and drawers of water, tied in bondage, and all our substance being eaten out.

In the last three or four or five years the Western people have come to realize that the condition of the South and the condition of the West were identical. Hence we find to-day that the Democratic party of the West is here almost in solid phalanx appealing to the South, and the South has responded —to come to their help and remove this yoke. Some of my friends from the South and elsewhere have said that this is not a sectional issue. I say it is a sectional issue. (Long prolonged hissing.)

The truth is mighty and will prevail. Facts can neither be sneered out of existence nor obliterated by hisses. I present you some figures from the United States census, which will prove that it is a sectional issue and nothing else. I will give it to you by the way of comparison.

And first I want to put before you the fifteen Southern

States, if you may count Delaware and Maryland as Southern, as extending clear to the Mississippi river, and across it, and including Louisiana and Arkansas. They have 566,000 square miles. Now I want you to watch and see how much of this gets into the papers. It is not going to get there, and you watch and see if it gets there. These Southern States have 566,000 square miles and a population in 1890 of 17,000,000. The one State of Pennsylvania has an area of 45,000 square miles and a population of 5,258,000. The Southern States are twelve times the area of Pennsylvania and have three and three-tenths times as much population. These Southern States increased in population 2,555,000; Pennsylvania increased 975,000 in the decade between 1880 and 1890. The Southern States were assessed at $2,607,000,000, Pennsylvania at $1,683,000,000. The Southern States had one and fifty-four one-hundredths times as much wealth and had increased twice in population. They should have gained in the ten years as compared with Pennsylvania as follows: Capital, 1.54, multiplied by the population, 3.3, multiplied by territory, 12.5, giving an advantage of 3½ times to 1. But instead of such a record, what did happen? During the ten years from 1880 to 1890 the fifteen Southern States gained $909,000,000 and the State of Pennsylvania gained $901,000,000.

Of course you say this rule won't work. I will give you another comparison. Take the State of Massachusetts and compare it with the five States of Ohio, Indiana, Illinois, Nebraska, Iowa and Missouri. Without going into details as to area and population and assessable values, which would tire you, I will simply jump to the ultimate result, and that is that during the decade these five Western States, the garden of the world, gained in wealth $572,000,000 while the 9,000 square miles of Massachusetts gained $569,000,000.

Now take New York. Add to the five States I have mentioned, the States of Kentucky and Tennessee and the States of Kansas and Nebraska, the richest agricultural portion of the globe, and compare it with the one State of New York. These nine States gained in wealth $1,094,000,000, while New York gained $1,123,000,000 or nearly $29,000,000 more than the whole nine.

Take the three States of Massachusetts, New York and Pennsylvania and compare them with the other twenty-five which I will not call, including the entire West this side of the Rocky Mountains and all the South. Did you get it honestly? Are you more industrious and economical? Ah! these figures cannot enter your brains until you read them; but the fact remains that the Southern and Western people have been hewers of wood and drawers of water, and that their substance has been going to the East by reason of the financial system that the misgovernment of the Republican party has fastened on it.

How much time have I, Mr. Chairman?

THE CHAIR: The Convention must be in order. The gentleman has twenty minutes remaining.

Mr. TILLMAN (continuing): Now, it is not worth while for me to say, so far as any purpose of stirring up sectional passions or breeding any discord between the sections, such a thought does not harbor in my breast. The South has no feeling of sectionalism; the South wants to be—(at this point the speaker was interrupted by a local band of music which began to play at the southern end of the hall. The Sergeant-at-Arms having caused them to be removed, the Chair said:)

THE CHAIR: The delegates will please resume their seats. Gentlemen must be seated and cease conversation. There is too much noise in front of the Chair and the Sergeant-at-Arms will preserve order.

Mr. TILLMAN (continuing): I deny utterly having one ill thought or angry passion in my bosom in contemplating the wrongs which we have endured. But if you will listen to the truth, and will let it enter your brain, you are bound to acknowledge that as to most of these improvements and money in the Eastern and Southern States where all this wealth has gone, it has not gone for the benefit of the people, but the wealth is owned by a few thousand men. The people in that section—for I have been among them in New York ten days ago—have submerged the gold men, and I should think that 90 per cent. of the honest population are in sympathy to-day with this demand for the restoration of the currency of our fathers. The two political machines, Democratic and Republican, of that section, have used their money to darken the minds of the people by not telling the truth to them through their papers; and what they know of this question has just simply come by intuition and to them through such other sources of information as they could get privately. Look at this city here; not a paper in it in favor of the money of the Constitution and of the people; every one of them howling day by day and abusing the majority of their fellow citizens in this section, even, and further west, by calling them howling dervishes and silver lunatics. I am in receipt of letters daily from all classes of men in that part of the United States, and they say to me that if you people will come among us out in the Western country we will show you a ground-swell and under-current as will wash away these people in November. I say that in so far as this feeling is sectional it is sectional as between the Eastern bosses and not between the people of the East, and the West, and the South.

We have, instead of a slave oligarchy, a money oligarchy. The one is more insolent than the other was. The only thing which can keep the movement—this resolution—from succeeding in sweeping this country from end to end, is that we may submerge our patriotism here, forget the duty which we owe our people, follow after the banner of some individual rather than a principle, and fail to discharge that duty which we owe to the masses of selecting a man here whose record will fit this platform. There is one peculiarity about the condition and the aspect of this struggle which is in some sense amusing. In 1892 I attended the National Convention in this city. Then, as now, my State was arrayed in this cause. We were side by side with New York then. New York's candidate was hissed, as I have been. New York's orator and sponsor, this distinguished gentleman here (Senator HILL) was howled down. The conditions are reversed. Where is New York now? Where is New York's leader? The States which antagonized him then, to a man, when he was the logical and proper candidate of the Democracy, are here to-day behind him. It is not for me to criticise the motive of any man, nor to call in question the honesty of any man. I give and accord to every man here who opposes me on this proposition the same liberty I claim for myself—that is, independence of thought and independence of action, and credit for honesty of purpose. But when I have done that don't let them call in question ours; don't let them, through their newspapers, sneer at, and abuse and lie about us as they are doing.

(At this point the speaker was interrupted by a great uproar, hisses and calls for "HILL.")

Senator TILLMAN said: "The audience might just as well understand that I am going to have my say if I stand here until sundown."

After order was restored Mr. TILLMAN said:

Mr. President, the Senator from New York, under the arrangement that has been made, is to follow me. I will have no reply. I tried yesterday to get him to go in front, but he would not do it. I do not say that he feared to go in front, because he fears no man. But, lest you think I am making a wanton assault on him—and I am not; I am just simply pointing out the anomalous condition into which we have gotten, the new allies with which he has allied himself—and to leave it to your judgment and to his explanation, if he can, what has produced the change.

He despised the President of the United States in 1892. He has had cause since to more than despise him. But for some inscrutable reason, although he has been betrayed by his own party, in his own State, he appears here, and has appeared in the Senate as the sponsor and apologist for the administration. This fight as to the administration is not of my seeking. The entire Committee, as represented by the silver men yesterday, begged him not to precipitate the issue. He forced it on us. Why, he will tell you. I therefore merely meet what I know is coming, and give expression to the reason and explanation of why I shall offer a substitute.

I am sure that, as I said in the beginning, this speech cannot have any connection hardly with the platform. But, as GROVER CLEVELAND stands for gold monometallism, and we have repudiated it, then, when we are asked to indorse GROVER CLEVELAND's administration, we are asked to write ourselves down as asses and liars. They want us to say that he is honest, and they link with him all of his Cabinet in order to try to bolster him up. The only thing that I have ever seen that smacked of dishonesty in his career is that he signed a contract in secret, with one of his partners as a witness, which gave ten millions of dollars of the American people's money to a syndicate, and appointed that syndicate receiver of the Government for the same. They ask us to indorse his courage. Well, now, no one disputes the man's boldness and obstinacy, because he had the courage to ignore his oath of office and redeem in gold paper obligations of the Government, which were payable in coin—both gold and silver—and, furthermore, he had the courage to over-ride the Constitution of the United States and invaded the State of Illinois with the United States Army and undertook to over-ride the rights and liberties of his fellow-citizens.

They ask us to indorse his fidelity. He has been faithful unto death, or rather unto the death of the Democratic party, so far as he represents it through the policy of the friends that he had in New York and ignored the entire balance of the Union. I came here in 1892 opposed to CLEVELAND. We had denounced him in South Carolina as a tool of Wall street. I appear here to-day, and what was prophecy then is history now. Mr. HILL appears here in the attitude, as I said, of his sponsor and apologist. I will only quote the words of BYRON, which are applicable to the situation and apropos of the condition. It is more in condemnation of this attitude than any attempt at self-laudation:

> For, fallen on evil days and evil tongues,
> Milton appeals to the Avenger, Time;
> For Time, the Avenger, execrates his wrongs
> And makes the word Miltonic mean sublime.
> He never deigned to coin his brain in song,
> Nor turned his very talent to a crime;
> He never loathed the sire to laud the son,
> And closed the tyrant-hater he begun.

Now, one more illustration of the condition of this country and I will close. I desire to emphasize the proposition that a community of interest between the different sections of this Union will give us a revolution this year and give us victory. The Southern and Western producers, now impoverished by the financial system, cannot buy the products of the

Northern factories. The consequence is that those factories are idle. The home market, which the Republican party has always clamored for and which it now seeks to re-establish, in practice, by the McKinley tariff, has been partly or wholly destroyed. We cannot hope to have the wheels of prosperity move forward again until the foundation—the agricultural interests, which furnish three-fourths of our exports—is set upon its feet again, and the farmers of the South and West are given an opportunity to make more than a bare living.

With no money to spend we cannot patronize the local merchants; the local merchant cannot order from the jobber, the jobber cannot order from the factory, and you see the sequence of consequence. The farmers of the Northeastern States are just as poor and just as hard up as we are. They are ready to join this army of emancipation.

Now one word in reference to the claim of the Republican party that the Democratic party should be turned out because of its incompetency. I have here the utterance of a distinguished Senator of the Republican party and a leader of that party in its financial policy, delivered in the Senate of the United States about three months ago, and I will read it for you:

"The President and the Secretary of the Treasury were perfectly justified in pursuing the course they have followed; they could not have done otherwise. Suppose they had refused payment of the notes of the United States in gold; the result would have been that our money would at once have fallen below par and a disturbance in foreign and domestic trade would have occurred. They did right. Though I hold far different opinions from them on many questions, yet I stand here and say boldly and openly that in managing our financial affairs during the present condition of things I think the Secretary of the Treasury and the President have done their full duty, and I could not say any more if there were a Republican President in office."

A Voice: "Who is that?"

Mr. Tillman: John Sherman. That is a certificate of Cleveland Republicanism, so far as his policy goes. Sherman, with his Republican gold-bugs, joined Cleveland and his Southern silver traders and struck down silver, and he now asks the American people to reward them for the treachery of our President. Will the American people turn out or turn down the Democratic party which has spurned and repudiated this man's policy? If you adopt anything squinting at sympathy or an indorsement of him or his administration, you dare not go to the people of this country and ask them to support your ticket, no matter whom you nominate. Having been called on to indorse or repudiate, you dare not dodge the issue. You have got to meet it and meet it like men, however distasteful it be, and however much their pleadings for harmony and unity in the Democracy may call on you not to do it. The Democracy are face to face with this issue, and it must be met. We of the South have burned our bridges as far as the Northwestern Democracy is concerned, as now organized.

We have turned our faces to the West, asking our brethren of those States to unite with us in restoring the government to the liberty of our fathers, or which our fathers left us. The West has responded by its representatives here. The West, however, is in doubt, while the South can deliver its electoral vote. But you must get the Republican silver men West, and the Populists in those States, to indorse your platform and your candidate, or you are beaten.

If this Democratic ship goes to sea on storm-tossed waves without fumigating itself, without express repudiation of this man who has sought to destroy his party, then the Republican ship goes into port and you go down in disgrace, defeated, in November. That is the situation as I see it. I know an appeal will be made to you not to listen to the mouthings of this ranter from South Carolina. I know that the timeserving politician, the man who follows public opinion but never leads it, the man who simply wants to be with the procession, will hesitate and halt and falter before he passes on this bridge. We would not have laid the bridge down had we not been forced to the issue. We have denounced this sin in the platform without mentioning the sinner. We have repudiated everything that he has done, almost. Now, we are forced either to repudiate him and his administration, or, as I said before, we will go before the country stultified.

I therefor offer as a substitute, or an amendment to the amendment, the following resolution. Now, please keep quiet and listen to it, and if any man here—if any considerable number of these delegates deny the truth they can express it by their votes, but those of you who know it is true are called on to face the responsibility of declaring so by your votes:

"We denounce the administration of President CLEVELAND as undemocratic and tyranical—(This created great confusion throughout the hall; when it had subsided he continued:) and as a departure from those principles which are cherished by all liberty-loving Americans.

"The veto power has been used to thwart the will of the people, as expressed by their Representatives in Congress. The appointive power has been used to subsidize the press and debauch Congress, and to overawe and control citizens in the free exercise of their constitutional rights as voters. A plutocratic despotism is thus sought to be established on the ruins of the Republic. We repudiate the construction placed on the financial plank of the last National Democratic Convention by President CLEVELAND and Secretary CARLISLE as contrary to the plain meaning of English words, and as being an act of bad faith deserving the severest censure.

"The issue of bonds in time of peace with which to buy gold to redeem coin obligations payable in silver or gold at the option of the government and the use of the proceeds towards defraying the ordinary expenses of the government are both unlawful and usurpations of authority deserving of impeachment." (Great confusion, noise, hisses, cheers, etc.)

Now, one more word, Mr. President, and I will relieve these howlers who have been brought in here on tickets given to them, many of them, of the disagreeable duty or obligation to listen to me. I say to you, fellow-Democrats, those of you who are Democrats, who have not gone off after false gods, who stand by the principles of Jefferson and Jackson, and I say to all other parties, all representatives of parties or members of parties in this audience, that if we do not unite the disjointed and contending or jealous elements in the ranks of the silver people of this country that we cannot win.

Mr. MARSTON, of Louisiana: Mr. Chairman, I rise to a question of information.

THE CHAIR: Senator TILLMAN has the floor; he must not be interrupted; he declines to yield it and I cannot recognize the gentleman from Louisiana.

Mr. TILLMAN: For myself, and for those of my State who came with me, we came here primarily to see that we had a platform which meant what it said and said what it meant. We have got it. Now give us any man you please who is a true representative of that platform—we have no choice—and we pledge you that every vote South of the Potomac will go to him.

Senator JONES, of Arkansas: Gentlemen, I will not occupy much of your time, but will give way to another. I did not intend to open my mouth as to this platform. I believe it means what it says and says what it means; that it did not require one word of explanation. And I would not have uttered one syllable but for the charge that has just been made here by the distinguished Senator who has just left the platform that this was a sectional question. I am a Southern man, was born in the South and carried a musket as a private soldier during the war. There is not one thing connected with the upbuilding and good of that section of the country for which I am not willing to lay down my life. But above the South and above section, I love the whole of this country.

The great cause in which I and those who feel as I do are engaged in is not sectional. It is not confined to any part of this great country. It is not confined to any one country on the face of God's green earth. It is a great question, involving all the interests of mankind, as we believe all over the world; and when we find such men as this magnificent Democrat from Maine, ARTHUR SEWALL, when we find such men as GEORGE FRED WILLIAMS, from Massachusetts, when we find in every hamlet of this country men who believe as we believe, in the name of God how can any man say the question is sectional? I, and those who believe as I do, believe in fraternity, in liberty, in union, and we believe that we ought to stand together as one great people. I simply rose to say that for myself, and, as I believe, for the most of those who agree with me, that I utterly repudiate the charge that this question is sectional.

THE CHAIR: The Chair recognizes Hon. DAVID B. HILL, of New York.

Senator HILL: Mr. Chairman and Gentlemen of the Convention: I do not know that it is necessary to pursue the course of the distinguished Senator from South Carolina and introduce myself. But if I were to follow him in that respect, I would say at the outset, I am a Democrat; but I am not a revolutionist. South Carolina, with all its power, cannot drive me out of the Democratic party. Without intending to specially reply to the remarks of the distinguished Senator from South Carolina, I will only say that it was a waste of time on his part to assume that we were so ignorant as not to know that it was his State that attempted to break up the Democratic party in 1860.

But that party has survived the attempts of every section of the country to permanently divide it—to distract it. It lives to-day, and I hope it will live forever. My mission here to-day is to unite, not to divide; to build up, not to destroy; to plan for victory, not to plot for defeat. I know that I speak to a Convention which, as now constituted, probably does not agree with the financial views of the State that I especially represent upon this occasion; but I know that notwithstanding the attack which has been made upon that State, you will hear me for my cause.

New York makes no apology to South Carolina for her Democracy. We get our Democracy from our fathers, and not from South Carolina. We do not need to learn it from those whom my friend represents. Need I defend New York and her people? No, it is not necessary. That State defends herself. Need I defend the attack made upon her citizens —the charge of being men of wealth, of being men of intelligence and character? No, it is not necessary. Need I remind this Democratic National Convention that it is in the great State of New York and in its great city where the wealth that he inveighs against is situated, and that it is that great city that never but once in its history that I recall, ever gave a Republican majority. While other cities throughout the country have failed to respond, New York has ever been the Gibraltar of Democracy.

The question which this Convention is now to decide is which is the best position to take at this time upon the financial question. In a word, the precise question presented is between international bimetallism and local bimetallism. If there be gold monometallists here they are not represented either in the majority report or in the minority report. I therefore start out with this proposition: That the Democratic party stands to-day in favor of gold and silver as the money of the country. We stand in favor of the proposition of a double standard of gold and silver, but we differ as to the means to bring about that result. Those I represent and for whom I speak—the sixteen members of the minority committee—insist that we should not attempt the experiment of free and unlimited coinage of silver without the co-operation of other great nations.

It is not a question of patriotism. It is not a question of courage. It is not a question of loyalty. It is not a question of valor. The majority platform speaks of the subject as though it were simply a question as to whether we were a brave enough people to enter upon this experiment. It is a question of business. It is a question of finance. It is a question of economics. It is not a question, which men, ever so brave, can solve, as a mere matter of bravery.

Mr. President, I think the safest, the best course for this Convention to have pursued, was to take the first step forward in the great cause of monetary reform by declaring in favor of international bimetallism.

I am not here to assail the honesty or sincerity of a single man who disagrees with me. There are those around me who know that in every utterance made upon this subject I have treated the friends of free and unlimited coinage of silver at the ratio of 16 to 1 with respect. I am here to pursue that course to-day. I do not think that we can safely ignore the monetary system of other great nations. I concede that it is a question about which honest men may differ. I believe we cannot ignore the attitude of other nations upon this subject any more than we can ignore their attitude upon other questions of the day. I know it is said by enthusiastic friends that America can mark out a course for herself. I know that it appeals to the pride of the average American to say that it matters not what other countries may do, we can determine this matter for ourselves. But I beg to remind you that if that suggestion is carried out to its legitimate conclusion you might as well do away with commercial treaties with other countries; you might as well do away with all the provisions in your tariff bills that have relation to the laws of other countries. In this great age, when we are connected with all portions of the earth by our ships, by our cables, and by all modern methods of intercourse, we of the minority think that it is unwise to attempt alone a change of our money standard.

Mr. President, I want to call your attention to another point. I think it is unwise further for this Convention to hazard this contest upon a single ratio. What does this majority platform provide? It should have contented itself with the single statement that it was in favor of the remonetization of silver and the placing it upon equality with gold, but instead of that your Committee has recommended for adoption a platform which makes the test of Democratic loyalty to hang upon a single ratio, and that 16 to 1. I doubt the wisdom of having entered into details. I doubt the propriety of saying that 15½ or 17 is heresy, and 16 is the only true Democratic doctrine. Permit me to remind you—I see distinguished Senators before me who, in the Senate of the United States, friends of free silver, who have introduced bills for the free and unlimited coinage of silver at the ratio of 20 to 1—I beg to remind this Convention that some of your candidates proposed for nomination, men whom I respect and whose Democracy I admit, have voted time and time again in Congress for other ratios than 16 to 1; and yet you are proposing to nominate those men upon a platform that limits and restricts the adhesion to Democracy to one single ratio. With all due respect I think it an unwise step. I think it an unnecessary step; and I think it will return to plague us in the future. I think we have too many close business relations with other great nations of the world for us to ignore their attitude. Your proposed platform says that the policy of gold monometallism is a British policy. Mr. President, they forget to tell the people of this country that it is a French policy also; they forget to tell the people of this country that it is a German policy also; they fail to remind you that it is a Spanish policy also. They fail to tell you that it is the policy of the whole number of governments represented in what was called the Latin Union. Therefore, I think—I think—it looks a little —just a trifle like demagogism to suggest that this is the policy of the British nation alone. Mr. President, I regret also to see that the majority platform contains not a single word in favor of international bimetallism—not necessarily inconsistent with this platform—and there is no declaration whatever that it is the policy of this government to attempt to bring it about. The minority platform declares expressly that it is the policy of this government to make steady efforts to bring about international bimetallism. It would be safer to do it; it would be wiser to do it. We would then run no risk upon the great question of the finances of this republic. I do not intend in the brief time alloted me to enter into any elaborate argument upon this question.

I assume that this Convention desires, as the people of this country desire, that every silver dollar coined shall be the equal of every other dollar coined. I find no words in this platform in favor of the maintenance of the parity of the two metals. I find no suggestion of what is to be done in case the experiment fails. I find no suggestion of how you are to brace up this now depreciated currency. Everything is risked upon the mere fact that it shall be given free coinage at the mints. I beg to call your attention to this fact: That in my humble opinion the very financial policy condemned in this platform is the policy that has kept your greenback currency and your silver dollars at a parity with gold during the past years. We think that times and conditions have changed. We think that you can not ignore the fact of the great production of silver in this country. We think you cannot safely ignore the fact, in the preparation of a financial system, that the cost of the production of silver has greatly fallen.

Why, it is the very pregnant fact that confronts all the world in the solving of this question, of the immense discovery of silver everywhere. The great fact confronts the world that the cost of silver production has been largely reduced. If the American people were brave, were courageous, if they had the spirit of 1776, as this platform says, could they, single and alone, make and maintain copper the equal of gold? Could they make lead the equal of gold? Must you not take into consideration the great fact of production, the great fact of the lessening of the cost of production in the last fifteen or twenty years? If bravery, if courage, could solve monetary problems, then you could make any metal, no matter what it might be, a money metal.

But I tell you it is a question of economics, a question of business, a question of finance. It is a question of resources. And upon that point it is the judgment of the minority of the Committee that the safest course is to take the first great step in favor of international bimetallism, and stop there. I know it will be said that in some particulars this minority platform agrees with that of our Republican friends; that may be; it is not any better nor any worse for it. I call your attention to the fact that your plank upon pensions, that your plank upon the Monroe doctrine, that your plank upon Cuba, that your plank upon territories, that your plank upon Alaska, that your plank even upon the civil service, are exactly or substantially like the Republican planks. Therefore, I do not think that that criticism will detract from the value of the minority proposition. Mr. President, I said a few moments ago I thought the safest course for this Convention to have pursued was simply to have said that this government should through international agreement place and treat gold and silver alike as the currency of the country, and stop there. I do not think, as I said and will repeat it, it is wise to hazard everything upon a single ratio.

Let me go further. I object to various other provisions of this platform, and I think if the counsels of the wise, level, cool-headed men, far-sighted men, such as the distinguished senator from Arkansas who addressed you, had prevailed, that majority platform would have been different.

What was the necessity for opening up the old and vexed question of greenback circulation? What was the necessity for putting in this platform an implied pledge that this Government might issue greenback currency and make it legal tender?

The Democratic party is opposed to legal tender paper money; the Democratic party from its earliest history has been in favor of hard money. The Democratic party believes that the best way is to eliminate United States notes and treasury notes from our currency. They are a drag upon your money metals. You have to constantly keep supplied a fund for their redemption, unless you propose to repudiate them. Therefore, when my friend from South Carolina and my friend from Arkansas say that this platform "says what it means and means what it says," I would like to have some one who follows me tell what this platform means upon the subject of the issue of paper money hereafter.

I am not violating, I think, the secrets of the Committee-room when I say that it was avowed that this Government might desire to pursue the course of issuing unlimited legal tender paper money, and this is an attempt at this late day to commit the Democratic party to the suicidal policy of the issuing of such paper money. You say you wanted a clear and distinct platform. You have not got it upon that question. This plank cannot be defended successfully.

Another suggestion permit me to make. What was the necessity for putting into the platform other questions which have never been made the tests of Democratic loyalty before? Why revive the disputed question of the policy and constitutionality of an income tax. What! Has it come to this, that the followers of SAMUEL J. TILDEN, who during all his life was the opponent of that iniquitous scheme which was used against him in his old age to annoy him and harass him and humiliate him—why, I say, should it be left to this Convention to make as a tenet of Democratic faith belief in the propriety and constitutionality of an income tax law?

Why was it wise to assail the Supreme court of your country? Will some one tell what that clause means in this platform? "If you meant what you said and said what you meant," will some one explain that provision? That provision, if it means anything, means that it is the duty of Congress to reconstruct the Supreme court of the country. It means, and such purpose was openly avowed, it means the adding of additional members to the court, or the turning out of office and reconstructing the whole court. I said I will not follow any such revolutionary step as that. Whenever before in the history of this country has devotion to an income tax been made the test of Democratic loyalty? Never! Have you not undertaken enough, my good friends, now without seeking to put in this platform these unnecessary, foolish and ridiculous things?

What further have you done? In this platform you have declared, for the first time in the history of this country, that you are opposed to any life tenure whatever for office. Our fathers before us, our Democratic fathers, whom we revere, in the establishment of this government gave our Federal judges a life tenure of office. What necessity was there for reviving this question? How foolish and how unnecessary, in my opinion. Democrats, whose whole lives have been devoted to the service of the party, men whose hopes, whose ambitions, whose aspirations, all lie within party lines, are to be driven out of the party upon this new question of life tenure for the great judges of our Federal courts. No, no; this is a revolutionary step, this is an unwise step, this is an unprecedented step in our party history.

Another question that I think should have been avoided, and that is this: What was the necessity, what was the propriety of taking up the vexed question of the issue of bonds for the preservation of the credit of the nation? Why not have left this financial question of the free coinage of silver alone? What have you declared? You have announced the broad policy that under no circumstances shall there ever be a single bond issued in times of peace. You have not excepted anything. What does this mean? It means the virtual repeal of your resumption act; it means repudiation per se and simple.

The statement is too broad, the statement is too sweeping; it has not been carefully considered. You even oppose Congress issuing bonds; you even oppose the President doing it; you oppose them doing it either singly or unitedly; you stand upon the broad proposition that for no purpose, whether to redeem the currency or not, whether to preserve your national credit or for any other purpose—shall there be a bond issued. Why, how surprising that will be to my Democratic associates in the Senate who for the last two or three years have introduced bill after bill for the issuing of bonds for the Nicaragua Canal and other purposes.

No, no, my friends, this platform has not been wisely considered. In your zeal for monetary reform you have gone out of the true path; you have turned from the true course, and in your anxiety to promote and aid the silver currency you have unnecessarily put in this platform provisions which cannot stand a fair discussion. Let me tell you, my friends, without going into a discussion of the bond question proper, which is somewhat foreign to this subject—let me tell you what would be the condition of this country to-day if the President of the United States, in the discharge of the public duty that is imposed upon him, had not seen fit to issue bonds to protect the credit of the government. The Democratic party has passed a tariff bill, which, unfortunately, has not produced a sufficient revenue as yet to meet the necessities of the government. There has been a deficit of between twenty-five and fifty millions a year. It is hoped that in the near future this bill will produce ample revenues for the support of the government, but in the meantime your greenback currency and your treasury notes must be redeemed when they are presented, if you would preserve the honor and the credit of the nation. Where would the money have come from if your President and your southern Secretary of the Treasury had not discharged their duty by the issuing of bonds to save the credit of the country?

Let me call your attention to the figures. There has been issued during this administration $262,000,000 of bonds. What amount of money have you in the treasury to-day? Only just about that sum. Where would you have obtained the means with which to redeem your paper money if it had not been procured by the sale of bonds? Why, my friend TILLMAN would not have had money enough out of the treasury for his salary to pay his expenses home.

Mr. President, I reiterate that this bond question has brought into this Convention an unnecessary, a foolish issue, which puts us on the defense in every school district in the country.

I do not propose to detain you by any other criticism of this platform at this time. It is unfortunate enough that you have entered upon a financial issue upon which the Democracy is largely divided. In addition to that, you have unwisely brought into this platform other questions foreign to the main question, and made the support of them the test of Democracy. I do not think that this was the course that should have been pursued. Mr. President, there is time enough yet to retrace these false steps. The burdens you have imposed upon us in the Eastern States in the support of this platform relating to silver are all that can be reasonably borne. But in addition to that, you have put upon us the question of the preservation of the public credit. You have brought into it the question of the reconstruction of the Supreme Court. You have brought into it the question of the issuing of bonds. You have brought into it the question of the issuing of paper money. You have brought into it the great question of life tenure in office. And this platform is full of incongruous and absurd provisions which are proposed to be made the test of true Democracy.

Mr. President, it is not for me to revive any question of sectionalism, and I shall not do it. This country is now at peace in all sections of it, and let it so remain. I care not from what section of the country a Democrat comes, so long as he is true to the fundamental principles of our fathers. I will take him by the hand and express my friendly sentiments toward him. The question of sectionalism under this platform will creep in in spite of the efforts of our best men to keep it out. I oppose this platform because I think it makes our success more difficult. I want the grand old party with which I have been associated from my boyhood, to win. I have looked forward to the day when it should be securely entrenched in the affections of the American people. I dislike the Republican party. I dislike all their tenets. I have no sympathy with their general principles; but I do think that we ourselves are here to-day making a mistake in the venture which we are about to take. Be not deceived. Do not attempt to drive old Democrats out of the party, who have grown gray in its service, to make room for a lot of Republicans and Populists and political nondescripts who will not vote your ticket at the polls.

Do not attempt to trade off the vote of New Jersey, that never failed to give us its electoral vote, and take the experiment of some State out West that has always given its vote to the Republican ticket. I tell you that no matter who your candidate may be in this Convention, with possibly one exception, your Populist friends, upon whom you are relying for support in the West and South, will nominate their own ticket, in whole or in part, and your silver forces will be divided. Mark the prediction which I make. (A voice. "No, no!")

Someone says "No!" Who are authorized to speak for the Populist party in a Democratic Convention? I saw upon this platform the other day an array of Populists—former Republicans—giving countenance and support to this movement, men who never voted a Democratic ticket in their lives, and never expect to. They have organized this Populist party. They are the men who attempted to proscribe Democrats all over this Union. They are the men who were crying against us in the days that tried men's souls—during the war.

My friends, I thus speak more in sorrow than in anger. You know what this platform means to the East; you know that we who are identified with the fortunes of the party there must suffer the result. But, calamitous as it may be to us, it will be more calamitous to you if, after all, taking these risks, you do not win this fight. My friends, we want the Democratic party to succeed. We want to build it up. We do not want to tear it down. We want our principles—the good old principles of JEFFERSON, of JACKSON, of TILDEN, of hard money, of safe money. We want no greenback currency on our plates. We want no legal tender paper currency whatever. We want to stand by the principles under which we have won during the history of the country, and made it what it is. If we keep in the good old paths of the party, we can win. If we depart from them we shall lose the great contest which awaits us.

THE CHAIR: The Chair desires to make a statement to the Convention. Under the arrangement which has been made for debate, the Chair was informed that there was to be one hour and twenty minutes of debate. The Senator from South Carolina has used fifty minutes. The Senator from New York has used forty-nine minutes. That leaves thirty-one minutes remaining for the minority. The Chair now presents to the Convention Hon. WILLIAM F. VILAS, of the State of Wisconsin.

Senator VILAS: Mr. Chairman and Fellow Democrats of this National Convention: A majority of the Committee on resolutions has graciously accorded to the minority the privilege of presenting their views to the Convention. They have conceded nothing more. Upon the subject of overshadowing present importance they propose to lead this body to a declaration which the minority believe abhorrent to Democratic faith, denounced as folly by all history, and to menace dire calamity to this country.

We shall present, summarily, of course, the reasons which we entertain, or some of them. We present them, however, recognizing that they now constitute only the earnest and solemn protest of a minority against the purposed revolution in party faith and conduct and threatened injury to our country. For myself, my opinions are the result of long and sincere study. I cannot alter them for majorities nor personal consequence; but as a Democrat who has always maintained a reasonable obedience to be the first duty to accomplish the party's mission, I ask a hearing for the party's sake, which from youth I have devotedly believed necessary for our country and our liberty. I speak for a State which has maintained the Democratic faith under circumstances of trial and with constant fidelity. The question which you are about to decide is momentous; painfully so. Its right decision demands intelligence and reasoning. Oratory will reverse no law of nature, and theory will range itself in vain against principles of finance. This Convention has power over neither; but will be powerful for good as it shall respect that higher law which it cannot alter, though it may disobey and encounter. The minority believe the proposal of the majority to be disobedient to that law, recklessly and flagrantly so, and sure of a fearful penalty. I will not protract the argument. The Senator from New York—our illustrious and able friend—has already stated the argument. I will summarize the conclusion. This indirect proposal, its iniquities hidden to some, perhaps, its source of injury to the country lies in the proposed change in the standard of values, if that proposition is carried out. It will not produce bimetallism; far from it. It is in diametric opposition to the platform of 1892, which proposed an honest bimetallism, if the thing be possible at all, when conditions shall make it possible. And the superlative iniquity of this scheme will be to the honest bimetallist who lends his aid to it in the belief that he will thereby secure bimetallism. Hence will it deceive those who expect an abundance of money from it. It will shrink and not swell our currency. The silver dollar is no new thing to the United States. This scheme of silver monometallism is no new thing to this country, however novel to the ignorance, perhaps, of some of this generation. The silver standard had its day of unlimited rule in the United States, beginning with our early poverty and weakness and abiding until 1834; then money was scant in this country. It possessed no gold; it was to get gold and with it abundance so far as a sound currency can give it, that the act of 1834 was passed. That was a Democratic measure. That was a measure created under Democratic leadership by BENTON, with the favor of ANDREW JACKSON.

That was distinctly accused then as a gold measure and it raised the standard of gold in this country; but it raised this country from the grade of China and Japan and Mexico to a place among the foremost nations that maintain and rule the world's commerce and carry the colors of civilization to the farthest regions of the globe.

The gold standard is now accused of responsibility for falling prices; but it is never credited when prices rise. In truth, it is entitled neither to the credit nor to the fault. The argument is a false deduction. Would you stop the fall of prices, suppress invention, extinguish enterprise, discard improvements in transportation—in short, smite with paralysis the forces of civilization! Take from the farmer the harvester and the threshing machine and wheat will rise; snatch away from the planter the cotton gin, and the press, and cotton will rise. Burn your mills and woolen goods will rise. Let loose on society the fiends of destruction and they will soon deliver you from this supposed curse of civilization,—a cheap abundance. But the gold standard has nothing to do with it. When any standard be fixed with continuing stability, it has no more to do with prices than a yard stick or a pair of scales. The one test which must infallibly prove the fact, and prove the excellence of this standard shows that gold has fallen, not risen, in value; and that test ought above all others to receive favor in a Democratic Convention, the wages of labor. During this generation now just passed the average wage of labor throughout the United States skilled and unskilled has increased three-fifths—66 per cent. But in the same time the power of a day's wages has more than doubled by reason of lower prices for what the labor has to buy. Will you insult the intelligent wage-earners of the United States by proffering to them the state and condition of a Mexican, Portuguese, a Chinese or Japanese laborer in place of the American workmen of this country? And, Mr. Chairman, how will you justify the effect of the sudden transition upon the value of contracts? Are we to be told that contracts may be reduced one-half? Why will you not adopt this amendment proposed by the Convention, which shall limit the effect of a change of standard to future contracts? Thus will you deliver your platform from the imputation of a purpose to plunder.

If you shall not, then do not be accepting the McKinleyism that the foreigner will pay the tax. Our foreign debt is stipulated in gold. For every debtor profited you will have a creditor injured, and one of your own fellow citizens. Is that right?

I desire to read a word or two from a distinguished legal writer who, since he referred to the record of others, will not complain if I use his great authority to satisfy this Convention of what right and justice is. I refer to the work of the distinguished and illustrious Temporary Chairman of this Convention. This is what he said, speaking on this question in this aspect, in his law book on negotiable notes, as it is quoted in a newspaper slip I have at hand:

"But," said he, "in construing a bill or note it is to be interpreted according to the meaning of the words used at the time and the place where the instrument was drawn or made; and accordingly if the coin which is expressly agreed to be paid be alloyed by the Government between the time of contract and the time of payment, the debtor should be required to make good the full value of the coin at the time of the contract. And so, if the name of the coin be changed so as to apply to a lesser value, the amount to be paid should be estimated according to the value at the time of drawing the instrument, if payment in that coin then of higher value was contemplated. On this subject the authorities exhibit great contrariety of opinion. We have simply stated the conclusions which seem to us just and right."

What pretext in the face of such simple propositions can any man find to his conscience who shall refuse such a measure as an amendment to this? Who loves the name of Democrat must welcome it; who believes silver will rise cannot refuse it. Standing upon that simple doctrine and driven by lapse of time to a rapid conclusion, I say that I protest against the assumption that this is a nation of dishonest debtors. I deny that Democratic doctrine can be based on iniquity. When and where, fellow Democrats, did robbery by law come to be Democratic doctrine. Can we believe that the American people will give their final judgment to so unjust, so reckless a course of action? In the language of LINCOLN, "you may fool all of the people some of the time; you may fool some of the people all of the time, but you cannot fool *all* of the people *all* of the time." Sound and sober sense will in the end prevail. Will not thinking men soon see that if you can by force of law make sixteen ounces of silver equal to one of gold, though thirty to thirty-two be the market rating, you can just as well declare the two metals equal, ounce for ounce?

If you can lawfully take one-half of the debt, why cannot you take the whole? What distinguishes the confiscation of one-half the credits of the nation for the benefit of debtors from a universal distribution of property, except a difference in degree? What in short is this radical scheme but the beginning of the overthrow of all law, of all justice, of all security and repose in the social order? I solemnly believe you fearfully misjudge the people of America. In the vastness of this country there may be some MURAT unknown, some DANTON or ROBESPIERRE, but we have not the people who will tolerate an approach to the first step towards the atrocities of the French revolution.

I will even venture a special prediction: Should this Centaur ever receive a temporary majority it will be quickly turned to flight by universal distress; but should it ever have a seeming success and become a real menace, such wide spread disaster will befall as will teach what reason seems to fail to show. When that day of calamity comes let it be remembered who were not its authors. Oh, fellow Democrats, why must you launch our old party on this wild career? What inspiration warrants our pursuit of that which the wisdom of mankind condemns? Who teaches us, with authority, a lesson in finance which the world of the highest civilization stands aghast at? Is it possible that this old party of JEFFERSON, this old Democratic party of constitutional law and liberty, shall thus fall to the machinations of a propaganda in the interest of protection maintained by silver mine owners for their benefit which had its origin many years ago?

It was not for such uses, it was not for such an end that the Democratic party was created. I protest with solemn earnestness, with sincerity and personal kindness, that the Democrats of the North ought not to have expected this result. For thirty years they have stood at great personal cost, fighting devotedly for the principles of Democracy, until in a restored Union, with equal rights shared by every part and every portion of the people, they have seen the triumph apparently of Democracy. And now, in the hour when we thought everything before us was well, are we to have this newly-given strength exerted to pull down the pillars of the temple and crush us all beneath the ruins? So I hope for a better future for the Democratic party. The evil times, the evil days, though filled with darkness and with dangers and compassed around with clouds, may pass. I hope to live to see a Democratic Convention assembled here when all shall be united and the whole party restored to the vigor and power which is necessary for its service to the Constitution.

THE CHAIR: The Chair presents to the Convention Governor WILLIAM E. RUSSELL, of Massachusetts.

Hon. WILLIAM E. RUSSELL: Mr. Chairman and Members of this Convention: I have but one word to say. The time is past for debate upon the merits of this issue. I am conscious, painfully conscious, that the mind of this Convention is not and has not been open to argument and reason. I know that the will of its great majority, which has seen fit to override precedent, to trample down rights, to attack the sovereignty of States, is to be rigidly enforced.

I know that an appeal, even, will fall upon deaf ears. There is but one thing left to us, and that is the voice of protest; and that voice, not in anger, not in bitterness, not questioning the sincerity, the honesty, of any Democrat—that voice I utter with a feeling of infinite sorrow. And, mark my words, my friends, the country, our country, if not this Convention, will listen to our protest. I speak for one of the smallest States of this Union; not great in territory or population; not prominent in her material resources; but glorious in her history; great in her character, in her loyalty to truth, in her devotion to principle and duty, and in the sacrifices she has willingly made for independence, liberty and our country. That mother State has taught us, her children, to place principle above expediency; courage above time-serving, and patriotism above party. And in the cause of justice and of right not to flinch, no matter how great the majority or how overbearing may be its demands.

I speak, and I have a right to speak, for the Democracy of my commonwealth. I have seen it for a generation in darkness and defeat following steadfastly the old principles of an abiding faith. I have followed it when it was rejected and proscribed. It mattered not to us. We knew that its principles would triumph and we lived to see the day when we planted the banner of Democracy for three successive years victorious in that stronghold of Republicanism and protection. These victories were for the great principles of a national party. They were the assertions of Massachusetts, of the rights of the States, her protest against sectionalism, and against paternal government, which, either by force or by favor, should seek to dominate a dependent people. This was then the Democracy of South Carolina and of Illinois and bound us together from ocean to ocean. We did not think that we should live to see the time when these great Democratic principles which have triumphed over Republicanism should be forgotten in a Democratic Convention, and we should be invited under new and radical leadership to a new and a radical policy; that we should be asked to give up vital principles for which we have labored and suffered, repudiate Democratic platforms and administrations, and at the demands of a section urging expediency be asked to adopt a policy which many of us believe invites peril to our country and disaster to our party.

In the debates of this Convention I have heard one false note from the commonwealth of Massachusetts. I answer it, not in anger, but in sorrow, and I appeal to you, my associates of the Massachusetts delegation, do I not speak the true sentiment of my State, and of our party, when I declare that they and we utter our earnest, emphatic and unflinching protest against this Democratic platform.

I have heard from the lips of some of the old leaders of our party, at whose feet we younger men have loved to learn the principles of our faith, that this new doctrine was the bright dawn of a better day. I would to God that I could believe it. I have heard that Democracy was being tied to a star—not the lone star, my Texas friends, that we gladly would welcome—but to the falling star, which flashes for an instant and then goes out in the darkness of the night. No, my freinds, we see not the dawn, but the darkness of defeat and disaster. Oh, that from this great majority, with its power, there might come the one word of concession and conciliation. Oh, that from you there might be held out the olive branch of peace, under which all Democrats united would rally to a great victory. Mr. Chairman, I have finished my word of protest. Let me, following the example of the Senator from South Carolina, utter my word of prophecy. When this storm has subsided, when the dark clouds of passion and prejudice have rolled away, and there comes after the turmoil of this Convention the sober, second thought of Democrats and of our people, then the protests we of the minority here make, will be hailed as the ark of the covenant of the faith where all Democrats, reunited, may go forth to fight for old principles and carry them to triumphant victory.

THE CHAIR: The Chair will present to this Convention Hon. WILLIAM J. BRYAN, of Nebraska.

Mr. BRYAN: Mr. Chairman and Gentlemen of the Convention: I would be presumptuous, indeed, to present myself against the distinguished gentlemen to whom you have listened if this were but a measuring of ability; but this is not a contest among persons. The humblest citizen in all the land, when clad in armor of a righteous cause, is stronger than all the whole hosts of error that they can bring. I come to speak to you in defense of a cause as holy as the cause of liberty—the cause of humanity. When this debate is concluded a motion will be made to lay upon the table the resolution offered in commendation of the administration and also the resolution in condemnation of the Administration. I shall object to bringing this question down to a level of persons. The individual is but an atom; he is born, he acts, he dies but principles are eternal; and this has been a contest of principle.

Never before in the history of this country has there been witnessed such a contest as that through which we have passed. Never before in the history of American politics has a great issue been fought out, as this issue has been, by the voters themselves.

On the 4th of March, 1895, a few Democrats, most of them members of Congress, issued an address to the Democrats of the nation asserting that the money question was the paramount issue of the hour; asserting also the right of a majority of the Democratic party to control the position of the party on this paramount issue; concluding with the request that all believers in free coinage of silver in the Democratic party should organize and take charge of and control the policy of the Democratic party. Three months later, at Memphis, an organization was perfected, and the silver Democrats went forth openly and boldly and courageously proclaiming their belief and declaring that if successful they would crystallize in a platform the declaration what they had made; and then began the conflict with a zeal approaching the zeal which inspired the crusaders who followed PETER the Hermit. Our silver Democrats went forth from victory unto victory until they are assembled now, not to discuss, not to debate, but to enter up the judgment rendered by the plain people of this country.

But in this contest, brother has been arrayed against brother, and father against son. The warmest ties of love and acquaintance and association have been disregarded. Old leaders have been cast aside when they refused to give expression to the sentiments of those whom they would lead, and new leaders have sprung up to give direction to this cause of freedom. Thus has the contest been waged, and we have assembled here under as binding and solemn instructions as were ever fastened upon the representatives of a people.

We do not come as individuals. Why, as individuals we might have been glad to compliment the gentleman from New York (Senator HILL), but we knew that the people for whom we speak would never be willing to put him in a position where he could thwart the will of the Democratic party. I say it was not a question of persons; it was a question of principle, and it is not with gladness, my friends, that we find ourselves brought into conflict with those who are now arrayed on the other side. The gentleman who just preceded me (Governor RUSSELL) spoke of the old State of Massachusetts. Let me assure him that not one person in all this Convention entertains the least hostility to the people of the State of Massachusetts.

But we stand here representing people who are the equals before the law of the largest cities in the State of Massachusetts. When you come before us and tell us that we shall disturb your business interests, we reply that you have disturbed our business interests by your action. We say to you that you have made too limited in its application the definition of a business man. The man who is employed for wages is as much a business man as his employer. The attorney in a country town is as much a business man as the corporation counsel in a great metropolis. The merchant at the crossroads store is as much a business man as the merchant of New York. The farmer who goes forth in the morning and toils all day, begins in the spring and toils all summer, and by the application of brain and muscle to the natural resources of this country creates wealth, is as much a business man as the man who goes upon the Board of Trade and bets upon the price of grain. The miners who go a thousand feet into the earth or climb 2,000 feet upon the cliffs and bring forth from their hiding places the precious metals to be poured in the channels of trade are as much business men as the few financial magnates who in a back room corner the money of the world.

We come to speak for this broader class of business men. Ah, my friends, we say not one word against those who live upon the Atlantic coast; but those hardy pioneers who braved all the dangers of the wilderness, who have made the desert to blossom as the rose—those pioneers away out there, rearing their children near to nature's heart, where they can mingle their voices with the voices of the birds—out there where they have erected school houses for the education of their children and churches where they praise their Creator, and the cemeteries where sleep the ashes of their dead—are as deserving of the consideration of this party as any people in this country.

It is for these that we speak. We do not come as aggressors. Our war is not a war of conquest. We are fighting in the defense of our homes, our families and posterity. We have petitioned, and our petitions have been scorned. We have entreated and our entreaties have been disregarded. We have begged, and they have mocked when our calamity came.

We beg no longer; we entreat no more; we petition no more. We defy them!

The gentleman from Wisconsin has said he fears a ROBESPIERRE. My friend, in this land of the free you need fear no tyrant who will spring up from among the people. What we need is an ANDREW JACKSON to stand as JACKSON stood, against the encroachments of aggregated wealth.

They tell us that this platform was made to catch votes. We reply to them that changing conditions make new issues; that the principles upon which rest Democracy are as everlasting as the hills; but that they must be applied to new conditions as they arise. Conditions have arisen and we are attempting to meet those conditions. They tell us that the income tax ought not to be brought in here; that is not a new idea. They criticise us for our criticism of the Supreme Court of the United States. My friends, we have made no criticism. We have simply called attention to what you know. If you want criticisms read the dissenting opinions of the Court. That will give you criticisms.

They say we passed an unconstitutional law. I deny it. The income tax was not unconstitutional when it was passed. It was not unconstitutional when it went before the Supreme Court for the first time. It did not become unconstitutional until one judge changed his mind; and we cannot be expected to know when a judge will change his mind.

The income tax is a just law. It simply intends to put the burdens of government justly upon the backs of the people. I am in favor of an income tax. When I find a man who is not willing to pay his share of the burden of the government which protects him I find a man who is unworthy to enjoy the blessings of a government like ours.

He says that we are opposing the national bank currency. It is true. If you will read what Thomas Benton said you will find that he said that in searching history he could find but one parallel to Andrew Jackson. That was Cicero, who destroyed the conspiracies of Cataline and saved Rome. He did for Rome what Jackson did when he destroyed the bank conspiracy and saved America.

We say in our platform that we believe that the right to coin money and issue money is a function of government. We believe it. We believe it is a part of sovereignty, and can no more with safety be delegated to private individuals than can the power to make penal statutes or levy laws for taxation.

Mr. Jefferson, who was once regarded as good Democratic authority, seems to have a different opinion from the gentleman who has addressed us on the part of the minority. Those who are opposed to this proposition tell us that the issue of paper money is a function of the bank, and that the Government ought to go out of the banking business. I stand with Jefferson, rather than with them, and tell them, as he did, that the issue of money is a function of the Government, and that the banks should go out of the governing business.

They complain about the plank which declares against the life tenure in office. They have tried to strain it to mean that which it does not mean. What we oppose in that plank is the life tenure that is being built up in Washington which establishes an office-holding class and excludes from participation in the benefits the humbler members of our society. I cannot dwell longer in my limited time upon these things.

Let me call attention to two or three great things. The gentleman from New York says that he will propose an amendment providing that this change in our law shall not affect contracts which, according to the present laws, are made payable in gold. But if he means to say that we cannot change our monetary system without protecting those who have loaned money before the change was made, I want to ask him where, in law or in morals, he can find authority for not protecting the debtors when the act of 1873 was passed, when he now insists that we must protect the creditor. He says he also wants to amend this platform so as to provide that if we fail to maintain the parity within a year that we will then suspend the coinage of silver. We reply that when we advocate a thing which we believe will be successful we are not compelled to raise a doubt as to our own sincerity by trying to show what we will do if we are wrong. I ask him, if he will apply his logic to us, why he does not apply it to himself. He says that he wants this country to try to secure an international agreement. Why doesn't he tell us what he is going to do if they fail to secure an international agreement.

There is more reason for him to do that than for us to expect to fail to maintain the parity. They have tried for thirty years—thirty years—to secure an international agreement, and those are waiting for it most patiently who don't want it at all.

Now, my friends, let me come to the great paramount issue. If they ask us here why it is we say more on the money question than we say upon the tariff question, I reply that if protection has slain its thousands the gold standard has slain its tens of thousands. If they ask us why we did not embody all these things in our platform which we believe, we reply to them that when we have restored the money of the constitution all other necessary reforms will be possible, and that until that is done there is no reform that can be accomplished.

Why is it that within three months such a change has come over the sentiments of the country? Three months ago, when it was confidently asserted that those who believed in the gold standard would frame our platforms and nominate our candidates, even the advocates of the gold standard did not think that we could elect a President; but they had good reasons for the suspicion, because there is scarcely a State here to-day asking for the gold standard that is not within the absolute control of the Republican party. But note the change. Mr. McKinley was nominated at St. Louis upon a platform that declared for the maintenance of the gold standard until it should be changed into bimetallism by an international agreement. Mr. McKinley was the most popular man among the Republicans and everybody three months ago in the Republican party prophesied his election. How is it to-day? Why, that man who used to boast that he looked like Napoleon, that man shudders to-day when he thinks that he was nominated on the anniversary of the battle of Waterloo. Not only that, but as he listens he can hear with ever-increasing distinctness the sound of the waves as they beat upon the lonely shores of St. Helena.

Why this change? Ah, my friends, is not the change evident to anyone who will look at the matter? It is because no private character, however pure, no personal popularity, however great, can protect from the avenging wrath of an indignant people the man who will either declare that he is in favor of fastening the gold standard upon this people, or who is willing to surrender the right of self-government and place legislative control in the hands of foreign potentates and powers.

My friends, the prospect——

(The continued cheering made it impossible for the speaker to proceed. Finally Mr. Bryan raising his hand, obtained silence, and said: I have only ten minutes left, and I ask you to let me occupy that time.)

We go forth confident that we shall win. Why? Because upon the paramount issue in this campaign there is not a spot of ground upon which the enemy will dare to challenge battle. Why, if they tell us that the gold standard is a good thing, we point to their platform and tell them that their platform pledges the party to get rid of a gold standard, and substitute bimetallism. If the gold standard is a good thing why try to get rid of it? If the gold standard, and I might call your attention to the fact that some of the very people who are in this convention to-day and who tell you that we ought to declare in favor of international bimetallism and thereby declare that the gold standard is wrong, and that the principles of bimetallism are better—these very people four months ago were open and avowed advocates of the gold standard and telling us that we could not legislate two metals together even with all the world.

I want to suggest this truth, that if the gold standard is a good thing we ought to declare in favor of its retention and not in favor of abandoning it; and if the gold standard is a bad thing why should we wait until some other nations are willing to help us to let it go?

Here is the line of battle. We care not upon which issue they force the fight. We are prepared to meet them on either issue or on both. If they tell us that the gold standard is the standard of civilization we reply to them that this, the most enlightened of all nations of the earth, has never declared for a gold standard, and both the parties this year are declaring against it. If the gold standard is the standard of civilization, why, my friends, should we not have it? So if they come to meet us on that we can present the history of our nation. More than that. We can tell them this, that they will search the pages of history in vain to find a single instance in which the common people of any land ever declared themselves in favor of a gold standard. They can find where the holders of fixed investments have.

Mr. CARLISLE said in 1878 that this was a struggle between the idle holders of idle capital and the struggling masses who produce the wealth and pay the taxes of the country; and my friends, it is simply a question that we shall decide upon which side shall the Democratic party fight? Upon the side of the idle holders of idle capital, or upon the side of the struggling masses? That is the question that the party must answer first; and then it must be answered by each individual hereafter. The sympathies of the Democratic party, as described by the platform, are on the side of the struggling masses, who have ever been the foundation of the Democratic party.

There are two ideas of government. There are those who believe that if you just legislate to make the well-to-do prosperous that their prosperity will leak through on those below. The Democratic idea has been that if you legislate to make the masses prosperous their prosperity will find its way up and through every class that rests upon it.

You come to us and tell us that the great cities are in favor of the gold standard. I tell you that the great cities rest upon these broad and fertile prairies. Burn down your cities and leave our farms, and your cities will spring up again as if by magic. But destroy our farms and the grass will grow in the streets of every city in this country.

My friends, we shall declare that this nation is able to legislate for its own people on every question, without waiting for the aid or consent of any other nation on earth, and upon that issue we expect to carry every single State in this Union.

I shall not slander the fair State of Massachusetts nor the State of New York by saying that when its citizens are confronted with the proposition, "Is this nation able to attend to its own business?"—I will not slander either one by saying that the people of those States will declare our helpless impotency as a nation to attend to our own business. It is the issue of 1776 over again. Our ancestors, when but 3,000,000, had the courage to declare their political independence of every other nation upon earth. Shall we, their descendants, when we have grown to 70,000,000, declare that we are less independent than our forefathers? No, my friends, it will never be the judgment of this people. Therefore, we care not upon what lines the battle is fought. If they say bimetallism is good, but we cannot have it till some nation helps us, we reply that, instead of having a gold standard because England has, we shall restore bimetallism, and then let England have bimetallism because the United States have.

If they dare to come out and in the open defend the gold standard as a good thing, we shall fight them to the uttermost, having behind us the producing masses of the Nation and the world. Having behind us the commercial interests and the laboring interests and all the toiling masses, we shall answer their demands for a gold standard by saying to them, you shall not press down upon the brow of labor this crown of thorns. You shall not crucify mankind upon a cross of gold.

The conclusion of Mr. BRYAN's speech was the signal

for a tremendous outburst of noise, cheers, etc. The standards of many States were carried from their places and gathered around the Nebraska delegation. Finally order having been restored, the Chair recognized Senator HILL, of New York.

Mr. HILL: I desire to make a formal motion for the substitution of the financial plank of the minority platform in place of the financial plank of the majority. I make that motion at this time, and upon that I ask a call of the States.

Mr. JONES, of Arkansas: I move the previous question upon the adoption of the platform and upon the substitution for the amendment offered by the gentleman from New York.

THE CHAIR: The question first is upon the demand for the previous question.

Mr. TILLMAN, of South Carolina: I move as an amendment to the substitution of the gentlemen from New York, the resolution which I offered.

THE CHAIR: If the Convention will be in order, the Chair will state the question. The gentleman from Arkansas demands the previous question upon the motion to adopt the platform and upon the motions of the gentleman from New York to amend that platform, and the motion of the gentleman from South Carolina, which he offers as a further amendment. The Chair thinks, however, that the questions should be separated; and therefore, will submit the question first upon the amendments of the gentleman from New York and afterward of the gentleman from South Carolina.

Mr. HILL: I call the attention of the Chair to the fact that there have been other motions made. Some motions have been sent to the platform. I ask the Chair whether the previous question is intended to cut off those motions.

THE CHAIR: The Chair does not intend to cut them off. Does the gentleman from New York desire the question submitted on his amendment as a whole?

Mr. Hill: The gentleman desires a call of the States upon the motion for a substitution of one financial plank for the other. Afterward there may be a call of the States upon the other motion. After that I will be content, so far as I am concerned, with a *viva voce* vote upon the motion to adopt the platform.

The motion was put upon the previous question, and the Chair declared the previous question ordered.

The Chair: The Clerk will now report the first amendment offered by the gentleman from New York, representing the minority of the Committee.

The Secretary read the proposed amendment as follows:

" But it should be carefully provided by law at the same time that any change in the monetary standard should not apply to existing contracts."

Mr. Hill: Does the Chair now intend to put that as a separate motion? I move to substitute one financial plank for the other. That is a separate and distinct amendment which will come up afterward, and upon which I do not care whether we have the roll of the States called or not.

The Chair: Then the gentleman desires the first substitute as read, or the amendment as read.

Mr. Hill: The substitute read. The first of the report upon the financial plank.

The Chair: The Clerk will read the proposed substitute.

Mr. Hill: He will read the substitute of one financial plank for the other.

The Secretary read the proposed substitute, as follows:

We declare our belief that the experiment on the part of the United States alone of free silver coinage and a change of the existing standard of value independently of the action of other great nations would not only imperil our finances, but would retard or entirely prevent the establishment of international bimetallism, to which the efforts of the Government should be steadily directed. It would place this country at once upon a silver basis, impair contracts, disturb business, diminish the purchasing power of the wages of labor, and inflict irreparable evils upon our nation's commerce and industry. Until international co-operation among the leading nations in the coinage of silver can be secured we favor the rigid maintenance of the existing gold standard as essential to the preservation of our national credit, the redemption of our public pledges and the keeping inviolate of our country's honor.

We insist that all our paper and silver currency shall be kept absolutely at a parity with gold. The Democratic party is the party of hard money, and is opposed to legal-tender paper money as a part of our permanent financial system, and we therefore favor the gradual retirement and cancellation of all United States notes and Treasury notes under such legislative provisions as will prevent undue contraction. We demand that the national credit shall be resolutely maintained at all times and under all circumstances.

THE CHAIR: The gentleman from New York now moves to substitute that plank which has just been read for the original plank reported by the Committee on Platform.

The motion was seconded.

Mr. J. M. DUNCAN, of Texas: I move to lay the motion of the gentleman from New York on the table.

THE CHAIR: The Chair thinks the gentleman from Texas will not insist on this motion, because, under the rules of the House of Representatives, if this amendment was laid on the table it would carry with it the main proposition. The question is upon agreeing to the substitute.

The question was put to the Convention and a *viva voce* vote taken.

A roll call being demanded, the secretary proceeded to call the roll of the States as follows:

	Yeas.	Nays.
Alabama		22
Arkansas		16
California		18
Colorado		8
Connecticut	12	

THE CHAIR: The Chair hopes these votes will not be applauded; we will get along much more rapidly.

The roll call of the States was continued as follows:

	Yeas.	Nays.
Delaware	5	1
Florida	3	5
Georgia		26
Idaho		6
Illinois		48
Indiana		30
Iowa		26
Kansas		20

When Kentucky was called, the Chairman of the delegation said, "Blackburn's home casts 26 votes no."

The Chair recognized Mr. W. B. HALDEMAN, of Kentucky:

Mr. HALDEMAN: In the name of two members of the Kentucky delegation sent to this Convention under specific instructions by the Democrats of the Fifth Kentucky district, I protest against the application on a question of principle of that abomination of abominations, the gag law known as the unit rule. The delegates from the Fifth Congressional district of Kentucky vote in favor of the minority report.

Mr. O. M. JAMES, of Kentucky: Mr. Chairman: Kentucky votes under the unit rule. By the courtesy and kindness of Kentucky these gentlemen are here, and the unit rule applies in Kentucky, and we vote no.

The vote of Kentucky was recorded in the negative, and the roll call was proceeded with, and Louisiana cast 16 noes.

When Maine was called, the Chairman of the delegation announced the vote of 10 ayes and 2 noes. The announcement was challenged by Mr. HOLMAN, and the Chair ordered the Secretary to call the roll of the delegation, which was done. The Secretary announced the result of the vote in the State of Maine as 10 ayes, 2 noes. The roll call proceeded:

	Yeas.	Nays.
Maryland	12	4
Massachusetts	37	3
Michigan	11	17

The Chairman of the Michigan Delegation: Under the unit rule Michigan casts her twenty-eight votes no.

The roll call was continued as follows:

	Yeas.	Nays.
Minnesota (one absent)	11	6
Mississippi		18
Missouri		34
Montana		6
Nebraska		16
Nevada		6
New Hampshire	8	..
New Jersey	20	..
New York	72	..
North Carolina	..	22
North Dakota	..	6
Ohio	4	42

Mr. L. E. HOLDEN, of Ohio: Under our unit rule Ohio casts forty-six votes no.

The accuracy of the count was challenged and the Chair directed the roll of delegates to be called, which was done. When Mr. HOLLIDAY's vote was announced the point of order was raised that Mr. HOLLIDAY was not in the hall and his vote could not be counted.

Mr. LONG, of Ohio, said that Mr. HOLLIDAY voted on the call of the State, and his vote was recorded no; whereupon the Chairman announced that it would be so recorded now, and overruled the point of order. The call of the roll of the State proceeded. The Secretary announced the result as four ayes, forty-two noes.

The roll call proceeded.

	Yeas.	Nays.
Oregon		8
Pennsylvania	64	
Rhode Island	8	
South Carolina		18
South Dakota	8	
Tennessee		24
Texas		30
Utah		6
Vermont	8	
Virginia		24
Washington	3	5
West Virginia		12
Wisconsin	24	

Mr. E. J. Dockery, of Wisconsin: I challenge the accuracy of the count.

The Chair: The Clerk will then call the roll of the delegates from Wisconsin.

The State of Wisconsin was polled with the following result: 4 nays, 20 yeas.

The roll was resumed as follows:

	Yeas.	Nays.
Wyoming		6
Alaska	6	
Arizona		6
District of Columbia	2	4
New Mexico		6
Oklahoma		6
Indian Territory		6

The Clerk announced the result of the vote as follows: Ayes, 303; Noes, 626; Absent, 1.

The vote in detail follows:

States.	Total Vote.	Ayes.	Nays.	States.	Total Vote.	Ayes.	Nays.
Alabama	22	..	22	New York	72	72	..
Arkansas	16	..	16	North Carolina	22	..	22
California	18	..	18	North Dakota	6	..	6
Colorado	8	..	8	Ohio	46	..	46
Connecticut	12	12	..	Oregon	8	..	8
Delaware	6	5	1	Pennsylvania	64	64	..
Florida	8	3	5	Rhode Island	8	8	..
Georgia	26	..	26	South Carolina	18	..	18
Idaho	6	..	6	South Dakota	8	8	..
Illinois	48	..	48	Tennessee	24	..	24
Indiana	30	..	30	Texas	30	..	30
Iowa	26	..	26	Utah	6	..	6
Kansas	20	..	20	Vermont	8	8	..
Kentucky	26	..	26	Virginia	24	..	24
Louisiana	16	..	16	Washington	8	3	5
Maine	12	10	2	West Virginia	12	..	12
Maryland	16	12	4	Wisconsin	24	24	..
Massachusetts	30	27	3	Wyoming	6	..	6
Michigan	28	..	28	*Territories.*			
Minnesota*	18	11	6	Alaska	6	6	..
Mississippi	18	..	18	Arizona	6	..	6
Missouri	34	..	34	Dist. of Columbia	6	2	4
Montana	6	..	6	New Mexico	6	2	4
Nebraska	16	..	16	Oklahoma	6	..	6
Nevada	6	..	6	Indian Territory	6	..	6
New Hampshire	8	8	..				
New Jersey	20	20	..	Total	930	303	626

*One Absent from Minnesota.

Mr. HILL: Mr. President, I now ask for a call by States on the other resolution which I offered.

THE CHAIR: Does the gentleman desire a separate vote on each one?

Mr. HILL: No, I do not. I have already stated that upon the last two amendments I did not care for a call of the roll by States to take up the time of this Convention, but I do ask for a roll call upon the amendment relating to the National Administration. I ask for the reading of that amendment, and on that amendment I ask for a call of the roll by States. After that, the others may be voted upon *viva voce*.

The Chair: Does the gentleman desire that the roll shall be called now upon this amendment?

Mr. Hill: That is what I wish.

The Chair: The Clerk will report the amendment offered by the gentleman from New York.

The Clerk read as follows: "We commend the honesty, economy, courage and fidelity of the present Democratic National Administration."

The Chair: Upon this amendment the gentleman from New York demands a vote by States. Is that demand seconded?

Mr. Holman, of Maine: I second the motion.

The Chair: The Clerk will call the roll of the States again, commencing with Alabama.

Alabama was called several times without response, and no announcement of the vote was made until the amendment had been read again for the information of the delegation. Then the roll call proceeded thus:

	Aye.	No.
Alabama		22
Arkansas		16

When the Secretary called the State of California the chairman of the delegation asked that the roll be called, which was done with the following result: Ayes 7; nays 6; absent 5.

The roll call of the States was then continued as follows:

	Yeas.	Nays.
Colorado		8
Connecticut	12	
Delaware	5	1
Florida	7	1
Georgia		26
Idaho		6
Illinois		48
Indiana		30

When the Secretary called the State of Iowa, the delegates from that State asked that the resolution be read again, but objection was made and the request was not complied with. The chairman of the delegation announced the vote of the State as 26 nays, which was challenged by Mr. STACKHOUSE. The Chair said: "Does the gentleman deny the accuracy of the count?"

Mr. STACKHOUSE: Yes, sir, I do.

THE CHAIR: The Secretary will call the roll of Iowa.

Mr. VAN WAGANEN, of Iowa: Mr. Chairman, let me call your attention to the fact that the federal officeholder who makes the objection took the count himself.

The Secretary called the roll of the Iowa delegation, with the following result: Nays 19, ayes 6, and one not voting. Under the unit rule the vote was 26 nays.

	Yeas.	Nays.
Kansas		20
Kentucky		26
Louisiana	16	

THE CHAIR: The Chair desires to ask if the unit rule is in force at Louisiana.

Mr. MARSTON: I challenge the vote.

THE CHAIRMAN: Does the gentleman deny the accuracy of the count?

Mr. MARSTON: I wish to have it put on record.

THE CHAIR: No matter. Does the gentleman deny the accuracy of the count? (No response.) The chair overrules the point. (The Clerk continues to call.) "Maine."

THE CHAIR: The clerk will call the names of the delegates from Maine, the demand therefor being made.

This was done with the following result—One nay and 11 yeas.

	Yeas.	Nays.
Maryland	16	
Massachusetts (one not voting)	28	1
Michigan	20	8
Minnesota	17	1
Mississippi		18
Missouri		24
Montana (two decline to vote)		4
Nebraska		16
Nevada		6
New Hampshire	8	
New Jersey	20	
New York	72	
North Carolina		22
North Dakota (one absent)		5
Ohio (under the unit rule)		46
Oregon		8
Pennsylvania	64	
Rhode Island	8	
South Carolina		18
South Dakota	8	
Tennessee		24
Texas		30
Utah		6
Vermont	8	
Virginia		22

When the State of Virginia was reached, Mr. BRADLEY of that delegation challenged the vote and called for a polling of the delegation, with the following result: Ayes 2; nays 22. Under the unit rule, twenty-four votes were declared to be cast in the negative.

The Secretary proceeded with the call of the states as follows:

	Yeas.	Nays.
Washington	3	5

The State of West Virginia was called and the vote was announced as nays 11, one not voting.

After West Virginia had been called and the vote

announced Mr. WALLACE, of Washington, challenged the vote of his own State, and the Secretary called the roll of the delegation from Washington, with the following result: Ayes 3, Nays 5.

The Secretary proceeded with the call of States as follows:

	Yeas.	Nays.
Wisconsin	20	4

Mr. JAMES E. MALONE, of Wisconsin: I challenge the accuracy of the vote.

THE CHAIR: Does the gentleman deny the accuracy of the count?

Mr. MALONE: I challenge the accuracy of the vote.

THE CHAIR: Unless the gentleman denies the accuracy of the count the delegates will not be polled.

Mr. MALONE: I deny the accuracy of the count.

THE CHAIR: The Clerk, then, will call the list of delegates.

The delegates were polled with the following result: Four nays, twenty ayes.

General EDWARD S. BRAGG: Under the unit rule Wisconsin's vote will be recorded twenty-four ayes.

THE CHAIR: It will be so recorded.

The Secretary resumed the roll call as follows:

	Yeas.	Nays.
Wyoming		6
Alaska	6	
Arizona		6
District of Columbia	1	5
New Mexico		6
Oklahoma		6
Indian Territory		6

Mr. J. J. DWYER, of California: I wish you would

246   OFFICIAL PROCEEDINGS OF THE

call the roll of the absentees of California. Four or five of us were absent and we want the vote to be recorded.

THE CHAIR: The gentleman from California asks to have the names of the gentlemen who did not vote now called. The Clerk will call them.

The Secretary called the list of those who were absent during the former call of the California delegates.

Mr. DWYER: JAMES V. COLEMAN desires to change his vote from no to aye. Mr. LANE desires to change his vote from no to aye.

THE SECRETARY: The State of California is recorded 11 ayes, 3 nays, 4 not voting.

The result of the vote was as follows: Yeas, 357; nays, 564; not voting and absent, 9.

The vote in detail was:

STATES.	TOTAL.	YEAS.	NAYS.	NOT VOTING.
Alabama	22		22	
Arkansas	16		16	
California	18	11	3	4
Colorado	8		8	
Connecticut	12	12		
Delaware	6	5	1	
Florida	8	7	1	
Georgia	26		26	
Idaho	6		6	
Illinois	48		48	
Indiana	30		30	
Iowa	26		26	
Kansas	20		20	
Kentucky	26		26	
Louisiana	16		16	
Maine	12	11	1	
Maryland	16	16		
Massachusetts	30	28	1	1
Michigan	28	28		
Minnesota	18	17	1	
Mississippi	18		18	
Missouri	34		34	
Montana	6		4	2
Nebraska	16		16	
Nevada	6		6	
New Hampshire	8	8		
New Jersey	20	20		
New York	72	72		
North Carolina	22		22	
North Dakota	6		5	1
Ohio	46		46	
Oregon	8		8	
Pennsylvania	64	64		
Rhode Island	8	8		
South Carolina	18		18	
South Dakota	8	8		
Tennessee	24		24	
Texas	30		30	
Utah	6		6	
Vermont	8	8		
Virginia	24		24	
Washington	8	3	5	
West Virginia	12		11	1
Wisconsin	24	24		
Wyoming	6		6	
Alaska	6	6		
Arizona	6		6	
District of Columbia	6	1	5	
New Mexico	6		6	
Oklahoma	6		6	
Indian Territory	6		6	
Total	930	357	564	9

So the amendment was lost.

THE CHAIR: The question now is upon the amendment offered by the gentleman from New York. He offers it to be inserted immediately after the financial plank.

The amendment was read as follows by the Reading Clerk:

"But it should be carefully provided by law at the same time that any change in the monetary standard should not apply to existing contracts."

The question was put by the Chair and the amendment was declared lost.

THE CHAIR: The next amendment will be read.

Mr. HILL, of New York: All right. The next amendment.

The amendment was read by the Reading Clerk as follows:

"Our advocacy of the independent free coinage of silver being based on the belief that such coinage will effect and maintain a parity between gold and silver at the ratio of 16 to 1, we declare as a pledge of our sincerity that if such free coinage shall fail to effect such parity within one year from its enactment by law such coinage shall thereupon be suspended."

THE CHAIR: The question is upon agreeing to the amendment.

The question being put, the amendment was lost.

The Chair recognized Mr. HILL, of New York.

Mr. HILL: I rise simply for the purpose of calling for the roll of States upon the adoption of the platform.

THE CHAIR: Is there any second to the motion of the gentleman from New York?

Mr. GOODWIN, of Alabama: I second the motion.

THE CHAIR: The gentleman from South Carolina will be recognized on his amendment.

Mr. TILLMAN: I desire to say, sir, that the failure to indorse an express resolution according to parliamentary usage carries with it the converse of the proposition. No brave man strikes a fallen foe, so I withdraw my amendment.

THE CHAIR: The question is upon the adoption of the platform as reported by the majority of the committee. The Secretary will call the roll of States.

The Secretary called the roll as follows:

States.	Total Vote.	Yeas.	Nays.	States.	Total Vote.	Yeas.	Nays.
Alabama	22	22	..	New York	72	..	72
Arkansas	16	16	..	North Carolina	22	22	..
California	18	18	..	North Dakota	6	6	..
Colorado	8	8	..	Ohio	46	46	..
Connecticut	12	..	12	Oregon	8	8	..
Delaware	6	1	5	Pennsylvania	64	..	64
Florida	8	5	3	Rhode Island	8	..	8
Georgia	26	26	..	South Carolina	18	18	..
Idaho	6	6	..	South Dakota	8	..	8
Illinois	48	48	..	Tennessee	24	24	..
Indiana	30	30	..	Texas	30	30	..
Iowa	26	26	..	Utah	6	6	..
Kansas	20	20	..	Vermont	8	..	8
Kentucky	26	26	..	Virginia	24	24	..
Louisiana	16	16	..	Washington	8	5	3
Maine	12	2	10	West Virginia	12	12	..
Maryland	16	4	12	Wisconsin	24	..	24
Massachusetts	30	3	27	Wyoming	6		6
Michigan	28	28	..	Territories.			
*Minnesota	18	6	11	Alaska	6	..	6
Mississippi	18	18	..	Arizona	6	6	..
Missouri	34	34	..	Dist. of Columbia	6	6	..
Montana	6	6	..	New Mexico	6	6	..
Nebraska	16	16	..	Oklahoma	6	6	..
Nevada	6	6	..	Indian Territory	6	6	..
New Hampshire	8	..	8				
New Jersey	20	..	20	Total	930	628	301

*One not voting.

During the call of the roll, the following interruptions occurred. When Iowa's vote was announced, Mr. STACKHOUSE said:

Mr. STACKHOUSE: I challenge the vote of the State of Iowa.

THE CHAIR: The Chair desires to know if the gentleman denies that the vote was correctly reported?

No such denial being made the roll call proceeded.

The State of Wisconsin was challenged by Delegate HOLGATE, but the accuracy of the count was not denied, and no action was taken by the Convention. The Secretary announced the result of the roll call as follows: Yeas, 628; nays, 301; absent, 1.

On motion of Senator JONES, of Arkansas, the Convention took a recess until 8 o'clock P. M.

OFFICIAL COPY OF PLATFORM.

We, the Democrats of the United States in National Convention assembled, do reaffirm our allegiance to those great essential principles of justice and liberty, upon which our institutions are founded, and which the Democratic Party has advocated from Jefferson's time to our own—freedom of speech, freedom of the press, freedom of conscience, the preservation of personal rights, the equality of all citizens before the law, and the faithful observance of constitutional limitations.

During all these years the Democratic Party has resisted the tendency of selfish interests to the centralization of governmental power, and steadfastly maintained the integrity of the dual scheme of government established by the founders of this Republic of republics. Under its guidance and teachings the great principle of local self-government has found its best expression in the maintenance of the rights of the States and in its assertion of the necessity of confining the general government to the exercise of the powers granted by the Constitution of the United States.

The Constitution of the United States guarantees to every citizen the rights of civil and religious liberty. The Democratic Party has always been the exponent of political liberty and religious freedom, and it renews its obligations and reaffirms its devotion to these fundamental principles of the Constitution.

THE MONEY PLANK.

Recognizing that the money question is paramount to all others at this time, we invite attention to the fact that the Federal Constitution named silver and gold together as the money metals of the United States, and that the first coinage law passed by Congress under the Constitution made the silver dollar the monetary unit and admitted gold to free coinage at a ratio based upon the silver-dollar unit.

We declare that the act of 1873 demonetizing silver without the knowledge or approval of the American people has resulted in the appreciation of gold and a corresponding fall in the prices of commodities produced by the people; a heavy increase in the burden of taxation and of all debts, public and private; the enrichment of the money-lending class at home and abroad; the prostration of industry and impoverishment of the people.

We are unalterably opposed to monometallism which has locked fast the prosperity of an industrial people in the paralysis of hard times. Gold monometallism is a British policy, and its adoption has brought other nations into financial servitude to London. It is not only un-American, but anti-American, and it can be fastened on the United States only by the stifling of that spirit and love of liberty which proclaimed our political independence in 1776 and won it in the War of the Revolution.

We demand the free and unlimited coinage of both silver and gold at the present legal ratio of 16 to 1 without waiting for the aid or consent of any other nation. We demand that the standard silver dollar shall be a full legal tender, equally with gold, for all debts, public and private, and we favor such legislation as will prevent for the future the demonetization of any kind of legal-tender money by private contract.

We are opposed to the policy and practice of surrendering to the holders of the obligations of the United States the option reserved by law to the Government of redeeming such obligations in either silver coin or gold coin.

INTEREST-BEARING BONDS.

We are opposed to the issuing of interest-bearing bonds of the United States in time of peace and condemn the trafficking with banking syndicates, which, in exchange for bonds and at an enormous profit to themselves, supply the Federal Treasury with gold to maintain the policy of gold monometallism.

AGAINST NATIONAL BANKS.

Congress alone has the power to coin and issue money, and President JACKSON declared that this power could not be delegated to corporations or individuals. We therefore denounce the issuance of notes intended to circulate as money by National banks as in derogation of the Constitution, and we demand that all paper which is made a legal tender for public and private debts, or which is receivable for dues to the United States, shall be issued by the Government of the United States and shall be redeemable in coin.

TARIFF RESOLUTION.

We hold that tariff duties should be levied for purposes of revenue, such duties to be so adjusted as to operate equally throughout the country, and not discriminate between class or section, and that taxation should be limited by the needs of the Government, honestly and economically administered. We denounce as disturbing to business the Republican threat to restore the McKINLEY law, which has twice been condemned by the people in National elections, and which, enacted under the false plea of protection to home industry, proved a prolific breeder of trusts and monopolies, enriched the few at the expense of the many, restricted trade and deprived the producers of the great American staples of access to their natural markets.

Until the money question is settled we are opposed to any agitation for further changes in our tariff laws, except such as are necessary to meet the deficit in revenue caused by the adverse decision of the Supreme Court on the income tax. But for this decision by the Supreme Court, there would be no deficit in the revenue under the law passed by a Democratic Congress in strict pursuance of the uniform decisions of that court for nearly 100 years, that court having in that decision sustained Constitutional objections to its enactment which had previously been overruled by the ablest Judges who have ever sat on that bench. We declare that it is the duty of Congress to use all the Constitutional power which remains after that decision, or which may come from its reversal by the court as it may hereafter be constituted, so that the burdens of taxation may be equally and impartially laid, to the end that wealth may bear its due proportion of the expense of the Government.

IMMIGRATION AND ARBITRATION.

We hold that the most efficient way of protecting American labor is to prevent the importation of foreign pauper labor to compete with it in the home market, and that the value of the home market to our American farmers and artisans is greatly reduced by a vicious monetary system which depresses the prices of their products below the cost of production, and thus deprives them of the means of purchasing the products of our home manufactories; and as labor creates the wealth of the country, we demand the passage of such laws as may be necessary to protect it in all its rights.

We are in favor of the arbitration of differences between employers engaged in interstate commerce and their employes, and recommend such legislation as is necessary to carry out this principle.

TRUSTS AND POOLS.

The absorption of wealth by the few, the consolidation of our leading railroad systems, and the formation of trusts and pools require a stricter control by the Federal Government of those arteries of commerce. We demand the enlargement of the powers of the Interstate Commerce Commission and such restriction and guarantees in the control of railroads as will protect the people from robbery and oppression.

DECLARE FOR ECONOMY.

We denounce the profligate waste of the money wrung from the people by oppressive taxation and the lavish appropriations of recent Republican Congresses, which have kept taxes high, while the labor that pays them is unemployed and the products of the people's toil are depressed in price till they no longer repay the cost of production. We demand a return to that simplicity and economy which befits a Democratic Government and a reduction in the number of useless offices the salaries of which drain the substance of the people.

FEDERAL INTERFERENCE IN LOCAL AFFAIRS.

We denounce arbitrary interference by Federal authorities in local affairs as a violation of the Constitution of the United States and a crime against free institutions, and we especially object to government by injunction as a new and highly dangerous form of oppression by which Federal Judges, in contempt of the laws of the States and rights of citizens, become at once legislators, judges and executioners; and we approve the bill passed at the last session of the United States Senate, and now pending in the House of Representatives, relative to contempts in Federal courts and providing for trials by jury in certain cases of contempt.

PACIFIC RAILROAD.

No discrimination should be indulged in by the Government of the United States in favor of any of its debtors. We approve of the refusal of the Fifty-third Congress to pass the Pacific Railroad Funding bill and denounce the effort of the present Republican Congress to enact a similar measure.

PENSIONS.

Recognizing the just claims of deserving Union soldiers, we heartily indorse the rule of the present Commissioner of Pensions, that no names shall be arbitrarily dropped from the pension roll; and the fact of enlistment and service should be deemed conclusive evidence against disease and disability before enlistment.

ADMISSION OF TERRITORIES.

We favor the admission of the Territories of New Mexico, Arizona and Oklahoma into the Union as States, and we favor the early admission of all the Territories, having the necessary population and resources to entitle them to Statehood, and, while they remain Territories, we hold that the officials appointed to administer the government of any Territory, together with the District of Columbia and Alaska, should be bona fide residents of the Territory or District in which their duties are to be performed. The Democratic party believes in home rule and that all public lands of the United States should be appropriated to the establishment of free homes for American citizens.

We recommend that the Territory of Alaska be granted a delegate in Congress and that the general land and timber laws of the United States be extended to said Territory.

SYMPATHY FOR CUBA.

The Monroe doctrine, as originally declared, and as interpreted by succeeding Presidents, is a permanent part of the foreign policy of the United States, and must at all times be maintained.

We extend our sympathy to the people of Cuba in their heroic struggle for liberty and independence.

CIVIL SERVICE LAWS.

We are opposed to life tenure in the public service, except as provided in the Constitution. We favor appointments based on merit, fixed terms of office, and such an administration of the civil service laws as will afford equal opportunities to all citizens of ascertained fitness.

THIRD TERM RESOLUTION.

We declare it to be the unwritten law of this Republic, established by custom and usage of 100 years and sanctioned by the examples of the greatest and wisest of those who founded and have maintained our Government that no man should be eligible for a third term of the Presidential office.

IMPROVEMENT OF WATERWAYS.

The Federal Government should care for and improve the Mississippi river and other great waterways of the Republic, so as to secure for the interior States easy and cheap transportation to tide water. When any waterway of the Republic is of sufficient importance to demand aid of the Government such aid should be extended upon a definite plan of continuous work until permanent improvement is secured.

CONCLUSION.

Confiding in the justice of our cause and the necessity of its success at the polls, we submit the foregoing declaration of principles and purposes to the considerate judgment of the American people. We invite the support of all citizens who approve them and who desire to have them made effective through legislation, for the relief of the people and the restoration of the country's prosperity.

WASHINGTON, D. C., August 31, 1896.

I certify that the above is the correct copy of the platform adopted at Chicago, Ill., by the National Democratic Convention, July 9th, 1896.

JAMES D. RICHARDSON,
Chairman, pro tempore.

THIRD DAY.

EVENING SESSION.

CHICAGO, ILL., July 9, 1896.

The Convention was called to order by acting Chairman Mr. RICHARDSON, of Tennessee, at 8:26 P. M., in the following words:

THE CHAIR: The Convention will be in order. The Chair appeals to the gentlemen on the floor to cease their conversation.

Senator JONES, of Arkansas: I move that the roll of the States be called, that nominations may be made for President and Vice President of the United States.

This motion was adopted.

THE CHAIR: The roll of the States will be called. The Chair desires to say that by an agreement entered into by and between the friends of the candidates the nominating and seconding speeches will be confined to thirty minutes time; these thirty minutes may be used when the principal speech is made, or they may be used by gentlemen who second the nominations. The Clerk will now call the roll.

The State of Arkansas being called, Senator JONES, of that State, said: "Arkansas yields the floor to Senator GEORGE G. VEST, of Missouri."

THE CHAIR: The Chair presents to the Convention the Senator from Missouri, Mr. VEST, who will address you for ten minutes.

Senator VEST: Gentlemen of the Convention: Through the courtesy of the Arkansas delegation, for which we are very grateful, the Democrats of Missouri are able at this time to present as a candidate for the Presidential nomination from this Convention the name of RICHARD PARKS BLAND, of Missouri.

Revolutions do not begin with the rich and prosperous. They represent the protest of those who are suffering from present conditions, and whose demands for relief are unheeded by the beneficiaries of unjust and oppressive legislation.

When a profound sense of wrong, evolved from years of distress, fastens upon the public mind in a free country, and the people are determined to have redress, a leader is always found who is a platform in himself, and to whom they instinctively turn as the logical exponent of their hopes.

The people are not iconoclasts nor false to their convictions. They followed JEFFERSON when he assailed the centralizing and monarchial doctrines of the old Federalists and was denounced as a communist and leveler by the wealth and culture of New England and New York.

They followed JACKSON when he took the United States bank by the throat, and was proclaimed a tyrant and ruffian by the usurers and money kings.

They followed LINCOLN when he attacked the slave power and declared that this country could not exist "half slave and half free."

The great movement of bimetallism—the free and unlimited coinage of gold and silver at the ratio of 16 to 1—and the restoration of silver to its constitutional status is

"No sapling chance-sown by the fountain,
Blooming at Beltane, in winter to fade."

It has come to stay.

It is a protest against the wrong and outrage of 1873, when, without debate, and with the knowledge of only a few men in Congress, the silver dollar was stricken from the coinage and the red despot of gold made supreme as to all values.

It is a declaration by the freemen of America that the United States must withdraw from the conspiracy which was formed to destroy one-half of the metallic money of the world.

in order to establish the slavery of greed and usury, more degrading than the tyranny of armed force.

It is the stern demand from unrequited toil, bankrupt enterprise and ruined homes, for a change in the money system which for years has brought disaster and desolation.

In this crisis of our country and party we must take no step backward in platform nor candidate. We want no uncertain nor doubtful leader. No "Laggard in peace or dastard in war," no latter-day silver saint, but a grizzled and scarred veteran, who has borne the heat and burthen of the day, and whose breast is marked from edge of sword and point of lance on a hundred fields.

Twenty years ago the battle for silver was begun in the halls of Congress by a modest, unpretending, brave man, not an iridescent or meteoric statesman, but of the people and from the people, who has never faltered for an instant in the great struggle. Others doubted and wavered, some yielded to blandishment and patronage, and are now holding office under the gold power; other misrepresented their constituents and have been provided for in the national infirmary of the present administration; but RICHARD PARKS BLAND stands now where he stood then, the living, breathing embodiment of the silver cause.

He struck with steel point the golden shield of the money monopolists, as did IVANHOE that of the proud templar in the lists at Ashby, and has neither asked nor given quarter.

Nor is he a narrow, one-ideaed man. For twenty-two years in Congress he fought in the front ranks for Democratic principles and policies, as taught by JEFFERSON.

He stood by the side of RANDALL and risked health and life to defeat the first Force bill. He opposed ably and earnestly that crowning tariff infamy, the McKINLEY Act, and again was among the foremost opponents of the last Force bill, which passed the House, but was defeated in the Senate.

He introduced the first free coinage measure in Congress, and was the author of the Seigniorage bill, which passed both Houses and was vetoed by President CLEVELAND.

If this be an obscure record, where can be found the career of any public servant which deserves the plaudits of his countrymen?

The Democrats of Missouri, who have passed through the fiery furnace of Republican proscription seven times heated, and whose State flag has always been placed beneath the great oriflamme of the National Democracy, make no apology nor excuse when offering such a candidate for the Presidency.

If you ask "Whence comes our candidate?" we answer: "Not from the usurers' den nor temple of Mammon, where the clink of gold drowns the voice of patriotism; but from the farm, the workshop, the mine—from the hearts and homes of the people."

To reject him is to put a brand upon rugged honesty and undaunted courage, and to chill the hearts and hopes of those who, during all these years, have waited for this hour of triumph. To nominate him is to make our party again that of the people, and to insure success.

> "Give us SILVER DICK, and silver quick,
> And we will make MCKINLEY sick
> In the ides of next November."

When the confusion and applause which greeted the close of this speech subsided, the Chair said:

THE CHAIR: I present to the Convention, Hon. DAVID OVERMYER, of Kansas.

Mr. OVERMYER: Mr. President and Gentlemen of the Convention: In the name of the Democracy of Kansas; in the name of the farmers of Kansas; in the name of the farmers of the United States; in the name of the homeless wanderers who throng your streets in quest of bread; in the name of that mighty army of the unemployed; in the name of that mightier army which has risen in insurrection against every form of economic despotism, I second the nomination of that illustrious statesman and patriot, that TIBERIUS GRACCHUS, Silver DICK BLAND, of Missouri. A man who understands the significance of the fact that the American Democracy took the Constitution when it was a mere commission of public authority and added to it the ten great amendments which stand forever as an impassable barrier against the invasive instincts of power; a man who knows that if power is not required to stop somewhere power will stop nowhere; that the first lesson of liberty is jealousy of power, and that the first maxim of liberty is that safety lies in distrust of power; a man who knows that no nation ever enriched itself by taxing itself; that no tax is either constitutional or just, except it be levied for a public purpose and that any tax which places the burden of government upon the backs of the poor while exempting the rich, is iniquitous; a man who knows that there are things dearer than gold—character, exalted character; manhood, unconquerable manhood; honor, immortal honor—and that these high qualities cannot long be retained by men menaced with mortgages, dominated by landlords and bowed down under the bitter and hopeless bondage of perpetual debt; that all which dignifies, all which elevates, all which exalts our mortal life, must wither and perish under the desolating touch of gold.

> Ill fares that land, to hastening ills a prey,
> Where wealth accumulates and men decay;
> Princes and lords may flourish or may fade
> A breath may make them as a breath has made;
> A bold yeomanry, their country's pride,
> When once destroyed can never be supplied.

A man who knows that money is the life-blood of the body commercial, and that no man or set of men can ever have a right to ligate the limbs of that body or to arrest or impede the normal circulation of that blood; a man who knows that money coined from either of the precious metals is sound money, as attested by the experience and wisdom of all the ages past; a man who knows that the money of the Constitution is sound money; that money which is good enough to pay every private debt is good enough to pay every public debt; that money which was good enough to pay GEORGE WASHINGTON for his expenses incurred in establishing our liberty, is good enough to pay ICKLEHEIMER or MORGAN or any other man in the wide, wide world; that the money of JEFFERSON, of JACKSON, of MADISON, of MONROE and of BENTON is honest money, and that he who says it is not insults the memory of those "dead but sceptered sovereigns who rule our spirits from their urns." A man who knows that international agreement is a mere device to appease the people and once more disappoint and betray them; and that they who would place this nation under subjection to Great Britain in the matter of the standard of values are no friends of their country or their kind; and that the true ratio between the metals is sanctioned by time, 16 to 1. A man who knows that this nation's honor is not in the keeping of that predatory and piratical element, that leagued and confederated scoundrelism which loots the treasury, stifles commerce, paralyzes industry and plunders the world; a man who cannot be ruled by consolidated monopoly or aggregated diabolism; a man who knows that no nation ever prospered where agriculture has languished, and that commerce has never languished where agriculture has prospered.

He knows that a vast majority of the American people are farmers; that when prosperity shall return it will come first to these dust-covered millions, whose hard, sun-browned hands never touch a polluted dollar, who work in the fields under the open skies, under the burning sun of summer and through the frosts and storms of winter from the time the stars grow dim in the West till they rise in the East; and when these prosper all who trade and who transport, all who buy and all who sell will prosper, and that until this happens none can prosper except those who speculate in human misery. A man who is in complete sympathy with the common people; who knows the tragedy of poverty and the pathos of the short but simple annals of the poor; a man around whose simple rural home is no wall of iron to keep out his fellow men; a man who needs not, and who has no bodyguard, but whose shield and protection are the love and sympathy of his fellow men. Such a man is RICHARD P. BLAND. He is as patient as WASHINGTON, as sympathetic as JEFFERSON, as brave and as just as JACKSON, and as wise and sagacious as any man who ever occupied the presidential chair. He can command the suffrages of more Democrats than any other man standing upon a free silver platform, and he can command the suffrages of more silver men who are not Democrats than any other Democrat. He can carry every State of the South.

He can carry the prairie States and the mountain States and the Pacific States, and he can carry more States of the central and eastern part of the country than any other man standing in the position which the great Democratic party has here taken. Nominate him and he will be elected by such a majority as has never been witnessed in this country. Then will be fulfilled the Californian's prophecy of

> "That land from out whose depths shall rise
> The new-time prophet; that wide domain
> From out whose awful depths shall come,
> All clad in skins with dusty feet,
> A man fresh from his Maker's hand,
> A singer singing ever sweet.
> A charmer charming very wise,
> And then all men shall not be dumb;
> Nay, not be dumb, for he shall say;
> 'Take heed, for I prepare the way for weary feet.'"

The eyes of the whole country, the eyes of the whole world are upon us; the great heart of mankind beats with anxious expectation of the issue of this Convention. Upon that result hangs the future weal or woe of this country. By the ashes of your ancestors; by the memories of your great and venerated dead; by the love which you bear to your children; by the duty which you owe to posterity; in the name of all that men hold sacred. I appeal to you to resolve this great issue aright, and there is one name the very utterance of which is a complete solution—BLAND, BLAND, BLAND.

THE CHAIR: The Chair desires to say that the nomination of Mr. BLAND will now be seconded by J. R. WILLIAMS, of Illinois.

Mr. WILLIAMS: Mr. Chairman and Gentlemen of the Convention: In behalf of the great and growing Democracy of Illinois I rise to second the nomination of a candidate who has done more than any other living American for the restoration of silver and for this triumphant victory. A candidate who is not an orator, but a statesman of sound judgment and many years of useful experience; a man whose long and loyal services for free coinage of silver has made his illustrious name a watchword in every home of America.

Having served four years with Mr. BLAND on the Coinage Committee and six years in the House of Representatives, I know him well. He is honest, he is able, he is positive and he is brave. He has all the noble attributes of a noble man, Democratic on all questions and at all times. I have seen his ability tried. I have seen his Democracy tested. There never was an occasion during my six years of observation when Mr. BLAND was not ready and able to discuss intelligently any of the great public measures that came before the American Congress for its consideration. The records of his public services will demonstrate to the country his superior intelligence and ability as a statesman.

It is true he has not the eloquence of a WEBSTER; but his statements of public questions are always clear, concise and intelligent and his twenty years of public service have given him an acquaintance with public men and public measures that but few other candidates have. The Democracy of Illinois is proud of all the illustrious names that will be presented to this Convention. We would rejoice to honor them all. But this great silver question which is now boiling over in this Convention, rises far above any and all candidates. And there is no man in America whose name is so identified with this great issue of silver as "Silver DICK" BLAND of Missouri.

The people of the United States have been deceived so often with straddling platforms and straddling candidates that we cannot afford to nominate a candidate whose breathless silence on this great silver question would cast any suspicion upon his devotion to our cause.

Nominate BLAND, and the people will know you are in earnest. Nominate BLAND, and you will have a candidate whose high character, whose splendid ability, whose true Democracy, whose devotion to silver has been tested by twenty years of public service. Take BLAND, and you know what he is. But if you take a candidate whose life and character have been less subjected to the great sunlight of public life, you may find in him many weak spots after his nomination.

Take BLAND and you will not be asked how long has he been a Democrat or how does he stand on silver. Nominate BLAND and no Republican words of his against Democracy will rise up before us in the campaign to chill our enthusiasm or weaken our support.

It has been said that we must nominate a man who will get Republican votes. I say, first of all, let us nominate a man who can get Democratic votes—a man whose name will enthuse the Democracy of this country and bring to the polls thousands and thousands of disappointed men who remained at home four years ago. Nominate BLAND, and $100,000,000 of silver dollars under the BLAND act will rise up before the American people and appeal for his election.

Nominate him and you will have a candidate strong in his integrity, strong in his Democracy, strong in his devotion to silver and strong in the hearts of his countrymen. Nominate BLAND—name him now—and the great silver waves of public sentiment will begin to rise higher and roll faster across the grand Republic until they have buried beneath their mighty force that British policy of a single standard. Let us do this, my fellow Democrats, in all fairness, and our patriotic efforts in this great cause of humanity will be crowned with gold and silver—victory and prosperity.

When Mr. WILLIAMS had concluded his remarks, the call of the States was continued. When the State of California was called W. W. FOOTE said:

Mr. FOOTE: California desired to nominate STEPHEN M. WHITE, the distinguished presiding officer of this Convention, but under the instructions of Mr. WHITE, he positively declines to let us present his name. Therefore you may pass California.

The call of the states was proceeded with, and no further name was placed before the Convention until the State of Georgia was reached, when the Chairman of the delegation announced that Hon. H. T. LEWIS would place in nomination the candidate who was to receive the vote of the Georgia delegation.

THE CHAIR: The Chair desires to present to the Convention Hon. HENRY T. LEWIS, of Georgia.

Mr. LEWIS: Mr. President and Gentlemen of the Convention: I do not intend to make a speech, but simply in behalf of the Democratic party of the State of Georgia, to place in nomination as the Democratic candidate for the President of the United States a distinguished citizen, whose very name is an earnest of success, whose public record will insure Democratic victory, whose public life and public record are loved and honored by the American people. Should public office be bestowed as a reward for public service, then no man merits the reward more than he.

Is public office a public trust? Then in no hands can be more safely lodged this greatest trust in the gift of the American people than in his. In the political storms that have swept over this country he has stood on the field of battle among the leaders of the Democratic hosts like SAUL among the Israelites, head and shoulders above all the rest. As Mr. PRENTISS said of the immortal CLAY, so we can truthfully say of him, "That his civil rewards will not yield in splendor to the brightest helmet that ever bloomed upon a warrior's brow."

He needs no speech to introduce him to this Convention. He needs no encomium to commend him to the people of the United States. Honor him, fellow Democrats, and you will honor yourselves; nominate him and you will reflect credit upon the party you represent; honor him and you will win for yourselves the plaudits of your constituents and the blessings of posterity. I refer, fellow citizens, to WILLIAM J. BRYAN, of Nebraska.

This announcement was followed by a long period of noise, cheers and confusion. When it abated the Chair said:

THE CHAIR: The Chair will now introduce to the Convention Hon. T. K. KLUTZ, of North Carolina, who will second the nomination of Mr. BRYAN.

Mr. KLUTZ: Mr. Chairman and Gentlemen of the Convention: At the behest of the yeoman Democracy of the good old State of North Carolina, I second the nomination of that young giant of the West, that friend of the people, that champion of the lowly, that apostle and prophet of this great crusade for financial reform, WILLIAM J. BRYAN, of Nebraska.

He can poll every Democratic vote in every section of this great country that any other candidate here named can do. And more than that, he can poll more votes from persons of different political affiliations and do more to unite the friends of free silver than all of them put together.

Cynics tell us that oratory is dead; that the admiration of civic virtues is lost to our people, but this splendid ovation that you gave to-day to WILLIAM J. BRYAN, the splendid tribute that you paid to his manhood, to his oratory, to his patriotism and to his sincerity, gives the lie to both of those observations. In the young prime of his great powers, known as a fearless tribune of the people, known for his advocacy of the cause of the lowly, known as the friend of free silver and as the champion of financial reform, eloquent as CLAY, patriotic as WEBSTER or LINCOLN, if he is elected, as he will be if he is nominated, he will be the President of all classes and all sections of this great country of ours.

THE CHAIR: I now present to the Convention Hon. GEORGE F. WILLIAMS, of Massachusetts, who will second the nomination of Mr. BRYAN.

Mr. WILLIAMS: The State of Georgia has requested me to add voice to its wish in this Convention, and as we are about to crown a leader in this great agricultural movement which is giving new hope and life to the Democracy, I beg to submit as a new sign and token the gold sheath of Nebraska's waving grain. We want the strength of youth for the hardships of a new cause. We want a loyal heart that can burn hot with the fire of purpose. We want a young arm to wield the sword for an indignant people; new, fresh sympathies for new woes, unfailing vigor in a desperate contest, a young giant out of the loins of a great Republic. We want no NAPOLEON, whose conception of government is too near the image of a throne to be consistent with the genius of American liberty. Whom I present now is a new CICERO to meet the new CATALINES of to-day.

THE CHAIR: The Chair now desires to present to the Convention Hon. THOMAS J. KERNAN, of Louisiana.

Mr. KERNAN: Mr. Chairman and fellow Democrats: The United States of America no longer kneel like credulous children at the feet of Europe. Long enough ago, as you have often enough been told, this great Republic of the West declared our political independence of the mother country; but it has remained for you, this grand gathering of the

Democratic hosts of this great Republic to declare our independence of the monetary despotism of the same hard old step-mother. We have to-day declared that we will no longer await her royal pleasure, nor that of her nursling dependents, to give us leave to be free in fact as well as in name. We have this day declared, unlike our Republican brethren, that we will not bow down and worship the Golden Calf which England has set up for the perpetual adoration of her underlings. We have refused to permit this idol to command us in the words of the Deity, " I am the Lord thy God; thou shalt have no other gods before me." We have proclaimed another deity; we have declared this day, that henceforth both gold and silver shall rule equal sovereigns in the world of finance.

This is not a revolution; it is a restoration. It determines not that gold shall be despoiled of any of her just power, but only that silver shall have her own again. To every assertion from Republicans, and I may say also from our *quasi* Democratic friends, who say that to pay in silver means repudiation of obligations made payable in coin, we reply that " we believe that we can make silver equally as valuable as gold without your help; with your help we know we can do it. Then join us in re-establishing universal bimetallism and then repudiation becomes impossible."

Upon this occasion, as upon all others in the great crises of the nation, the Democratic party stands forth as the champion of the people, the friend of the poor, and the protector of the oppressed. Not only by this declaration of industrial independence do we this day send forth tidings of great joy to all the toiling millions of this overburdened land; but every principle declared in the platform you have made here to-day, breathes the spirit of American freedom, and bids them be of good cheer, for the day of deliverance is at hand. To substantially complete this great work, it is only necessary——

(At this point the speaker was interrupted by noise and confusion, to which he said) I note with pleasure that I am receiving the respectful attention of the delegates upon this floor; and for the jeers of the gallery I care no more than I care for the jeers of the Republicans.

I say that to substantially complete the work of this Convention it only remains to name the candidate who will fit the platform. I say, in the nomination of the candidate, whose nomination I have the honor to second on behalf of the State of Louisiana, that it is difficult to determine whether the platform was made for him, or whether he was made for the platform.

Now, gentlemen of the Convention, in the name of the Democracy of the State of Louisiana, in the name of the farmers of this broad land everywhere, from the waving grain fields of the North, and the blossoming cotton fields of the South, they who know in the man whom I shall name a friend who believes with them that if the golden rays of the summer sun must ripen the harvest, that there is need of the silver beams of the harvest moon to gather it in safety. I name the silver-tongued orator of Nebraska, WILLIAM J. BRYAN. I believe that to nominate him is to elect him; I believe that to elect him is to restore business and to return to prosperity; and when his term of office shall have ended, I believe that we Democrats can truly say what has been so well said of another, that "he smote the rock of the public resources and it streamed with revenue; that he touched the portal of the public credit and it rolled open at his feet."

The call of the States was proceeded with, and no candidate was presented until the State of Indiana was reached, when Hon. DAVID TURPIE ascended the platform.

THE CHAIR: The Chair will present to the Convention Hon. DAVID TURPIE, of Indiana.

Hon. Mr. TURPIE: The choice of a candidate for the Presidency by the National Democratic Convention, of one who is to be the Chief Magistrate of this country for the next official term, of a successor to the many illustrious statesmen of our political faith who have served in that exalted position, so easily becomes the subject of glowing zeal and fancy, that the act and duty of selection are prone to be obscured by the glamor of the theme. Yet we ought to realize that the result is a plain question of arithmetic, depending upon a simple count of numbers, and that for many other reasons our action herein should be determined only by the most rigid scrutiny, and by the most careful calculation.

We ask then, as practical men, where should this nomination be placed? Indiana has long been known as the arena of the most severe and closely fought political contests. It is a member of the great Democratic phalanx of the North, including New York, New Jersey and Connecticut, but, strangely isolated, it has stood alone.

Upon the East and West, and upon the North, we have, ordinarily, hostile borders of intense spirit and activity; and even upon the South, the migration to us across the water of the Ohio, which occurs regularly in the Presidential year, is usually of such complexion as only to give aid and comfort to the enemy. In a State so nearly balanced that for years there has not been, in a Presidential election, a majority, either way, of ten thousand, in a total vote of four or five hundred thousand, the condition requires that our Democracy stand always embattled, whether awaiting victory or defeat—always prepared.

We submit to the delegations from the great States of Tennessee, of Georgia, of Mississippi, and others more certainly situated as to their political life and progress, what would you give, what would you not give, to make this State as certain as your own? How and when shall you help us to send you the message, in November next, of victory? This is the place, the time is now, to write that message. You can write that message to-day, ready for transmission, if your favor shall make the man of our choice the nominee of this Convention.

Survey the field, examine its various positions, throw the searchlight of inspection upon the situs of the different candidacies; you will find that Indiana is the strategic point and pivot of this conflict. The prestige, the power, the honor of this nomination are great, but not too great to be used as a means of assured success.

Let us not be misled by the fervid predictions of over confidence, by the contagious and stirring enthusiasm of the passing hour. Remember, gentlemen, that the returns of the election are not yet received; they will not begin to arrive until many months hence. We must overcome an enemy strongly fortressed against attack, reinforced by influences, to-day unnamed, unknown, flushed with the shout of recent triumph. We may make an error which shall cost us the whole stake, an error irretrievable. The opportunity for success is here, but also that of defeat. Let every man so act that he may not have to say hereafter, "Ah, I had not thought of that," as has been done more than once before. We may court defeat and disaster, as a lover woos his bride, by failing to put the right man in the right place.

Let us then, consult reason. Let us calmly weigh probabilities, and compute the chances at such a ratio as shall include and cover all contingencies. Let us dispose of the aid of this prestige of nomination where it will be most highly appreciated, where it will be most effective, where it is most needed, and where it must win.

Our candidate had the good fortune to be born in the State of Kentucky, was reared to manhood in one of the old Kentucky homes as near to mansions in the skies as any habitation on this planet. He was educated and graduated at Center College, Danville, in its palmiest days of yore, from whose doors came McCreary, Vest, Blackburn, Stevenson and others, men of National fame and distinction. He belongs, by birth and lineage, to the South. The South has no worthier or more noble son.

He married early in life the daughter of one well known in the history of our State, Governor and Senator Whitcomb. He commenced life as a farmer in one of the most fertile sections of the valley of the Wabash. Prosperity, well pleased and justly earned, has waited upon his footsteps.

Protection he needed not, save that of his pure heart and stalwart arm. He is now, and always has been a farmer. He has walked for years in the furrow; he has stepped off the "lands", he is not only a hearer, but a doer of the word noted in the old adage,

> "He who by the plow would thrive,
> Himself must either hold or drive."

Our candidate belongs to the largest, the most ancient and honorable business association of the world. Much is now said about the business, and business interests of this country. The business of a country is that vocation in which the larger number of the inhabitants are engaged. Agriculture employs a greater number of workmen than any other calling, hardly less than that of all others combined. We ask the delegates of this Convention to deliberately consider whether it may not be well worth the while to make a choice of one who is in the closest natural alliance with this most numerous and most influential body of our fellow citizens, one who has been all his life a member of this grand confraternity of the field and farm.

It is fifty-five years since a farmer appeared at the East front of the Capitol to take the oath as President upon Inauguration day. The inauguration and service of Indiana's choice would be a reminder of the earlier, the ideal days of this Republic when, as tradition relates, JEFFERSON left his farm at Monticello, traveled on horseback to the seat of Government, without ceremony took the constitutional obligation, and was inducted into office.

Our candidate is, and has been from his youth up to this hour, after the straightest sect of our political school, a Democrat. An intelligent, able, earnest and most diligent laborer in the cause. His first public service was that of a member of the General Assembly, to which he had been chosen by his friends and neighbors in and near the county of his residence. In 1890 he was elected Secretary of State of the State of Indiana. After a very exciting and laborious canvass, in 1892, he was chosen Governor of Indiana, the office he now holds, and in which he has shown those rare qualities of wise administration, executive skill and genius, unwearied and conscientious discharge of duty, in such manner as to have challenged, alike, the admiration and approval of men of all parties in our Commonwealth.

In this friend of ours, for whom, not for his sake, but for our own, we solicit your favor and support, you will find the best attainments of the scholar and the statesman fitly joined together, and a most intimate acquaintance with the wants and interests of the many upon whose suffrages the success of these, our labors, must depend.

The person whose name we shall present has never been beaten in a popular election in his own State. Our State, the State which by every sort of accent and emphasis is pushed, at this juncture, to the front, where the men in the gap of this great controversy abide, this State which danger haunts, which doubt has known and marked, this State we offer while we ask the man.

He whose name we shall announce for your consideration, comes, not as a guest or sojourner to this great National Council. He comes as a member and inmate of the family to his house and home wherein he has gained a right of domicile by lifelong fealty to the cause of American Democracy.

Upon the issue of the tariff, of federal election laws, of the liberty of the citizen, of the disposition of the public domain to actual settlers only, in opposition to all subsidies to private corporations, in favor of all the rights and privileges of Organized Labor, and of still further legislation toward that beneficent end, our candidate has stood with us, and for us through many years of heated quarrel and debate, and upon that question, now so conspicuous, his opinions have long been known, and have often, both in his own State and elsewhere, been the subject of the most public and explicit declaration.

Our candidate believes in the immediate restoration of silver to the full franchise of the mint, that the standard silver dollar should be coined, without restriction, at the same ratio of sixteen to one, as was formerly by our law established, and when so coined, that it shall be a legal tender for all debt.

He is not in favor of waiting for the action of European nations upon this subject, and perceives no reason for deferring or postponing our legislation for the remonetization of silver, to suit the convenience, assent or agreement of other governments.

Ardently sympathizing with the Republic of Cuba, he is also strongly attached to the doctrine of MONROE.

An American in every fiber, he would resist foreign aggression in any form. He heartily denounces as un-American the Republican platform adopted at St. Louis, which would maintain, and continue in this country that alien rule of foreign policy, the English single standard of gold and which proposes to reduce the government and the people of the United States, financially, to their ancient condition as a colonial possession of the British crown. He thinks that the freedom and independence of the mint and coinage of the United States are as necessary to the national prosperity as any other of our liberties; these rights, once ours, now lost, from whatever causes, must and shall be regained.

Thus the State, the man, the cause are merged, merged at last into one, the one request, the single entreaty, the momentous ultimate appeal, an appeal to your wisdom, to your serious judgment, to your most discreet discernment.

And I now, therefore, in pursuance of the instructions of the united Democracy of our State, expressed in Convention, and of the unanimous action of the delegates here present, do in all confidence place in nomination as a candidate for the Presidency, the name of CLAUDE MATTHEWS, of Indiana.

Senator TURPIE'S voice not being powerful proved inadequate to the task of filling the hall; during the delivery of his speech, which was barely audible at the table of the Official Stenographer, the noise and confusion became so great that the Chair instructed the police in the galleries to eject any one who disturbed the proceedings of the Convention.

Senator JOHN MARTIN, of Kansas: That declaration has been made so often from the platform, that the audience has lost faith in its efficacy. I want to see you do it, and we shall expect you to do it; and the best thing you can do is to commence now, and clear out these people. There are hundreds of men inside this hall who have no right here, and who interrupt the business of the Convention.

Mr. G. S. LONG, of Ohio: I move you, sir, that if the same disrespect is shown another speaker as was shown Senator TURPIE, that we adjourn until to-morrow morning, then the delegates and the officers can have control of the order of this Convention.

THE CHAIR: The Chair will again make the announcement that unless order is restored there will be no one admitted to the hall to-morrow except the delegates and the alternates. The Chair desires to say that persons in the gallery, in front and in the rear, are the guests of this

Convention, and they should favor us with good behavior; they should favor us with common politeness, and the Chair appeals to persons in the audience to give us perfect quiet, to the end that the business of the Convention may be conducted in an orderly manner.

I now present Hon. OSCAR A. TRIPPET, of California, who will second the nomination of Governor MATTHEWS.

Mr. TRIPPET: Gentlemen of the Democratic Convention: California is the greatest gold-producing State in the Union, but notwithstanding this great fact and the advantage she would gain by reason of a single gold standard, she is not jealous of her silver-producing sister States, and joins with the demand of the people for a free and unlimited coinage of silver at the ratio of 16 to 1. In recognition of the wishes of her people the Republican party of that great State sent to the recent convention at St. Louis a delegation instructed in favor of the free and unlimited coinage of silver. That delegation returned to their homes in defeat and disgrace, wearing the gold badges dictated by Wall street and the money sharks of Europe.

The Democracy of California recently assembled in the largest and most enthusiastic Convention ever held within the State, and that Convention also unanimously instructed its delegates to this Convention to vote as a unit for the free and unlimited coinage of silver at the ratio of 16 to 1.

The delegates of this Convention will return to their homes, flushed with victory to receive the plaudits of a grateful people.

At St. Louis was heard the voice of Wall street, at which England rejoiced. To-day is heard the voice of the people of America; and John Bull will groan.

How often have we heard from the Republican platform the denunciation of the Democratic party for a financial alliance with England, and now this same party with singular inconsistency has joined heart and soul with England against the demands of a suffering people.

This Convention having adopted a platform which declares in favor of the honest money of our forefathers, the delegates of the empire State of the Pacific coast desire the nomination by this Convention of a man in harmony with the principles announced. This great State extends her hand toward the Atlantic seaboard and asks to be met half way, and that a western man be selected as the nominee of this Convention. Without wishing to say aught in disparagement of other gentlemen whose names have been presented to this Convention, I take great pleasure in seconding the nomination of Governor MATTHEWS, of Indiana.

This is a Convention of the people, and what is more proper for this Convention to do than to select as its standard bearer a man who springs from that great class of American people—the farmers of the United States.

Like a CINCINNATUS, he was called from the plow to preside over the destinies of the great State of Indiana, and so fully has he met every expectation that he has sprung into National prominence and respect more rapidly than any other man of his generation.

I think with other delegates coming here from the Pacific slope that if this Convention will nominate this distinguished citizen of the great middle west he will lead to victory the Democratic cohorts in November.

At the close of Mr. LONG's speech, the Secretary resumed the call of States, the first then reached being the State of Iowa. Mr. FRED WHITE, of Iowa, came to the platform.

THE CHAIR: The Chair desires to present to the Convention Hon. FREDERICK WHITE, of Iowa.

Mr. WHITE: Mr. Chairman and Gentlemen of the Convention: I am authorized by the Democracy of Iowa to present to this Convention for nomination to the high office of President the name of HORACE BOIES, of our State. I want to assure this Convention in advance that this is not the result of any question of mere local pride, nor is it the result of any consideration of the question of mere availability. We ask you to nominate the candidate of our choice upon far broader grounds—upon the ground that HORACE BOIES is emphatically a broad man. Those of us who know him best do not hesitate, either here or elsewhere, to declare with all the confidence that a thorough knowledge of the truth can inspire that he is a man of the staunchest character, possessing a powerful personality and equipped with a combination of mental qualities that will make him, if elected, an ideal executive. Knowing as we all do that the political situation of the country is a grave and ominous one, this Convention must not ignore, nor even evade, the responsibility this situation creates, which is to give to the American people a candidate the mention of whose name, wherever known, will carry with it an overwhelming strength, and stand, in case of election, as an unqualified guarantee for the entire safety in the management of all public affairs, and the just settlement of every pressing question, and the speedy inauguration of a vigorous reign of exact justice.

Neither in formulating a policy nor in the execution of the same, nor yet in presenting an argument upon the merits or demerits of any public question, has Governor BOIES ever striven in the least degree to create a sensation. To his everlasting honor it must be said that in the doing of these things he has never failed to make a deep impression. This is the ideal test by which the capacity of a public man should be judged; this is the highest standard by which a statesman's reliability and usefulness should be ascertained and determined.

If you select Governor BOIES as your candidate and the people ratify your decision in November we can promise you no pyrotechnical display from the White House during his administration; there will be no rockets sent up, the explosion of which will frighten the timorous or furnish a subject for foolish talk of the superficial. There will be no sensational performances upon the political trapeze at the executive mansion while HORACE BOIES is its occupant; he will write no startling messages upon exciting public topics. We will promise you none of these performances; but I will tell you what we can and do promise you; and that is the inauguration and the faithful execution of a policy that will commend itself to every philosophic mind and be applauded by every sincere patriot; a policy that will be characterized throughout by the invigorating course of hard common sense and be all aglow with the everlasting sunshine of noble intentions— a policy the primary object of which will not be the creation of opportunities for the unnatural increase of the already excessive fortunes of an avaricious class, but the strict maintenance of the natural and constitutional right of every citizen carefully preserved, including that great body of our population, the working classes; the people who produce our national wealth; who never tire in their devotion to the constitution; who never desert their country's cause at any stage of any peril; who are always true and steadfast, even in the very midst of an overwhelming crisis; who furnish the volunteer soldiers and sailors in time of war, and earn the wherewith to pay the cost of war when it is over; the people who are the very mainstay of free government—to secure to these a larger share of the fruit of their labor; to secure to these impartial justice will be one of the cardinal principles, fully developed in the policy of the BOIES administration. To secure to him who earns the dollar the dollar he earns is the task that will be vigorously exacted of the statesmanship of the future. That type of statesmanship which so persistently and successfully plotted to pilfer from the industrious, that the idle may thrive, will be given its death next November if you men here are wise in your counsels and provide the opportunity to the people to strike the blow.

HORACE BOIES was born in New York State and came to Iowa in his early manhood. He came not as an adventurer, but with a fixed purpose of building up a permanent home, which he did at the town of Waterloo. While he was thus voluntarily and resolutely incurring all the inconveniences of a frontier life, the result is that in his mature years the people of his State have loaded him down with the richest honors and rewards in their power to bestow; he is to-day an inseparable figure in the conspicuous part of the phenomenal history of our State.

Let me beg of this Convention the privilege of one glimpse of Iowa history. With the question of Iowa's being a great State, concerning the capacity of her soil to produce uniformly abundant crops, I will not deal. It is enough to say that the diplomas awarded to Iowa by the management of the World's Columbian Exposition is the official declaration which secures to us what has been before conceded by all—viz., the crowning glory of standing at the head of the long column of the agricultural States of this nation. Neither drought nor flood has ever been powerful enough in Iowa to constitute what in other localities was a natural calamity. I have raised fifty bushels of solid corn to the acre, upon which not one drop of rain fell from the time it came up until the ear was fully grown. There is perhaps not another spot in this wide world where such a thing is possible.

But while we are easily supreme in the corn field, our Democrats have had a hard road to hoe in politics. The torments inflicted by the seven plagues of Egypt must have been a solid chunk of comfort compared with the treatment accorded Iowa Democrats by the 60,000, 70,000 and 80,000 uninterrupted Republican majority which for more than a generation delighted them in making an annual picnic out of election day, and just for the fun of the thing, trampled the Iowa Democracy into the very earth. This huge army of Republican voters was dominated by the spirit of inexplicable fanaticism, and the more we combatted this spirit the fiercer it grew. Naturally Democrats became disheartened and scarce. When this Republican recklessness was nearing the culminating point, and through sumptuary legislation every guaranty of personal liberty was endangered; when acts which throughout the civilized world are regarded as natural and treated as lawful were in Iowa defined as crimes and compared to capital offenses; when the constitutional protection, trial by jury, which for centuries has been esteemed as the very climax of all the glory of Anglo-Saxon civilization; when this was about to be eliminated from our judicial system, and the cold, barbarous system of Russia was to be substituted; when the whole machinery of our local government, the greatest of all democratic principles, the principle of home rule, was about to be swept out of existence; when every lover of freedom was on the point of despairing; when there was no Democratic leader anywhere in sight wise and bold enough to face the crisis, there was heard the voice of one as speaking from the wilderness; it was the magic voice of HORACE BOIES summoning disheartened men to heroic action. He it was who leaped to the very front and alone defied the seemingly irresistible column of an exultant foe—a foe that had never been chastened by defeat. He accomplished what all men united in declaring the impossible; for in two great contests which followed, which in many respects have no parallel in the history of American politics, HORACE BOIES came off victor, and thus did he forever avert the danger of having a veritable despotism planted upon the fruitful soil of a free State.

A soldier can show his courage only in battle; a sailor his fearlessness only while a storm is raging; the fireman in a great city can only exhibit that sublime type of heroism which we all so much admire during the time of an actual conflagration, when property is to be saved and imperiled lives are to be rescued; so a statesman can only show his real capacity, can only demonstrate the full measure of his wisdom and power during a crisis, and it is only during an actual crisis that the higher qualities of statesmanship can be developed and tested. That HORACE BOIES possesses this rarest of all humane capacities, the power to rise equal and superior to a crisis and control it, is attested by the history of our State and concurrent testimony of political friend and foe. This is the man, who stands before the American people equipped with these supreme qualifications, whom we ask this Convention to nominate.

Upon the overshadowing issue of this campaign Governor BOIES stands upon an invulnerable platform, the Constitution of his country, inasmuch as the Constitution, in defining what the State shall use as "legal tender in the payment of debts," designates not gold or silver, but gold and silver. Governor BOIES believes that the bimetallic system thus provided for in the fundamental law of the land is the system the Democratic party must indorse and uphold. He believes that so long as the Constitution remains unchanged Congress has no power to demonetize either metal. Hence, in common with the great mass of the American people, he believes that the demonetization of silver was not an ordinary political blunder, but an actual crime, and he can conceive of no condition which can possibly arise that would justify the Democratic party in justifying that crime or in helping to perpetuate its direful results. Governor BOIES does not believe in a dishonest 50-cent dollar, as it would work injury to the creditor class;

neither does he believe in the 200-cent dollar, which is still more dishonest, as it unquestionably involves the bankruptcy of the debtor class. Governor BOIES believes in an honest American dollar, authorized not by the Parliament, but by the law of the American Congress, and coined for use among the American people. He believes in a gold dollar of 22.2 grains of gold and a silver dollar just sixteen times heavier.

Having rebelled against British influence over a century ago, winning the fight when a mere weakling; having now developed into the strongest people on the face of the earth, clearly entitling us to the leadership among nations, Governor BOIES believes it would be not merely pitiable cowardice on our part, but actual treason to the people, should we now capitulate to English greed.

The finger of a kind fate points to the election of HORACE BOIES. History seems to be anxious to repeat itself. Give us the man from Waterloo and allies will flock to his standard which will destroy MARK HANNA's NAPOLEON No. 2 as effectually as the European allies destroyed the French NAPOLEON No. 1.

At the conclusion of the speech there occurred a repetition of the noise and confusion which had taken place at different times during the Convention. The appearance of a young woman at the eastern end of the hall, persistently cheering for BOIES, finally attracted the attention of the entire assemblage, and she was escorted by the Iowa delegation to the floor, and twenty minutes elapsed before the business of the Convention could be resumed.

THE CHAIR: The Chair presents Hon. T. A. SMITH, of Minnesota.

Mr. SMITH: In beginning the few remarks I have to make I shall have to make the same apology that old "JACK" FALSTAFF made on one occasion, that he was "hoarse with hollowing and singing of anthems." I am hoarse with hollowing and singing of anthems for this glorious silver cause, but my voice has not yet entirely died away to such an extent that I cannot raise it with a feeble shout for HORACE BOIES, the grand old commoner of the Hawkeye State.

My friends, you of the South with whom political strife is not a question of victory, but one simply of majorities; you gentlemen who live in the close States, what we might call the border States in politics, where a good, stout, fighting Democracy and a strong organization insures you victory a goodly portion of the time, you, perhaps, have no conception of the difficulties under which we, the Democrats of the Northwest, have labored prior to the last ten years.

In fact, the great Dr. SAMUEL JOHNSON described our condition well when he said on one occasion that a woman's preaching was like a dog's walking on its hind legs; you did not expect to see it done well; you were surprised to see it done at all. Well, that was very much like our fighting prior to the last ten years; and yet during those ten years what have we done? In several cases we have elected complete State tickets; in all of those States, without exception, we have grasped the brightest jewels from the Republican crown and have captured a great many of the Congressional districts, sending members to Congress to vote against iniquitous Republican schemes, against Force Bills and the SHERMAN Bill, and Tariff Bills, McKINLEY Bills—BILL McKINLEY's Bill.

Yes, gentlemen, even in Minnesota we have gone forth to battle—in darkest Minnesota, not fruitlessly, even; we have brought back spoils and are entitled to the honor of a triumph. But if that has been the case throughout the Northwest, how has it been in Iowa? I remember when HORACE BOIES first came upon the field of action. He was nominated in the face of an adverse majority of 75,000. No one dreamed that he would be elected, and yet, making a masterly canvass, he was elected by a good respectable majority, and a thrill of exultation went through the bosom of every Democrat in the Northwest when they learned that the stout fighting Democracy of Iowa had raised him on their shield and elected him their chosen chief.

But, my friends, there is another consideration which I wish to mention, and which ought to be a very potent one in this Convention. If it were not for HORACE BOIES we would not have a silver majority here at all. You remember the depressed condition that existed in the cause of silver prior to his appearance in the field. Michigan had just been carried by the gold standard. All at once HORACE BOIES threw down his gauge of battle to the federal officeholders marshaled against him in Iowa, and what was the result? The result was that the prairies were on fire with indignation. They came from the hamlets and from the farms and elected twenty-six majority—twenty-six delegates to sit in this Convention and to vote for free silver and HORACE BOIES. It was the crucial point of the battle. The cause of silver was then won. From the time when Iowa declared for HORACE BOIES and free silver the cause was won throughout the Union. It was like the charge of KELLERMANN at the battle of Marengo. It was like that of CROMWELL at the battle of Naseby.

Now, my friends, I say that we can do no better—my strength will not permit of me speaking any more, even if I had the inclination to do so—we cannot do any better than to nominate this grand old man. He is not a man of one idea. He is a man of broad mental grasp, capable of meeting and grappling with all these complicated questions that come up in public life. Therefore, my friends, I take pleasure in nominating, or seconding the nomination of HORACE BOIES, the grand old commoner of Iowa.

The Secretary resumed the call of States.

Kansas had no name to present, but when Kentucky was reached Mr. OLLIE JAMES, the chairman of the delegation, said:

Mr. JAMES: Mr. Chairman, I desire to announce that the Kentucky delegation have selected the Hon. JOHN S. RHEA, delegate from the State-at-large to present the State's greatest Democrat, JOE BLACKBURN.

THE CHAIR: The Chair presents to the Convention Hon. JOHN S. RHEA.

Mr. RHEA: Mr. Chairman and fellow Democrats: Kentucky greets her brethren of all this Union with the assurance that no matter from whence our candidate will come, Kentucky will support him. But she begs that you do remember that like NAPOLEON's drummer boy, when to NAPOLEON's legions the battle seemed lost at Marengo and he ordered the retreat, JOE BLACKBURN said to CARLISLE: "Sire, I do not know how. War has never taught me the retreat, but I can sound a charge. Oh, I can sound a charge that will call the dead back into line. I beat that charge at the bridge of Lodi, I beat it at the Pyramids. Oh may I beat it here to-day."

Kentucky presents JOE BLACKBURN to the Union, because to Kentuckians he is "JOE" BLACKBURN, and that means all. He is big enough and broad enough and brainy enough to satisfy every Democrat in the land. I know that he comes from the South: I know that he was a Confederate soldier; I know that he comes from a section the valor and patriotism of whose men has challenged the admiration, as it has elicited the wonder of the world, and whose women are the expression of God's tenderest beneficence to men, that have gladdened the eye or filled the heart of mankind with love, respect and admiration. When the tongue of slander and the heart of hate was hurled against his people he stood as a pillar of cloud by day and a pillar of fire by night and when the memory of HANCOCK, the superb, was attacked by INGALLS, JOE BLACKBURN was the first at the front to defend the stars and stripes under which HANCOCK fought. He has stood upon both floors of the American Congress, battling for the equal rights of all the states and all the people. Now, his candidacy is not sectional, nor is the issue upon which, if he be nominated, he will make the race a sectional one. The free and unlimited coinage of silver may have found its home in the South or West to start with; it has been nurtured under sunny skies, and comes laden with the perfume of the tropics, but its home is by the frozen lakes. The lightning starts in the clouds but its flash encircles the earth. Justice has its seat in the bosom of God, but its principles pervade the world.

The call to arms from California has been echoed back from Maine. Its potential adherents are found from ocean to ocean, from the gulf to the lakes. They come with the smell of fresh plowed earth upon their garments, or they may come with their faces begrimed with smoke, and bear the stain that labor bears, but they are the people who pay the taxes and fight the battles for their country. Freedom's battles are never fought at bankers' banquets. No board of trade, no chamber of commerce, no clearing house association crossed lofty heights nor blazed their way through trackless forests to fight this battle of the American revolution. When this great nation of ours was threatened with dissolution, where were these banqueting bankers, these boards of trade, these chambers of commerce? They were engaged in the laudable and patriotic business of buying bonds with 40-cent paper, irredeemable dollars that they might thereafter now demand here that they should be paid back again in a 200-cent gold dollar.

Now the candidacy of Senator BLACKBURN appeals to the whole Union of States and in no sectional spirit, asking no sectional fight, because if nominated and elected he will be no sectional president, but he will be a president of the whole people. Now, what does that signify? You will remember that three years ago he stood upon the floors of your American Congress and refused to bend the supple hinges of the knee where thrift might follow fawning. He said to the President of the United States: Let your collectorships, your post-offices and your federal patronage go. They cannot buy my manhood and cannot buy my principle, or my loyalty to the people. His whole career, covering quite one-third of a century, has been a lifelong expression of his sympathy and love for the interests of labor. Why, had he his way he would coin into legal tender dollars every drop of sweat which falls from labor's brow. As to the man I present, who can challenge his Democracy? Why, he fights with the boys in the trenches. Who can doubt his honor? Who can impeach his capacity? He has shown himself the peer in the American Congress, of the ablest in the land. His voice has been heard in the forty five States of the American Union, battling for the supremacy of Democratic principles and the election of Democratic candidates. It may be said of him, as it has been said of another great Kentuckian, who has been gathered to his fathers, that his greatness stood confessed in the people's tears.

He is resolute and courageous and clean of envy, and yet not wanting in that finer ambition which makes men greater and better. His honor is unimpregnable and his simplicity is sublime. No country every had a truer son, no cause a nobler champion, no people a bolder defender; and if he goes down in defeat it may still be said, no cause had a purer victim. Put your standard in his hands and he will carry it to success; but if it be the will of this great Convention of Democrats that he shall remain longer in the ranks, obeying now as he always has, the will of his party, which to him is supreme, he will step down and out and be found battling for any man who is your choice.

THE CHAIR: The Chair will now present Hon. W. W. FOOTE, of California.

Mr. FOOTE: Mr. Chairman and Delegates of the National Convention: California, the greatest gold-producing State in the world, has sent to this Convention eighteen delegates who are pledged to the unlimited coinage of silver at the ratio of 16 to 1, without any foreign interference whatever. California has further instructed her delegates to present the name of the Hon. STEPHEN M. WHITE, the distinguished Senator from that State, and the presiding officer of this Convention. But Senator WHITE has declined to permit his name to be presented, and I am here, with the consent of my delegation, to second the nomination of a man whom I believe to be as good if not a better representative of the free silver cause as any other man who has been named, in the person of the Hon. J. C. S. BLACKBURN, of Kentucky.

We have adopted a platform of principles here to-day which speaks in no uncertain tone to the people of the United States. The silver plank of this Convention can be understood by any man who can read the English language. The grand army of Democracy is to-day enlisted under the silver banner; and my experience is that when you have an army you ought to have a leader in whom they have confidence. Who could lead the silver forces to victory better than JOE BLACKBURN, of Kentucky? Who fought the combined cohorts of the Treasury Department and of the Federal Administration all during the session of that legislature? The news was wafted to distant California; JOE BLACKBURN appeared, like the white-plumed Knights of Navarre, battling for that cause; and, although the State went Republican, JOE BLACKBURN achieved a victory of which he may well be proud. The only objection that I have heard to his nomination to the Presidency, is that his wise counsels might be missed in the Senate of the United States.

I have no words to say against any other candidate who

has been nominated in this Convention. JOE BLACKBURN is a candidate upon principle. He is not being paraded around here by any JOAN OF ARC; and he has undertaken to appeal, not to your prejudices, but to your principles. California, however she may vote, has the highest respect for the distinguished Senator from Kentucky, and when we come to our sober second-sense, JOE BLACKBURN ought to receive the nomination of this Convention. You have seen him here upon this platform—a gallant and a distinguished man—a man who would honor the Presidency of the United States— and for myself and other delegates from the State of California I take pride and pleasure in seconding his nomination.

Louisiana, Maine and Maryland had no names to present. When Massachusetts was reached, Hon. JOHN W. CORCORAN, the chairman of the delegation, said:

Mr. CORCORAN: By unanimous vote of the Democrats of Massachusetts, the delegation is instructed to present the name of Governor RUSSELL; but, by his direction and because of the platform, he declined the use of his name. Therefore we have no candidate to offer, and ask that we be passed. That is the sentiment of Massachusetts—not by proxy, but by its delegates.

Michigan, Minnesota and Mississippi had no candidates, but when Missouri was called, Governor STONE announced that the State of Missouri would yield to the State of Arkansas.

THE CHAIR: The Chair presents to the Convention Hon. PAUL JONES, of Arkansas.

Mr. JONES: For President of the United States of America I nominate RICHARD P. BLAND, of Missouri. A few years ago the mutterings of a storm were heard all over this union. The storm clouds gathered and burst in all their might and majesty over the west and the south. That storm was the mighty uprising of a great and free people in defense of their rights and against wrong and oppression. They looked about to find a leader worthy of their cause, and their eyes turned to that peerless Democrat of Missouri and from the Mississippi River to the east and to the west the name of BLAND was shouted over this country until the echoes died in the expanse of two oceans.

BLAND is no new man, no experiment in Democracy. For twenty-two years he has fought the battles of our party under the terrible blaze of a political search light and no spot has been found on his escutcheon, no flaw in his political armor. He is the logical candidate upon the great issue that now confronts the American people, and which the American people must settle in November. When we speak of THERMOPYLÆ we think of LEONIDAS; when we talk of the triumphant Roman eagles we think of the CÆSARS; when we speak of the Revolution our minds go back to WASHINGTON; of the Declaration of Independence, and we worship a JEFFERSON; of the National Bank, and we admire JACKSON; when we speak of the free and unlimited coinage of silver our minds go back instinctively to RICHARD P. BLAND.

Since silver was murdered in the house of her friends by the stealth of a cowardly assassin, BLAND has fought incessantly for its restoration. He is the very embodiment, the incarnation of the doctrine of silver. When we want to know what the character of a man is we ask what his neighbors say about him. Who is BLAND, and what do his neighbors say? On the east we have the empire State of Illinois with this imperial city by the lake, a State which has given this nation the great LINCOLN and to its people the fearless ALTGELD.

Tested by every rule he stands before you in the full measure of a Democrat and in the full measure of a citizen. His life has been pure and as spotless as the snows of the north and his heart is as warm and genial as the suns of the south. I say to you in all honesty he is worthy to be your nominee. The nomination of BLAND would mean more to the American people than all the silver planks you can put into your platform. This is an issue that was made by the people, and BLAND is the people's man.

No politician is directing this grand Ship of State which the Democracy has launched in this campaign. The people are at the helm and they demand the leader of their choice. They demand not only the choice of this great Convention, but they demand a majority of the silver delegates of this

Convention. Nominate him upon the platform which you have, and every true, every honest Democrat will support him. Not only that, but under his banner will enlist every patriot, who for his country's good, for the honor and prosperity of the people has broken political allignments and is willing to do battle for his country.

Fellow citizens, you have given us free silver and now I want you to give us "Free Silver DICK" and, by the gods, we will carry the election in November. I thank you.

Montana was called, but had no candidate to present. When the Secretary gave Nebraska its opportunity the Chairman of that delegation said:

For the present the State of Nebraska passes, but at the proper time will take pleasure in casting its votes for the man whom we honor and love, the Hon. WILLIAM J. BRYAN.

Neither Nevada nor New Hampshire had any candidate to put in nomination, and when New Jersey was called the Chairman of the delegation said:

New Jersey does not desire to nominate any man upon the platform of this Convention.

New York being called, Senator HILL announced:

New York has no candidate to present to this Convention.

The Secretary then resumed the calling of the roll. North Carolina and North Dakota were passed, but when Ohio was reached the Chairman introduced Col. A. W. PATRICK, of that State:

Col. PATRICK: Mr. President and Gentlemen of the Convention: Considering your arduous labors for the last three days and the great patience with which you have heard the eulogiums passed upon the different candidates, it seems to me that brevity in the announcement of candidates is now the soul of sense. Therefore, gentlemen of the Convention, in no set phrases of speech, but inspired by the love that I have for one of the most magnificent characters that grace this country, I at once, in the name of the Democracy of the great State of Ohio, put in nomination as candidate for President, the Hon. JOHN R. MCLEAN, of Cincinnati.

I shall pass no extravagant eulogium on the man. His whole life speaks for itself. He is honest, he is capable, he is a Democrat, he is the son of a sire that did more to mold the Democracy of Ohio into triumph than any man in it. I will say another thing here, and brother delegates, listen and give me your attention while I say it. There are fine eulogies passed upon the favorite sons that have been mentioned here to-night. Some of them may carry Ohio against WILLIAM MCKINLEY, but, by the eternal gods, JOHN MCLEAN will carry Ohio against WILLIAM MCKINLEY. If you give us JOHN R. MCLEAN I promise you here that Ohio will be the Waterloo of that NAPOLEON, and Salt River his St. Helena.

Here I might halt, but bear with me, for I promise you that I will be brief. I will not trespass upon your time, but bear with me when I tell you that from the beginning of this great war of millionaires against the millions, of the plutocrats against the people, of the classes against the masses, JOHN MCLEAN'S heart and soul have been with the people. Let me say another thing; in all great efforts for the benefit of the people, there are what we call pioneers, men who go ahead of the army, who go ahead even of the vanguard, who, in the darkness of a political night raise the beacon of hope and right and of relief in behalf of the people. I say to you when the cause of free silver was weak, when the members supporting it were few, JOHN R. MCLEAN was one of the bravest soldiers, and the noblest pioneer of them all.

Let me say further, that his great journal, filled with arguments in favor of the people, was scattered every day in the year, like snowflakes, into the ranks of the people of twenty States; and that great organ did more to educate the people and develop the growth of bimetallism and free coinage of silver than any other one influence west of the Allegheny mountains. Then, brother Democrats, I ask you this: If he was with you in this cause when you were weak, what will you do for him now in the majesty of your strength? In the triumph of the cause, will you forget the pioneers that led the way? I hope not. I believe not. I say to you delegates, into whose faces I am looking, that we hand over the claims of JOHN R. MCLEAN into your hands, into your hearts, relying upon the integrity and gratitude of the great Democratic masses. I thank you, gentlemen, for your attention.

At this point Hon. JOHN A. BANKHEAD, of Alabama, took the chair. The Secretary resumed the call of the roll at Oregon, which had no candidate to present.

When Pennsylvania was next called Hon. WILLIAM F. HARRITY, the Chairman of the delegation from that State, said:

Mr. Chairman: Pennsylvania has no candidate to present at this time, but when the roll of States shall be called for the purpose of ascertaining preferences as to candidates, Pennsylvania will express her wishes upon that subject.

The Secretary resumed the call of the roll. Rhode Island, South Carolina and Tennessee having no candidates. When Texas was reached the Chairman of that delegation announced that the State of Texas wished to express the preferences of that delegation through one of its members, Hon. J. W. BAILEY. Mr. BAILEY went upon the stand. Chairman BANKHEAD said:

THE CHAIR: Gentlemen of the Convention: I have the honor of introducing to you Hon. JOSEPH W. BAILEY, of the State of Texas.

Mr. BAILEY: Mr. Chairman and Gentlemen of the Convention: For the first time since the close of our unhappy Civil war a large majority of those who vote in the coming Presidential contest will be governed in the casting of their ballots by their convictions upon the great economic question of the day. This Convention has already adopted a platform which defines with admirable force and clearness the position of our party upon the question, and it is now our duty to perfect our work by nominating a candidate whose words and deeds are better than a written pledge that he will faithfully keep the promises which our platform makes. Who most completely fulfills this supreme requirement? If I should ask this audience, or if I should ask any audience assembled on the American continent, and under the American flag, what Democrat among all these splendid leaders of our party best represents the issue which to-day divides the American people and which must be decided at the polls on the 3rd day of next November, I should be answered with the name of RICHARD BLAND. And, gentlemen of the Convention, he not only best typifies the issue which is to be paramount in the next election, but he has been a fearless and consistent advocate of those immortal principles of Democracy which our Democratic forefathers cherished and defended. Those who doubt the wisdom of his nomination sometimes venture to express the fear that he is not great enough to be our President. To them I say, examine his record. For twenty-two years he sat in the Federal House of Representatives, and during all those years he voted right as often and he voted wrong as seldom as any man who occupied the same position for an equal length of time. No ordinary man could safely pass through this crucial test. The American voters are willing to believe that the man who is wise enough always to be right is wise enough to be the Chief Magistrate of this great Republic.

Yea, my countrymen, better even than his unerring common sense, is his rugged and unyielding honesty. In his person he unites the highest qualities of an ideal candidate. He is so patriotic that he has always put love of country above the love of self. He is so honest that no tainted dollar ever touched his hand. He is so firm that a legion of his country's enemies could not drive him from his post of duty. The nomination of Mr. BLAND will proclaim to all the millions who are proud to own their allegiance to Democracy that the public good is again to be exalted above selfishness and private greed. It will assure the doubters, it will recall the Democratic wanderers, it will inspire the masses with hopeful courage. Nominate him, and in every home from the mountains to the sea, in palace and cabin, it will be told how a great and successful party has crowned a private citizen with its highest honor because he always has been true to his own convictions and loyal to the best interests of his countrymen.

Fellow Democrats, whether your choice shall be BLAND or BOIES, MATTHEWS or MCLEAN, BLACKBURN or BRYAN, the imperial commonwealth of Texas, with her more than 100,000 will take her place at the head of your victorious column.

When the Secretary called Utah, the chairman of that delegation said: Utah desires to be heard through her distinguished son, Hon. J. L. RAWLINS.

Mr. RICHARDSON having resumed the Chair said: I have the pleasure to present to the Convention Hon. J. L. RAWLINS.

Mr. RAWLINS: Mr. Chairman and Gentlemen of the Convention: In the few remarks which I shall make I despair of attaining to that high level of exact truth and eloquence which has characterized all that has been said previously in respect to candidates before this Convention. Our surest justification of the hope of success is to deserve it. The Democratic party, as old as the Nation, as broad as the continent, and as free as the air, since the election of THOMAS JEFFERSON as President has never failed to command the support of the majority of the people when it has been true to its faith and selected for its candidates those who, under all circumstances, have faithfully maintained its doctrines. We must maintain self-respect, exalt our principles, and in gratitude cherish and honor those whose unselfish devotion to our cause has brought us so near to the goal of victory. In this connection, at this time, there is one name which is pre-eminent. His ancestors were of Virginia—the mother of Presidents. The "old Kentucky home" consecrated and blessed the spot where he was born. Away off in California he is loved. He resided in Nevada and held office in Utah; the newest and brightest star placed upon the flag delights to shine for him. His name is a household word in Colorado; his home is in the great State of Missouri, but he dwells everywhere in the hearts of the people. Has he not been brave, and honest, and true for twenty years without hope of reward? He has unselfishly consecrated his life to the cause which is now predominant. With the persistence and faith of the Christian in the story of "Pilgrim's Progress" his pursuit of the cause, in spite of obstacles, has been unfaltering. This cause is now the paramount issue. He has guarded and nurtured it with the loving devotion a mother would bestow in the care of her child. When others have faltered he has been steadfast; when many have been lured away by the blandishments of wealth and power, he has never swerved; when all around him others have yielded to the seduction of place and patronage, he has stood erect, maintained his honor and spurned their offers.

Conscious of the dignity and justice of the cause, while the shafts of contumely, derision and insult were being hurled against his intelligence and manhood, by a debauched but powerful press, in calmness and dignity, and with unflinching courage he stood by his convictions until he commanded the eulogy and respect of his most virulent adversaries. He is capable. He has never courted popularity. His is not the career of the weather-cock, or the time-fly. His life is an open book. He has spoken honestly, clearly, and with the wisdom of foresight of a statesman upon all the great questions which concerned our country's welfare. As the cause is greater than the man you cannot ignore or pass this man by without exemplifying your ingratitude, raising doubts as to your sincerity and imperiling the success of our cause. You cannot, you dare not do it. In his person the hopes of the people are centered. He is the incarnation of their convictions, the personification of their purpose. In him their assurance against betrayal is supreme; with their trust committed to his care by the victory to be achieved in November, in spite of all the machinations of MOLOCH, their purpose they know will be by him faithfully executed. Utah seconds the nomination of RICHARD P. BLAND.

The State of Vermont had no candidate to present. When Virginia was called Colonel W. A. JONES of that delegation said:

The Democrats of Virginia, in Convention assembled, requested their delegates to present the name of Hon. JOHN W. DANIEL; but at his earnest request and insistance Virginia will not present his name as a candidate to this Convention.

Washington seconded the nomination of BLAND, of Missouri, through the Chairman of the delegation and promised him the electoral vote in November.

When West Virginia was called the Chair presented to the Convention Hon. J. W. ST. CLAIR, who addressed the Convention as follows:

Mr. ST. CLAIR: Mr. Chairman and Gentlemen of the Convention: I recognize on behalf of our delegation that you have presented to you names of many distinguished Democrats to-night. We honor BLAND, we venerate BOIES, we love MATTHEWS, we love McLEAN; we love all Democrats, but for purposes of this contest grander than them all is JOSEPH S. C. BLACKBURN, of the State of Kentucky. Gentlemen, who sounded the tocsin for free silver in this contest? JOE BLACKBURN. Gentlemen, this battle was not begun until the State of Kentucky held her Convention on the 5th day of last June. The people of this land watched that brave soldier, the nominee of the Democratic party for the Senate of the United States in the State of Kentucky fighting against odds, bolters, and every class of people who could concentrate their power and forces against him. After he went down before the Legislature the people stood by him on the 5th of June and gave him the flag of free silver to bear to this Convention. You say, gentlemen, that he has been a Confederate soldier. We, the people of the South, have paid our share of taxes. We have stood by the principles of our country and have helped to pay your pensions, and now let that issue be buried and give us a Southern candidate once more. Gentlemen, when the Democracy of the country gave to it a leader, you found in every instance not only a brave and courageous man, but a statesman as eminent as this continent has ever produced, and "JOE" BLACKBURN walks in his footsteps. You can make no mistake in giving BLACKBURN to our country and making him standard bearer of the Democratic party in 1896.

The Secretary resumed the calling of the roll of States. The State of Wisconsin being called, General EDWARD S. BRAGG said: Wisconsin cannot participate in nominating a Democrat to stand upon the platform.

Hon. JAMES MALONE, of Wisconsin, said: I arise to second the nomination of Senator BLACKBURN and the delegation from Wisconsin will express its views through Mr. E. J. Dockery.

Mr. Dockery: Gentlemen of the Convention: The undemocratic unit rule has throttled my vote in this great Convention. Whoever may be nominated by this Convention will receive, they tell us, no votes at the hands of those who represent the State of Wisconsin here. But I want to say to this Convention and through them to the people of this great Nation, that Wisconsin in November will cast her electoral votes for the nominee of this Convention. Gentlemen, the hour is late and I will not detain you by any extended speech. All I ask, gentlemen, at the hands of this Convention, is that it nominate the idol of this Convention, WILLIAM J. BRYAN, of Nebraska, and we will elect him.

General BRAGG, of Wisconsin, mounted his chair and said: We will, with your permission, search for another straggler and get another candidate for this Convention.

The Secretary then proceeded with the reading of the roll and Wyoming, Alaska, Louisiana, District of Columbia, New Mexico, Oklahoma, Indian Territory, announced that they had no candidates to present.

Upon the conclusion of the roll call Senator JONES, of Arkansas, moved that the Convention adjourn until 10 o'clock to-morrow morning.

A number of voices were raised in a demand that 12 o'clock be substituted for 10. The Chair put the motion which was adopted and the Convention adjourned to July 10, 1896, at 10 o'clock A. M.

FOURTH DAY.

MORNING SESSION.

Chicago, Ill., July 10, 1896.

The Convention was called to order by the Chairman, Senator White, at 11 o'clock a. m., in the following words:

Gentlemen, come to order. Prayer will be offered by Rev. Dr. Greene.

PRAYER.

Almighty God, unto whom all hearts are open, all desires known, and from whom no secrets are hidden, cleanse our hearts by the inspiration of Thy holy spirit, that we may perfectly love Thee and do those things that are pure and acceptable in Thy sight. As Thou hast given us another day, give us grace for its duties, and guide our minds, which are frail and feeble, by the infinite wisdom of Thy grace, that we may be kept from evil and from sin and be guided in the paths of righteousness.

We pray again for Thy blessing upon this representative assembly of the people of these United States. For the great concern of their duty, guide Thou them aright. Overrule their mistakes for good. Pardon, we pray Thee, all that Thou may find amiss in what is done, and whatever we may think and whatever we may be, over and above us may Thy kingdom come. May human life be made better and purer, and may the gospel of Thy blessed Son, our Savior, rule throughout all the world. We pray for our land and nation. Prosper us with plenty and with peace. Rule Thou over us, for Thou art mighty; and grant that that righteousness which exalteth a people may be ours, and that we may be free from that sin which is a reproach to any nation. And so unto Thee, Father, Son and Holy Ghost, we praise forever more. Amen.

At the conclusion of the prayer, the Chair said: The Chair requests gentlemen upon the floor and in the galleries to be as quiet as possible. Instead of making a vast amount of disturbance, try to hypnotize your neighbors into silence.

The Chair then recognized Hon. WILLIAM F. HARRITY, of Pennsylvania.

Mr. HARRITY: I desire to say, Mr. Chairman, that in obedience to the instructions given by the Democratic State Convention of Pennsylvania, the Pennsylvania delegation presents the name of Hon. ROBERT E. PATTISON, of Pennsylvania, as a candidate for the Presidency.

The Chair inquired if there were any other nominations. Mr. MATTINGLY, of the District of Columbia, secured recognition, and said:

"Last evening, before adjournment, the roll call was concluded rather unceremoniously. On behalf of the District of Columbia, I desire to second the nomination of the peerless champion of free silver, that great Democrat of Ohio and friend of the farmer and laboring man, JOHN R. McLEAN."

Mr. MILLER, of Oregon, then said: On behalf of the delegation of Oregon, we desire to present to this Convention the name of ex-Governor SYLVESTER PENNOYER for President of the United States.

THE CHAIR: Are there any other nominations? There being no response I will declare nominations for President closed, and order the Secretary to call the roll of States.

Mr. SMITH, of Ohio: On behalf of the Ohio delegation I wish to say that we have just received the news of the sudden and unexpected death of that eloquent Democrat, FRANK H. HURD, of Ohio, and we ask the Convention to join with us in our sorrow for the loss of our friend and our Democratic associate.

THE CHAIR: Does the gentleman from Ohio make any motion?

MR. SMITH: I do not think it is a matter on which a motion should be made.

THE CHAIR: The announcement is all that is desired at this time. Call the roll.

At this point Mr. RICHARDSON was called to the Chair.

The Clerk began by calling Alabama, the first State on the roll. TENNETT LOMAX, chairman of the delegation, said:

Mr. Chairman, there are a number of delegates from Alabama who desire to express their preferences in this vote. They are JOHN B. KNOX, H. B. FOSTER, S. J. CARPENTER, J. H. MINGE and D. R. BURGESS. They desire to cast their votes for that splendid type of New England Democracy, ex-Governor RUSSELL, of Massachusetts, but under the operation of the unit rule I cast the twenty-two votes of Alabama for HORACE BOIES, of Iowa.

Arkansas being called, sixteen votes were cast for BLAND.

California being challenged, the roll of delegates was called with the following result: BLACKBURN, 9; MATTHEWS, 2; BRYAN, 4; BOIES, 2; CAMPBELL, 1.

Colorado was passed at the request of its delegation.

When Connecticut was called ex-Governor WALLER, of that State, made the following announcement:

Mr. WALLER: Connecticut has twelve votes. Two of those twelve it casts for Governor RUSSELL, of Massachusetts.

Delaware being called, the chairman of the delegation said:

Delaware casts three votes for ROBERT E. PATTISON, of Pennsylvania, one for WILLIAM J. BRYAN, of Nebraska, two votes are not cast and those delegates have no desire to express as to the candidates of this Convention.

Florida gave two votes to BLAND and MATTHEWS and one each to BOIES, BRYAN, BLACKBURN and PATTISON.

Georgia cast twenty-six votes for BRYAN.

Idaho six for BLAND.

Illinois forty-six votes for BLAND.

Iowa twenty-six votes to HORACE BOIES.

Indiana recorded her vote as follows: Thirty votes for her great and distinguished Governor, CLAUDE MATTHEWS.

Kansas twenty votes for BLAND.

When Kentucky was called the chairman of the delegation announced that there were two gold men in her delegation, Mr. PHELPS and Mr. HALDEMAN, but under the unit rule Kentucky's twenty-six votes were cast for JOE BLACKBURN, of Kentucky.

Chairman BLANCHARD, of the Louisiana delegation: As the unit rule prevails in this state, its sixteen votes are for BRYAN. I am requested to state that Mr. MARSTON expresses his personal preference for BLAND.

Mr. MARSTON (holding in his hand a silver dollar): I only wish to say, sir, that the reason my preferences are given to RICHARD P. BLAND is because I hold a talisman in my hand which will carry us to victory in November.

Maine cast its vote, BLAND, 2; BRYAN, 2; PATTISON, 5; not voting 3.

Maryland: BRYAN, 4; PATTISON, 11; not voting, 1.

When Massachusetts was reached Delegate HAMILTON, of that State said:

Mr. HAMILTON: In the absence of the Chairman and the vice-Chairman of our delegation, the majority of the delegation desire that Massachusetts shall be passed for the present.

Mr. O'SULLIVAN, a delegate from the same State, said:

Mr. O'SULLIVAN: In the absence of the gold leaders of this delegation we demand the call of the roll. They are away because they intend to stay away.

THE CHAIR: The Chair will state that speeches are not in order in the midst of a roll call. Let us remember this, gentlemen. Massachusetts will be passed for the present.

When Michigan was called the Chairman of the delegation announced nine votes for BRYAN, four for BOIES, five for BLAND and ten not voting. Mr. STEVENSON challenged the vote, and the delegation was polled with the following result: BLAND, 4; BOIES, 5; BRYAN, 9; not voting, 10.

Mr. STEVENSON: I would like to know how Mr. POWERS in the Third District is recorded.

The Secretary informed him that Mr. POWERS voted for BLAND.

Mr. STEVENSON. He is not present, Mr. Chairman.

Mr. HUMMER, of Michigan: His alternate is here.

Mr. STEVENSON: His alternate is not here. Mr. CHESTER is his alternate and Mr. KNIGHT is the alternate for the other delegate, and I challenge the right of an alternate for another delegate to vote for Mr. POWERS.

THE CHAIR: That is a question of fact. If the delegation cannot tell what the fact is the Chair certainly cannot.

Mr. HUMMER: The fact is Mr. KNIGHT is here and has been acting all the time as Mr. POWERS' proxy.

THE CHAIR: Has any objection been made heretofore by any member of the delegation to his voting?

Mr. HUMMER: No.

THE CHAIR: Then the vote will stand.

Mr. STEVENSON: The record shows that Mr. CHESTER is the alternate for Mr. POWERS.

Mr. HUMMER: The record shows no such thing.

THE CHAIR: The gentlemen will resume their seats. The Chair has ruled.

The roll of the States continued as follows:

Minnesota: BOIES, 4; BRYAN, 2; BLACKBURN, 1; PATTISON, 2; STEVENSON, 1. Eight not voting.

Mississippi: BOIES, 18.

Missouri: BLAND, 34.

Montana: BLAND, 4; BLACKBURN, 2.

Nebraska: BRYAN, 16.

Nevada: MATTHEWS, 3; McLEAN, 3.

When New Hampshire was reached Mr. DOYLE announced the vote as follows: One vote for PATTISON, and seven declining to vote.

When New Jersey was reached the Chairman of that delegation announced that it declined to cast its vote.

THE CHAIR: Gentlemen will abstain from any manifestations of approval or disapproval of the votes in the future.

When New York was reached ex-Governor FLOWER said:

Mr. FLOWER: In view of the platform adopted by this Convention and of its action and proceedings I am instructed by the delegation from the State of New York to say that we decline to further participate in the selection of candidates for President and Vice-President, and therefore we decline to vote.

When North Carolina was called the Chairman said:

In view of the platform adopted by this Convention and the proceedings going before it, I am requested by the delegates of North Carolina to cast twenty-two votes for WILLIAM J. BRYAN.

The vote of Ohio was challenged and the Secretary called the roll of delegates. JOHN R. McLEAN, the first on the list was called, and his alternate voted as follows:

In the absence of Mr. McLEAN, I assume the duties of delegate and cast my vote for JOHN R. McLEAN.

The roll call proceeded, JOHN C. PATTERSON was called, and in his absence the Chairman of the delegation said:

Mr. PATTERSON directed me to cast his vote for JOHN R. MCLEAN.

Mr. HOLDEN: I object to this. Let his alternate cast his vote.

THE CHAIR: If the Chairman of the delegation states that he has authority to cast the vote of the delegate the Chair will accept his statement.

The vote of Ohio was announced as follows:

Absent, 2; BLAND, 1; MCLEAN, 40; BRYAN, 1; PATTISON, 1. The Chair then said that under the unit rule the 46 votes would be cast for MCLEAN.

Oregon: PENNOYER, 8.

Pennsylvania: PATTISON, 64.

Rhode Island: PATTISON, 6; 2 not voting.

South Carolina: TILLMAN, 17; not voting, 1.

This announcement having been received with hisses, Mr. POWERS, of Utah, said:

Mr. POWERS: I rise to a question of privilege; my question is whether, when delegates sitting here in convention permit guests to occupy the galleries, they are to be allowed to hiss when any Democrat is nominated or voted for in a National Convention, or whether this Convention will require them to conduct themselves as ladies and gentlemen, and whether they are here through our courtesy or not.

THE CHAIR: That is a very pertinent inquiry.

In the delegation of Rhode Island two delegates declined to vote.

South Carolina cast her seventeen votes for BENJAMIN R. TILLMAN.

When Tennessee was reached the Chairman of that delegation announced that under the unit rule he was instructed to cast the twenty-four votes of that State for BLAND.

Mr. BOYD: Mr. Chairman, I demand a poll of the vote of the delegation from Tennessee.

THE CHAIR: Does the gentleman from Tennessee deny that a majority of the delegation are for the candidate for whom the votes are cast?

Mr. BOYD: He does.

Mr. BATE: It is, perhaps, necessary for me to state that under the unit rule I was instructed to cast twenty-four votes for Mr. BLAND, but I will state that of this vote fourteen are for BLAND and ten for BOIES, but under the instructions of the delegation twenty-four votes are cast for BLAND.

THE CHAIR: The Chair will state that, it having been denied that a majority of the delegates are for the candidate named, the roll must be called regardless of the opinion of its Chairman.

Senator BATE: I desire it to be called.

The Secretary proceeded to call the roll of Tennessee.

The result of the vote was announced as follows: BLAND, 16; BOIES, 5; BRYAN, 3.

THE CHAIR: The Chair suggests that when gentleman demand a roll call upon a specific statement that a wrong has been done in the announcement they should advise themselves accurately. Go on with the roll call.

Texas: BLAND, 30.
Utah: BLAND, 6.
Vermont: BRYAN, 4; not voting, 4.
Virginia: BLACKBURN, 24.
West Virginia: BLACKBURN, 12.

When Washington was called the Chairman of the delegation said:

There are in this delegation five silver men and three gold standard men. The State of Washington desires to cast her vote for a man who can stand upon the platform and win upon the platform. She therefore casts one vote for WILLIAM J. BRYAN and seven votes for RICHARD P. BLAND.

When Wisconsin was called General BRAGG was recognized and said:

General BRAGG: Wisconsin has not directed her delegates how and when to vote. Therefore she declines at present to vote.

Mr. HOLDGATE: The delegation of the State of Wisconsin not having been polled, and being instructed to vote as a unit when the vote has been polled, I ask for a calling of the roll.

THE CHAIR: Is there any denial that there is a unit rule in Wisconsin, General BRAGG?

General BRAGG: I have the rule in my hand, and there are thirty-five copies of it in the credentials from our State. It is a part of the agreement by which we took our seats upon the floor. We have precocious children in our State and the instruction was given to keep them from —

General BRAGG was interrupted by cries of "Call the roll," many of them coming from Virginia and West Virginia. When quiet reigned sufficiently he continued:

General BRAGG: The gentlemen from West Virginia or from old Virginia cannot direct the Democracy of Wisconsin how they shall act or how they shall vote.

Mr. HOLDGATE, of Wisconsin, was then recognized by the Chairman and said:

Mr. HOLDGATE: I have the directions, the original, certified, right here, wherein it is said "We hereby direct the delegates from Wisconsin to the National Democratic Convention to be held at Chicago on July 7 next to vote as a unit on all subjects and candidates when and as a majority of the delegation may direct." We are directed to vote as a unit when we are polled.

General BRAGG: The Wisconsin delegation upon its meeting yesterday, voted twenty votes to four to sustain and conform to the instructions of its State, and to make up that four the gentleman who challenged the count was counted as one.

The delegation roll was then ordered called. When General BRAGG's name was called he said:

General BRAGG: I decline to vote, and I am instructed by twenty of our delegation to cast their votes as I cast mine.

The Secretary then called the name of WILLIAM F. VILAS, who said:

Mr. VILAS: Mr. Chairman, the delegation from Wisconsin was instructed to vote as a unit when the majority of the delegation directed. I have, as one, voted to direct the Chairman to withhold the vote of Wisconsin.

Mr. VILAS's name was again called, in answer to which he said:

Mr. VILAS: I decline to vote.

The name of JAMES D. FLANDERS was then called. He said:

Mr. FLANDERS: Mr. Chairman, in accordance with the instruction of our State Convention, instructing us to vote when and as directed by the majority of the delegation, and having been instructed by the majority of that delegation not to vote, I decline to cast my vote for a candidate for President upon this platform.

The Secretary then called the name of JAMES J. HOGAN, who said:

Mr. HOGAN: Under the instruction, I decline to vote.

GEORGE M. MCKEE also stated that he declined to vote. Under instructions THOMAS M. KEARNEY said he respectfully declined. There was no response to the call of JAMES E. MALONE. When WILLIAM H. ROGERS was called, General BRAGG arose, and said:

General BRAGG: He declines to vote, and so instructed me.

Dr. HERMANN GASSER also declined. In response to his name Dr. W. A. SYNON said:

Dr. SYNON: I place a different construction on the instructions, and I vote for W. J. BRYAN.

WILLIAM BERGENTHAL, M. C. MEADE, Dr. HENRY BLANK, H. P. HAMILTON, JOHN J. WOOD, JR., declined to vote. When ROBERT LEES' name was called General BRAGG said he was instructed on behalf of Mr. LEES to decline to vote. A. C. LARSON voted for BRYAN. JOHN L. BRENNAN and JOHN WATTAWA both declined to vote. E. J. DOCKERY and AMOS HOLGATE voted for BRYAN. R. J. SHIELDS and W. F. MCNALLY both declined to vote.

As soon as the Secretary had completed the polling of the delegation from Wisconsin the Chair recognized Senator MONEY, of Mississippi, who said:

Senator MONEY: I make this point of order, that when a delegation is instructed to vote as a unit, and any number of these gentlemen decline to vote, they cannot stifle the voice of a delegate who does desire to vote.

THE CHAIR: For information, the Chairman will have read the instruction of the Wisconsin delegation.

The Secretary read the instruction referred to, which is as follows:

We hereby direct the delegates from Wisconsin to the Democratic National Convention, to be held in Chicago, July 7, next, to vote as a unit on all subjects and candidates when and as a majority of the delegation may direct.

The Chair then recognized General BRAGG, who stood upon a chair in the Ohio delegation, and said:

General BRAGG: I make a point of order, Mr. Chairman, on that vote.

Mr. SMITH, of Ohio: He does not represent Ohio.

Ex-Governor HOGG invited General BRAGG to speak from the Texas delegation, and helped him upon a chair.

General BRAGG: I make the point of order that the vote of Wisconsin, under its instructions, must be entered as declining to vote. The instruction reads: "To vote as a unit on all subjects and candidates when and as a majority of the delegation may direct." There are but four votes cast in our delegation out of twenty-four here, contrary to the wish of the majority, and unless this Convention seeks to make that four a majority of twenty-four they cannot bind the twenty nor disgrace our State by forcing it to vote the way those gentlemen wish.

Mr. DOCKERY, of Wisconsin, speaking from the platform, said:

Mr. DOCKERY: Gentlemen of the Convention: I am one of the men who are standing before this Convention asking for the privilege of casting a vote. The gentleman who stands here and acts as the spokesman for Wisconsin (General BRAGG) claims the privilege of sitting in this great Convention and refusing to cast any vote upon any subject. We ask that those of us who are ready and willing to cast our vote be permitted to vote and that they be received.

The resolution which was passed by the Convention in the State of Wisconsin gave to those gentlemen the right to say that a majority of that Convention should control the votes of the delegates here, but there are no words in that resolution which say that they forbid us to vote if we desire. Four of us stand here and cast our votes in harmony with this Convention, and being the only votes that are cast here, we claim that we, and we alone, are the members of that delegation who should be heard; and if the great State of Wisconsin were able to give her voice to-day as to what her sentiments are, she would be for silver. If we cannot express our feelings and beliefs to-day, I want to say to you, gentlemen, as I said last night, we will give it to you in November. We appeal to this Convention, and we ask that those gentlemen either vote or allow us to vote.

Mr. FINLEY, of Ohio, rose to a point of order, and asked to have re-read the resolution of the Wisconsin Convention instructing its delegates. The Secretary read the resolution, and Mr. FINLEY said:

Mr. FINLEY: My point of order is that the delegation

may direct a vote, but by abstaining from voting it is not directing a vote, and that therefore the gentleman (Mr. DOCKERY) has the right to vote.

Mr. McCONNELL, of Tennessee: I move you, sir, that the delegates present and voting in any delegation in this Convention shall be entitled to cast—

THE CHAIRMAN (interrupting): That is out of order; out of order. There is a point of order pending before the house which has not been decided.

Mr. MONEY, of Mississippi: I ask the Chair if he has ruled upon the point of order that I made a while ago, or if he is ready to do so?

THE CHAIR: The Chair is ready to rule upon this question. The point raised by the delegation from Wisconsin is that its Convention directed the delegation from Wisconsin to vote as a unit on all subjects and candidates as a majority of the delegation may direct. That is the point of order. The Chair rules that this instruction is not an instruction to abstain from voting, but to regulate the voting of the delegation. The Chair further rules that when the roll is called a delegate absent shall be recorded as absent, and if a minority of the delegation vote, that their votes shall be individually recorded, but that the minority cannot cast the entire vote of the delegation. The vote of Wisconsin will be announced.

The Secretary announced the vote as follows: Declining to vote, 19; W. J. BRYAN, 4; BLACKBURN, 1.

The call of the States was proceeded with as follows:

Wyoming: PATTISON, 5.

Alaska: BLAND, 6.

Arizona: BLAND, 6.

District of Columbia: BOIES, 1; McLEAN, 5.

New Mexico: BLAND, 6.

Oklahoma: BLAND, 6.

Indian Territory: BLAND, 6.

The Chair then directed that those States which had been omitted should be called, which was done. California was first called, and the missing votes were recorded.

Colorado was then called and cast her eight votes for HENRY M. TELLER.

The vote of Massachusetts was recorded as follows: PATTISON, 3; STEVENSON, 5; BLAND, 2; HILL, 1; BRYAN, 1; those absent and declining to vote, 18.

On motion of GEORGE B. HUMMER, of Michigan, the name of JOHN B. SHIPMAN was called and he cast his vote for BRYAN.

The Chair recognized a delegate from Minnesota, who stated that two members of the delegation, who had come in since the roll call, desired to have their votes recorded.

THE CHAIR: Hereafter, if there should be another roll call, the Chair will not go back, unless it be where a State was passed by consent; and, unless the entire delegation of a State desires to change its vote, there will not be undivided changes made during the counting of the ballot, nor until after the first announcement is made. The Secretary will foot the returns, and until that is done no further business will be transacted.

The following is the result of the first ballot as finally corrected:

DEMOCRATIC NATIONAL CONVENTION.

FIRST BALLOT.

STATES.	Total Vote	Bryan	Bland	Boies	Matthews	McLean	Pattison	Blackburn	Stevenson	Teller	Russell	Tillman	Campbell	Pennoyer	Hill	Not Voting
Alabama	22		22													
Arkansas	16	16														
California	18	4		2	2		9					1				
Colorado	8									8						
Connecticut	12										2					10
Delaware	6	1				3										2
Florida	8	1	2	1	2	1	1									
Georgia	26	26														
Idaho	6		6													
Illinois	48	48														
Indiana	30					30										
Iowa	26			26												
Kansas	20		20													
Kentucky	26							26								
Louisiana	16	16														
Maine	12	2	2			5										3
Maryland	16	4				11										1
Massachusetts	30	1	2			3		5							1	18
Michigan	28	9	4	5												10
Minnesota	18	2		4			2	1	1							8
Mississippi	18	18														
Missouri	34		34													
Montana	6		4							2						
Nebraska	16	16														
Nevada	6			3	3											
New Hampshire	8					1										7
New Jersey	20															20
New York	72															72
North Carolina	22	22														
North Dakota	6			6												
Ohio	46				46											
Oregon	8														8	
Pennsylvania	64					64										
Rhode Island	8						6									2
South Carolina	18											17				1
South Dakota	8	6				1										1
Tennessee	24		24													
Texas	30		30													
Utah	6		6													
Vermont	8	4														4
Virginia	24							24								
Washington	8	1	7													
West Virginia	12						12									
Wisconsin	24	4						1								19
Wyoming	6							6								
Alaska	6		6													
Arizona	6		6													
District of Columbia	6			1		5										
Oklahoma	6		6													
Indian Territory	6		6													
New Mexico	6		6													
Totals	930	137	235	67	37	54	97	82	6	8	2	17	1	8	1	178

The Secretary announced the result of the first ballot as follows:

Bland	235
Boies	67
Matthews	37
McLean	54
Bryan	137
Blackburn	82
Pattison	97
Pennoyer	8
Campbell	1
Russell	2
Stevenson	6
Tillman	17
Hill	1
Teller	8
Absent or not voting	178

THE CHAIR: The Secretary will call the roll of the States for the second ballot.

The Secretary then called the roll of the States.

Alabama the first State on the roll was called, and Mr. LANE of that delegation said:

Mr. LANE: In the poll of the Alabama delegation there was one absent, not voting. There were six for BRYAN, fifteen votes for "Silver Dick" BLAND of Missouri and I cast the twenty-two votes of Alabama for RICHARD P. BLAND.

Arkansas: BLAND, 16.

California having been reached the vote of the delegates was challenged and the polling resulted as follows: BLACKBURN, 5; BRYAN, 7; BLAND, 2; BOIES, 1; MATTHEWS, 2; McLEAN, 1.

When Maine was reached a delegate from that commonwealth desired to have the names of the delegates polled.

THE CHAIR: Does the gentleman claim that the vote of the delegation from that State has not been correctly announced?

Democratic National Convention.

The Delegate: I do not.

The Chair: The vote having been correctly announced the Chair declines to have any call of the roll.

When Massachusetts was reached Hon. John W. Corcoran said:

Mr. Corcoran: Mr. Chairman, I desire to have the list of delegates voting on the former ballot corrected. We cast now five votes for Stevenson as we did on the first ballot; three for Pattison, two votes for Bland, one for Hill, one for Bryan and one for Matthews, seventeen not voting.

When New Jersey was called Mr. McDermott, of that State, said:

Mr. McDermott: New Jersey desires to have two of her votes cast for Pattison.

The Secretary announced the vote as "two for Bryan," upon which Mr. McDermott said:—

Mr. McDermott: You can't come that on us. It was not two votes for Bryan, but two votes for Pattison.

The Secretary announced the vote as given and passed on to New York, which State declined to vote.

Under the operation of the unit law the whole vote of Ohio was cast for John R. McLean, but in explanation Mr. Long, Chairman of that delegation, stated that there was one vote for Bland, two for Pattison, seven for Bryan and three not voting.

Pennsylvania recorded her vote through Mr. Harrity, Chairman of the Pennsylvania Delgation, as "sixty-four votes for Pattison."

Tennessee was passed.

The Secretary then called Virginia and the Chairman of the delegation said:

I am requested to state that upon the poll there were six votes for Bryan, but under the operation of the unit rule the twenty-four votes are cast for Bland.

When Wisconsin was called General BRAGG said under instructions nineteen of the delegates declined to vote.

Mr. MALONE asked that the roll be called.

THE CHAIR: Under the ruling on the previous vote, four votes being cast for Mr. BRYAN and one for Mr. BLACKBURN, if there is no objection the vote will be so entered.

The vote was then announced as four for BRYAN, one for BLACKBURN and nineteen not voting.

When Arizona was called her chairman announced that she cast five votes for BLAND and one for BRYAN, but under the unit rule the six votes would be cast for BLAND.

At the conclusion of the list the Chair announced that the Clerk would call the States that had been passed. Minnesota was the first called. The Chair then stated that as the Chairman of the Minnesota delegation was unable to recapitulate the vote the Clerk would call the roll of the State. This was done, with the following result: BOIES, 2; BLACKBURN, 2; PATTISON, 1; BRYAN, 4; STEVENSON, 4; not voting, 5.

When the Secretary called the State of Tennessee, which had also been passed, Senator BATE, Chairman of the delegation, said:

Senator BATE: When the name of Tennessee was called her delegates were in consultation. In that consultation the delegation decided by a majority vote that her solid vote should be cast for RICHARD P. BLAND, of Missouri, and I hereby give 24 votes from Tennessee for RICHARD P. BLAND, of Missouri.

The Chairman of the delegation from California here arose and said:

Mr. Chairman, under the instructions from the California delegation I now desire to poll the vote differently: 14 for BRYAN; 1 for MATTHEWS; 2 for BLAND, and 1 for BOIES.

On the second ballot the roll call resulted as follows:

Bland... 281
Boies... 37
Matthews... 34
McLean... 53
Blackburn... 11
Pattison.. 100
Bryan... 197
Teller... 8
Stevenson... 10
Hill... 1
Pennoyer.. 8
Not voting.. 160

The following is the ballot as corrected:

SECOND BALLOT.

STATES.	Total	Bryan	Bland	Boies	Matthews	McLean	Pattison	Blackburn	Stevenson	Teller	Pennoyer	Hill	Not Voting
Alabama	22		22										
Arkansas	16		16										
California	18	14	2	1	1								
Colorado	8									8			
Connecticut	12						2						10
Delaware	6	1					3						2
Florida	8	2		1	1	2	1		1				
Georgia	26	26											
Idaho	6		6										
Illinois	48		48										
Indiana	30				30								
Iowa	26			26									
Kansas	20		20										
Kentucky	26							26					
Louisiana	16	16											
Maine	12	2	2				5						3
Maryland	16	4					11						1
Massachusetts	30	1	2		1		3		5			1	17
Michigan	28	28											
Minnesota	18	4		2			1	2	4				5
Mississippi	18	18											
Missouri	34		34										
Montana	6		6										
Nebraska	16	16											
Nevada	6					6							
New Hampshire	8						1						7
New Jersey	20						2						18
New York	72												72
North Carolina	22	22											
North Dakota	6				6								
Ohio	46					46							
Oregon	8										8		
Pennsylvania	64						64						
Rhode Island	8						6						2
South Carolina	18	18											
South Dakota	8	7					1						
Tennessee	24		24										
Texas	30		30										
Utah	6		6										
Vermont	8	4											4
Virginia	24		24										
Washington	8	1	7										
West Virginia	12						12						
Wisconsin	24	4					1						19
Wyoming	6	6											
Alaska	6		6										
Arizona	6		6										
District of Columbia	6	3	1	1		1							
New Mexico	6		6										
Oklahoma	6		6										
Indian Territory	6		6										
Totals	930	197	281	37	34	53	100	41	10	8	8	1	160

At this point of the proceedings E. W. MARSTON, of Louisiana, said: "Mr. Chairman!"

THE CHAIR. For what purpose does the gentleman arise?

Mr. MARSTON: I move, sir, that it is the sense of this Convention that the majority should rule, and that the two-thirds precedent heretofore governing Democratic Conventions is a cowardly subterfuge, and should be repealed.

Mr. JONES, of Arkansas: Mr. Chairman, I rise to a point of order. My point is this: That under the rules governing this Convention any resolution or motion looking to a change of these rules must be referred to the Committee on Rules, considered by them and reported back to the Convention for its action.

THE CHAIR: The Chair sustains the point of order.

Mr. MARSTON: I appeal from the Chair to this Convention, and on that motion I desire to address the Convention on the appeal.

Mr. MARSTON took the platform to state his point. Before he began the Chairman said:

THE CHAIR: The Chair desires to state the question. The gentleman from Louisiana (Mr. MARSTON) on the right of the Chair has offered a resolution to the effect that the two-thirds rule be abrogated and repealed.

Mr. MARSTON: No, no.

THE CHAIR: Will the gentleman (Mr. MARSTON) state his own motion without debate.

Mr. MARSTON: My motion is that it is the sense of this Convention that the majority should rule, and that the precedent established by Democratic Conventions heretofore upon the two-thirds rule is a cowardly subterfuge.

THE CHAIR: The Chair decides that the gentleman from Louisiana has not made any motion. In order to be entirely fair the Chair will state that the gentleman desires to offer a resolution repealing the two-thirds rule, as he understands it.

Mr. MONEY, of Mississippi: I move that this motion be referred to the Committee on Rules and Order of Business without debate.

THE CHAIR: The gentleman from Arkansas (Mr. JONES) has made a point of order, which is pending, and therefore the motion of the gentleman would not be in order until the point of order is disposed of.

Mr. MONEY: Then, under the rules, it is referable only to the Committee on Rules without debate.

Mr. BLANCHARD: I am directed by the delegates from Louisiana to state that the gentleman from Louisiana on the stand (Mr. MARSTON) in making the motion that he did, did not do so by the direction of the delegation from Louisiana, and I am further requested by the delegation to move to lay his motion on the table.

THE CHAIR: The Chair will now decide the question of order, which has first to be disposed of. The gentleman from Arkansas (Mr. JONES) has made the point of order that this motion by the gentleman from Louisiana (Mr. MARSTON) must first be considered by the Committee on Rules, and the Chair sustains the point of order and the Clerk will proceed with the call of the roll for a third ballot.

Mr. MARSTON: You will hear from me later.

The call of the roll for a third ballot being ordered, the Secretary proceeded to call the roll of States.

When the State of Ohio was called the Chairman of the delegation announced that Ohio, under the unit rule, would cast 46 votes for McLEAN, but the preferences had been pressed by individual delegates as follows: Not voting, 2; PATTISON, 2; BLAND, 1; BRYAN, 10.

When Alabama was reached, Mr. TENNETT LOMAX said:

Mr. LOMAX: I rise to make a statement in reference to the Alabama delegation. Upon the poll of this delegation there were two absent and not voting, six voting for BRYAN and the rest for BLAND. Under the unit rule I cast the vote of Alabama for Mr. BLAND.

The following is the result of the third ballot:

DEMOCRATIC NATIONAL CONVENTION.

THIRD BALLOT.

STATES	TOTAL	BRYAN	BLAND	BOIES	MATTHEWS	McLEAN	PATTISON	BLACKBURN	STEVENSON	HILL	NOT VOTING
Alabama	22	22									
Arkansas	16		16								
California	18	13	2	1	1		1				
Colorado	8	8									
Connecticut	12						2				10
Delaware	6	1					3				2
Florida	8	5			3						
Georgia	26	26									
Idaho	6		6								
Illinois	48		48								
Indiana	30					30					
Iowa	26			26							
Kansas	20		20								
Kentucky	26							26			
Louisiana	16	16									
Maine	12	2	2				5				3
Maryland	16	5					10				1
Massachusetts	30	1	2				3		5	1	18
Michigan	28	28									
Minnesota	18	9	1						2		6
Mississippi	18	18									
Missouri	34		34								
Montana	6		6								
Nebraska	16	16									
Nevada	6					6					
New Hampshire	8						1				7
New Jersey	20						2				18
New York	72										72
North Carolina	22	22									
North Dakota	6			6							
Ohio	46					46					
Oregon	8	5	2			1					
Pennsylvania	64						64				
Rhode Island	8						6				2
South Carolina	18	18									
South Dakota	8	7					1				
Tennessee	24		24								
Texas	30		30								
Utah	6		6								
Vermont	8	4									4
Virginia	24		24								
Washington	8	1	7								
West Virginia	12	1	7	2					2		
Wisconsin	24	3	2								19
Wyoming	6	6									
Alaska	6		6								
Arizona	6		6								
District of Columbia	6	4		1		1					
New Mexico	6		6								
Oklahoma	6		6								
Indian Territory	6		6								
Totals	930	219	291	36	34	54	97	27	9	1	162

The Secretary announced the result of the third ballot as follows:

```
Bland..................................................291
Boies...................................................36
Matthews...............................................34
McLean.................................................54
Bryan.................................................219
Blackburn..............................................27
Pattison...............................................97
Stevenson..............................................9
Hill....................................................1
Absent and not voting................................162
```

Immediately upon the announcement of this vote the Chair directed the Secretary to call the roll for the fourth ballot, which was then proceeded with.

When Wisconsin was reached General BRAGG said:

General BRAGG: Mr. Chairman, the State of Wisconsin, by a vote of 19 of its delegates instructed by its State Convention have directed me to announce to this Convention that the 24 votes of Wisconsin are not voting.

THE CHAIR: The roll-call having been finished, the secretaries will compute the result.

Pending the computation the Pennsylvania delegation withdrew from the hall for consultation.

Illinois also withdrew for a like purpose.

The Secretary announced the result of the fourth ballot as follows:

```
Bland.................................................241
Boies..................................................33
Matthews..............................................36
McLean.................................................46
Bryan.................................................280
Blackburn..............................................27
Pattison...............................................97
Stevenson..............................................8
Hill....................................................1
Absent or not voting.................................161
Whole number of votes cast...........................768
Necessary to a choice................................512
```

The following is the fourth ballot in detail:

DEMOCRATIC NATIONAL COMMITTEE.   321

FOURTH BALLOT.

STATES	TOTAL	BLAND	BOIES	BRYAN	MATTHEWS	BLACKBURN	PATTISON	MCLEAN	STEVENSON	HILL	NOT VOTING OR ABSENT
Alabama	22			22							
Arkansas	16	16									
California	18	2	1	12	2	1					
Colorado	8			8							
Connecticut	12						2				10
Delaware	6			1			3				2
Florida	8			5	3						
Georgia	26			26							
Idaho	6			6							
Illinois	48	48									
Indiana	30				30						
Iowa	26		26								
Kansas	20			20							
Kentucky	26					26					
Louisiana	16			16							
Maine	12	2		2			5				3
Maryland	16			5			10				1
Massachusetts	30	2		1			3		5	1	18
Michigan	28			28							
Minnesota	18	1		10					2		5
Mississippi	18			18							
Missouri	34	34									
Montana	6	6									
Nebraska	16			16							
Nevada	6			6							
New Hampshire	8						1				7
New Jersey	20						2				18
New York	72										72
North Carolina	22			22							
North Dakota	6		6								
Ohio	46							46			
Oregon	8			8							
Pennsylvania	64						64				
Rhode Island	8						6				2
South Carolina	18			18							
South Dakota	8			7			1				
Tennessee	24	24									
Texas	30	30									
Utah	6	6									
Vermont	8			4							4
Virginia	24	24									
Washington	8	6		2							
West Virginia	12	10		1						1	
Wisconsin	24			5							19
Wyoming	6			6							
Alaska	6	6									
Arizona	6	6									
District of Columbia	6			5	1						
New Mexico	6	6									
Oklahoma	6	6									
Indian Territory	6	6									
Total	930	241	33	280	36	27	97	46	8	1	161

THE CHAIR: The proceedings of the Convention have reached a stage when it is necessary for the Chairman to announce his construction of the rule with reference to the two-thirds vote. A careful examination of the records heretofore made leaves open to the Chair but one decision.

The last Democratic Convention adopted rules which we have re-enacted here. Among others they adopted the rules of the last Convention. On page 29 of the official record of the last Convention I find a reference to the antecedent rule which has stood upon this record without objection ever since.

It was adopted in the Ohio Convention of 1852, and in so far as is pertinent here it is as follows: that two-thirds of the whole number of votes given shall be necessary for a nomination for President or Vice-President.

The rules of the House of Representatives, which have also been adopted, are clear and positive that when a quorum is ascertained, that the rule which I am now about to enforce must be held the true and proper rule of conduct and therefore, in the opinion of the Chair, two-thirds of the vote given will nominate a candidate for President and Vice-President of the United States.

THE CHAIR: The Secretary will again call the roll.

Mr. MARSTON, of Louisiana: I appeal from the Chair to the Convention.

THE CHAIR: You can appeal later, when the result is announced.

The Secretary then called the roll of States.

When Kentucky was called, Hon. OLLIE JAMES, the Chairman of its delegation, said:

Mr. JAMES: Mr. Chairman: While Kentucky loves her great Democrat and would be glad to see him President of the United States, yet because he was in the Confederate army they seem not to want him. Therefore we take great pleasure in casting the twenty-six votes of Kentucky for the world's greatest orator, WILLIAM J. BRYAN.

Ohio cast her 46 votes for McLEAN, but the Chairman

of the delegation stated that there were 9 preferences for BRYAN; 1 for BLAND; 2 for PATTISON and 2 not voting.

The roll call having been completed in regular course, the Secretary returned to call the names of the States which had been passed. Upon the second call the State of West Virginia was still not ready to vote.

Illinois upon the second call cast her forty-eight votes for WILLIAM J. BRYAN.

Mr. McLEAN, of Ohio, said: Ohio withdraws the name of JOHN R. McLEAN and casts forty-six votes for WILLIAM J. BRYAN.

Ex-Governor STONE, of Missouri: Mr. Chairman and Gentlemen of the Convention: Two or three days since I received this note (holding up a letter) which I will now read in your hearing, from RICHARD PARKS BLAND.

"I wish it to be understood that I do not desire the nomination unless it is the judgment of the free silver delegates that I would be the strongest candidate. If it should at any time appear that my candidacy is the least obstruction to the nomination of any candidate who is acceptable to the free coinage delegates in the Convention, or one more acceptable to a majority of those delegates than myself, I wish my name at once unconditionally withdrawn from further consideration. I am willing to waive the State instructions for me if need be and let the free silver delegates decide the whole matter. The cause must be put above the man."

I came to this great city as one of the delegates from Missouri, voicing the sentiment of the Democracy of that State to present for your deliberate consideration the name of that illustrious commoner, for whom many of you have expressed preference by your votes in this Convention. To those who have been our friends in the struggle, I desire now to return my grateful appreciation. But, following the directions of Mr. BLAND himself, that whenever a majority of the silver delegates in this Convention shall have expressed a preference for another he desired his name unconditionally and peremptorily withdrawn, I now, in the name of Missouri, lower the standard under which we have fought throughout this Convention, and in its place I lift that of the gifted and glorious son of Nebraska.

Gentlemen, we have chosen a splendid leader, beautiful as Apollo, intellectual beyond comparison, a great orator, a great scholar, but above all, beating in his breast there is a heart that throbs in constant sympathy with the great masses of the people and instinct with the highest sentiments of patriotism.

We will not only nominate him, but I believe, with as much confidence as I can believe anything in the future, that we will elect him by an overwhelming majority in November, and that we will inaugurate not only a Democratic administration at Washington, but one which at its close will be set down as among the purest and ablest and the most illustrious of American history. So now, gentlemen, I withdraw the name of RICHARD PARKS BLAND, and cast the thirty-four votes of our State for WILLIAM J. BRYAN, of Nebraska.

THE CHAIR: I present to the Convention A. VAN WAGENEN, of Iowa.

Mr. VAN WAGENEN: Gentlemen of the Convention: When the delegation from Iowa came to Chicago they bore with them a message from our great Democratic leader. It was this: "I have in my heart but one desire, and that is the success of the great cause in which we are all engaged." He said to us: "If I am not nominated at Chicago it will be no personal disappointment to me. If the cause for which we are fighting shall not succeed in November it will be a great personal disappointment to me. My advice and my request to you is that, notwithstanding your strong instructions, if, when you get to the Chicago Convention, you are satisfied there is any man who can poll more votes than I, I ask you to cast the vote of Iowa for him." Now, my friends, while we have great confidence in HORACE BOIES, while we have understood here what was his strength, perhaps as you do not, we at this time believe, after looking at this great assemblage, that WILLIAM J. BRYAN, of Nebraska, can poll more votes than any other candidate before this Convention. I am, therefore, instructed by the delegation from Iowa to withdraw Governor BOIES' name from your consideration, and cast our 26 votes for WILLIAM J. BRYAN, of Nebraska. I want further to say to you, right here, that, his health permitting, you will find Governor BOIES upon the stump for Mr. BRYAN, and, we believe, knowing his great power as an orator, his great character as a man, that you will find no other such an ally upon the stump for this great cause in November. I thank you, gentlemen, for your kind attention.

The Secretary announced that Iowa cast her 26 votes for W. J. BRYAN. The Chair then recognized Senator JONES, of Arkansas, the Chairman of the Arkansas delegation, who said:

Senator JONES: The name of RICHARD P. BLAND having been withdrawn, the State of Arkansas desires to change her vote from BLAND to BRYAN.

The Chair then recognized the Chairman of the Montana delegation, who addressed the Convention as follows:

Mr. CHAIRMAN: The delegation from Montana has been placed between the two great states of Missouri and Nebraska. We have upon each ballot cast our votes unanimously for our first choice, RICHARD P. BLAND. But, as we have stood by Mr. BLAND from first to last, we just as cheerfully now give our votes to the man from Nebraska—to WILLIAM J. BRYAN.

After considerable effort the Chairman succeeded in restoring sufficient order for Senator TURPIE, who had come upon the stand, to be heard.

Senator TURPIE said: Mr. Chairman and Gentlemen of the Convention: The delegation from our State has stood first to last by our distinguished Chief Executive of Indiana, but I am now authorized by the delegation from Indiana and the great Democratic constituency which it represents, to cast the 30 votes of our State for W. J. BRYAN, of Nebraska. Mr. President, I also further move you and the delegates of this Convention, in the interest of unity, which should make unanimity—I move that the nomination of W. J. BRYAN for the office of President of the United States be made unanimous.

Gov. CULBERSON, of Texas: Mr. Chairman, in view of the fact that the friends of Mr. BLAND have withdrawn his name from this contest, I am instructed by the majority of the delegates from Texas to cast the votes of that State for WILLIAM J. BRYAN.

A TEXAS DELEGATE: I am one of the minority, and I refuse to change my vote to BRYAN. I want to say further, Mr. Chairman, that no man of the same capacity—

At this point the Chair ruled that the delegate was out of order.

Mr. EVANS, of Utah, came upon the platform, was recognized by the Chair and spoke as follows:

Mr. CHAIRMAN: Young Utah desires to cast its 6 votes for young WELLINGTON J. BRYAN, and I second the motion that his nomination be made unanimous.

Following is the fifth and final ballot on the presidential nomination, as changed and corrected:

DEMOCRATIC NATIONAL CONVENTION.   327

FIFTH BALLOT.

STATES.	Total	Bryan	Bland	Pattison	Stevenson	Hill	Turpie	Not Voting
Alabama	22	22						
Arkansas	16	16						
California	18	18						
Colorado	8	8						
Connecticut	12			2				10
Delaware	6	1		3				2
Florida	8	8						
Georgia	26	26						
Idaho	6	6						
Illinois	48	48						
Indiana	30	30						
Iowa	26	26						
Kansas	20	20						
Kentucky	26	26						
Louisiana	16	16						
Maine	12	4		4				4
Maryland	16	5		10				1
Massachusetts	30	6		3	2	1		18
Michigan	28	28						
Minnesota	18	11			2			5
Mississippi	18	18						
Missouri	34	34						
Montana	6	6						
Nebraska	16	16						
Nevada	6	6						
New Hampshire	8			1				7
New Jersey	20			2				18
New York	72							72
North Carolina	22	22						
North Dakota	6	4			2			
Ohio	46	46						
Oregon	8	8						
Pennsylvania	64			64				
Rhode Island	8			6				2
South Carolina	18	18						
South Dakota	8	8						
Tennessee	24	24						
Texas	30	30						
Utah	6	6						
Vermont	8	4						4
Virginia	24	24						
Washington	8	4	4					
West Virginia	12	2	7		2		1	
Wisconsin	24	5						19
Wyoming	6	6						
Alaska	6	6						
Arizona	6	6						
District of Columbia	6	6						
New Mexico	6	6						
Oklahoma	6	6						
Indian Territory	6	6						
Totals	930	652	11	95	8	1	1	162

The Chairman then put the motion of Senator TURPIE, from Indiana, to make the nomination unanimous and declared the vote carried. The Chairman declared an informal recess of an indefinite length. When quiet was partially restored the Reading Clerk announced that Chairman HARRITY, of the Democratic National Committee, informed the members of that Committee that in the event of the Convention adjourning *sine die* to-day there would be a meeting of the present Democratic National Committee held in the main parlor of the Palmer House on Saturday; but should a session of the Convention be held on Saturday, the hour of the meeting of the National Committee would be duly announced.

The Sergeant-at-Arms then announced, at the request of the Chair, that the Convention was in recess until 8 o'clock this evening.

The Convention thereupon took a recess until 8 o'clock P. M.

FOURTH DAY.

EVENING SESSION.

CHICAGO, ILL., July 10, 1896.

The Chairman, Senator WHITE, called the Convention to order at 8:55 P. M., in the following words:

THE CHAIR: The gentlemen will come to order. The Chair is requested to announce that after the nominations for Vice-President are made, whenever that may be, the Committee upon Notification will at once meet in the rooms of the Committee on Resolutions at the right of the Chairman's desk.

Permit me to introduce to you the eloquent and unsuccessfully protesting Chairman of the Wisconsin delegation, my friend General BRAGG.

General BRAGG: Gentlemen of the Convention: I rise, Mr. Chairman, on a question of State privilege; the gentlemen of the South know what that is (cries of louder). I have no fireman's trumpet with me. While the delegation of Wisconsin was to-day engaged in a private consultation as to what should be done by them in the future some gentleman (I suppose he was a gentleman—in fact, I know him to be such,) stole the colors of our State and passed them as the representation of my delegation and of my State into the trail of the victor, for whom we had refused to cast our votes. I make this statement not with regard to any gentleman who did it, but simply to place the State which I represent as its Chairman right, so that the record will show that we trailed not the Wisconsin "Badger" behind the votes of the majority of this Convention.

Mr. DOCKERY attempted to take the stand to answer General BRAGG's remarks.

General BRAGG said: If you make any personal remarks about me you will suffer for it.

THE CHAIR: The Chair knows the distinguished soldier from Wisconsin and believes that whatever asperity might exist between the gentlemen from Wisconsin ought not to enter into a National Convention. I am satisfied that the gentlemen in the end will be found supporting the ticket, and I refuse to recognize Mr. DOCKERY for the purpose of addressing the Convention on factional disputes.

The question before the Convention is the nomination of Vice-President of the United States. I present Governor STONE, of Missouri.

Governor STONE: Gentlemen of the Convention: Up to this date the attention of the Convention has been wholly absorbed with the platform to be made and the candidate to be named for the Presidency. The work so far done has been, in my judgment, so well done that it will receive the instant and enthusiastic approval of the people. But the work yet to be performed by this Convention is of great importance. We have yet to name a Democrat to be associated with our great leader upon the ticket. I believe, Mr. Chairman, that this important work ought not to be hastily or inconsiderately performed. It should, on the contrary, be performed after the most mature deliberation possible under the circumstances. So far no attention has been paid to this.

To the end that the delegates may have an opportunity to confer with each other and to arrive at a conclusion which in the end will strengthen the ticket, and to the end that no mistake shall be made, I desire to move that this Convention do now adjourn until 12 o'clock noon to-morrow.

Mr. HENRY, of Mississippi, moved to amend by making the hour 10 o'clock instead of 12 and Gov. STONE accepted the amendment.

Mr. MENZIES, of Indiana, demanded a call of the roll of

States, and the Chairman ordered the Secretary to call the roll, which was done, with the following result:

	Yeas.	Nays.
Alabama	22	
Arkansas	16	
California	18	
Colorado	8	
Connecticut		12
Delaware	1	33
Florida	8	
Georgia	26	
Idaho	6	
Indiana		30
Iowa	26	

At this point Mr. MORRIS obtained the recognition of the Chair and said:

Mr. MORRIS: Mr. Chairman: Illinois desires to be called.

THE CHAIR: Call the roll of Illinois, if we are to be annoyed by such roll calls.

Mr. MORRIS: We do not want the roll called. We simply want to have our State called.

The Secretary again called the State of Illinois and Mr. MORRIS said:

Mr. MORRIS: Illinois, in order that no mistakes may be made, insists that there be an adjournment until to-morrow morning and casts forty-eight votes yea.

The roll call was proceeded with as follows:

	Yeas.	Nays.
Kansas	20	
Kentucky	26	

Mr. DONOVAN, of Illinois, secured the attention of the Chair and demanded a call of the delegates. The Chair said:

THE CHAIR: Illinois shall have the opportunity. The delegate will please sit down.

The roll of delegates of the State of Illinois was called by the Secretary, with the following result:

THE CLERK: The State of Illinois casts 24 votes aye, 16 votes nay, 8 absent.

The Secretary continued the calling of the roll as follows:

	Yeas.	Nays.
Maine	12	..
Louisiana	16	..

The Secretary, continuing, called the roll of Maryland. A delegate from that State attempted to make an explanation and got as far as to say: We will agree—

THE CHAIR: What will you agree to?

THE DELEGATE: I want to say—

THE CHAIR: Call the roll.

The Secretary obeyed the instruction of the Chair and Maryland voted sixteen votes no. The Secretary proceeded calling Massachusetts next, which voted twenty-seven no, three not voting.

	Yeas.	Nays.
Michigan	28	..
Mississippi	18	..
Minnesota (7 absent)	11	..
Missouri	24	..
Montana	6	..
Nebraska	6	..
Nevada	16	..
New Hampshire, not voting	..	..
New Jersey, not voting	..	..
New York, declining to vote	..	..
North Carolina	22	..
North Dakota	6	..

When Ohio was called HORACE ALFORD, of that State, arose and said:

Mr. ALFORD: There has been no poll of the Ohio delegation, and the only way to cast a vote is by having the roll called.

THE CHAIR: I disagree with you. Take your seat.

Mr. ALFORD: I ask for a call of the roll.

THE CHAIR: It will not be called. Go and sit down.

Ohio was then called by the reading clerk and responded with 46 yeas.

	Yeas.	Nays.
Oregon	8	
Pennsylvania		69
Rhode Island		6
South Carolina	18	
South Dakota	8	
Tennessee	24	
Texas	30	
Utah	6	
Vermont		8
Virginia	24	
Washington	8	
West Virginia	10	2
Wisconsin	24	
Wyoming	6	
Alaska	6	
Arizona	6	
New Mexico	6	
Oklahoma	6	
Indian Territory	6	

A delegate from Rhode Island obtained recognition, and said that Rhode Island wanted a chance to vote, and the Chair said:

THE CHAIR: Well, what is the vote of Rhode Island?

The delegate said that Rhode Island desired to cast 6 votes no; and the Secretary recorded the votes accordingly.

The Secretary announced to the audience that the tickets without coupons would be good for admission to-morrow.

THE CHAIR: For everybody who does not talk too much.

Without waiting for the result of the roll call to be announced the Convention adjourned to July 11, 1896, at 10 o'clock A. M.

FIFTH DAY.

CHICAGO, ILL., July 11, 1896.

The Convention was called to order by the Chairman, Senator WHITE, at eleven o'clock, in the following words:

THE CHAIR: The Convention will come to order. Mr. HARRITY, of Pennsylvania, desires to make an announcement.

Mr. HARRITY: Gentlemen of the Convention: Through the kindness of your Chairman I am permitted to announce that the meeting of the present Democratic National Committee which was called to meet in the main parlor of the Palmer House at 12 o'clock, noon, will not be held until 3 o'clock this afternoon, this change having been made necessary because of the session of the Convention this morning. The meeting of the present Committee will be held at 3 o'clock, and the members of the new Committee will be welcome, if they will attend.

General FINLEY, of Ohio: You will remember that the State of Michigan and the State of Nebraska, and perhaps one other, have not elected their members of the National Committee, and it was referred to the Committee on Permanent Organization. I have since learned that the Chairmen of these respective States have passed in the names of their National Committeemen. I now move that this Convention ratify and adopt the action of the Chairmen of these State Committees.

NICHOLAS M. BELL, of Missouri: The State of Missouri has not made any selection, but will do so in a few moments and will report.

General FINLEY: I will include the name of whatever gentleman the delegation of Missouri may select.

Senator TILLMAN, of South Carolina: I move that the doors of the Convention be thrown open to the public so that the people may occupy those vacant seats.

THE CHAIR: That has already been done.

Senator JONES, of Arkansas: I move that the roll of States be called, and that the speeches nominating candidates be limited to five minutes to each candidate.

This motion was adopted.

Mr. BELL, of Missouri: Missouri presents the name of Governor W. J. STONE as a member of the National Committee from that State.

Mr. G. V. MENZIES, of Indiana: We have selected for member of the National Committee JOHN G. SHANKLIN.

THE CHAIR: The question now is upon the ratification of the selections made by the various delegations for National Committeemen. If there is no objection it is so ordered.

The Chair then recognized Mr. O'SULLIVAN, of Massachusetts.

Mr. J. T. O'SULLIVAN: Mr. Chairman and Democrats of this Convention: I am a free coinage man from the Commonwealth of Massachusetts. I am here to present a man from that old Commonwealth for the suffrages of this Convention. He is not a millionaire and he has no money to offer in this contest for the people's rights. I come from a city and a district that BENJAMIN F. BUTLER represented in the Charleston Convention in 1860, and from which he bolted, but I do not bolt, nor do my people from whom I come.

In this great hall where were gathered 16,000 people we witnessed yesterday a scene unparalleled in the history of the world in time of war or in time of peace. We saw a man come here who had no voices pleading for him, nor a blare of trumpets to announce his candidacy; but he stood here and by the simple force of his magnificent presence he swept this Convention of delegates off its feet, and we, for the first time in many years, saw a representative Convention nominate a man who was not slated by its leaders. We were in the presence of a scene that rivaled the gatherings in the Coliseum in the days of Roman triumph, and the only incident in the history of the world that equals it is when NAPOLEON returned from Elba, and without striking a blow or firing a musket took an empire by the magic of his name. And the people of this country, in opposition to the daguerreotype imitation of a NAPOLEON, nominated by a HANNA-led Convention, have nominated a man from the loins of the people.

Now, you have given the South and West the platform. Carry the war into Africa and give us the candidate. We nominate a man from Massachusetts who had the courage of his convictions; who came out for silver in a country where fifty out of fifty-one bankers cannot tell what 16 to 1 means, while every boy west of the Missouri and south of Mason and Dixon's line can tell you that. Gentlemen, the war is over. If you want to answer that sullen delegation from New York that sits there, if you want to prove to the Nation that you turned down the illustrious leader of that State because he represented gold and not the East, you will come to the East for your candidate.

Gentlemen, I nominate a man who was once a gold man, but who saw the error of his way, and I propose to you, my friends, to have ocean join hands with ocean, to have the man from the wheat fields of Nebraska, where live the producers, join hands with the plain people of my country, where they go in the gray dawn of morning by the thousands to earn their bread by the sweat of their brows, as God Almighty told them; the consumers, who buy your wheat and who will vote for silver to give you a fair price for that wheat, in order that you may buy clothes and cloth from them; and I have the honor and the pleasure to name for Vice-President of the United States and this Republic a man whose voice has ever been raised against corporations, GEORGE FRED WILLIAMS, of Massachusetts.

The Chair says I have one minute more. I can do a great deal in a minute. I can tell you why the delegation from Massachusetts is divided on this issue. Two years ago in the grand old commonwealth, under the gilded dome of the State house, across to the east of which lies the shadow of Bunker

Hill, in which thronged the fathers of Concord and Lexington, GEORGE FRED WILLIAMS opposed the greedy schemes of the West End to buy the legislature. The president of the West End is HENRY WHITNEY; HENRY WHITNEY is the brother of the magnate of the Standard Oil Company from New York who sits here and does not vote, and who went into our organization and used his influence against GEORGE FRED WILLIAMS.

We do not want a man with a "barrel." We are going to inaugurate a new revolution here—a peaceful revolution—and when we want funds we will take the dimes and half-dollars of the people, and we will appeal for a popular subscription which will come from our friends who propose to prosper in their happy homes, which lie all the way from Texas to the great lakes on the north, and from ocean to ocean.

Mr. W. B. MARSTON: Gentlemen of the Convention: I assure you that I have not tasted a drop of water this morning. I rise upon this floor as a delegate from Louisiana, representing not myself alone upon the Louisiana delegation, as was proven yesterday when I undertook to take this floor. But, sir, before high heaven, I declare here in the presence of this assembled multitude, that I do represent the State of Louisiana. I come here by the unanimous consent of my district, and I come here, sirs, as a patriot. I am not a politician; I am simply a Louisiana planter; but my rights upon this floor I dare to maintain, and, sirs, looking over this whole situation and seeing the magnificent platform we have adopted, and the candidate we have put upon that platform to be landed next November in the White House—I say that I think it is necessary to put a man by his side—an old stager who is well broken into the harness—to keep this young colt, if necessary, in the traces. I know he is a thoroughbred, and therefore, we should take the better care of him.

Who is the grandest wheel-horse in the Democratic party? Which is the pivotal State of this Union? JOHN R. MCLEAN, of Ohio, is the man, and Ohio is the pivotal State. Nominate him, fellow delegates of this Convention, and we will sweep this country as a prairie on fire, and we will land our man in the Presidential house next November, and give the interests of this country into the keeping of the Democratic party of this nation for the next twenty-five years.

THE CHAIR: If there be no other nominations the Clerk will proceed to call the roll of States.

THOMAS MALONEY, of Washington: I don't want to get up on the platform, but I want to put in nomination JAMES HAMILTON LEWIS, of the great State of Washington.

THE CHAIR: Who are you anyway, and what do you want?

Mr. MALONEY: I am Delegate THOMAS MALONEY, of the great State of Washington.

THE CHAIR: Well, come up on the platform and say what you want to.

Mr. MALONEY: No, I won't go up on the platform. I will speak from the floor. In behalf of the State of Washington, I place in nomination her honored son, JAMES HAMILTON LEWIS. That will do; that's all I want to say.

THE CHAIR: I present Hon. J. H. CURRIE, of North Carolina.

Mr. CURRIE: Mr. Chairman and Gentlemen of the Convention: I come here to this platform to place in nomination a man who, I think, when I mention his name will be known not only within the confines of his own State, but from one end of this broad land to the other. I know not how it may be to-day, I know not who will lead this Convention; or what occasion may arise when such a baptism of patriotism will be poured out on it that may it make no mistake, but I name a man who will follow our great leader to victory. We are aware, Mr. Chairman, and I can congratulate this Convention on one thing, that they came here with one purpose, and that was to serve their country and the cause for which they have been battling for years. And I think it is the greatest compliment that can be paid to this Convention to say that there is not one single state, there is not one single banner, that was placed in the hands of this great Convention from any State it represented that was trailed, that was lowered, that was placed in jeopardy, but they all come here in obedience to their States, and the papers of this city paid this Convention a great compliment when they said that it was governed by a firm, determined, solid silver delegation from all the States that stand for silver. I say, Mr. Chairman and gentlemen of this Convention, that that is one of the things that we ought to be congratulated on, and if this Coliseum is to be the future place for the meetings of all the Conventions may we hope and pray that God in His majesty will rule all Conventions of all parties who come here in obedience to the wish and to do the will of their constituents, and show to the world that they were not for sale, that they would not waver in the ranks, but stand steady to do the duty which was placed upon them.

Gentlemen of the Convention, I come to place in nomination a man who is revered and honored in his own State and all over the country where he is known; and what can a man ask more than to be honored by all the people? In the last election he was the nominee of the great Democratic party of North Carolina for a position on the supreme bench. He received the indorsement of all his party, and received the votes of the two other parties, both Republican and Populist.

Now, my fellow countrymen and gentlemen of this Convention, there is no man—there is no citizen of North Carolina that would have this Convention do other than the very wisest thing—place the strongest man that you can possibly find in the lead with that great champion that is now holding the banner of Democracy, and I will place in nomination the name of Judge WALTER CLARK, our honored and gifted son on the supreme bench of North Carolina.

The Chair introduced Mr. THOMAS JOHNSON as follows:

THE CHAIR: Gentlemen of the Convention. It gives me great pleasure now to present to you a gentleman who seems to be well known to many of you. I had the honor to serve in two Congresses at Washington with this gentleman. I saw him there when the WILSON tariff bill was under consideration, and although he stood upon the floor and admitted that he belonged, or that he knew of the steel trust, as it was called— the trust for the manufacture of steel rails—and although he was engaged in a business occupation which derived immense profits from that trust, he had the honor and the courage to vote and contend that steel rails should be put upon the free list. I present to you the big hearted, the honest, the brave and courageous Tom Johnson, of Ohio.

Mr. Johnson: Mr. Chairman, Ladies, Gentlemen and Fellow Democrats: I come before you to-day to put in nomination for the Vice Presidency George W. Fithian, of Illinois. He was six years a member of Congress; and his action on every vote there places him in entire accord with our platform, and he has the merit; and I think the thing that is absolutely necessary for the Vice Presidency, he is not a wealthy man. This fight will have to be won by the plain people, by the people on one side who are interested in humanity against property on the other side. If it is a race between money and men, gentlemen, money will be altogether on the other side. What few wealthy Democrats the Democratic party had have mostly gone over to the support of McKinley. You cannot win this fight except you stand for humanity, and I am not a free silver man. But I do believe that the Democratic party has started a great revolution for the interests of the people; and in free silver, although I think it is wrong, you have a movement for the good of humanity, and therefore I am with you heartily.

Make not the mistake of thinking that you can, by merely nominating men with money, accomplish anything. It will chill the ardor of this Convention; it will chill the people. Have both men poor men. Mr. Fithian fills the bill. He was an honorable member of Congress; he comes from a State that is pivotal; he is in just the position to add to the strength of the ticket, and I hope to God you will nominate him.

The Chair then introduced Mr. Miller, of Oregon.

Hon. M. A. Miller: Mr. Chairman and Fellow Democrats of the National Convention: I rise before you this morning to place in nomination for the office of Vice President a man who will unite under our banner all the labor movements in this country; a man who comes from the common people; a man who has been twice elected Governor of the great State of Oregon as a Democratic nominee, notwithstanding the fact that the State was 10,000 Republican; a man who has recently been almost unanimously elected Mayor of the great metropolis of the Northwest; who in all his acts has been for the common people of this country; and I say to you to-day, in all candor and in all honesty, that if you place upon this ticket, alongside of the distinguished WILLIAM J. BRYAN, of Nebraska, the name of the distinguished Governor of Oregon, SYLVESTER PENNOYER, you will make no mistake.

When PENNOYER was Governor of the great State of Oregon the railroad companies had trouble with their employes. He went upon the scene of action, and he said to those corporations: "Pay your men and you will have no more trouble." And the trouble ceased there, and he failed to call out the militia to protect the corporations of that State. He comes from the common people. His heart is in sympathy with this great movement. I say to you that PENNOYER will unite the people all over this country, and as election day approaches the name of PENNOYER will add strength and faith to the great labor movements, and this country will indorse him, and he will be triumphantly elected. I appeal to you to recognize the Pacific coast and place upon this ticket the name of SYLVESTER PENNOYER, of Oregon.

The Chairman then presented to the Convention WILLIAM R. BURK, of California.

Mr. BURK: Mr. Chairman and Ladies and Gentlemen of the Convention: What I say to you at this juncture I know in one respect will commend itself to you. I shall be brief. Gentlemen, taking into account the great mission which has called us into Convention, it seems to me that we should consider matters far beyond the reach of this great body. We should consider that there are people whom we represent who have to vote on this great question, and those people represent forty-seven of the great Northern States, starting from Maine, reaching to the Pacific, touching the Atlantic coast on the south and extending far beyond into the State of Texas. Therefore, Mr. Chairman, as I have said, geographical consideration should prompt us, as well as the question of ability.

It would not become me to say aught of any gentleman whose name has been brought before you in this connection. I would not say aught of the gentleman from North Carolina or from Oregon or from any of the great western States, but it seems to me that when we come to make up the remaining portion of this ticket we should consider those States beyond the Blue Ridge mountains, and in that connection I present a candidate who represents every element which is presented to you in your platform and in your distinguished candidate for the President, WILLIAM J. BRYAN. I take pleasure in presenting for your careful consideration the name of ARTHUR SEWALL, of Maine. Mr. President, it may be well said of him, in connection with the great questions involved in this matter and the interests which are before you, that he will fulfill the pledges which have been made by your platform at this time. You will make no mistake in nominating him.

The Chairman then presented J. D. SHEWALTER, of Missouri.

Mr. SHEWALTER: Mr. Chairman and fellow Democrats: I ask your attention for a short time, promising that I will not detain you but a few minutes. When a great crisis arises a great statesman is produced to meet it. Great issues produce great men. On yesterday the star of destiny took its flight westward and pointed its index finger to the fair and fertile plains of Nebraska, and the man whom you selected will be a modern MOSES, who will lead our people from the land of bondage into the regions of freedom.

Perish the thought that the utterances that were heard during the proceedings of this Convention that we were governed by sectional interests and sectional impulses in our choice. I say that we love rock-ribbed Massachusetts; we love her great and enduring fame. And here and now I say that we reverently bow at the base of Plymouth Rock and gather inspiration for the Democracy amid the high aspirations that cluster there. We revere and love the great State of New York. We admire her grand achievements for the Democracy in the past. We well remember that her virgin soil was pressed by the feet of those who have fought to fulfill the promises and carry out the principles of Democracy. We recall with pride her MORRISES, her TILDENS, her SEYMOURS, and the Democracy remembers with gratitude and reflects upon the magnificent service of her great Senator. We nominate a man in the interest of no section. We recognize as Democrats an indissoluble union of indissoluble and equal States, divided as the billows, but one as the sea.

I now go to the East and produce a name known to every delegate present for his distinguished services in the cause of humanity and Democracy; a statesman most profound; an orator eloquent; indeed, a man who, seizing the banner of the people in the people's righteous cause, threw it in the face of aggregated power and challenged it to the conflict. I name for the second place upon this ticket a man who will add strength to it; I name the man who in a Republican district was elected by an overwhelming majority to Congress; I nominate JOSEPH C. SIBLEY, of the grand commonwealth of Pennsylvania.

The Chair then introduced to the Convention C. S. THOMAS, of Colorado.

Mr. THOMAS: Mr. Chairman and Gentlemen of the Convention: My voice is in no condition this morning for speaking. I only desire to second a nomination already made. The West has secured the first place upon this ticket in the person of the brilliant and magnetic orator from Nebraska. We should turn our eyes now to the East and look to the solid attainments of a business man for the second choice on this ticket. We should unite as far as possible the diversified interest and feeling of the Democracy of the United States by placing upon the ticket as our second choice a man whose business interests, business experience, business training and life-long devotion to the cause of Democracy make him eminently fitted to fill out as a full and rounded whole the work which, so auspiciously begun, has up to this time been so well performed. In the ranks of the Democratic party for political distinction we recognize neither wealth nor poverty. Every man who expresses and by his conduct testifies his devotion to the great principles of our Democratic faith, regardless of his condition or standing, is entitled to respectful consideration at the hands of a National Convention.

A man has already been presented to the consideration of

this Convention, who all his life has been a devoted follower of Democratic faith. He obtained the inspiration of his belief from JEFFERSON and from JACKSON, and, inspired by the splendid diction and unanswerable logic of a great son of Kentucky years and years ago, became a disciple of the great bimetallic principle, which you have crystallized into a cardinal principle of Democratic faith by placing it in your platform.

This gentleman comes from one of the remote corners of the United States, where, if I am correctly informed, he was born; there he spent the best days of his young manhood, and there to-day he is enjoying in its full fruition the fruits, the harvest of a life well spent, and as a citizen has long enjoyed the confidence and esteem not only of his Democratic brethren but of all with whom he has come in contact.

I desire, therefore, without extended eulogy, although upon that name I might speak far greater length of time, perhaps, than would be consonant with your wishes, but I recognize that you desire to have the roll called as soon as possible without saying anything beyond this, that his name is that of a solid, conservative, sound substantial business man, whose interests are extensive and extended, the sails of whose vessels whiten the seas of the world; I desire to second the nomination of ARTHUR SEWALL, of Maine.

The Chair recognized Governor CULBERSON, of Texas.

Gov. CULBERSON: Mr. Chairman. I am instructed by the delegation from Texas to say that on the call of the roll by States the vote of Texas will be cast for RICHARD P. BLAND, of Missouri.

The Chair then introduced Mr. O. W. POWERS, of Utah.

Mr. POWERS: Mr. Chairman and Gentlemen of the Convention: After years of industrial misery; after sorrow and suffering and travail; after despair has driven thousands to suicide and filled the penitentiaries to overflowing; after hope had nearly left the breasts of the people, Democracy has parted the clouds, and behold there is a silver lining. Democracy points toward the doorway of prosperity, she bids all to enter; and she will do all in her power to restore the halcyon days even as they existed before gold and greed blighted this land and bound the faces of the people to the great grindstone of distress. Nations may rise and nations may fall; parties may become recreant to their principles; men may come and men may go, but Democracy will live forever. It was born when God said "Let there be light," when the birds sang and the trees burst into bloom and the great orb of day thrust life into the breast of earth with its golden shaft. Its undying creed is equal rights to all and unjust privileges to none. It is the life, the light, the soul of liberty. It will light this people through the dead sea of a financial disaster into the bright garden of prosperity. Animated by this great principle, you have reaffirmed the Declaration of Independence; you have inaugurated a new era, wherein silver and gold, the twin money metals that lie locked in each other's embrace, shall go forth hand in hand, as God intended, scattering blessings upon every side.

You have placed upon that platform a typical American; one familiar with the needs of the entire country; one who is aware that west of Chicago there are thousands of homes filled with patriotic, intelligent and Christian people. I desire, now, on behalf of the youngest State of the Union, a State whose star was placed upon the flag on Saturday last, amid the booming of cannon, the forty-sixth State, the State of Utah, and suggest the name for your consideration which, linked with that of BRYAN, I believe will be carried forward to victory. I shall name one who comes from the South.

If it be said that he comes from a section of the country that is not yet ready for recognition, let me say to those who raise that objection that the South, risen from her ashes, has grasped the standard of our common country, and is leading the people forward in this great movement. I shall name one who is a scholar and who is a statesman.

If it be said of him that I should not present the name because he comes from the South, let me say that I come from Abolition parents; and I desire in this Convention to present the name of one whom my ancestors would have honored could they have known him. I also present him because our State owes to him more than it owes to almost any of the statesmen.

I present it by the unanimous voice of the delegation, by the wish of our people who are at home. Let me ask you, then, that we shall have no sectionalism. This is the people's fight.

Our candidate for the Presidency received votes from the whole section of the country. Even the distinguished gentlemen from New York who abstained from their annual visits to the crowned heads of Europe, in order that they might have a softening and humanizing influence here, will know, when the ides of November shall come, that the people are about all right and they are all wrong, and they will fall into this procession and aid us in carrying Democracy on to victory. I should say no more, perhaps, than to present the name of my candidate. I present the name of the peerless orator, one fit to join hands with the peerless BRYAN. I present the name of a man of pure character, one fit to sit in the highest seat of the nation. I present the name of a statesman who is without a peer in the Senate of the United States. I present and I ask of you that you shall vote for him and unite all sections. I present, without his knowledge and without the knowledge of his State, the name of JOHN W. DANIEL, of Virginia.

Mr. W. A. JONES, of Virginia: Mr. Chairman and Gentlemen of the Convention: We delegates from Virginia greatly appreciate the beautiful tribute that has been paid to Virginia's honored and gifted son; but, Mr. Chairman, I am instructed by Senator DANIEL to say that if his name should be presented to this Convention, under no circumstances will he permit it to be used in connection with this high and exalted position. Therefore, I am constrained by his earnest desire to ask that his name shall not be considered in connection with this position.

The Chair then presented FREE P. MORRIS, of Illinois.

Mr. MORRIS: Mr. Chairman and Gentlemen of the Convention: While many distinguished men have been named for the high office of Vice-President of these United States, yet we adjourned last night with a view of deliberating upon the advisability of selecting a candidate whose name, whose personality would mean for us when election day comes around, that success which we hoped and prayed for and which has led us to assemble in this Convention. Unless we act with wisdom the great efforts which have been made, will have been made in vain. This is no slight office. The office is next to the highest and grandest one that can possibly be conferred upon any citizen. I desire, without disparaging any gentleman whose name has been mentioned, to say that we should select one of wide business experience and capacity—a man who has been engaged in business so long that his name will stand before the people and assure them so that they may have the utmost confidence that if he is nominated and put upon the ticket he will be elected.

Such a gentleman I propose to mention. He is one whose heart beats in sympathy with the downtrodden of the world. He is one whose name and personality would consume iniquities and destroy corruption. He is one who believes that the stars that were emblazoned upon our national flag, like the stars in heaven, are sent forth as a message of liberty to our people and announce such to the world. I desire to say that if you link with the name of that masterful orator whom you named yesterday the gentleman whom I shall give to you, you will inscribe upon your banners as certain as the news shall go forth that his name has been put there the word "Victory."

I have the honor on behalf of the great commonwealth of the State of Illinois, to second the nomination of JOSEPH C. SIBLEY, of the State of Pennsylvania.

The Chairman then introduced ULRIC SLOAN, of Ohio.

Mr. SLOAN: Gentlemen of the Convention: The sturdy silver Democrats of Ohio highly appreciate the compliment conferred upon her beloved son, JOHN R. MCLEAN, by his being placed in nomination by her sister State, Louisiana. Ohio came here asking for the nomination of her son for the first place on this ticket; asking for it in the name of the services since the demonetization of silver that he has rendered in the cause of its rehabilitation; asking for it by reason of the fact that his strong individuality combined with and through the Cincinnati Enquirer has made this Convention of silver men possible. Asking it because she has made possible the seats of Kentucky, Indiana and West Virginia on this floor.

She failed to get the nomination for him, and she now does not present him because he does not wish his name presented for the second place. But he bids me, as the acting chairman of his delegation, and speaking in the name of the silver, not the gold Democrats of Ohio, to say in his name that the same patriotism and the same power that enabled this Convention to be here in the cause of free silver will be exerted to its utmost, gentlemen of the Convention, to place Ohio in the column of Democratic States in November.

The Chair then presented to the Convention GEORGE FITHIAN, of Illinois.

Mr. FITHIAN: Gentlemen of the Convention: I am deeply grateful for the compliment that has been paid me by my distinguished friends from the State of Ohio, but I desire to say to this Convention that I am not a candidate for Vice-President. On behalf of the great State of Illinois which next November will roll up a Democratic majority for the national ticket, and again elect that distinguished son, the present Governor of this State, to the Governorship; on behalf of the State of Illinois, I desire to second the nomination of JOSEPH C. SIBLEY, Pennsylvania's noble son.

I had the honor and the pleasure to serve with him in Congress, and while some of his political enemies, hoping to destroy his usefulness in the battle for Democratic principles, have circulated the report that he was not a Democrat, but a Populist, I desire to say to the members of this Convention, who have not a personal acquaintance with him, that he is as good a Democrat as has a seat as a delegate to this Convention upon this floor. It is true, gentlemen, that he differed with the President upon questions of policy, and he had the courage to express his opinion upon the great public questions of the day, regardless and fearless of the administration and of everybody else.

But, if I am a Democrat, JOE SIBLEY is a Democrat, and I believe I am as good a Democrat as ever walked in shoe leather. The only thing that can be said against JOE SIBLEY's Democracy can be said by the gold standard men alone, and that is that he favors the free coinage of gold and silver at the ratio of 16 to 1. But it has been said that we ought not to nominate him because, in a speech in the House of Representatives, in differing with the Federal administration upon matters of public policy, he used language that was, perhaps, too severe toward the President of the United States. I want to remind this Convention that a majority, yea, nearly two-thirds majority of this Convention, have, by voting down the resolution that was offered by the distinguished Senator from the State of New York—recognizing and indorsing the President of the United States for his courage, his honesty and his integrity—when this Convention, by a majority of nearly two-thirds, refused to say that the President of the United States was a man of courage, a man of honesty, a man of integrity, then it seems to me that this Convention should not object to anything that JOE SIBLEY said, criticising the federal administration in the Fifty-third Congress.

The Chairman announces to me that my time is exhausted, and I will only add as a last remark that this Convention will do itself a great honor, and the Democratic party great honor and great good, by putting that distinguished Pennsylvanian upon its ticket.

The Chair recognized Mr. JOHN SCOTT, of Maine.

Mr. SCOTT: Mr. Chairman and Gentlemen of the Convention: Maine is still in the Union; Maine Democrats are still Maine Democrats, and next September we intend to come out of the woods and vote. If you think that the lot of a Maine Democrat has been a happy one—if you think that the path of a pioneer free-silver man of Maine has been strewn with roses—you have no conception of the land where we mount guard over the rising sun. Yet we have such a man in Maine—the star in the East of the silver Democracy—found in a quarter of the nation where you would last look for such a one—a leading business man, a New England president of a National bank, a man whose ships have spread their white wings to the breeze of every ocean and carried the American flag to the uttermost parts of the earth. Because he would not desert the cause of the people it has been decreed by those who came here to thwart the will of this delegation that he should be slaughtered in the house of his friends. I cannot, therefore, promise you that he will have the entire Maine delegation behind him, but I can promise that next September he will have the Democracy of Maine behind him.

In behalf of every man who admires matchless ability, inflexible integrity, and that courage which will stand without flinching even in the face of death, I second the nomination of ARTHUR SEWALL, of Maine. In behalf of every Democrat who believes that even every suspicion of sectionalism should be removed from our ticket, I ask you that you place with the sunflower of Nebraska the pine cone of Maine, and next September the whispering pine shall sound a Democratic note which will sound more threatening to the ears of the little NAPOLEON at Canton than the march of the Prussians did to the great NAPOLEON at Waterloo.

THE CHAIR: The Clerk will now announce the gentlemen who have been placed in nomination.

THE CLERK: The following gentlemen have been nominated for Vice-President: Mr. WILLIAMS, Mr. MCLEAN, Mr. LEWIS, Mr. CLARK, Mr. FITHIAN, Governor PENNOYER, Mr. SEWALL and Mr. SIBLEY.

The CHAIR: The Clerk will now call the roll of the States.

The Clerk then called the roll, as follows:

Alabama: WILLIAMS, of Massachusetts, 4; SEWALL, 4; CLARK, 4; LEWIS, 3; BOIES, 4; WILLIAMS, of Illnois, 3.

Arkansas: SEWALL, 16.

California: SEWALL, 10; BOIES, 7; WILLIAMS, of Massachusetts, 1.

Colorado: SEWALL, 4; WILLIAMS, of Massachusetts, 4.

Connecticut: WILLIAM F. HARRITY, 2; ten not voting.

Delaware: WILLIAM F. HARRITY, 3; SIBLEY, 1; two not voting.

Florida: SEWALL, 8.

Georgia: The State of Georgia for the present was passed.

Idaho: BLAND, 6.

Illinois: SIBLEY, 48.

Indiana: SIBLEY, 2; FITHIAN, 1; WILLIAMS, of Illinois,

4; WILLIAMS, of Massachusetts, 4; BLACKBURN, 4; McLEAN, 15.

Iowa: SIBLEY, 14; WILLIAMS, of Massachusetts, 11; TELLER, 1.

Kansas: WILLIAMS, of Massachusetts, 20.

Kentucky: SIBLEY, 21; SEWALL, 4; WILLIAMS, of Massachusetts, 1.

Louisiana: BLACKBURN, 16.

When the State of Maine was reached the Chairman said:

Mr. Chairman, I am authorized on behalf of the State of Maine to say that, while a majority of our delegation is absent, as a matter of State pride, at least, we give the vote of Maine to ARTHUR SEWALL, 12 votes.

The Chairman of the delegation of Maryland said:

Mr. Chairman, our delegation, thinking the Convention would adjourn last night, made their arrangements to return home this morning at 10 o'clock. Before leaving, however, five of the delegates instructed me to vote for JOHN R. McLEAN, of Ohio. The other delegates will be recorded as absent and not voting.

The State of Massachusetts requested to be passed.

Michigan: McLEAN, 28.

Minnesota: DANIELS, 1; SEWALL, 2; SIBLEY, 10; absent, 5.

Mississippi: SEWALL, 18.

Missouri: WILLIAMS, of Massachusetts, 3; WILLIAMS, of Illinois, 15; SIBLEY, 6; SEWALL, 10.

Montana: SEWALL, 6.

When Nebraska was called the Chairman of that delegation arose and said:

Nebraska, grateful for the very high honor that has been conferred upon it, is prepared to accept the result of the combined wisdom of this Convention, and it is not willing to take any part in this contest, and therefore requests to be excused from voting.

Nevada: McLean, 6.

New Hampshire, passed.

New Jersey and New York announced that they declined to vote.

When North Carolina was reached the Chairman of that delegation arose and said:

North Carolina never misses an opportunity to vote in a good cause. She now casts her twenty-two votes for her distinguished son, Judge Walter Clarke.

North Dakota: Sewall, 6.

When Ohio was called Chairman Long of that delegation said:

Mr. Long: While Mr. McLean personally is not a candidate, my delegation insists that the forty-six votes of Ohio be cast for John R. McLean.

As the Reading Clerk announced the vote Mr. Claypool, of Ohio, demanded the poll of the vote of the Ohio delegation, saying that he challenged the accuracy of the announcement of the vote, whereupon the Chair ordered the roll called, which was done, with the following result: McLean, 34; Sewall, 1; Sibley, 4; Williams (Mass.), 1; Fithian, 1; absent, 5.

The Chairman of the Ohio delegation announced that, under the unit rule, Ohio's vote would be cast for McLean.

The roll call was continued as follows:

Oregon: Pennoyer, 8.

Pennsylvania: Sibley, 7; Pattison, 2; absent or not voting, 55. (William F. Harrity, of Pennsylvania, requested that the delegates from Pennsylvania should not vote for him, as he was not a candidate.)

Rhode Island: Harrity, 6; Not voting, 2.

South Carolina: Sibley, 18.

South Dakota: Sewall, 8.

Tennessee: BOIES, 9; SIBLEY, 7; WILLIAMS (of Massachusetts), 4; DANIEL, 4.

Texas: BLAND, 30.

When Utah was called the Chairman of her delegation said:

Utah lays, as a tribute to the feet of one whom she honors, her six votes for JOHN W. DANIEL, of Virginia.

Vermont: McLEAN, 4; not voting, 4.
Virginia: CLARKE, 24.
Washington: LEWIS, 8.
West Virginia: WILLIAMS, 12.

Wisconsin was next called, General BRAGG was recognized. He said:

General BRAGG: Wisconsin declines to vote.

Delegate WHITE, of Wisconsin, stated that their delegation cast five votes for SIBLEY. This was announced by the Secretary, and the call of the States was proceeded with.

Wyoming: SIBLEY, 6.
Alaska: Declined to vote.
Arizona: WILLIAMS, 6.
District of Columbia: McLEAN, 6.
New Mexico: WILLIAMS, 6.
Oklahoma: WHITE, 1; SIBLEY, 4; McLEAN, 1.
Indian Territory: FITHIAN, 1; SIBLEY, 6.

Under the unit rule the six votes of Indian Territory were cast for SIBLEY.

Delegate MILLER, of Oregon, was recognized by the Chair and said:

Mr. MILLER: I rise for the purpose of changing the eight votes of Oregon from PENNOYER to that distinguished statesman from Pennsylvania, JOSEPH C. SIBLEY.

The State of Georgia was then called and the Chairman of her delegation said:

Georgia has instructed me to vote for a man for Vice-President who ought to be nominated by this Convention by acclamation. RICHARD P. BLAND.

The Chairman of the Massachusetts delegation said:

I am directed by the delegation of Massachusetts to state that she unanimously leaves the fortune of her distinguished son in the hands of this Convention.

The Chair inquired if the State of Nebraska still declined to vote, and the Chairman of the delegation stated that Nebraska still desired to be passed.

The Chair recognized Mr. STEELE, of South Dakota, who announced that his State wished to change her eight votes from ARTHUR P. SEWALL, of Maine, to WILLIAM F. HARRITY, of Pennsylvania.

The Chair ordered the Secretary to make the change requested.

Mr. POWERS, of Utah: Utah desires to change its votes from DANIEL to BLAND.

THE CHAIR: It is impossible to make changes at present. The Chair will recognize the gentleman later on if he desires it. The Clerk will now announce the result of the first ballot.

The Secretary announced the result of the first ballot as follows:

```
Sibley..................................163
McLean.................................111
Sewall.................................100
Williams, of Massachusetts............. 76
Bland.................................. 62
Clarke................................. 50
Williams, of Illinois.................. 22
Blackburn.............................. 20
Boies.................................. 20
Harrity................................ 21
Lewis.................................. 11
Daniel................................. 11
Pattison...............................  1
```

Fithian... 1
Teller... 1
White... 1
Absent and not voting........................... 258
Whole number of votes cast..................... 682
Necessary to choice.............................. 455

A. VAN WAGENEN: Mr. Chairman.

THE CHAIR: The gentleman from Iowa—for what purpose does he rise?

Mr. VAN WAGENEN: Gentlemen of the Convention. I am instructed by the delegation from Iowa to say to you that we do not deem the nomination of Governor BOIES for Vice-President wise, and therefore we withdraw his name. Let no man construe this as abating one particle from our zeal in the great cause. Let no man think, in saying this that Governor BOIES is not willing to-day to make all the sacrifices necessary, but after carefully considering this matter, we want to say to you that we do not think it wise to permit his nomination for the second place, and therefore, gentlemen, thanking you kindly for the compliment you have conferred upon him by your vote, I will ask you not further to consider his name, but to elect one who will add to your ticket and who will be acceptable to the Convention.

The Secretary then commenced the calling of the roll for the second ballot, beginning with Alabama. When that State was called TENNENT LOMAX arose in his place and said:

Mr. LOMAX: On behalf of the unterrified Democracy of the great State of Alabama I desire to cast her vote in this Convention for a gentleman whose addition to the ticket will make victory certain in November. I propose to cast that vote for a distinguished gentleman whose name has not been presented as a candidate to this Convention, and whose delegates now are willing that his name should be presented.

A. D. SMITH, of Minnesota: Mr. Chairman, I rise to a point of order. No speechmaking is in order during the call of the ballot.

THE CHAIR: The Chair decides the point of order well taken.

Mr. LOMAX, unmindful of the ruling of the Chair, continued: But the great Democratic party has a right to call upon any of its servants to serve it, and I cast the vote of the State of Alabama for that man whose name means 16 to 1, RICHARD P. BLAND, of Missouri.

Then the roll call proceeded thus:

Arkansas, 16 votes for BLAND.
California, 18 votes for BLAND.
Colorado, 8 votes for JOHN R. MCLEAN.
Connecticut, 2 votes for WILLIAM F. HARRITY, of Pennsylvania, 10 not voting.
Delaware, 3 votes for WILLIAM F. HARRITY, 1 vote for BLAND, 2 not voting.
Florida, 8 votes for BLAND.
Georgia, 26 votes for BLAND.
Idaho, 6 for BLAND.
Illinois, 48 for SIBLEY.
Indiana, 15 for BLAND, 15 for MCLEAN.
Iowa, passed.
Kansas, 20 for BLAND.
Kentucky, passed.
Louisiana, 16 for MCLEAN.
Maine, 8 for SEWALL, 4 not voting.
Maryland, 5 for MCLEAN, 11 absent and not voting.
Massachusetts, 9 for WILLIAMS, of Massachusetts, and 21 absent and not voting.
Michigan, 28 for MCLEAN.
Minnesota, 5 for SIBLEY, 6 for MCLEAN, 2 for SEWALL, 6 absent.
Mississippi, 18 for BLAND,
Missouri, passed.
Montana, 6 for BLAND.
Nebraska, passed.
Nevada, 6 for BLAND.
New Hampshire, passed.
New Jersey, declined to vote.

New York, declined to vote.
North Carolina, 22 for CLARKE.
North Dakota, 6 for SEWALL.

When Ohio cast its forty-six votes for McLEAN, Mr. CLAYPOOL, of that state, again challenged the vote, but the Chairman stated that under the unit rule the vote would be cast for McLEAN.

The roll call then continued:

Oregon, 4 for BLAND, 4 for SIBLEY.
Pennsylvania, 5 for SIBLEY, 2 for BLAND, 1 for PATTISON, 56 absent or declining to vote.

When Rhode Island was called Chairman RICHARDSON stated to the Convention:

Mr. RICHARDSON: The Chairman of the Rhode Island delegation called upon the Chair a few moments ago and said that the delegation was compelled to leave the hall to take its train returning home, but he authorized the present occupant of the Chair to cast the vote of that state. If there be no objection the Chair will name the gentleman for whom they authorized him to cast the vote. He is WILLIAM F. HARRITY, of Pennsylvania.

There being no objection, Chairman RICHARDSON cast the eight votes of Rhode Island for WILLIAM F. HARRITY.

Then the call proceeded thus:

South Carolina, 18 for SIBLEY.
South Dakota, 8 for WILLIAM F. HARRITY.
Tennessee, passed.
Texas, 39 for BLAND.
Utah, 6 for BLAND.
Vermont, 4 for BLAND, 4 not voting.
Virginia, 24 for BLAND.

When Washington was called, Mr. WHITE, of that State, said:

Mr. WHITE: Washington, unfortunately, is divided on this question through the influence of the gold bugs of this Convention. She casts—

At this point the Chair ruled that debate was out of order. Mr. WHITE thereupon said:

Mr. WHITE: Washington casts three votes for BLAND and five for SEWALL.

West Virginia, 12 for BLAND.
Wisconsin, 3 for BLAND, 3 for SIBLEY, 19 not voting.
Wyoming, 6 for BLAND.
Alaska, not voting.
Arizona, 6 for BLAND.
District of Columbia: McLEAN, 6.
New Mexico: BLAND, 6.
Oklahoma: BLAND, 6.
Indian Territory: BLAND, 6.

The Chair then directed that the States that were passed be called, which was done, with the following result:

Iowa: SIBLEY, 26.
Kentucky: McLEAN, 16; WILLIAMS, of Massachusetts, 1; SIBLEY, 1; BLAND, 2; SEWALL, 6.

When Missouri was called Governor STONE arose and said:

The State of Missouri presented the name of one of its citizens for the presidential nomination. In the wisdom of this Convention another was selected. The delegation has no authority to present the name of that citizen for the second place upon the ticket. If it is done by this Convention it must be done of its own accord, without solicitation by the Missouri delegation. Missouri casts ten votes for SEWALL, five for SIBLEY, six for WILLIAMS, of Massachusetts, and thirteen for WILLIAMS, of Illinois.

The call of the passed States was then ended by Tennessee casting twenty-four votes for BLAND.

The Secretary announced the result of the second ballot as follows:

Sibley..113
McLean...158
Sewall.. 37
Williams, of Massachusetts...................... 13
Bland..294
Clarke 22
Williams, of Illinois............................ 16
Harrity.. 21
Pattison... 1
Not voting......................................255

No candidate having received the necessary vote, the Chairman ordered the Secretary to call the roll for a third ballot, when Amos Cummings, of New York, ascended the platform and the Chair requested the Secretary to suspend the roll call while he introduced Mr. Cummings.

The Chair: The Chair thinks that the roll call should be suspended that he may present to the Convention Amos J. Cummings, member of the famous Tammany Society of New York, who will read a telegram of interest to the Convention.

Mr. Cummings then presented the following:

Meadville, Pa., July 11.
Amos Cummings. Please do not permit my name to be presented. I so instructed my friends yesterday.
Joseph C. Sibley.

The Secretary then called the roll of States by the third ballot with the following result:

Alabama: Bland, 22.
Arkansas: Sewall, 16.
California: Sewall, 18.
Colorado: Sewall, 8.
Connecticut: No response.
Delaware: Harrity, 3; Sewall, 1; not voting, 2.
Florida: Sewall, 8.
Georgia: Bland, 26.
Idaho: Bland, 6.
Illinois: Sibley, 48.

Indiana: McLean, 30.
Iowa: McLean, 26.
Kansas: Bland, 20.
Kentucky: McLean, 16; Bland, 3; Sewall, 7.
Louisiana: McLean, 16.
Maine: Sewall, 12.
Maryland: McLean, 5; 11 not voting.
Massachusetts: George Fred Williams, 9; 21 absent and not voting.
Michigan: Sewall, 28.
Minnesota: Sibley, 2; Bland, 3; McLean, 5; 8 absent.
Mississippi: McLean, 18.
Missouri: Bland, 34.
Montana: Bland, 6.
Nebraska: Excused from voting.
Nevada: McLean, 6.
New Hampshire: Passed.
New Jersey: Declined to vote.
New York: Declined to vote.
North Carolina: Clark, 22.
North Dakota: Sewall, 6.
Ohio: McLean, 46.
Oregon: Bland, 8.
Pennsylvania: Sewall, 4; McLean, 3; Pattison, 1; declining to vote, 56.
Rhode Island: Harrity, 8.
South Carolina: Bland, 18.
South Dakota: Harrity, 8.
Tennessee: Bland, 24.
Texas: Bland, 30.
Utah: John W. Daniel, 6.
Vermont: Bland, 4; not voting, 4.
Virginia: Bland, 14.
Washington: Bland 4; Sewall, 4.
West Virginia: Bland, 1; Williams, of Massachusetts, 6; McLean, 5.
Wisconsin: Bland, 4; Sewall, 1; not voting, 19.
Wyoming: Bland, 6.
Alaska: Declined to vote.
Arizona: Bland, 6.

District of Columbia: McLean, 6.
New Mexico: Bland, 6.
Oklahoma: Sewall, 6.
Indian Territory: Sewall, 6.

Michigan having been passed, Mr. Hummer, of that State, arose and cast the twenty-eight votes of Michigan for McLean.

The Clerk announced the result of the third ballot as follows:

Sibley	50
McLean	210
Sewall	97
Williams, of Massachusetts	15
Bland	255
Clarke	22
Harrity	19
Daniel	6
Pattison	1
Absent and not voting	255

After the announcement of the vote, the Chairman recognized Governor Stone, of Missouri.

Gov. Stone: Gentlemen of the Convention: I desire, on behalf of Missouri, and as the friend of Mr. Bland, to express to you our grateful appreciation of your kindness. I am now in receipt of a telegram from Mr. Bland, in which he says substantially that he would deem it unwise and impolitic to nominate both candidates from the west side of the Mississippi river. He directs me to say that the nomination of Mr. Bryan has his warm and hearty approval, and he thinks the nomination for the Vice-Presidency should be made with one object alone in view, and that is of strengthening the ticket. Accordingly, he directs me to say that he wishes his name withdrawn from the consideration of this Convention for that purpose.

The Chair then instructed the Clerk to call the roll for the fourth ballot. When Alabama was called she asked leave to retire for consultation, and her delegates were permitted to do so. The call then proceeded, as follows:

Arkansas: SEWALL, 16.
California: SEWALL, 18.
Colorado: SEWALL, 8.
Connecticut: Passed.

When Delaware was called Chairman RICHARDSON announced that he had been instructed to cast Delaware's vote, and, if there was no objection, would do so. He announced the vote as follows: HARRITY, 3; SEWALL, 1; not voting, 2.

Florida: SEWALL, 8.
Georgia: McLEAN, 26.
Idaho: SEWALL, 6.
Illinois: Passed.
Indiana: McLEAN, 30.
Iowa: McLEAN, 26.
Kansas: SEWALL, 20.
Kentucky: Passed.
Louisiana: McLEAN, 16.
Maine: SEWALL, 12.

When Maryland was called, Delegate-at-Large WARFIELD said:

Mr. WARFIELD: The Chairman of our delegation said that they were compelled to go because they had made their arrangements, and the delegates have instructed me positively to vote for Mr. McLEAN. In addition to that, four delegates instructed me to use my best judgment for them. Believing it is the best thing for the party to nominate Mr. McLEAN, I now declare nine votes from Maryland for Mr. McLEAN, seven absent and not voting.

The roll call then continued as follows:

Massachusetts: WILLIAMS, of Massachusetts, 9; Mr. WILLIAMS not voting for himself; twenty absent and not voting.

Michigan: McLean, 28.
Minnesota: McLean, 11; absent and not voting, 7.
Mississippi: McLean, 18.
Missouri: Sewall, 34.
Montana: Sewall, 4; McLean, 2.
Nebraska: Passed.
Nevada: McLean, 6.

New Hampshire, New Jersey and New York each declined to vote.

When North Carolina was reached the Chairman of the delegation said:

We of this wilderness wish to do what North Carolina does—vote for Walter Clark, of North Carolina. We cast twenty-two votes for Clark.

North Dakota: Sewall, 6.
Ohio: McLean, 46.

When the Secretary called the State of Oregon the Chairman of the delegation said:

Eight votes for that distinguished Democrat that believes in the free coinage of silver at 16 to 1, Mr. Sewall, of Maine.

Pennsylvania: Sewall, 3; McLean, 4; Pattison, 1; absent or declining to vote, 56.
Rhode Island: Harrity, 8.
South Carolina: Sewall, 18.
South Dakota: Sewall, 8.

The State of Tennessee was passed, the members of the delegation being engaged in consultation.

Texas: Daniel, 30.
Utah: Daniel, 6.
Vermont: McLean, 4; not voting, 4.
Virginia: Passed.
Washington: Sewall, 8.
West Virginia: Daniel, 12.
Wisconsin: Sewall, 5; 19 not voting.

Wyoming: DANIEL, 6.
Alaska: Passed.
Arizona: SEWALL, 6.
District of Columbia: MCLEAN, 6.
New Mexico: MCLEAN, 3; SEWALL, 3.
Oklahoma: SEWALL, 6.
Indian Territory: SEWALL, 6.
Alabama: SEWALL, 22.

When the State of Illinois was called by the Secretary, Mr. FITHIAN said:

Mr. FITHIAN: Mr. Chairman, this Convention cannot afford to nominate JOHN R. MCLEAN, and I challenge the vote of this delegation.

THE CHAIR: The gentleman from Illinois, Mr. FITHIAN, challenges the vote of Illinois, and the Secretary will call the roll of that State.

The Secretary then called the roll.

When H. W. MASTERS' name was called he said:

Mr. MASTERS: Mr. Chairman, I have voted for SEWALL and I was for him, but I bow to the will of the majority. I cast my vote for JOHN R. MCLEAN.

When A. M. BELL's name was called he said:

Mr. BELL: While my preference was for SEWALL, I am with the majority, and I cast my vote for JOHN R. MCLEAN.

The Clerk announced the result of the poll as, 28 for MCLEAN, 10 for SEWALL, 10 absent, and the Chairman stated that under the unit rule the vote of Illinois was cast for Mr. MCLEAN.

California then announced through its Chairman that the vote of that state should be corrected, and should be 16 for SEWALL and 2 for MCLEAN.

The Secretary then called the states which had been passed when they were called in their order. The call resulted as follows:

Kentucky: McLean, 16; Sewall, 10.
Tennessee: Sewall, 24.

New Mexico announced a change in her vote as follows: Sewall, 6.

Virginia, which had been passed, recorded her vote as follows: Clark, 24.

During the count of the ballot the Secretary made the following announcements:

Mr. Chairman: The Coliseum Garden Amusement Company desires to extend to you and the National Committeemen and Delegates an invitation to attend this evening's performance of "America" at which they will display the likeness of William Jennings Bryan. All delegate badges will be recognized at the gate, also badges of National Committeemen.

C. J. Smith (Nebraska): In connection with the invitation just extended, I desire to inquire how we poor unfortunate fellows who have no badges can get in?

The vote was announced by the Secretary as follows:

```
McLean ............................................. 296
Sewall .............................................. 261
Williams, of Massachusetts ..........................   9
Clark ...............................................  46
Harrity .............................................  11
Daniel ..............................................  54
Pattison ............................................   1
Total votes cast .................................... 678
Absent and not voting ............................... 250
Necessary for choice ................................ 453
```

As soon as the result of the fourth ballot had been announced Mr. McConnell, of Ohio, obtained recognition and stated that the Ohio delegation had a telegram from Mr. McLean, which they wished to read to the Convention. Mr. Long, of the Ohio delegation, came forward and spoke as follows:

Mr. Long: Two telegrams have been received by the

Ohio delegation from Mr. McLean. They state substantially what I stated here in the opening—that he is not a candidate, but that you may have the exact words, I read his telegram. He speaks for himself, not for the Ohio delegation: "Any vote cast for me for Vice-President is against my expressed wish and without my authority. Please so announce to the Convention." That is Mr. McLean; that is not the Ohio delegation statement.

The Chairman then ordered the Secretary to call the roll of States for a fifth ballot. When Alabama was called, Chairman Lomax of that delegation, said:

Mr. Lomax: Upon a poll of the vote of the State of Alabama three votes were cast for Mr. McLean, but under the operation of the unit rule I cast twenty-two votes for Mr. Sewall, of Maine.

The Secretary then proceeded with the roll call.

Arkansas: Sewall, 16.
California: Sewall, 16; McLean, 2.
Colorado: Sewall, 8.
Connecticut: Declined to vote.
Delaware: Harrity, 3; Sewall, 1; not voting, 2.
Florida: Sewall, 8.
Georgia: Sewall, 26.
Idaho: Sewall, 6.
Illinois: McLean, 48.
Indiana: Sewall, 30.

Mr. Menzies (of Indiana): If Mr. McLean had not authorized the withdrawal of his name, Indiana would have cast thirty votes for him, but now it casts thirty votes for Mr. Sewall.

Iowa: Sewall, 26.
Kansas: Sewall, 20.
Kentucky: McLean, 13; Sewall, 13.
Louisiana: Sewall, 16.
Maine: Sewall, 12.
Maryland: McLean, 5; Sewall, 4; not voting, 7.

Massachusetts: WILLIAMS, of Massachusetts, 9; 21 absent and not voting.
Michigan: SEWALL, 28.
Minnesota: SEWALL, 11; not voting, 7.
Mississippi: McLEAN, 18.
Missouri: SEWALL, 34.
Montana: SEWALL, 6.
Nebraska: Passed.
Nevada: SEWALL, 6.
New Hampshire: Not voting.
New Jersey: Declines to vote.
New York: Declines to vote.

North Carolina was called and the Chairman of the delegation said:

Mr. Chairman, the delegation of North Carolina is not committed to the East in this vote; and we believe that the name of a Southern or a Western man should be presented here; I cast the vote of this delegation for Mr. CLARKE, of North Carolina.

North Dakota: SEWALL, 6.

Ohio being called, Mr. LONG said:

Mr. LONG: Mr. Chairman, notwithstanding the telegram read from Mr. McLEAN, the delegation from Ohio casts its 46 votes for JOHN R. McLEAN.

Oregon: SEWALL, 8.
Pennsylvania: SEWALL, 5; McLEAN, 1; PATTISON, 1; 57 absent or declining to vote.
Rhode Island: HARRITY, 8.
South Carolina: SEWALL, 18.
South Dakota: SEWALL, 8.
Tennessee: SEWALL, 24.
Texas: DANIEL, 30.
Utah: DANIEL, 6.
Vermont: McLEAN, 4; 4 not voting.
Virginia: CLARK, 24.
Washington: SEWALL, 8.
West Virginia: SEWALL, 12.
Wisconsin: SEWALL, 4; McLEAN, 1; 19 not voting.

Wyoming: SEWALL, 6.
Alaska: Not voting.
Arizona: SEWALL, 6.
District of Columbia: McLEAN, 6.
Territory of New Mexico: SEWALL, 6.
Oklahoma: SEWALL, 6.
Indian Territory: SEWALL, 6.

At the conclusion of the roll call, and before the tellers could announce the result, Mr. DONOVAN, of Illinois, was recognized by the Chair and said:

Mr. DONOVAN: Mr. Chairman: The State of Illinois, which proposes to assist in the election of a President on the 3d of next November with its electoral vote, desires now to assist in the nomination of the Vice-President by changing its forty-eight votes from McLEAN to SEWALL.

Mr. JAMES, of Kentucky, stated that the vote of his State was changed and cast for SEWALL.

Mr. SLOAN, of Ohio, announced that the vote of his State was changed and cast in favor of the man from Maine, when he moved that the nomination of Mr. SEWALL be made unanimous.

Maryland and Mississippi were the next to change their votes, Maryland giving 9 and Mississippi 18 to Mr. SEWALL.

Nebraska then cast its first vote for the Vice-Presidency and recorded its 16 votes for SEWALL. Mr. HAMMILL, of Michigan, moved that the nomination be made unanimous.

The Reading Clerk said: I am requested by the Chair to announce that the gentlemen who have been appointed upon the committee to notify the Presidential and Vice-Presidential candidates of their nominations are to meet immediately upon the adjournment of the Convention in the room of the Committee upon Resolutions; and also requested to announce that the National Committee, both the old and the new, instead of meeting at 3 o'clock this afternoon, will meet at 5 o'clock this evening at the Palmer House.

Virginia asked to have her vote changed to SEWALL, and Mr. BAUMGARDEN, of Ohio, moved on behalf of the

Ohio delegation that the rules be suspended and that the nomination of Mr. Sewall be made by acclamation.

The Chairman then put the motion to make the nomination unanimous, and the motion was adopted by the States which voted. New York, New Jersey, New Hampshire and Alaska not voting.

The announcement by the Chair of the nomination of Mr. Sewall was made at 3 o'clock.

Senator Jones, of Arkansas, was recognized by the Chair, and said:

I am directed by the Committee on Resolutions to present the following and move its adoption:

"*Resolved*, That the National Committee are hereby empowered and directed to fix the time and place for holding the next National Convention and that the basis of representation herein be the same as fixed for this Convention, and in its discretion to select as its Chairman and members of the Executive Committee persons who are not members of the said National Committee."

The resolution was adopted. Senator Jones also offered the following resolution and moved its adoption:

Resolved, That the thanks of this Convention are hereby tendered to Hon. John W. Daniel, the temporary president; the Hon. Stephen M. White, the permanent president, and Hon. James D. Richardson, the acting president, and the other officers of the Convention for their services.

The resolution was unanimously adopted.

The following was also offered by Senator Jones and adopted:

Resolved, That the thanks of this Convention be hereby tendered to the Secretary and the other Secretaries of this Convention.

Senator Jones also offered the following resolution on behalf of the Committee on Resolutions:

Resolved, That the official stenographer be directed to prepare the proceedings of this Convention to be printed in proper form, and that the National Committee cause a suitable number of copies to be distributed to the delegates to this Convention, and to such others as may be entitled to receive them.

The Chairman announced that there being no objection, the resolution would be agreed to. The Chair then recognized Senator BLANCHARD, of Louisiana, who said:

Senator BLANCHARD: I move that the thanks of this Convention and the individual delegates thereto be extended to the city and to the people of Chicago for many courtesies received at their hands, and that we vote Chicago the greatest convention city on earth.

This resolution was adopted.

The Chair then recognized Hon. BARTON SMITH, of Ohio, who said:

Mr. SMITH: I move that Hon. WILLIAM F. HARRITY, Chairman of the Democratic National Committee, be included in the first resolution, thanking the officers of the Convention, and that the thanks of the Convention are due, and are hereby tendered to him, for his faithful services to the party.

This motion was unanimously adopted.

The following resolution was thereupon offered by Senator JONES, of Arkansas, on behalf of all the friends of free silver in the Convention:

Resolved, That the thanks of this Convention are due and are hereby tendered to Hon. WILLIAM F. HARRITY, Chairman of the National Committee, for the able and impartial manner in which he has discharged his duties while presiding over the deliberations of this Convention.

This resolution was unanimously adopted.

The Chair then recognized Mr. LADD, of Illinois, who said:

Mr. LADD: I move you, sir, as the sense of this Convention, that the next National Convention abolish the two-thirds rule, and let the majority rule in all things.

THE CHAIR: This Convention can make no rules for subsequent conventions.

The following tables show the vote in detail of the five ballots for Vice-President:

DEMOCRATIC NATIONAL CONVENTION.

FIRST BALLOT.

STATES	Total	Sibley	McLean	Sewall	Williams (Mass.)	Bland	Clark	Williams (HcLs.)	Blackburn	Boies	Hargrity	Lewis	Daniel	Pattison	Pitman	Teller	White	Absent, Excused or Not Voting
Alabama	22		4	4		4	3		4	3								
Arkansas	16		16															
California	18		10	1					7									
Colorado	8		4	4														
Connecticut	12										2							10
Delaware	6	1									3							2
Florida	8		8															
Georgia	26					26												
Idaho	6					6												
Illinois	48	48																
Indiana	30	2	15		4		4	4						1				
Iowa	26	14			11										1			
Kansas	20				20													
Kentucky	26	21		4	1													
Louisiana	16								16									
Maine	12		12															
Maryland	16		5															11
Massachusetts	30																	30
Michigan	28		28															
Minnesota	18	10		2									1					5
Mississippi	18			18														
Missouri	34	6		10	3			15										
Montana	6			6														
Nebraska	16																	16
Nevada	6		6															
New Hampshire	8																	8
New Jersey	20																	20
New York	72																	72
North Carolina	22						22											
North Dakota	6			6														
Ohio	46		46															
Oregon	8	8																
Pennsylvania	64	7												2				55
Rhode Island	8									6								2
South Carolina	18	18																
South Dakota	8									8								
Tennessee	24	7			4					9		4						
Texas	30				30													
Utah	6											6						
Vermont	8		4															4
Virginia	24						24											
Washington	8											8						
West Virginia	12				12													
Wisconsin	24	5																19
Wyoming	6	6																
Alaska	6																	6
Arizona	6				6													
Dist. of Columbia	6		6															
New Mexico	6				6													
Oklahoma	6		1	4												1		
Indian Territory	6			6														
Total	930	163	111	100		76	62	50	22	20	20	19	11	11	2	1	1	260

SECOND BALLOT.

STATES	Sibley	McLean	Sewall	Williams (Mass.)	Bland	Clark	Williams (Ill.)	Harrity	Pattison	Not Voting or Absent
Alabama					22					
Arkansas					16					
California					18					
Colorado		8								
Connecticut								2		10
Delaware					1			3		2
Florida					8					
Georgia					26					
Idaho					6					
Illinois	48									
Indiana		15			15					
Iowa	26									
Kansas					20					
Kentucky	1	16	6	1	2					
Louisiana		16								
Maine			8							4
Maryland		5								11
Massachusetts				9						21
Michigan		28								
Minnesota	4	6	2							6
Mississippi		18								
Missouri	5		10	6			13			
Montana					6					
Nebraska										16
Nevada					6					
New Hampshire										8
New Jersey										20
New York										72
North Carolina					22					
North Dakota			6							
Ohio		46								
Oregon	4				4					
Pennsylvania	5				2				1	56
Rhode Island								8		
South Carolina	18									
South Dakota								8		
Tennessee					24					
Texas					30					
Utah					6					
Vermont					4					4
Virginia					24					
Washington			5		3					
West Virginia					12					
Wisconsin	2				3					19
Wyoming					6					
Alaska										6
Arizona					6					
District of Columbia					6					
New Mexico					6					
Oklahoma					6					
Indian Territory					6					
Total	113	158	37	16	294	22	13	21	1	255

THIRD BALLOT.

STATES	SIBLEY	MCLEAN	SEWALL	WILLIAMS (MASS.)	BLAND	CLARK	HARRITY	DANIEL	PATTISON	ABSENT OR NOT VOTING
Alabama					22					
Arkansas			16							
California			18							
Colorado			8							
Connecticut										12
Delaware			1				3			2
Florida			8							
Georgia					26					
Idaho					6					
Illinois	48									
Indiana		30								
Iowa		26								
Kansas					20					
Kentucky		16	7		3					
Louisiana		16								
Maine			12							
Maryland		5								11
Massachusetts				9						21
Michigan		28								
Minnesota	2	5			3					8
Mississippi		18								
Missouri					34					
Montana					6					
Nebraska										16
Nevada		6								
New Hampshire										8
New Jersey										20
New York										72
North Carolina						22				
North Dakota			6							
Ohio		46								
Oregon					8					
Pennsylvania		3	4						1	56
Rhode Island							8			
South Carolina					18					
South Dakota							8			
Tennessee					24					
Texas					30					
Utah								6		
Vermont					4					4
Virginia					24					
Washington			4		4					
West Virginia		5		6	1					
Wisconsin			2		4					19
Wyoming					6					
Alaska										6
Arizona					6					
District of Columbia										
New Mexico					6					
Oklahoma			6							
Indian Territory			6							
Total	50	210	97	15	255	22	19	6	1	255

FOURTH BALLOT.

STATES	McLean	Sewall	Williams (Mass.)	Clark	Harrity	Daniel	Pattison	Absent or Not Voting
Alabama		22						
Arkansas		16						
California	2	16						
Colorado		8						
Connecticut								12
Delaware		1			3			2
Florida		8						
Georgia	26							
Idaho		6						
Illinois	48							
Indiana	30							
Iowa	26							
Kansas		20						
Kentucky	16	10						
Louisiana	16							
Maine		12						
Maryland	9							7
Massachusetts			9					21
Michigan	28							
Minnesota	11							7
Mississippi	18							
Missouri		34						
Montana	2	4						
Nebraska								16
Nevada	6							
New Hampshire								8
New Jersey								20
New York								72
North Carolina				22				
North Dakota		6						
Ohio	46							
Oregon		8						
Pennsylvania	4	3					1	56
Rhode Island					8			
South Carolina		18						
South Dakota		8						
Tennessee		24						
Texas						30		
Utah						6		
Vermont	4							4
Virginia				24				
Washington		8						
West Virginia						12		
Wisconsin		5						19
Wyoming						6		
Alaska								6
Arizona		6						
District of Columbia	6							
New Mexico		6						
Oklahoma		6						
Indian Territory		6						
Total	298	261	9	46	11	54	1	250

DEMOCRATIC NATIONAL CONVENTION.

FIFTH BALLOT.

STATES	McLean	Sewall	Williams (Mass.)	Clark	Harrity	Daniel	Pattison	Absent or not voting
Alabama		22						
Arkansas		16						
California	2	16						
Colorado		8						
Connecticut								12
Delaware		1				3		2
Florida		8						
Georgia		26						
Idaho		6						
Illinois		48						
Indiana		30						
Iowa		26						
Kansas		20						
Kentucky		26						
Louisiana		16						
Maine		12						
Maryland		9						7
Massachusetts			9					21
Michigan		28						
Minnesota		11						7
Mississippi	18							
Missouri		34						
Montana		6						
Nebraska								16
Nevada		6						
New Hampshire								8
New Jersey								20
New York								72
North Carolina				22				
North Dakota		6						
Ohio		46						
Oregon		8						
Pennsylvania	1	5					1	57
Rhode Island					8			
South Carolina		18						
South Dakota		8						
Tennessee		24						
Texas							30	
Utah							6	
Vermont	4							
Virginia		24						
Washington		8						
West Virginia		12						
Wisconsin	1	4						19
Wyoming		6						
Alaska								6
Arizona		6						
District of Columbia	6							
New Mexico		6				2		
Oklahoma		6						
Indian Territory		6						
Total	32	568	9	22	11	36	1	251

The following are the Committees on Notification, and the Democratic National Committee, as handed to the Secretary by the delegations from the several States:

COMMITTEE ON NOTIFICATION.

Alabama—J. J. WILLETT.
Arkansas—PAUL JONES.
California—A. CARMINETTI.
Colorado—T. J. O'DONNELL.
Connecticut—(Not announced).
Delaware—J. F. SAULSBURY.
Florida—G. B. SPARKMAN.
Georgia—J. T. HILL.
Idaho—B. N. HILLIARD.
Illinois—H. W. MASTERS.
Indiana—U. S. JACKSON.
Iowa—L. T. GENUNG.
Kansas—FRANK BACON.
Kentucky—JOHN S. GARNER.
Louisiana—VICTOR MAUBARRET.
Maine—FRED W. PLAISTED.
Maryland—JOHN HANNIBAL.
Massachusetts—JAMES DONOVAN.
Michigan—F. W. HUBBARD.
Minnesota—F. H. VOREIS.
Mississippi—R. H. HENRY.
Missouri—HUGH J. BRADY.
Montana—PAUL A. FUSZ.
Nebraska—JOHN A. CREIGHTON.
Nevada—JACOB KLEIN.
New Hampshire—HERBERT J. JONES.

New Jersey—GOTTF'D KRUGGER.
New York—ELLIOTT DANFORTH.
North Carolina—GEO. F. POWELL.
North Dakota—W. N. ROACH.
Ohio—L. E. HOLDEN.
Oregon—CHARLES NICKELL.
Pennsylvania—JOHN T. LENAHAN.
Rhode Island—GEO. W. GREENE.
South Carolina—E. P. McSWEENEY
South Dakota—S. V. ARNOLD.
Tennessee—JOHN K. SHIELDS.
Texas—J. L. SHEPARD.
Utah—FRED J. KISSELL.
Vermont—M. MAGIFF.
Virginia—T. B. MURPHY.
Washington—JAMES F. GIRTON.
West Virginia—L. E. TIERNEY.
Wisconsin—JAMES E. MALONE.
Wyoming—M. L. BLAKE.
Alaska—GEO. R. TINGLE.
Arizona—W. E. JONES.
Dist. of Columbia—GEO. KILLEEN
Indian Ter.—D. M. HALEY.
N. Mexico—DEMETRIUS CHAVEZ.
Oklahoma—TEMPLE HOUSTON.

DEMOCRATIC NATIONAL COMMITTEE.

Alabama—HENRY D. CLAYTON.
Arkansas—THOMAS C. McRAE.
California—J. J. DWYER.
Colorado—ADAIR WILSON.
Connecticut—CARLOS FRENCH.
Delaware—R. R. KENNEY.
Florida—SAMUEL PASCO.
Georgia—CLARK HOWELL, JR.
Idaho—GEORGE AINSLIE.
Illinois—THOMAS GAHAN.
Indiana—JOHN G. SHANKLIN.
Iowa—CHARLES A. WALSH.
Kansas—J. G. JOHNSON.

Kentucky—UREY WOODSON.
Louisiana—N. C. BLANCHARD.
Maine—SETH C. GORDON.
Maryland—ARTHUR P. GORMAN.
Massachusetts—JOHN W. CORCORAN.
Michigan—DANIEL J. CAMPAU.
Minnesota—DANIEL W. LAWLER.
Mississippi—W. V. SULLIVAN.
Missouri—W. J. STONE.
Montana—J. J. MACHATTON.
Nebraska—WM. H. THOMPSON.
Nevada—R. P. KEATING.
New Hampshire—A. W. SULLOWAY.

New Jersey—JAMES SMITH, JR.
New York—WM. F. SHEEHAN.
N. Carolina—JOSEPHUS DANIELS.
North Dakota—W. C. LIESTIKOW.
Ohio—JOHN R. MCLEAN.
Oregon—J. TOWNSEND.
Pennsylvania—WM. F. HARRITY.
Rhode Island—R. B. COMSTOCK.
S. Carolina—BENJ. R. TILLMAN.
South Dakota—JAS. M. WOODS.
Tennessee—J. M. HEAD.
Texas—J. G. DUDLEY.
Utah—A. W. MCCUNE.
Vermont—BRADLEY B. SMALLEY.
Virginia—P. J. OTEY.
Washington—HUGH C. WALLACE.
West Virginia—J. T. MCGRAW.
Wisconsin—E. C. WALL.
Wyoming—W. H. HOLLIDAY.
Alaska—C. D. ROGERS.
Arizona—MARCUS A. SMITH.
District of Columbia—LAWRENCE GARDNER.
Indian Ter.—THOMAS MARCUM.
N. Mexico—F. A. MANZANARES.
Oklahoma—WHITE M. GRANT.

On motion of Senator JONES, of Nebraska, the Convention adjourned at 3:30 P. M., *sine die*.

APPENDIX.

DEMOCRATIC NATIONAL COMMITTEE MEETING.

PALMER HOUSE, CHICAGO, ILL., July 11, 1896.

At 5 P. M., the meeting of the Democratic National Committee was called to order with Hon. WILLIAM F. HARRITY, of Pennsylvania, in the Chair.

Mr. HARRITY said: Gentlemen: In pursuance of the usual practice of having a meeting of the Committee after the conclusion of the work of the Convention, for the purpose of closing up the business of the Committee and in order that we may leave nothing (or, if anything, as little as possible) to give trouble to our successors, this meeting has been called.

The Chair thinks it proper to add that the view of the Chair is that the Sub-Committee which was appointed for the purpose of making arrangements for this Convention shall be continued or consider itself continued until it closes its work, which is now largely a matter of the payment of bills and the return of the unexpended balance, if any; to the contributors of the fund raised for the purpose of defraying the expenses of the Convention. The amount raised, so far as we are able to judge, is ample; and there probably will be a balance or surplus, which will be handed over to the Treasurer of the Committee that furnished the funds to this Committee. The subscribers have had as their Treasurer, Mr. JOSEPH DONNERSBERGER, of Chicago, who has been most faithful and efficient. He has been industrious in the collection of the funds and has been successful. Although some of the subscribers were a little tardy, the money is now in hand so that nothing more need be said about that. The Secretary will present the report of the Sub-Committee on Arrangements for the Convention.

If there be any business that occurs to any of the gentlemen that requires the attention of the outgoing Committee, the Chairman will be pleased to receive and entertain any motion for such purpose.

REPORT OF SUB-COMMITTEE ON CONVENTION ARRANGEMENTS.

To the Democratic National Committee:

Gentlemen: Your Committee appointed for the purpose of making the necessary arrangements for the meeting of the Democratic National Convention to be held at Chicago, Illinois, on Tuesday, July 7, 1896, at 12 o'clock, noon, respectfully reports:

That your Committee made suitable arrangements to have the Convention held in the Chicago Coliseum, a permanent building, which is admirably adapted for National Conventions and other large gatherings of people. The building is convenient of access and is capable of comfortably accommodating an audience of from 15,000 to 30,000 persons, depending upon whether or not all of the Coliseum building is used for the purpose.

The expenses, which were paid by subscriptions and contributions made by the people of Chicago, amounted to $38,206.68 and covered the expenditures for rent of Coliseum and headquarters, decorations, music, expenses of members of the Democratic National Committee, as well as of the members of the Committee of Arrangements, Sergeant-at-Arms, Doorkeepers, Clerks, Stenographers, Stationery, etc. All of the bills contracted by your Committee of Arrangements have been paid. Representative citizens of Chicago guaranteed that a fund of not exceeding $40,000.00 would be raised to cover the expenses incident to the Convention; but only the sum of $38,206.68, which is the exact amount of the aggregate of expenses incurred by your Committee, was paid into its Treasury.

Your Committee further desires to report that it is under many obligations to Mr. F. E. CANDA, of New York, for invaluable services, voluntarily and cheerfully rendered, as advisory engineer and architect of the Committee. To his skill, industry and experience are we largely indebted for the excellent arrangements of the Convention hall.

    Respectfully,
      WILLIAM F. HARRITY, Chairman.
      SIMON P. SHEERIN, Secretary.
      THOMAS H. SHERLEY.
      JOHN G. PRATHER.
      EDWARD C. WALL.
      BEN. T. CABLE.
      HUGH C. WALLACE.

July 11, 1896.

Hon. CHARLES W. BLAIR, of Kansas, was recognized and said:

Mr. CHAIRMAN: As the business of the Committee is not of a private character, I move that one or more of the leading representatives of the press be admitted to this meeting.

An amendment to this motion was offered by Hon. SAMUEL PASCO, of Florida, "to admit all representatives of the press." The motion, as amended, was carried.

The Chair then announced that the courtesies of the floor were extended to the representatives of the press.

Hon. CHARLES W. BLAIR, of Kansas, then said: Mr. Chairman and Gentlemen of the committee: To me, as one of the oldest members of this Committee, has been delegated an important duty now immediately to be performed; and I assure you that in the course of my life I have been called upon for the performance of few duties which I discharge so proudly and so thankfully. I need not say to those of us who have been associated with our distinguished Chairman for many years in the past, that we have not only learned to know him but that we have learned to love him. (Applause.)

We honor him for his uprightness and impartiality. We have respected him for the stern and unflinching determination with which he performs the duty that falls to his lot either in a political or representative capacity; and I venture the assertion that those of us who have served with him four years will go back fully convinced that at no period in the future will there be a man occupying the distinguished position that he is about to resign who will be more closely identified with Democratic tradition and duty, and who reflects or may reflect in the future more credit upon the Democratic organization (applause), and if we had not entertained this opinion prior to the present Convention, I hazard nothing in asserting that that conviction would have been born of the recent events through which we have just passed. There is no man under the difficult circumstances that surround him who could have discharged the high duties which he discharged with more absolute and perfect impartiality than he has discharged them, (applause), and whoever may be his successors (as was stated by the honorary presiding officer of the Convention), will look to him as a model and for guidance in the discharge of their duties. I, therefore offer this resolution :

Resolved, That the Democratic National Committee extend to the Hon. WILLIAM F. HARRITY its thanks for the able, upright and impartial manner in which he has discharged his duties as Chairman of the Committee.

And in order to spare the modesty of our presiding officer, I claim the privilege of putting it to the Committee myself. (Gen. BLAIR then put the question upon his resolution, whereupon it was unanimously adopted by a rising vote.)

Gen. BLAIR continuing, said : I am happy to notice that the Committee is in thorough accord with my resolution.

Now, Mr. Chairman, I offer another resolution ; and before offering it, I wish to say that, whilst we are indebted to the Chairman of this Convention for absolute impartiality, for universal kindly feeling toward us, there is no man from whom we have received more favors than we have from the Secretary of the Committee. For the last eight years that we have been associated with him, it matters little what we wanted, if we did not know where to get it, all we had to do was to ask Secretary SHEERIN and he got it for us. He seemed to take a great pleasure in serving the members of this Committee, and no better man for the position will occupy it in the future. (Applause.) I offer the following:

Resolved, That this Committee extend its thanks to Hon.

S. P. SHEERIN for the able, honest and efficient manner in which he has discharged his duties as Secretary of this Committee.

THE CHAIR: What is the pleasure of the Committee as to this resolution?

Hon. CHARLES S. THOMAS, of Colorado, arose and said:

Mr. THOMAS: Mr. Chairman and Gentlemen: I desire to second the motion that has just been offered, as I am anxious to second the other with all my heart. What was said by the gentleman from Kansas, who, I believe, is the oldest member in point of service upon the Committee, finds an answering echo in the hearts and the recollections of every member of this Committee. I desire especially, Mr. Chairman, in seconding this motion to say in addition to what has already been said and so well said by the gentleman from Kansas, that I do not know of a single instance during the administration of the affairs of the Committee by your honored self in which anything was said or thought or could have been said or thought that would have amounted to even imputation or suspicion of disrespect to you, except it might have been the something which in the heat of debate some few days ago had fallen from my lips. It is, therefore, my duty to doubly say that I know of no instance or of any occasion under which any member of this Committee during the administration of its affairs by yourself or Secretary SHEERIN which could in any wise be construed except as in the faithful discharge of a given line of duty and as pleasant and beautiful associations which spring up between men when brought together. I do not know, sir, who your successor will be; but if those who shall take our places shall be half so fortunate in procuring a presiding officer for their Committee, and if the candidates can secure for the management of their campaign a man who will devote time, labor and ability, and the constant endeavor to do what is best and right, there can be but one result. We have had many Chairmen and Secretaries of the Democratic National Committee, but none more deserving or more thoroughly satisfactory to all than those who are about to retire. I second the motion of the gentleman from Kansas.

Hon. HENRY D. CLAYTON, of Alabama, said:

Mr. Chairman: Before that motion is put, I desire to say, as a Democrat and as a man, that no one appreciates more than I do the unswerving fidelity of our Chairman and our Secretary; that no man appreciates more than I do their impartiality and their great ability; and I want to say, Mr. Chairman, with all my heart, feeling it in every fibre of my being, saturated as I am with the love for the Chairman and the Secretary of this Committee, that I want to give my hearty support of the resolution to the Secretary, as I have for the resolution to the Chairman. (Applause.)

THE CHAIR: The question is on the resolution of the gentleman from Kansas, referring to the fidelity and efficiency with which the Secretary of the Committee, Hon. SIMON P. SHEERIN, of Indiana, has discharged his duties.

The resolution was unanimously adopted by a rising vote.

Hon. M. S. TARPEY, of California, said:

Mr. Chairman, I desire to request, sir, on behalf of the members of this Committee, that those resolutions shall be spread at length in the minutes of this meeting and become a part of the archives of this Committee. I now make a motion to that effect.

Unanimously adopted.

The Chair (Mr. HARRITY) then said:

Gentlemen of the Committee: I desire to express my profound appreciation of the passage of the resolution just adopted, and to sincerely thank you for it. It has been my effort since I became associated with you as one of the members of the Committee, and particularly since I have had the honor and the pleasure of being the Chairman of your body, to so conduct myself, to so discharge such duties as were assigned to me or that devolved upon me as the Chairman of the Committee, as to merit, at least, in some degree, your approval. It is certainly very gratifying, I hope I may say without too much vanity, that there is some indication that I have, at least made the effort and, at least, partially succeeded. It is with feelings of regret that I am obliged to part company with so many, certainly quite a large number, of the gentlemen who have been members of the Committee and who have been succeeded by other gentlemen. Our successors, I have no doubt, will just as efficiently, just as ably and just as successfully represent their constituents and represent the Democracy as a National organization. It is my wish, my hope, it is my expectation that they will. I desire, gentlemen, to thank you cordially and kindly for this manifestation of your confidence and approval of my course.

The Secretary (Mr. SHEERIN) said:

Mr. Chairman and Gentlemen of the Committee: I thank you one and all most sincerely for this kind expression of your confidence and good will. My service upon the Committee has been a very great pleasure to myself. It is not hard to work when we find the associations in any kind of labor so entirely agreeable as I have found them in this Committee from the very moment I entered it until this time. I carry away with me recollections of the most pleasurable character, that will endure with me always. I thank you again, gentlemen, for your kind expressions and your generous approval of my official course.

THE CHAIR: The Chair thinks it would not be out of order to have the present Secretary of the Committee call the roll of States with the view of verifying the list of members of the new Committee, if I may so call it. The list has been published, and I take it that the list has been furnished to the officers of the Convention; but it may devolve upon the present Secretary to notify the members of the new Committee of the meeting that may be called when indicated from the gentlemen who ought to be consulted about the matter of the time and place of such meeting. The Chair assumes that the members of the new Committee, of the new Democratic National Committee, are not all present, and that probably the matter of organization, etc., will not be taken up now.

THE CHAIR: The Chair is requested to state that the members of the new Committee shall remain after this meeting shall adjourn for the purpose of, at least, a formal conference or for such other purpose as may be deemed proper by that body.

Hon. JAMES JEFFRIES, of Louisiana, moved that this Committee do now adjourn, without day; whereupon the Chair (Mr. HARRITY) put the motion, which was carried, and then arose and declared the Committee adjourned *sine die*.

ORGANIZATION OF NEW COMMITTEE.

The newly elected National Committee, composed of the following gentlemen, met for the purpose of organization. Hon. JAMES K. JONES, of Arkansas, was unanimously elected Chairman of the Committee, with power to select a Secretary and a Treasurer. Mr. JONES subsequently selected Hon. CHARLES A. WALSH, member of the National Committee from Iowa, as Secretary, and WILLIAM P. ST. JOHN, of the State of New York, as Treasurer of the Committee.

DEMOCRATIC NATIONAL COMMITTEE.

Alabama—HENRY D. CLAYTON.
Arkansas—THOMAS C. MCRAE.
California—J. J. DWYER.
Colorado—ADAIR WILSON.
Connecticut—CARLOS FRENCH.
Delaware—R. R. KENNEY.
Florida—SAMUEL PASCO.
Georgia—CLARK HOWELL, JR.
Idaho—GEORGE AINSLIE.
Illinois—THOMAS GAHAN.
Indiana—JOHN G. SHANKLIN.
Iowa—CHARLES A. WALSH.
Kansas—J. G. JOHNSON.
Kentucky—UREY WOODSON.
Louisiana—N. C. BLANCHARD.
Maine—SETH C. GORDON.
Maryland—ARTHUR P. GORMAN.
Massachusetts—JOHN W. CORCORAN.
Michigan—DANIEL J. CAMPAU.
Minnesota—DANIEL W. LAWLER.
Mississippi—W. V. SULLIVAN.
Missouri—W. J. STONE.
Montana—J. J. MACHATTON.
Nebraska—WM. H. THOMPSON.
Nevada—R. P. KEATING.
New Hampshire—A. W. SULLOWAY.
New Jersey—JAMES SMITH, JR.
New York—WM. F. SHEEHAN.
N. Carolina—JOSEPHUS DANIELS.
North Dakota—W. C. LIESTIKOW.
Ohio—JOHN R. MCLEAN.
Oregon—J. TOWNSEND.
Pennsylvania—WM. F. HARRITY.
Rhode Island—R. B. COMSTOCK.
S. Carolina—BENJ. R. TILLMAN.
South Dakota—JAS. M. WOODS.
Tennessee—J. M. HEAD.
Texas—J. G. DUDLEY.
Utah—A. W. MCCUNE.
Vermont—BRADLEY B. SMALLEY.
Virginia—P. J. OTEY.
Washington—HUGH C. WALLACE.
West Virginia—J. T. MCGRAW.
Wisconsin—E. C. WALL.
Wyoming—W. H. HOLLIDAY.
Alaska—C. D. ROGERS.
Arizona—MARCUS A. SMITH.
District of Columbia—LAWRENCE GARDNER.
Indian Ter.—THOMAS MARCUM.
N. Mexico—F. A. MANZANARES.
Oklahoma—WHITE M. GRANT.

EXECUTIVE COMMITTEE.

James K. Jones, Chairman.
Thos. O. Towles, Secretary.

Henry D. Clayton	Eufaula	Alabama.
Thomas C. McRae	Prescott	Arkansas.
J. J. Dwyer	San Francisco	California.
Adair Wilson	Durango	Colorado.
Richard R. Kenney	Dover	Delaware.
Samuel Pasco	Monticello	Florida.
George Ainslie	Boise City	Idaho.
John G. Shanklin	Evansville	Indiana.
C. A. Walsh	Ottumwa	Iowa.
Urey Woodson	Owensboro	Kentucky.
N. C. Blanchard	Shreveport	Louisiana.
Arthur P. Gorman	Laurel	Maryland.
D. J. Campau	Detroit	Michigan.
Wm. J. Stone	Jefferson City	Missouri.
W. H. Thompson	Grand Island	Nebraska.
James Smith, Jr	Newark	New Jersey.
Josephus Daniels	Raleigh	North Carolina.
Wm. C. Leistikow	Grafton	North Dakota.
B. R. Tillman	Trenton	South Carolina.
James M. Head	Nashville	Tennessee.
Peter J. Otey	Lynchburg	Virginia.
E. C. Wall	Milwaukee	Wisconsin.
Marcus A. Smith	Phœnix	Arizona.
Lawrence Gardner	Washington	Dist. of Columbia.
Thomas Marcum	Muscogee	Indian Territory.

CAMPAIGN COMMITTEE.

Chairman, Daniel J. Campau, Michigan.
Secretary, Frank Hosford, Michigan.

John R. McLean	Cincinnati	Ohio.
Wm. J. Stone	Jefferson City	Missouri.
J. G. Johnson	Peabody	Kansas.
Thos. Gahan	Chicago	Illinois.
Clark Howell, Jr	Atlanta	Georgia.
Wm. A. Clark	Butte	Montana.
James Kerr	Clearfield	Pennsylvania.

NOTIFICATION SPEECH OF GOV. W. J. STONE.

MADISON SQUARE GARDEN, NEW YORK,
August 12, 1896.

Mr. Chairman:

We are here this evening to give formal notice of their selection to the gentlemen nominated by the National Democratic Convention as candidates for President and Vice-President of the United States. Hitherto, by immemorial custom, the pleasing duty of delivering notifications of this character has devolved upon the permanent chairman of the National Convention acting, by virtue of his office, as chairman of the Notification Committee. Except for unfortunate circumstances, unexpected and unavoidable, the usual custom would not be departed from in the present instance. I regret to say, however, that unforeseen events of a personal nature have arisen which make it practically impossible for the Chairman of the Convention, the Hon. STEPHEN M. WHITE, of California, to be in New York at this time. A few days since he telegraphed me to that effect, and did me the honor to request me to represent him on this occasion. While I greatly appreciate the compliment conferred by this designation, I can not but deplore the enforced absence of the distinguished Senator from California, and I am directed by him to express his deep regret at his inability to be present and participate in the interesting ceremonies of this hour.

Mr. Chairman, the Convention which assembled at Chicago on the 7th day of July last was convened in the usual way, under a call issued in due form by the National Democratic Committee. There was nothing out of the ordinary in the manner of its assembling, and nothing in the action of the Committee under whose authority it was convoked to distinguish it from its predecessors. It was in all respects a regular National Convention of the Democratic party. Every State and Territory in the Union, from Maine to Alaska, were represented by a full quota of delegates, and I may add with perfect truth that a more intelligent and thoroughly representative body of Democrats was never assembled upon the American Continent. The Convention was called for two purposes: First, to formulate a platform declaratory of party principles, and, secondly, to nominate candidates for President and Vice-President of the United States. Both these purposes were fully accomplished according to the usages that have been recognized and the methods of procedure which have obtained in Democratic Conventions for fifty years. The acts of the Convention, therefore, were the acts of the Democratic party. Its work was done under the sovereign authority of the National organization; and that work was the direct outgrowth of the calm, well-matured judgment of the people themselves, deliberately expressed through their representatives chosen from among the wisest, most trusted, and patriotic of their fellow-citizens in all the States.

Although all I have said is literally true, yet the fact remains, of which every one is conscious, that there were extraneous circumstances leading up to the Convention which attracted unusual attention to its deliberations and invested them with unusual importance. To such an extent was this true that I may say without exaggeration that no other political convention has been assembled in this country since the civil war upon which public attention was riveted with such intensity, or in the outcome of whose deliberations not only the American people but the nations of the earth felt such deep concern. We are all familiar with the circumstances to which I refer. The existing National administration was created by the Democratic party. It is the result of the great victory won in 1892. The campaign of that year was fought almost wholly on the tariff issue. It was a war waged against the excessive, monopolistic, trust-breeding schedules of the McKinley law. The Democratic party was united almost as one man against that law, and thousands of those who believed in the policy of protection when conservatively administered for the public good and not for private enrichment, protested against this monstrous measure of extortion for individual and corporate emolument. Opposition to the McKinley law was the dominant issue of that campaign, and the measure was condemned by an overwhelming majority of the American people. But, Mr. Chairman, I desire to say that although the tariff was made the issue of 1892, there were thousands of Democrats who then believed that a reform in our monetary system was of far greater importance than a reform in our revenue policies. I was among those who so believed. Those holding to that belief did not in any degree underestimate the importance of the tariff issue—on the contrary, its importance was fully appreciated—but they believed nevertheless that the control of our fiscal affairs by a mercenary combination of Wall street bankers, dominated by foreign influences, was more perilous to national safety and more pernicious in its effect on national prosperity than all the tariffs the miserly hand of gluttonous greed could write. However, we acquiesced in the decision of our party Convention, accepted the issue as made, and as one man rallied with loyalty and alacrity to the standard of revenue reform. We rejoiced in Mr. CLEVELAND's election, and confidently expected, as we had a right to, that he would bring the tariff question to a speedy settlement and strip monopoly of its opportunity to plunder the people. But in this just expectation we were doomed to disappointment. Instead of devoting himself to a prompt and wise solution of the important issue upon which he was elected, he incontinently thrust it aside and began, almost at the threshold of his administration, to exercise the great powers of his office to commit the country to a financial system inaugurated by the Republican party, and which the Democratic party had time and again condemned in both State and National Conventions. In the beginning of this attempt the masses of the people, disappointed and distressed, looked on in amazement. With absorbing interest and with constantly increasing resentment they watched the rapid development of events. As these events passed before them one by one in quick succession, and when they came to understand their full meaning and effect, resentment turned to wrath and protest rose into revolt. Then began within the Democratic party one of the most remarkable struggles that has ever occurred in the political history of this country. It was a struggle for mastery between the National administration and the great masses of plain people, who constitute the party which created that administration. The prize they fought for was the National Convention. That convention was to determine whether the Democratic party should abide by the traditions of the fathers and adhere to its ancient faith, or whether it should obsequiously abandon the principles of true Democracy and become a pliant agent to advance the mercenary ends of an insolent plutocracy. The people won. They won a glorious victory. The full significance of their triumph cannot be estimated at a glance. Suppose they had lost; what then? Suppose the Chicago Convention had followed the servile example of the Republican Convention; what then? If that had happened what hue would the skies now reveal to the uplifted eyes of anxious millions? Would the star of hope then have risen luminous to the meridian or have fallen with waning light upon a clouded horizon? Upon what staff would the toiling millions in field and shop then have rested their tired hands? What bulwark of defense would then have stood between the great industrial and producing classes, who constitute the solid strength and safety of the State, and the combined aggressions of foreign money-changers and anglicized American millionaires? Upon what rock would the defenders of the Constitution, the champions of American ideas and the friends of American institutions have then anchored their hopes for the future? The paramount question before the country was and is—Shall this great Republic confess financial servitude to England, or act independently for itself? Shall this Government follow, or shall it lead? Shall it be a vassal or a sovereign? The Republican Convention declared for foreign supremacy—for American subserviency. It upheld the British policy of a single gold standard, fraudulently fastened upon this country, and declared that we are utterly incapable of maintaining an independent policy of our own. Confessing that the gold standard is fraught with evil to our people, and that bimetallism is best for this Nation and for the world, it yet declared that we are helpless—that we must stand idle, while our industries are prostrated and our people ruined, until England shall consent for us to lift our hands in our own defense. To this low state has MAMMON brought the great party of the immortal LINCOLN. For years plutocracy has been winding its slimy and poisonous coils around the Republican party, and it will strangle it to death as the sea serpents of old strangled the Trojan priest of Neptune and his sons. So also it laid its foul, corroding hand on the Democratic party—the party of JEFFERSON and JACKSON—and used all its giant strength to bend it to its purposes. Within both parties there was a mighty struggle for supremacy between those who believe in the sovereignty of the people and those who believe in the divinity of pelf. Upon the Republican party the hand of Marcus Aurelius Hanna has buckled a golden mail and sent it forth dedicated to the service of plutocracy in this free land of ours. But in the Democratic party, thank God, the people were triumphant. There the clutch of the money power, after a tremendous conflict, was broken. The priests of Mammon were scourged from the temple, and to-day, under the providence of high Heaven, the old party, rejuvinated, stands forth, stronger and better than ever, the undaunted champion of constitutional liberty, popular rights, and national independence. The guage of battle thrown down at St. Louis was taken up at Chicago. Against English ideas we place American ideas; against an English policy we place an American policy; against foreign domination we place American independence; and against the selfish control of privileged classes we place the sovereignty of the people. The Republican platform is the antithesis of the Democratic platform. One stands for gold monometallism, the other for gold and silver bimetallism. One proposes that we wait upon other nations; the other that we act for ourselves. One proposes that the Government shall lean upon the bankers of New York and London; the other that the Secretary of the Treasury shall stand erect, confident and fearless, and assert his power to protect the rights of the people and the honor the nation. One proposes to continue the policy of issuing bonds, the other to stop it. One declares for a European alliance, the other is a declaration for American independence. Upon these all-important questions issue is joined between the two great political parties of the Republic. Certainly there are other things of moment in which the people feel profound concern, but of all questions in the current political affairs of this day and generation the financial question rises to such supreme importance that all other objects are practically excluded from present consideration. The Chicago Convention declared in so many words that until this great, paramount issue was definitely settled, and settled right, the consideration of all other questions, upon which the people are seriously divided, should be postponed, or at least not pressed upon public or legislative attention. Around this one supreme issue the great battle of 1896 is to be fought. For the first time it has been fairly presented, without evasion or disguise. Both parties have taken position boldly. Both are confident and defiant. Between them the American people are the arbiters, and as such they are now to pass judgment upon the most important question presented to them since the storm of civil war wrecked happy homes and left its bloody trail upon the land. They are to pass judgment upon a question which I profoundly believe effects, as no other question can, not only the present happiness and prosperity of the people, but the felicity of their children, the perpetuity of American institutions, and the well-being of all mankind.

Mr. Chairman, in all great movements, in all concerted effort, when well directed, there must be leadership. A leader should be representative of the cause he champions. He should be more than that—he should be in all essential qualities, and in the highest degree, typical of those who invest him with the dignity and responsibility of leadership.

The Chicago platform has been denounced as un-Democratic and the delegates composing the Convention have been stigmatized as anarchists and socialists. We have heard much of this from a certain class of papers and individuals. On Saturday last in my own State an ex-Democratic, ex-Supreme Court Judge characterized the Chicago platform as "a bundle of Populistic notions, saturated brimful with socialism and anarchy," and at the same time an ex-Democratic corporation attorney of some distinction declared that American citizenship meant government "not by the unthinking, unheeding masses, but by the elements which are guided by judgment and reason." "Unthinking, unheeding masses" is very good. "The elements which are guided by judgment and reason" is extra good. It is at least a slight modification of VANDER-

BILT's arrogant anathema, "Damn the people," and for this small concession we ought no doubt to be duly grateful. Who composed the Chicago Convention? From the state in which reside the gentlemen from whom I have quoted, the delegation sent to that Convention was composed of farmers, lawyers, doctors, editors, merchants, manufacturers, and several of the most conspicuously successful business men in the Mississippi Valley. Among them also were eminent judges of high courts, Senators of the United States, Representatives in Congress, and the Treasurer and Governor of the state. That delegation was chosen by one of the greatest conventions ever assembled in that State, representing all classes of the very best people of the Commonwealth. What was true of Missouri was equally true of all the States. If these men could not speak for the Democratic party, who could? If these men do not understand Democracy, who are its exponents? But these are the men who are ridiculed as an unthinking, unheeding mob, who can not be trusted in the conduct of public affairs, and these are the men who must give way to English toadies and the pampered minions of corporate rapacity, who arrogate to themselves all the virtues and wisdom of the world! Sir, the man who holds up to opprobrium such men as constituted the Chicago Convention, who denounces them as cranks, anarchists, or socialists, or who in any respect impugns their intelligence or patriotism, does himself most rank injustice if he be not a knave, a slanderer, or a fool. That convention did indeed represent the "masses" of the people—the great industrial and producing masses of the people. It represented the men who plow and plant, who fatten herds, who toil in shops, who fell forests, and delve in mines. But are these to be regarded with contumely and addressed in terms of contempt? Why, sir, these are the men who feed and clothe the nation; whose products make up the sum of our exports; who produce the wealth of the Republic; who bear the heaviest burdens in times of peace; who are ready always to give their life-blood for their country's flag—in short, these are the men whose sturdy arms and faithful hands uphold the stupendous fabric of our civilization. They are the bravest and the tenderest, the truest and the best. These are the men who spoke at Chicago in tones that rang out clear, and high, and strong. They were in earnest, and did not mean to be misunderstood. It was the voice of true Democracy. It was also the voice of deep conviction, spoken without fear. They demanded what they want, and they mean to have it. They did not go to Wall street for their principles, nor over the sea for their inspiration. Their principles were inherited from the fathers and their inspiration sprang from an unconquerable love of country and of home.

For a leader they chose one of their own—a plain man of the people. His whole life and life work identify him, in sympathy and interest, with those who represent the great industrial forces of the country. Among them he was born and reared, and has lived and wrought all the days of his life. To their cause he has devoted all the splendid powers with which God endowed him. He has been their constant and fearless champion. They know him, and they trust him. Suave, yet firm; gentle, yet dauntless; warm-hearted, yet deliberate; confident and self-poised, but without vanity; learned in books and statecraft, but without pedantry or pretense; a superb orator, yet a man of the greatest caution and method; equipped with large experience in public affairs, true to his convictions, true to himself, and false to no man, WILLIAM J. BRYAN is a model American gentleman and a peerless leader of the people. This man is our leader. Under his banner and guided by his wisdom we will go forth to conquer. Let us rally everwhere, on hilltops and in the valleys, and strike for homes, our loved ones, and our native land. I have do doubt of victory. It is as sure to come as the rising of the sun. And it will come like a sunburst, scattering the mists, and the nation, exultant and happy, will leap forward like a giant refreshed to that high destiny it was designed to accomplish. This man will be President. His administration will be a shining epoch in our history, for he will leave behind him a name made illustrious by great achievements, and by deeds that will embalm him forever in the hearts and memory of his countrymen.

Mr. BRYAN. I esteem it a great honor, as it is most certainly a pleasure, to be made the instrument of informing you, as I now do, that you were nominated for the office of President of the United States by the Democratic National Convention which assembled in Chicago in July last. I hand you this formal notice of your nomination, accompanied by a copy of the platform adopted by the Convention, and upon that platform I have the honor to request your acceptance of the nomination tendered. You are the candidate of the Democratic party, but you are more than that—you are the candidate of all the people, without regard to party, who believe in the purposes your election is intended to accomplish. This battle must be fought upon ground high above the level of partisanship. I hope to see you unfurl the flag in the name of America and American manhood. In saying this I but repeat the expressed wish of the Convention which nominated you. Do this, and though you will not have millions of money at your command, you will have millions of sturdy Americans at your back. Lead on, and we will follow. Who will not follow here is unworthy to lead in any cause. Lead on with unfaltering step, and may God's blessing attend you and His omnipotent hand crown you with success.

MR. BRYAN'S SPEECH OF ACCEPTANCE.

NEW YORK CITY, August 12, 1896.

Mr. BRYAN: Mr. Chairman, Gentlemen of the Committee and Fellow-Citizens: I shall, at a future day and in a formal letter, accept the nomination which is now tendered by the Notification Committee, and I shall at that time touch upon the issues presented by the platform. It is fitting, however, that at this time, in the presence of those here assembled, I shall speak at some length in regard to the campaign upon which we are now entering. We do not underestimate the forces arrayed against us, nor are we unmindful of the importance of the struggle in which we are engaged; but relying for success upon the righteousness of our cause, we shall defend with all possible vigor the positions taken by our party. We are not surprised that some of our opponents, in the absence of better argument, resort to abusive epithets, but they may rest assured that no language, however violent, no invectives, however vehement, will lead us to depart a single hair's-breadth from the course marked out by the National Convention. The citizen, either public or private, who assails the character and questions the patriotism of the delegates assembled in the Chicago Convention, assails the character and questions the patriotism of the millions who have arrayed themselves under the banner there raised.

It has been charged by men standing high in business and political circles that our platform is a menace to private security and public safety; and it has been asserted that those whom I have the honor, for the time being, to represent, not only meditate an attack upon the rights of property, but are the foes both of social order and national honor.

Those who stand upon the Chicago Platform are prepared to make known and to defend every motive which influences them, every purpose which animates them, and every hope which inspires them. They understand the genius of our institutions; they are stanch supporters of the form of government under which we live, and they build their faith upon foundations laid by the fathers. ANDREW JACKSON has stated with admirable clearness and with an emphasis which cannot be surpassed, both the duty and the sphere of government. He said: "Distinctions in society will always exist under every just government. Equality of talents, of education or of wealth cannot be produced by human institutions. In the full enjoyment of the gifts of Heaven and the fruits of superior industry, economy and virtue, every man is equally entitled to protection by law." We yield to none in our devotion to the doctrine just enunciated. Our campaign has not for its object the reconstruction of society. We cannot insure to the vicious the fruits of a virtuous life; we would not invade the home of the provident in order to supply the wants of the spendthrift; we do not propose to transfer the rewards of industry to the lap of indolence. Property is and will remain the stimulus to endeavor and the compensation for toil. We believe, as asserted in the Declaration of Independence, that all men are created equal; but that does not mean that all men are or can be equal in possessions, in ability or in merit; it simply means that all shall stand equal before the law, and that government officials shall not, in making, construing or enforcing the law, discriminate between citizens.

I assert that property rights, as well as the rights of persons, are safe in the hands of the people. ABRAHAM LINCOLN, in his message sent to Congress in December, 1861, said: "No men living are more worthy to be trusted than those who toil up from poverty; none less inclined to take or touch aught which they have not honestly earned." I repeat his language with unqualified approval, and join with him in the warning which he added, namely: "Let them beware of surrendering a political power which they already possess, and which power, if surrendered, will surely be used to close the doors of advancement against such as they, and to fix new disabilities and burdens upon them, till all of liberty shall be lost." Those who daily follow the injunction: "In the sweat of thy face shalt thou eat bread," are now, as they ever have been, the bulwark of law and order—the source of our nation's greatness in time of peace, and its surest defenders in time of war.

But I have only read a part of Jackson's utterance—let me give you his conclusion: "But when the laws undertake to add to those natural and just advantages artificial distinctions—to grant titles, gratuities and exclusive privileges—to make the rich richer and the potent more powerful—the humble members of society—the farmers, mechanics and the laborers—who have neither the time nor the means of securing like favors for themselves, have a right to complain of the injustice of their government." Those who support the Chicago platform indorse all of the quotation from Jackson—the latter part as well as the former part.

We are not surprised to find arrayed against us those who are the beneficiaries of Government favoritism—they have read our platform. Nor are we surprised to learn that we must in this campaign face the hostility of those who find a pecuniary advantage in advocating the doctrine of non-interference when great aggregations of wealth are trespassing upon the rights of individuals. We welcome such opposition—it is the highest indorsement which could be bestowed upon us. We are content to have the co-operation of those who desire to have the Government administered without fear or favor. It is not the wish of the general public that trusts should spring into existence and override the weaker members of society; it is not the wish of the general public that these trusts should destroy competition and then collect such tax as they will from those who are at their mercy; nor is it the fault of the general public that the instrumentalities of government have been so often prostituted to purposes of private gain. Those who stand upon the Chicago platform believe that the Government should not only avoid wrongdoing, but that it should also prevent wrongdoing, and they believe that the law should be enforced alike against all enemies of the public weal. They do not excuse petit larceny, but they declare that grand larceny is equally a crime; they do not defend the occupation of the highwayman who robs the unsuspecting traveler, but they include among the transgressors those who, through the more polite and less hazardous means of legislation, appropriate to their own use the proceeds of the toil of others. The commandment: "Thou shalt not steal," thundered from Sinai and reiterated in the legislation of all nations, is no respecter of persons. It must be applied to the great as well as to the small; to the strong as well as the weak; to the corporate person created by law as well as to the person of flesh and blood created by the Almighty. No government is worthy of the name which is not able to protect from every arm uplifted for his injury the humblest citizen who lives beneath the flag. It follows as a necessary conclusion that vicious legislation must be remedied by the people who suffer from the effects of such legislation, and not by those who enjoy its benefits.

The Chicago platform has been condemned by some, because it dissents from an opinion rendered by the Supreme Court declaring the income tax law unconstitutional. Our critics even go so far as to apply the name Anarchist to those who stand upon that plank of the platform. It must be remembered that we expressly recognize the binding force of that decision so long as it stands as a part of the law of the land. There is in the platform no suggestion of an attempt to dispute the authority of the Supreme Court. The party is simply pledged to use "all the constitutional power which remains after that decision, or which may come from its reversal by the court as it may hereafter be constituted." Is there any disloyalty in that pledge? For a hundred years the Supreme Court of the United States has sustained the principle which underlies the income tax. Some twenty years ago this same court sustained without a dissenting voice an income tax law almost identical with the one recently overthrown; has not a future court as much right to return to the judicial precedents of a century as the present court had to depart from them? When courts allow rehearings they admit that error is possible; the late decision against the income tax was rendered by a majority of one after a rehearing.

While the money question overshadows all others questions in importance, I desire it distinctly understood that I shall offer no apology for the income tax plank of the Chicago platform. The last income tax law sought to apportion the burdens of government more equitably among those who enjoy the protection of the Government. At present the expenses of the Federal Government, collected through internal revenue taxes and import duties, are especially burdensome upon the poorer classes of society. A law which collects from some citizens more than their share of the taxes and collects from other citizens less than their share, is simply an indirect means of transferring one man's property to another man's pocket, and while the process may be quite satisfactory to the men who escape just taxation, it can never be satisfactory to those who are overburdened. The last income tax law, with its exemption provisions, when considered in connection with other methods of taxation in force, was not unjust to the possessors of large incomes, because they were not compelled to pay a total Federal tax greater than their share. The income tax is not new nor is it based upon hostility to the rich. The system is employed in several of the most important nations of Europe, and every income tax law now upon the statute books in any land, so far as I have been able to ascertain, contains an exemption clause. While the collection of an income tax in other countries does not make it necessary for this nation to adopt the system, yet it ought to moderate the language of those who denounce the income tax as an assault upon the well-to-do.

Not only shall I refuse to apologize for the advocacy of an income tax law by the National Convention, but I shall also refuse to apologize for the exercise by it of the right to dissent from a decision of the Supreme Court. In a government like ours every public official is a public servant, whether he hold office by election or by appointment, whether he serves for a term of years or during good behavior, and the people have a right to criticise his official acts. "Confidence is everywhere the parent of despotism; free government exists in jealousy and not in confidence"—these are the words of THOMAS JEFFERSON, and I submit that they present a truer conception of popular government than that entertained by those who would prohibit an unfavorable comment upon a court decision. Truth will vindicate itself; only error fears free speech. No public official who conscientiously discharges his duty as he sees it will desire to deny to those whom he serves the right to discuss his official conduct.

Now let me ask you to consider the paramount question of this campaign—the money question. It is scarcely necessary to defend the principle of bimetallism. No national party during the entire history of the United States has ever declared against it, and no party in this campaign has had the temerity to oppose it. Three parties—the Democratic, Populist and Silver parties—have not only declared for bimetallism, but have outlined the specific legislation necessary to restore silver to its ancient position by the side of gold. The Republican platform expressly declares that bimetallism is desirable when it pledges the Republican party to aid in securing it as soon as the assistance of certain foreign nations can be obtained. Those who represented the minority sentiment in the Chicago Convention opposed the free coinage of silver by the United States by independent action on the ground that, in their judgment, it "would retard or entirely prevent the establishment of international bimetallism, to which the efforts of the Government should be steadily directed." When they asserted that the efforts of the Government should be steadily directed toward the establishment of international bimetallism, they condemned monometallism. The gold standard has been weighed in the balance and found wanting. Take from it the powerful support of the money-owning and the money-changing classes and it cannot stand for one day in any nation in the world. It was fastened upon the United States without discussion before the people, and its friends have never yet been willing to risk a verdict before the voters upon that issue.

There can be no sympathy or co-operation between the advocates of a universal gold standard and the advocates of bimetallism. Between bimetallism—whether independent or international—and the gold standard there is an impassable gulf. Is this quadrennial agitation in favor of international bimetallism conducted in good faith, or do our opponents really desire to maintain the gold standard permanently? Are they willing to confess the superiority of a double standard when joined in by the leading nations of the world, or do they still insist that gold is the only metal suitable for standard money among civilized nations? If they are in fact desirous of securing bimetallism, we may expect them to point out the evils of a gold standard and defend bimetallism as a system.

If, on the other hand, they are bending their energies toward the permanent establishment of a gold standard under cover of a declaration in favor of international bimetallism, I am justified in suggesting that honest money cannot be expected at the hands of those who deal dishonestly with the American people.

What is the test of honesty in money? It must certainly be found in the purchasing power of the dollar. An absolutely honest dollar would not vary in its general purchasing power; it would be absolutely stable when measured by average prices. A dollar which increases in purchasing power is just as dishonest as a dollar which decreases in purchasing power. Professor Laughlin, now of the University of Chicago, and one of the highest gold-standard authorities, in his work on bimetallism, not only admits that gold does not remain absolutely stable in value, but expressly asserts "that there is no such thing as a standard of value for the future payments, either in gold or silver, which remains absolutely invariable." He even suggests that a multiple standard, wherein the unit is "based upon the selling prices of a number of articles of general consumption," would be a more just standard than either gold or silver, or both, because "a long-time contract would thereby be paid at its maturity by the same purchasing power as was given in the beginning."

It cannot be successfully claimed that monometallism or bimetallism, or any other system, gives an absolutely just standard of value. Under both monometallism and bimetallism the Government fixes the weight and fineness of the dollar, invests it with legal tender qualities and then opens the mints to its restricted coinage, leaving the purchasing power of the dollar to be determined by the number of dollars. Bimetallism is better than monometallism, not because it gives us a perfect dollar—that is, a dollar absolutely unvarying in its general purchasing power—but because it makes a nearer approach to stability, to honesty, to justice, than a gold standard possibly can. Prior to 1873, when there were enough open mints to permit all the gold and silver available for coinage to find entrance into the world's volume of standard money, the United

States might have maintained a gold standard with less injury to the people of this country; but now, when each step toward a universal gold standard enhances the purchasing power of gold, depresses prices and transfers to the pockets of the creditor class an unearned increment, the influence of this great nation must not be thrown upon the side of gold unless we are prepared to accept the natural and legitimate consequences of such an act. Any legislation which lessens the world's stock of standard money increases the exchangeable value of the dollar; therefore, the crusader against silver must inevitably raise the purchasing power of money and lower the money value of all other forms of property.

Our opponents sometimes admit that it was a mistake to demonetize silver, but insist that we should submit to present conditions rather that return to the bimetallic system. They err in supposing that we have reached the end of the evil results of gold standard; we have not reached the end. The injury is a continuing one, and no person can say how long the world is to suffer from the attempt to make gold the only standard money. The same influences which are now operating to destroy silver in the United States will, if successful here, be turned against other silver-using countries, and each new convert to the gold standard will add to the general distress. So long as the scramble for gold continues, prices must fall, and a general fall in prices is but another definition of hard times.

Our opponents, while claiming entire disinterestedness for themselves, have appealed to the selfishness of nearly every class of society. Recognizing the disposition of the individual voter to consider the effect of any proposed legislation upon himself, we present to the American people the financial policy outlined in the Chicago platform, believing that it will result in the greatest good to the greatest number.

The farmers are opposed to the gold standard because they have felt its effects. Since they sell at wholesale and buy at retail they have lost more than they have gained by falling prices, and, besides this, they have found that certain fixed charges have not fallen at all. Taxes have not been perceptibly decreased, although it requires more of farm products now than formerly to secure the money with which to pay taxes. Debts have not fallen. The farmer who owed $1,000 is still compelled to pay $1,000, although it may be twice as difficult as formerly to obtain the dollars with which to pay the debt. Railroad rates have not been reduced to keep pace with falling prices, and besides these items there are many more. The farmer has thus found it more and more difficult to live. Has he not a just complaint against the gold standard?

The wage-earners have been injured by a gold standard, and have expressed themselves upon the subject with great emphasis. In February, 1895, a petition asking for the immediate restoration of the free and unlimited coinage of gold and silver at 16 to 1 was signed by the representatives of all, or nearly all, the leading labor organizations and presented to Congress. Wage-earners know that while a gold standard raises the purchasing power of the dollar it also makes it more difficult to obtain possession of the dollar; they know that employment is less permanent, loss of work more probable, and re-employment less certain. A gold standard encourages the hoarding of money because money is rising; it also discourages enterprise and paralyzes industry. On the other hand, the restoration of bimetallism will discourage hoarding, because, when prices are steady or rising, money cannot afford to lie idle in the bank vaults. The farmers and wage-earners together constitute a considerable majority of the people of the country. Why should their interests be ignored in considering financial legislation? A monetary system which is peculiarly advantageous to a few syndicates has far less to commend it than a system which would give hope and encouragement to those who create the nation's wealth.

Our opponents have made a special appeal to those who hold fire and life insurance policies, but these policy-holders know that, since the total premiums received exceed the total losses paid, a rising standard must be of more benefit to the companies than to the policy-holders.

Much solicitude has been expressed by our opponents for the depositors in savings banks. They constantly parade before these depositors the advantages of a gold standard, but these appeals will be in vain, because savings bank depositors know that under a gold standard there is increasing danger that they will lose their deposits because of the inability of the banks to collect their assets; and they still further know that, if the gold standard is to continue infinitely, they may be compelled to withdraw their deposits in order to pay living expenses.

It is only necessary to note the increasing number of failures in order to know that a gold standard is ruinous to merchants and manufacturers. These business men do not make their profits from the people from whom they borrow money, but from the people to whom they sell their goods. If the people cannot buy, retailers cannot sell, and, if retailers cannot sell, wholesale merchants and manufacturers must go into bankruptcy.

Those who hold, as a permanent investment, the stock of railroads and of other enterprises—I do not include those who speculate in stocks or use stock-holdings as a means of obtaining inside advantage in construction contracts—are injured by a gold standard. The rising dollar destroys the earning power of these enterprises without reducing their liabilities, and, as dividends cannot be paid until salaries and fixed charges have been satisfied, the stockholders must bear the burden of hard times.

Salaries in business occupations depend upon business conditions, and the gold standard both lessens the amount and threatens the permanency of such salaries.

Official salaries, except the salaries of those who hold office for life, must, in the long run, be adjusted to the conditions of those who pay the taxes, and if the present financial policy continues we must expect the contest between the taxpayer and the taxeater to increase in bitterness.

The professional classes—in the main—derive their support from the producing classes, and can only enjoy prosperity when there is prosperity among those who create wealth.

I have not attempted to describe the effect of the gold standard upon all classes—in fact, I have only had time to mention a few—but each person will be able to apply the principles stated to his own occupation.

It must also be remembered that it is the desire of people generally to convert their earnings into real or personal property. This being true, in considering any temporary advantage which may come from a system under which the dollar rises in its purchasing power, it must not be forgotten that the dollar cannot buy more than formerly, unless property sells for less than formerly. Hence, it will be seen that a large portion of those who may find some pecuniary advantage in a gold standard will discover that their losses exceed their gains.

It is sometimes asserted by our opponents that a bank belongs to the debtor class, but this is not true of any solvent bank. Every statement published by a solvent bank shows that the assets exceed the liabilities. That is to say, while the bank owes a large amount of money to its depositors, it not only has enough on hand in money and notes to pay its depositors, but in addition thereto, has enough to cover its capital and surplus. When the dollar is rising in value slowly a bank may, by making short-time loans and taking good security, avoid loss; but when prices are falling rapidly the bank is apt to lose more because of bad debts than it can gain by the increase in the purchasing power of its capital and surplus.

Some bankers, however, combine the business of a bond broker with the ordinary banking business, and these may make enough in the negotiation of loans to offset the losses arising in legitimate banking business. As long as human nature remains as it is there will always be danger that, unless restrained by public opinion or legal enactment, those who see a pecuniary benefit for themselves in a certain condition may yield to the temptation to bring about that condition. JEFFERSON has stated that one of the main duties of government is to prevent men from injuring one another, and never was that duty more important than it is to-day. It is not strange that those who have made a profit by furnishing gold to the Government in the hour of its extremity, favor a financial policy which kept the Government dependent upon them. I believe, however, that I speak the sentiment of the vast majority of the people of the United States when I say that a wise financial policy administered in behalf of all the people would make our Government independent of any combination of financiers, foreign or domestic.

Let me say a word, now, in regard to certain persons who are pecuniarily benefited by a gold standard, and who favor it, not from a desire to tresspass upon the rights of others, but because the circumstances which surround them blind them to the effect of the gold standard upon others. I shall ask you to consider the language of two gentlemen whose long public service and high standing in the party to which they belong will protect them from adverse criticism by our opponents. In 1869 Senator SHERMAN said : " The contraction of the currency is a far more distressing operation than Senators suppose. Our own and other nations have gone through that operation before. It is not possible to take that voyage without the sorest distress. To every person, except a capitalist out of debt, or a salaried officer or annuitant, it is a period of loss, danger, lassitude of trade, fall of wages, suspension of enterprise, bankruptcy and disaster. It means ruin to all dealers whose debts are twice their business capital, though one-third less than their actual property. It means the fall of all agricultural production without any great reduction of taxes. What prudent man would dare to build a house, a railroad, a factory or a barn with this certain fact before him?" As I have said before, the salaried officer referred to must be the man whose salary is fixed for life, and not the man whose salary depends upon business conditions. When Mr. SHERMAN describes contraction of the currency as disastrous to all the people except the capitalist out of debt and those who stand in a position similar to his, he is stating a truth which must be apparent to every person who will give the matter careful consideration. Mr. SHERMAN was at that time speaking of the contraction of the volume of paper currency, but the principle which he set forth applies, if there is a contraction of the volume of the standard money of the world.

Mr. BLAINE discussed the same principle in connection with the demonetization of silver. Speaking in the House of Representatives on the 7th of February, 1878, he said : " I believe the struggle now going on in this country and other countries for a single gold standard would, if successful, produce widespread disaster in and throughout the commercial world. The destruction of silver as money, and the establishing of gold as the sole unit of value must have a ruinous effect on all forms of property, except those investments which yield a fixed return in money. These would be enormously enhanced in value, and would gain a disproportionate and unfair advantage over every other species of property." Is it strange that the "holders of investments which yield a fixed return in money" can regard the destruction of silver with complacency? May we not expect the holders of other forms of property to protest against giving to money a "disproportionate and unfair advantage over every other species of property?" If the relatively few whose wealth consists largely in fixed investments have a right to use the ballot to enhance the value of their investments, have not the rest of the people the right to use the ballot to protect themselves from the disastrous consequences of a rising standard?

The people who must purchase money with the products of toil stand in a position entirely different from the position of those who own money or receive a fixed income. The well-being of the nation—aye, of civilization itself—depends upon the prosperity of the masses. What shall it profit us to have a dollar which grows more valuable every day if such a dollar lowers the standard of civilization and brings distress to the people? What shall it profit us if, in trying to raise our credit by increasing the purchasing power of our dollar, we destroy our ability to pay the debts already contracted by lowering the purchasing power of the products with which those debts must be paid? If it is asserted, as it constantly is asserted, that the gold standard will enable us to borrow more money from abroad, I reply that the restoration of bimetallism will restore the parity between money and property, and thus permit an era of prosperity which will enable the American people to become loaners of money instead of perpetual borrowers. Even if we desire to borrow, how long can we continue borrowing under a system which, by lowering the value of property, weakens the foundation upon which credit rests?

Even the holders of fixed investments, though they gain an advantage from the appreciation of the dollar, certainly see the injustice of the legislation which gives them this advantage over those whose incomes depend upon the value of property and products. If the holders of fixed investments will not listen to arguments based upon justice and equity, I appeal to them to consider the interests of posterity. We do not live for ourselves alone; our labor, our self-denial and our anxious care—all these are for those who are to come after us.

as much as for ourselves, but we cannot protect our children beyond the period of our lives. Let those who are now reaping advantage from a vicious financial system remember that, in the years to come, their own children and their children's children may, through the operation of this same system, be made to pay tribute to the descendants of those who are wronged to-day.

As against the maintenance of a gold standard, either permanently or until other nations can be united for its overthrow, the Chicago platform presents a clear and emphatic demand for the immediate restoration of the free and unlimited coinage of silver and gold at the present legal ratio of 16 to 1, without waiting for the aid or consent of any other nation. We are not asking that a new experiment be tried; we are insisting upon a return to a financial policy approved by the experience of history and supported by all the prominent statesmen of our nation from the days of the first President down to 1873. When we ask that our mints be opened to the free and unlimited coinage of silver into full legal tender money, we are simply asking that the same mint privileges be accorded to silver that are now accorded to gold. When we ask that this coinage be at the ratio of 16 to 1 we simply ask that our gold coins and standard silver dollar—which, be it remembered, contains the same amount of pure silver as the first silver dollar coined at our mints—retain their present weight and fineness.

The theoretical advantage of the bimetallic system is best stated by a European writer on political economy, who suggests the following illustration: A river fed from two sources is more uniform in volume than a river fed from one source— the reason being that when one of the feeders is swollen the other may be low; whereas, a river which has but one feeder must rise or fall with that feeder. So in the case of bimetallism, the volume of metallic money receives contributions from both the gold mines and the silver mines, and therefore, varies less; and the dollar, resting upon two metals, is less changeable in its purchasing power than the dollar which rests upon one metal only.

If there are two kinds of money, the option must rest either with the debtor or with the creditor. Assuming that their rights are equal, we must look at the interests of society in general in order to determine to which side the option should be given. Under the bimetallic system, gold and silver are linked together by law at a fixed ratio, and any person or persons owning any quantity of either metal can have the same converted into full legal-tender money. If the creditor has the right to choose the metal in which payment should be made, it is reasonable to suppose that he will require the debtor to pay in the dearer metal if there is any perceptible difference between the bullion values of the metals. This new demand created for the dearer metal will make that metal dearer still, while the decreased demand for the cheaper metal will make that metal cheaper still. If, on the other hand, the debtor exercises the option, it is reasonable to suppose that he will pay in the cheaper metal if one metal is perceptibly cheaper than the other; but the demand thus created for the cheaper metal will raise its price, while the lessened demand for the dearer metal will lower its price. In other words, when the creditor has the option, the metals are drawn apart; whereas, when the debtor has the option, the metals are held together approximately at the ratio fixed by law; provided the demand created is sufficient to absorb all of both metals presented at the mint.

Society is, therefore, interested in having the option exercised by the debtor. Indeed, there can be no such thing as real bimetallism unless the option is exercised by the debtor. The exercise of the option by the debtor compels the creditor classes, whether domestic or foreign, to exert themselves to maintain the parity between gold and silver at the legal ratio, whereas they might find a profit in driving one of the metals to a premium if they could then demand the dearer metal. The right of the debtor to choose the coin in which payment shall be made extends to obligations due from the Government as well as contracts between individuals. A Government obligation is simply a debt due from all of the people to one of the people, and it is impossible to justify a policy which makes the interests of the one person who holds the obligation superior to the rights of the many who must be taxed to pay it. When, prior to 1873, silver was at a premium, it was never contended that national honor required the payment of Government obligations in silver, and the MATTHEWS resolution, adopted by Congress in 1878, expressly asserted the right of the United States to redeem coin obligations in standard silver dollars as well as in gold coin.

Upon this subject the Chicago platform reads: " We are opposed to the policy and practice of surrendering to the holders of the obligations of the United States the option reserved by law to the Government of redeeming such obligations in either silver coin or gold coin."

It is constantly assumed by some that the United States notes, commonly called greenbacks, and the Treasury notes, issued under the act of 1890, are responsible for the recent drain upon the gold reserve, but this assumption is entirely without foundation. Secretary CARLISLE appeared before the House Committee on Appropriations on January 21, 1895, and I quote from the printed report of his testimony before the committee:

Mr. SIBLEY: I would like to ask you (perhaps not entirely connected with the matter under discussion) what objection could there be to having the option of redeeming either in silver or gold lie with the Treasury instead of the note-holder?

Secretary CARLISLE: If that policy had been adopted at the beginning of the resumption—and I am not saying this for the purpose of criticising the action of any of my predecessors, or anybody else—but if the policy of reserving to the Government, at the beginning of resumption, the option of redeeming in gold or silver all its paper presented, I believe it would have worked beneficially, and there would have been no trouble growing out of it, but the Secretaries of the Treasury from the beginning of resumption have pursued a policy of redeeming in gold or silver at the option of the holder of the paper, and if any Secretary had afterward attempted to change that policy and force silver upon a man who wanted gold, or gold upon a man who wanted silver, and especially if he had made that attempt at such a critical period as we have had in the last two years, my judgment is it would have been very disastrous.

I do not agree with the Secretary that it was wise to follow a bad precedent, but from his answer it will be seen that the fault does not lie with the greenbacks and Treasury notes, but rather with the executive officers who have seen fit to surrender a right which should have been exercised for the protection of the interests of the people. This executive action has already been made the excuse for the issue of more than $250,000,000 in bonds, and it is impossible to estimate the amount of bonds which may hereafter be issued if this policy is continued. We are told that any attempt upon the part of the Government at this time to redeem its obligations in silver would put a premium upon gold, but why should it? The Bank of France exercises the right to redeem all bank paper in either gold or silver, and yet France maintains the parity between gold and silver at the ratio of 15½ to 1, and retains in circulation more silver per capita than we do in the United States.

It may be further answered that our opponents have suggested no feasible plan for avoiding the dangers which they fear. The retirement of the greenbacks and Treasury notes would not protect the Treasury, because the same policy which now leads the Secretary of the Treasury to redeem all Government paper in gold, when gold is demanded, will require the redemption of all silver dollars and silver certificates in gold, if the greenbacks and Treasury notes are withdrawn from circulation. More than this, if the Government should retire its paper and throw upon the banks the necessity of furnishing coin redemption, the banks would exercise the right to furnish either gold or silver. In other words, they would exercise the option, just as the Government ought to exercise it now. The Government must either exercise the right to redeem its obligations in silver when silver is more convenient, or it must retire all the silver and silver certificates from circulation and leave nothing but gold as legal-tender money. Are our opponents willing to outline a financial system which will carry out their policy to its legitimate conclusion, or will they continue to cloak their designs in ambiguous phrases?

There is an actual necessity for bimetallism as well as a theoretical defence of it. During the last twenty-three years legislation has been creating an additional demand for gold, and this law-created demand has resulted in increasing the purchasing power of each ounce of gold. The restoration of bimetallism in the United States will take away from gold

APPENDIX. 117

just so much of its purchasing power as was added to it by the demonetization of silver by the United States. The silver dollar is now held up to the gold dollar by legal-tender laws and not by redemption in gold, because the standard silver dollars are not now redeemable in gold either in law or by administrative policy.

We contend that free and unlimited coinage by the United States alone will raise the bullion value of silver to its coinage value, and thus make silver bullion worth $1.29 per ounce in gold throughout the world. This proposition is in keeping with natural laws, not in defiance of them. The best known law of commerce is the law of supply and demand. We recognize this law and build our argument upon it. We apply this law to money when we say that a reduction in the volume of money will raise the purchasing power of the dollar; we also apply the law of supply and demand to silver when we say that a new demand for silver created by law will raise the price of silver bullion. Gold and silver are different from other commodities, in that they are limited in quantity. Corn, wheat, manufactured products, etc., can be produced almost without limit, provided they can be sold at a price sufficient to stimulate production, but gold and silver are called precious metals, because they are found, not produced. These metals have been the objects of anxious search as far back as history runs, yet, according to Mr. HARVEY's calculation, all the gold coin of the world can be melted into a 22-foot cube, and all the silver coin in the world into a 66-foot cube. Because gold and silver are limited, both in the quantity now in hand, and in annual production, it follows that legislation can fix the ratio between them.

Any purchaser who stands ready to take the entire supply of any given article at a certain price can prevent that article from falling below that price. So the Government can fix a price for gold and silver by creating a demand greater than the supply. International bimetallists believe that several nations, by entering into an agreement to coin at a fixed ratio all the gold and silver presented, can maintain the bullion value of the metals at the mint ratio. When a mint price is thus established, it regulates the bullion price, because any person desiring coin may have the bullion converted into coin at that price, and any person desiring bullion can secure it by melting the coin. The only question upon which international bimetallists and independent bimetallists differ is: Can the United States by the free and unlimited coinage of silver at the present legal ratio create a demand for silver which, taken in connection with the demand already in existence, will be sufficient to utilize all the silver that will be presented at the mints? They agree in their defence of the bimetallic principle, and they agree in unalterable opposition to the gold standard. International bimetallists cannot complain that free coinage gives a benefit to the mine owner, because international bimetallism gives to the owner of silver all the advantages offered by independent bimetallism at the same ratio. International bimetallists cannot accuse the advocates of free silver of being "bullion owners who desire to raise the value of their bullion;" or "debtors who desire to pay their debts in cheap dollars;" or "demagogues who desire to curry favor with the people." They must rest their opposition upon one ground only, namely: That the supply of silver available for coinage is too large to be utilized by the United States.

In discussing this question we must consider the capacity of our people to use silver and the quantity of silver which can come to our mints. It must be remembered that we live in a country only partially developed, and that our people far surpass any equal number of people in the world in their power to consume and produce. Our extensive railroad development and enormous internal commerce must also be taken into consideration. Now, how much silver can come here? Not the coined silver of the world, because almost all of it is more valuable at this time in other lands than it will be at our mints under free coinage. If our mints are opened to free and unlimited coinage at the present ratio, merchandise silver cannot come here, because the labor applied to it has made it worth more in the form of merchandise than it will be worth at our mints. We cannot even expect all of the annual product of silver, because India, China, Japan, Mexico and all the other silver-using countries must satisfy their annual needs from the annual product; the arts will require a large amount, and the gold standard countries will need a considerable quantity for subsidiary coinage. We will be required to coin only that which is not needed elsewhere; but, if we stand ready to take and utilize all of it, other nations will be compelled to buy at the price we fix. Many fear that the opening of the mints will be followed by an enormous increase in the annual production of silver. This is conjecture. Silver has been used as money for thousands of years, and during all that time the world has never suffered from an over-production. If, for any reason, the supply of gold or silver in the future ever exceeds the requirements of the arts and the needs of commerce, we confidently hope that the intelligence of the people will be sufficient to devise and enact any legislation necessary for the protection of the public. It is folly to refuse to the people the money which they now need for fear they may hereafter have more than they need. I am firmly convinced that by opening our mints to free and unlimited coinage at the present ratio we can create a demand for silver which will keep the price of silver bullion at $1.29 per ounce measured by gold.

Some of our opponents attribute the fall in the value of silver, when measured by gold, to the fact that during the last quarter of a century the world's supply of silver has increased more rapidly than the world's supply of gold. This argument is entirely answered by the fact that, during the last five years, the annual production of gold has increased more rapidly than the annual production of silver. Since the gold price of silver has fallen more during these five years than it ever fell in any previous five years in the history of the world, it is evident that the fall is not due to increased production. Prices can be lowered as effectually by decreasing the demand for an article as by increasing the supply of it, and it seems certain that the fall in the gold price of silver is due to hostile legislation and not to natural laws. In other words, when gold leaves the country those who formerly owned it will be benefited. There is no process by which we can be compelled to part with our gold against our will, nor is there any process by which silver can be forced upon us without our consent. Exchanges are matters of agreement and if silver comes to this country under free coinage it will be at the invitation of some one in this country who will give something in exchange for it.

In answer to the charge that gold will go abroad under free coinage, it must be remembered that no gold can leave this country until the owner of the gold receives something in return for it which he would rather have.

Our opponents cannot ignore the fact that gold is now going abroad in spite of all legislation intended to prevent it, and no silver is being coined to take its place. Not only is gold going abroad now, but it must continue to go abroad as long as the present financial policy is adhered to, unless we continue to borrow from across the ocean, and even then we simply postpone the evil, because the amount borrowed, together with the interest upon it, must be repaid in appreciating dollars. The American people now owe a large sum to European creditors, and falling prices have left a larger and larger margin between our net national income and our annual interest charge. There is only one way to stop the increasing flow of gold from our shores, and that is to stop falling prices. The restoration of bimetallism will not only stop falling prices, but will—to some extent—restore prices by reducing the world's demand for gold. If it is argued that a rise in prices lessens the value of the dollars which we pay to our creditors, I reply that, in the balancing of equities the American people have as much right to favor a financial system which will maintain or restore prices as foreign creditors have to insist upon a financial system that will reduce prices. But the interests of society are far superior to the interests of either creditors or debtors, and the interests of society demand a financial system which will add to the volume of the standard money of the world, and thus restore stability to prices.

Perhaps the most persistent misrepresentation that we have to meet is the charge that we are advocating the payment of debts in fifty-three cent dollars. At the present time and under the present laws a silver dollar, when melted, loses nearly half its value, but that will not be true when we again establish a mint price for silver and leave no surplus silver upon the market to drag down the price of bullion. Under bimetallism silver bullion will be worth as much as silver coin, just as gold bullion is now worth as much as gold coin, and we believe that a silver dollar will be worth as much as a gold dollar.

APPENDIX. 421

The charge of repudiation comes with poor grace from those who are seeking to add to the weight of existing debts by legislation which makes money dearer, and who conceal their designs against the general welfare under the euphonious pretence that they are upholding public credit and national honor.

Those who deny the ability of the United States to maintain the parity between gold and silver at the present legal ratio without foreign aid point to Mexico and assert that the opening of our mints will reduce us to a silver basis and raise gold to a premium. It is no reflection upon our sister Republic to remind our people that the United States is much greater than Mexico in area, in population and in commercial strength. It is absurd to assert that the United States is not able to do anything which Mexico has failed to accomplish. The one thing necessary in order to maintain the parity is to furnish a demand great enough to utilize all the silver which will come to our mints. That Mexico has failed to do this is not proof that the United States would also fail.

It is also argued that, since a number of the nations have demonetized silver, nothing can be done until all of those nations restore bimetallism. This is also illogical. It is immaterial how many or how few nations have open mints, provided there are sufficient open mints to furnish a monetary demand for all the gold and silver available for coinage.

In reply to the argument that improved machinery has lessened the cost of producing silver, it is sufficient to say that the same is true of the production of gold, and yet, notwithstanding that, gold has risen in value. As a matter of fact, the cost of production does not determine the value of the precious metals, except as it may affect the supply. If, for instance, the cost of producing gold should be reduced 90 per cent without any increase in the output, the purchasing power of an ounce of gold would not fall. So long as there is a monetary demand sufficient to take at a fixed mint price all of the gold and silver produced, the cost of production need not be considered.

It is often objected that the prices of gold and silver cannot be fixed in relation to each other, because of the variation in the relative production of the metals. This argument also overlooks the fact that, if the demand for both metals at a fixed price is greater than the supply of both, relative production becomes immaterial. In the early part of the present century the annual production of silver was worth, at the coinage ratio, about three times as much as the annual production of gold; whereas soon after 1849, the annual production of gold became worth about three times as much, at the coinage ratio, as the annual production of silver; and yet, owing to the maintenance of the bimetallic standard, these enormous changes in relative production had but a slight effect upon the relative values of the metals.

If it is asserted by our opponents that the free coinage of silver is intended only for the benefit of the mine owners, it must be remembered that free coinage cannot restore to the mine owners any more than demonetization took away; and it must also be remembered that the loss which the demonetization of silver has brought to the mine owners is insignificant compared to the loss which this policy has brought to the rest of the people. The restoration of silver will bring to the people generally many times as much advantage as the mine owners can obtain from it. While it is not the purpose of free coinage to specially aid any particular class, yet those who believe that the restoration of silver is needed by the whole people should not be deterred because an incident benefit will come to the mine owners. The erection of forts, the deepening of harbors, the improvement of rivers, the erection of public buildings—all these confer incidental benefits upon individuals and communities, and yet these incidental benefits do not deter us from making appropriations for these purposes whenever such appropriations are necessary for the public good.

The argument that a silver dollar is heavier than a gold dollar, and that, therefore, silver is less convenient to carry in large quantities, is completely answered by the silver certificate, which is as easily carried as the gold certificate or any other kind of paper money.

There are some who, while admitting the benefits of bimetallism, object to coinage at the present ratio. If any are deceived by this objection, they ought to remember that there are no bimetallists who are earnestly endeavoring to secure it at any other ratio than 16 to 1. We are opposed to any change in the ratio for two reasons—first, because a change would produce great injustice, and, second, because a change in the ratio is not necessary. A change would produce injustice because, if effected in the manner usually suggested, it would result in an enormous contraction in the volume of standard money.

If, for instance, it was decided by international agreement to raise the ratio throughout the world to 32 to 1, the change might be effected in any of three ways:

The silver dollar could be doubled in size, so that the new silver dollar would weigh thirty-two times as much as the present gold dollar; or the present gold dollar could be reduced one-half in weight, so that the present silver dollar would weigh thirty-two times as much as the new gold dollar; or the change could be made by increasing the size of the silver dollar and decreasing the size of the gold dollar until the new silver dollar would weigh thirty-two times as much as the new gold dollar. Those who have advised a change in the ratio have usually suggested that the silver dollar be doubled. If this change were made it would necessitate the recoinage of four billions of silver into two billions of dollars. There would be an immediate loss of two billions of dollars either to individuals or to the Government, but this would be the least of the injury. A shrinkage of one-half in the silver money of the world would mean a shrinkage of one-fourth in the total volume of metallic money. This contraction, by increasing the value of the dollar, would virtually increase the debts of the world billions of dollars, and decrease still more the value of the property of the world as measured by dollars. Besides this immediate result, such a change in the ratio would permanently decrease the annual addition to the world's supply of money, because the annual silver product, when coined into dollars twice as large, would make only half as many dollars.

The people of the United States would be injured by a change in the ratio, not because they produce silver, but because they own property and owe debts, and they cannot afford to thus decrease the value of their property or increase the burden of their debts.

In 1878 Mr. CARLISLE said: "Mankind will be fortunate indeed if the annual production of gold and silver coin shall keep pace with the annual increase of population and industry." I repeat this assertion. All of the gold and silver annually available for coinage, when converted into coin at the present ratio, will not, in my judgment, more than supply our monetary needs.

In supporting the act of 1890, known as the SHERMAN Act, Senator SHERMAN, on June 5 of that year, said:

"Under the law of February, 1878, the purchase of $2,000,000 worth of silver bullion a month has by coinage produced annually an average of nearly $3,000,000 per month for a period of twelve years, but this amount, in view of the retirement of the bank notes, will not increase our currency in proportion to our increasing population. If our present currency is estimated at $1,400,000,000, and our population is increasing at the ratio of three per cent per annum, it would require $42,000,000 increased circulation each year to keep pace with the increase of population; but, as the increase of population is accompanied by a still greater ratio of increase of wealth and business it was thought that an immediate increase of circulation might be obtained by larger purchases of silver bullion to an amount sufficient to make good the retirement of bank notes and keep pace with the growth of population. Assuming that $54,000,000 a year of additional currency is needed upon this basis, that amount is provided for in this bill by the issue of Treasury notes in exchange for bullion at the market price."

If the United States then needed more than forty-two millions annually to keep pace with population and business, it now, with a larger population, needs a still greater annual addition; and the United States is only one nation among many. Our opponents make no adequate provision for the increasing monetary needs of the world.

In the second place, a change in the ratio is not necessary. Hostile legislation has decreased the demand for silver and lowered its price when measured by gold, while this same hostile legislation, by increasing the demand for gold, has raised the value of gold when measured by other forms of property.

We are told that the restoration of bimetallism would be a hardship upon those who have entered into contracts payable in gold coin, but this is a mistake. It will be easier to obtain the gold with which to meet a gold contract, when most of the people can use silver, than it is now, when every one is trying to secure gold.

The Chicago platform expressly declares in favor of such legislation as may be necessary to prevent for the future, the demonetization of any kind of legal tender money by private contract. Such contracts are objected to on the ground that they are against public policy. No one questions the right of Legislatures to fix the rate of interest which can be collected by law; there is far more reason for preventing private individuals from setting aside legal tender law. The money which is by law made a legal tender, must in the course of ordinary business, be accepted by ninety-nine out of every one hundred persons. Why should the one hundredth man be permitted to exempt himself from the general rule? Special contracts have a tendency to increase the demand for a particular kind of money, and thus force it to a premium. Have not the people a right to say that a comparatively few individuals shall not be permitted to derange the financial system of the nation in order to collect a premium in case they succeed in forcing one kind of money to a premium?

There is another argument to which I ask your attention. Some of the more zealous opponents of free coinage point to the fact that thirteen months must elapse between the election and the first regular session of the next Congress, and assert that during that time, in case people declare themselves in favor of free coinage, all loans will be withdrawn and all mortgages foreclosed. If these are merely prophecies indulged in by those who have forgotten the provisions of the Constitution, it will be sufficient to remind them that the President is empowered to convene Congress in extraordinary session whenever the public good requires such action. If, in November, the people by their ballots declare themselves in favor of the immediate restoration of bimetallism, the system can be inaugurated within a few months.

If, however, the assertion that loans will be withdrawn and mortgages foreclosed is made to prevent such political action as the people may believe to be necessary for the preservaiton of their rights, then a new and vital issue is raised. Whenever it is necessary for the people as a whole to obtain consent from the owners of money and the changers of money before they can legislate upon financial questions, we shall have passed from a democracy to a plutocracy. But that time has not yet arrived. Threats and intimidations will be of no avail. The people who, in 1776, rejected the doctrine that kings rule by right divine, will not, in this generation, subscribe to the doctrine that money is omnipotent.

In conclusion, permit me to say a word in regard to international bimetallism. We are not opposed to an international agreement looking to the restoration of bimetallism throughout the world. The advocates of free coinage have on all occasions shown their willingness to co-operate with other nations in the reinstatement of silver, but they are not willing to await the pleasure of other governments when immediate relief is needed by the people of the United States, and they further believe that independent action offers better assurance of international bimetallism than servile dependence upon foreign aid. For more than twenty years we have invited the assistance of European nations, but all progress in the direction of international bimetallism has been blocked by the opposition of those who derive a pecuniary benefit from the appreciation of gold. How long must we wait for bimetallism to be brought to us by those who profit by monometallism? If the double standard will bring benefits to our people, who will deny them the right to enjoy those benefits? If our opponents would admit the right, the ability and the duty of our people to act for themselves on all public questions without the assistance and regardless of the wishes of other nations, and then propose the remedial legislation which they consider sufficient, we could meet them in the field of honorable debate; but, when they assert that this nation is helpless to protect the rights of its own citizens, we challenge them to submit the issue to a people whose patriotism has never been appealed to in vain.

We shall not offend other nations when we declare the right of the American people to govern themselves, and, without let or hindrance from without, decide upon every question presented for their consideration. In taking this position, we simply maintain the dignity of seventy million citizens who are second to none in their capacity for self-government.

The gold standard has compelled the American people to pay an ever-increasing tribute to the creditor nations of the world—a tribute which no one dares to defend. I assert that national honor requires the United States to secure justice for all its citizens as well as to do justice to all its creditors. For a people like ours, blest with natural resources of surpassing richness, to proclaim themselves impotent to frame a financial system suited to their own needs, is humiliating beyond the power of language to describe. We cannot enforce respect for our foreign policy so long as we confess ourselves unable to frame our own financial policy.

Honest differences of opinion have always existed, and ever will exist, as to the legislation best calculated to promote the public weal; but, when it is seriously asserted that this nation must bow to the dictation of other nations and accept the policies which they insist upon, the right of self-government is assailed, and until that question is settled all other questions are insignificant.

Citizens of New York: I have traveled from the center of the continent to the seaboard that I might, in the very beginning of the campaign, bring you greeting from the people of the West and South and assure you that their desire is not to destroy but to build up. They invite you to accept the principles of a living faith rather than listen to those who preach the gospel of despair and advise endurance of the ills you have. The advocates of free coinage believe that, in striving to secure the immediate restoration of bimetallism, they are laboring in your behalf as well as in their own behalf. A few of your people may prosper under present conditions, but the permanent welfare of New York rests upon the producers of wealth. This great city is built upon the commerce of the nation and must suffer if that commerce is impaired. You cannot sell unless the people have money with which to buy, and they cannot obtain the money with which to buy unless they are able to sell their products at remunerative prices. Production of wealth goes before the exchange of wealth;

those who create must secure a profit before they have anything to share with others. You cannot afford to join the moneychangers in supporting a financial policy which, by destroying the purchasing power of the products of toil, must in the end discourage the creation of wealth.

I ask, I expect, your co-operation. It is true that a few of your financiers would fashion a new figure—a figure representing Columbia, her hands bound fast with fetters of gold and her face turned toward the East, appealing for assistance to those who live beyond the sea—but this figure can never express your idea of this nation. You will rather turn for inspiration to the heroic statue which guards the entrance to your city—a statue as patriotic in conception as it is colossal in proportion. It was the gracious gift of a sister Republic and stands upon a pedestal which was built by the American people. That figure—Liberty enlightening the world—is emblematic of the mission of our nation among the nations of the earth. With a Government which derives its powers from the consent of the governed, secures to all the people freedom of conscience, freedom of thought and freedom of speech, guarantees equal rights to all and promises special privileges to none, the United States should be an example in all that is good and the leading spirit in every movement which has for its object the uplifting of the human race.

LETTER OF ACCEPTANCE OF HON. W. J. BRYAN.

Lincoln, Neb., Sept. 9, 1896.

Hon. Stephen M. White and others, members of the Notification Committee of the Democratic National Convention:

Gentlemen: I accept the nomination tendered by you on behalf of the Democratic party, and in so doing desire to assure you that I fully appreciate the high honor which such a nomination confers and the grave responsibilities which accompany an election to the Presidency of the United States. So deeply am I impressed with the magnitude of the power invested by the Constitution in the Chief Executive of the nation, and with the enormous influence which he can wield for the benefit or injury of the people, that I wish to enter the office, if elected, free from every personal desire except the desire to prove worthy the confidence of my country. Human judgment is fallible enough when unbiased by selfish considerations, and in order that I may not be tempted to use the patronage of the office to advance any personal ambition, I hereby announce, with all the emphasis which words can express, my fixed determination not under any circumstances to be a candidate for re-election if this campaign results in my election.

I have carefully considered the platform adopted by the Democratic National Convention, and unqualifiedly indorse each plank thereof.

Our institutions rest upon the proposition that all men, being created equal, are entitled to equal consideration at the hands of the Government. Because all men are created equal it follows that no citizen has a natural right to injure any other citizen. The main purpose of government being to protect all citizens in the enjoyment of life, liberty, and pursuit of happiness, this purpose must lead the government, first, to avoid acts of affirmative injustice, and second, to restrain each citizen from trespassing upon the rights of any other citizen.

A democratic form of government is conducive to the highest civilization because it opens before each individual the greatest opportunities for development and stimulates to the highest endeavor by insuring to each the full enjoyment of all the rewards of toil except such contribution as is necessary to support the government which protects him. Democracy is indifferent to pedigree; it deals with the individual rather than with his ancestors. Democracy ignores differences in wealth. Neither riches nor poverty can be invoked in behalf of or against any citizen. Democracy known no creed, recognizing the right of each individual to worship God according to the dictates of his own conscience. It welcomes all to a common brotherhood, and guarantees equal treatment to all, no matter in which church or through what forms they commune with the creator.

Having discussed portions of the platform at the time of its adoption and again when your letter of notification was formally delivered, it will not be necessary at this time to touch upon all the subjects embraced in the party's declaration.

A DUAL GOVERNMENT.

Honest differences of opinion have ever existed and ever will exist as to the most effective means of securing domestic tranquility, but no citizen fails to recognize at all times and under all circumstances the absolute necessity for the prompt and vigorous enforcement of the law and the preservation of the public peace. In a government like ours law is but the crystalization of the will of the people; without it the citizen is neither secure in the enjoyment of life and liberty, nor protected in the pursuit of happiness. Without obedience to law government is impossible. The Democratic party is pledged to defend the Constitution, and enforce the laws of the United States, and it is also pledged to respect and preserve the dual scheme of government instituted by the founders of the Republic. The name, United States, was happily chosen. It combines the idea of national strength with the idea of local self-government and suggests "an indissoluble union of indestructible States." Our Revolutionary fathers, fearing the tendencies toward centralization as well as the dangers of disintegration, guarded against both, and national safety as well as domestic security is to be found in the careful observance of the limitations which they impose. It will be noticed that, while the United States guarantees to every State a republican form of government and is empowered to protect each State against invasion, it is not authorized to interfere in the domestic affairs of any State except upon application of the legislature of the State, or upon the application of the executive when the legislature cannot be convened.

This provision rests upon the sound theory that the people of the State, acting through their legally chosen representatives, because of their more intimate acquaintance with local conditions are better qualified than the President to judge of the necessity for Federal assistance. Those who framed our Constitution wisely determined to make as broad an application of the principles of local self-government as circumstances would permit, and we cannot dispute the correctness of the position taken by them without expressing a distrust of the people themselves.

ECONOMY.

Since governments exist for the protection of the rights of the people and not for their spoliation, no expenditure of public money can be justified unless that expenditure is necessary for the honest, economical and efficient administration of the Government. In determining what appropriations are necessary, the interest of those who pay the taxes should be consulted rather than the wishes of those who receive or disburse public moneys.

BONDS.

An increase in the bonded debt of the United States at this time is entirely without excuse. The issue of the interest-bearing bonds within the last few years has been defended on the ground that they were necessary to secure gold with which to redeem United States notes and Treasury notes, but this necessity has been imaginary rather than real. Instead of exercising the legal right vested in the United States to redeem its coin in either gold or silver, the executive branch of the Government has followed a precedent established by a former administration and surrendered the option to the holder of the obligations. This administrative policy leaves the government at the mercy of those who find a pecuniary profit in bond issues. The fact that the dealers in money and securities have been able to deplete or protect the Treasury, according to their changing whims, shows how dangerous it is to permit them to exercise a controlling influence over the Treasury Department. The Government of the United States, when administered in the interests of all the people, is able to establish and enforce its financial policy not only without the aid of syndicates, but in spite of any opposition which syndicates may present. To assert that the Government is dependent upon the good will or assistance of any portion of the people other than a constitutional majority is to assert that we have a government in form but without vital force.

NATIONAL BANK CURRENCY.

The position taken by the platform against the issue of paper money by national banks is supported by the highest Democratic authority as well as demanded by the interests of the people. The present attempt of the national banks to force the retirement of United States notes and Treasury notes in order to secure a basis for a larger issue of their own notes illustrates the danger which arises from permitting them to issue their paper as a circulating medium. The national bank note, being redeemable in lawful money, has never been better than the United States note, which stands behind it, and yet the banks persistently demand that these United States notes, which draw no interest, shall give place to interest-bearing bonds in order that the banks may collect the interest which the people now save. To empower national banks to issue circulating notes is to grant a valuable privilege to a favored class, surrender to private corporations the control over the volume of paper money, and build up a class which will claim a vested interest in the nation's financial policy. Our United States notes, commonly known as greenbacks, being redeemable in either gold or silver at the option of the government and not at the option of the holder, are safer and cheaper for the people than national bank notes based upon interest-bearing bonds.

THE MONROE DOCTRINE.

A dignified but firm maintenance of the foreign policy first set forth by President MONROE, and reiterated by the Presidents who have succeeded him, instead of arousing hostility abroad is the best guarantee of amicable relations with other nations.

It is better for all concerned that the United States should resist any extension of European authority in the Western hemisphere rather than invite the continued irritation which would necessarily result from any attempt to increase the influence of monarchical institutions in that portion of the Americas which has been dedicated to republican governments.

PENSIONS.

No nation can afford to be unjust to its defenders. The care of those who have suffered injury in the military and naval service of the country is a sacred duty. A nation which, like the United States, relies upon voluntary service rather than upon a large standing army, adds to its own security when it makes generous provisions for those who have risked their lives in its defense and for those who are dependent upon them.

THE PRODUCERS OF WEALTH.

Labor creates capital. Until wealth is produced by the application of brain and muscle to the resources of this country there is nothing to divide among the non-producing classes of society. Since the producers of wealth create the nation's prosperity in time of peace, and defend the nation's flag in time of peril, their interests ought at all times to be considered by those who stand in official positions. The Democratic party has ever found its voting strength among those who are proud to be known as the common people, and it pledges itself to propose and enact such legislation as is necessary to protect the masses in the free exercise of every political right and in their enjoyment of their just share of the rewards of their labor.

ARBITRATION.

I desire to give special emphasis to the plank which recommends such legislation as is necessary to secure the arbitration of differences between employers engaged in interstate commerce and their employees. Arbitration is not a new idea—it is simply an extension of the court of justice. The laboring men of the country have expressed a desire for arbitration and the railroads cannot reasonably object to the decisions rendered by an impartial tribunal. Society has an interest even greater than the interest of employer or employee, and has a right to protect itself by courts of arbitration against the growing inconvenience and embarrassment occasioned by disputes between those who own the great arteries of commerce on the one hand and the laborers who operate them on the other.

IMMIGRATION.

While the Democratic party welcomes to the country those who come with love for our institutions and with the determination and ability to contribute to the strength and greatness of our nation, it is opposed to the dumping of the criminal classes upon our shores and to the importation of either pauper or contract labor to compete with American labor.

INJUNCTIONS.

The recent abuses which have grown out of injunction proceedings have been so emphatically condemned by public opinion that the Senate bill providing for trial by jury in certain contest cases will meet with general approval.

TRUSTS.

The Democratic party is opposed to trusts. It will be recreant to its duty to the people if it recognizes either the moral or the legal right of these great aggregations of wealth to stifle competition, bankrupt rivals, and then prey upon society. Corporations are the creatures of law, and they must not be permitted to pass from under the control of the power which created; they are permitted to exist on the theory that they advance the public weal and they must not be allowed to use their powers for the public injury.

RAILROADS.

The right of the United States Government to regulate interstate commerce cannot be questioned, and the necessity for the vigorous exercise of that right is becoming more and more imperative. The interests of the whole people require such an enlargement of the powers of the Interstate Commerce Commission as will enable it to prevent discrimination between persons and places and protect patrons from unreasonable charges.

PACIFIC RAILROADS.

The government cannot afford to discriminate between its debtors, and must therefore prosecute its legal claims against the Pacific railroads. Such a policy is necessary for the protection of the rights of patrons as well as for the interests of the Government.

CUBA.

The people of the United States, happy in the enjoyment of the blessings of free government, feel a generous sympathy toward all who are endeavoring to secure like blessings for themselves. This sympathy, while respecting all treaty obligations, is especially active and earnest when excited by the struggles of neighboring peoples, who, like the Cubans, are near enough to observe the workings of a government which derives all its authority from the consent of the governed.

THE CIVIL SERVICE.

That the American people are not in favor of life tenure in the Government service is evident from the fact that they, as a rule, make frequent changes in their official representatives when those representatives are chosen by ballot. A permanent office-holding class is not in harmony with our institutions. A fixed term in appointive offices, except where the Federal Constitution now provides otherwise, would open the public service to a larger number of citizens without impairing its efficiency.

THE TERRITORIES.

The territorial form of government is temporary in its nature and should give way as soon as the territory is sufficiently advanced to take its place among the States. New Mexico, Oklahoma, and Arizona are entitled to statehood, and their admission is demanded by the material and political interests. The demand of the platform that officials appointed to administer the government of the Territories, the District of Columbia, and Alaska should be bona fide residents of the Territories or District is entirely in keeping with the Democratic theory of home rule. I am also heartily in sympathy with the declaration that all public lands should be reserved for the establishment of free homes for American citizens.

WATERWAYS.

The policy of improving the great waterways of the country is justified by the national character of those waterways and the enormous tonnage borne upon them. Experience has demonstrated that continuing appropriations are in the end more economical than single appropriations separated by long intervals.

THE TARIFF.

It is not necessary to discuss the tariff question at this time. Whatever may be the individual view of citizens as to the relative merits of protection and tariff reform, all must recognize that until the money question is fully and finally settled the American people will not consent to the consideration of any other important question. Taxation presents a problem which in some form is continually present, and a postponement of definite action upon it involves no sacrifice of personal opinion or political principles, but the crisis presented by financial conditions cannot be postponed. Tremendous results will follow the action taken by the United States on the money question, and delay is impossible. The people of this nation, sitting as a high court, must render judgment in the cause which greed is prosecuting against humanity. The dicision will either give hope and inspiration to those who toil or "shut the doors of mercy on mankind." In the presence of this overshadowing issue differences upon minor questions must be laid aside in order that there may be united action among those who are determined that progress toward an universal gold standard shall be stayed and the gold and silver coinage of the Constitution restored.

W. J. BRYAN.

MR. SEWALL'S SPEECH OF ACCEPTANCE.

NEW YORK CITY, August 12, 1896.

Mr. SEWALL: Mr. Chairman and Gentlemen of the Committee: You have given me official notice of my selection by the Democratic National Convention as its candidate for Vice-President.

For the courteous terms of your message, and the kind personal expressions, I thank you.

Having been present at that great Convention, I can more truly estimate the honor its action has conferred.

It was the greatest and most earnest Convention in the history of our party. It was closer and more in touch with the people. The delegates were there to voice the sentiments of their constituents, the people of the party, for the people of the party controlled and conducted that Convention.

The Democracy of the country realize that all the great principles of our party are as potent and essential to the wellbeing of the country to-day as they have always been, and as they ever will be, but the overshadowing issue before the country now, made dominant by the distressed condition prevailing throughout our land, is the demand for reform in our existing monetary system.

Our party, and, we believe, a great majority of the American people are convinced that the legislation of '73 demonetizing silver was a wrong inflicted upon our country which should and must be righted.

We believe that the single gold standard has so narrowed the base of our monetary structure that it is unstable and unsafe, and so dwarfed it, in its development and in its power to furnish the necessary financial blood to the nation, that commercial and industrial paralysis has followed.

We believe that we need, and must have, the broad and

expanding foundation of both gold and silver to support a monetary system strong and stable, capable of meeting the demand of a growing country and an industrious, energetic and enterprising people, a system that will not be weakened and panic stricken by every foreign draft upon us, a system that will maintain a parity of just values and the nation's money and protect us from the frequent fluctuations of to-day, so disastrous to every business and industry of the land.

We demand the free coinage of silver, the opening of our mints to both money metals without discrimination, the return to the money of our fathers, the money of the Constitution, gold and silver.

We believe this is the remedy and the only remedy for the evil from which we are now suffering; the evil that is now so fast devastating and impoverishing our land and people, bringing poverty to our homes and bankruptcy to our business, which, if allowed to continue, will grow until our very institutions are threatened.

The demonetization of silver has thrown the whole primary money function on gold, appreciating its value and purchasing power. Restore the money function to silver and silver will appreciate and its purchasing power increase. Take from gold its monopoly and its value will be reduced, and in due course the parity of the two metals will again obtain under natural causes.

We shall then have a broad and unlimited foundation for a monetary system commensurate with our country's needs and future development, not the unsafe basis of to-day reduced by half by the removal of silver and continually undermined by foreigners carrying from us our gold.

This is the reform to which we are pledged, the reform the people demand, the return to the monetary system of over eighty years of our national existence.

The Democratic party has already given its approval and its pledge. Our opponents admit the wisdom of the principle for which we contend, but ask us to await permission and co-operation of other nations.

Our people will not wait. They will not ask permission of any nation on earth to relieve themselves of the cause of their distress. The issue has been made. The people stand ready to render their verdict next November.

Mr. Chairman, unequivocally and through sincere conviction I endorse the platform on which I have been nominated.

I believe we are right; the people are with us, and what the people declare is always right and must prevail.

I accept the nomination, and with the people's conformation, every effort of which God shall render me capable will be exerted in support of the principles involved.

MR. SEWALL'S LETTER OF ACCEPTANCE.

Stephen B. White, Chairman, and Members of the Notification Committee:

GENTLEMEN:—I have the honor to accept in writing, as I have already done verbally, the nomination tendered me by you on behalf of the Democratic party as its candidate for Vice President of the United States. And in so doing I am glad, first, to express my satisfaction that the platform of our party, which has commanded my lifelong allegiance, is honestly and fully declaratory of all the principles, and especially of the absorbing financial issue upon which, as you say, I took my stand "when the hour of triumph seemed remote and when arrogant money-changers throughout the world boasted that the conquest of the American masses was completed."

These principles have been of late in abeyance, but only because those whom we trusted to maintain them have failed to do so. These principles can never die. We have rescued our party from those who, under the influence of the money power, have controlled and debased it. Our mission now is to rescue from this same power and its foreign allies our own beloved country. This is the first and highest duty imposed by our party's platform; upon the performance of this duty all other reforms must wait. The test of party principles is the government they assure; the proof of good government is a contented and happy people; the supreme test of both is the ability to guide the country through crises as well as to administer the government in ordinary times.

A CRISIS IS AT HAND.

Our people now face a crisis, a crisis more serious than any since the war. To what party shall they turn in their dire emergency? It is true that the present crisis may not involve all equally; that there are those who do not suffer now and who may not suffer should the crisis threatened by the gold standard come on in all its fury. Human selfishness makes these deaf to all appeals, but to these, fortunately, the Democratic party has never needed to appeal to win its battles, nor does it now, save as there are some among them who can rise superior to self in the sacrifice which such a crisis demands of every patriot. We are told that the country has prospered under the present monetary standard; that its wealth has enormously increased. Granted so, but in whose hands? In the hands of the toilers, the producers, the farmers, the miners, the fabricators in the factories, the framers of the nation's wealth in peace, its defenders in war? Have they the prosperity which was theirs so late as even twenty years ago? I deny it. They deny it. None affirm it save those whose interests it is to do so—whose profit would diminish as prosperity returns to those on whose distress they thrive.

All is indeed right between capital and labor. The "best money in the world" is none too good for those who have got it, but how is it with 90 per cent of our people who have "got it to get?" How is it with those who must buy this "best money in the world" with the products of their own labor? These are the people for whom the Democratic party would legislate. What is the best money for these? is the question for all to ask who really love this land. How else can you increase labor's purchasing power, but by increasing the price of labor's product? Is it a fair measure of values that in our great producing section ten bushels of potatoes must be paid for a dollar, ten bushels of oats for a dollar, six bushels of corn for a dollar, three bushels of wheat, and all other products of the soil and mines and the labor of all wage earners at the same ratio?

IS THIS HONEST MONEY?

Does any fair mind say this is honest money that forces such an exchange, and if it is not a fair exchange, is it honest, is it less than robbery? This is the condition to which the single standard has brought us. Under it the appreciation of the "best money of the world" has increased the wealth of the rich, and for the same reason has increased the debt of the debtor. So it has been, so under the present standard it must continue to be. With these object lessons about me, little need we have for history and statistics and the studies of scholars. Little satisfaction it is to us that they have warned us long since of the deadly evil of the gold standard. It has brought us at last to the parting of the ways. Whither shall the people go? In the way that has led to their enslavement, or into that which offers them their only chance to regain individual liberty, lasting prosperity and happiness?

Let our opponents charge us with creating class distinction. Alas for the republic, they are already here, created by the republican policy of the last thirty years; created by the very system we would now overthrow and destroy. Nor do we raise a sectional issue. The nomination you tender repels the charge. None know better than I that this nomination is meant as no personal tribute, but as an assurance that our party is a nonsectional party. Not by our policy, but only by the continuance of the gold standard can sectionalism be revived. Neither shall our opponents be permitted to terrify the people by predictions that temporary disturbance or panic will come from the policy we propose. The American people will be loyal to the nation's money, will stand behind and maintain it at whatever value they themselves may put upon it.

WHAT LINCOLN SAID.

Once before in the present generation have our people been called upon to face a momentous crisis. What then said Mr. Lincoln, the chosen leader of the plain people of the land? Was he awed by threats or weakened by the wily persuasion of the false friends who, as to-day, pleaded for compromise with wrong? His answer was:

"If our sense of duty forbids this, then let us stand by our duty fearlessly and effectively. Let us be diverted by none of these sophistical contrivances wherewith we are so industriously plied and belabored; contrivances such as groping for some middle ground between right and wrong, reversing the divine rule and calling not the sinner but the righteous to repentance; such as the invocations to Washington, imploring men to unsay what Washington said and undo what Washington did. Neither let us be slandered from our duty by false accusations against us. Let us have faith that right makes might, and in that faith let us to the end dare to do our duty as we understand it."

We know well the nature of the struggle in which we are engaged; we are anxious only that the people of the land shall understand it and then our battle is won. Behind the strong entrenchment of the gold standard are gathered all those favored classes of the land. Avarices and unholy greed are there; every trust and combination are there. Every monopoly is there, led by the greatest monopoly of all, the monopoly of the power of gold. With us in our assault upon these entrenchments are all these unselfish men who, not now suffering themselves, cannot rest content with conditions so full of suffering for others, and that vaster number of our people who have been sacrificed to the small and selfish class who now resist their attempts to regain their ancient rights and liberties. These are the patriots of 1896, the foes of a "dishonest dollar," which enriches 10 per cent of our people to rob the rest; the defenders of the homes of the land, the public morals and the public faith, both of which alike forbid the payment of government obligations in a coin costlier to those who have to pay it than that the contract calls for; the defenders of the honor of the nation whose most sacred charge is to care for the welfare of all its citizens.

The free and unlimited coinage of silver is the sole remedy with which to check the wrongs of today, to undo the ruin of of the past, and for our inspiration we have the justice of our cause and those cherished principles of Jefferson and Jackson which shall be our guide on our return to power—"Equal and exact justice to all men," absolute acquiescence in decisions of the majority, the vital principles of Republics, the honest payment of our debts and the sacred preservation of the public faith.

Profoundly sensible of the high honor of the nomination you tender, I am, truly yours.

ARTHUR SEWALL.

VICE PRESIDENTS AND ASSISTANT SECRETARIES.

The following are the Vice Presidents and Assistant Secretaries selected by the several delegations and adopted by the Committee on Permanent Organization, as per report at page 167.

VICE PRESIDENTS.

Alabama—JOHN W. TOMLINSON.
Arkansas—JAMES H. BERRY.
California—GEO. E. CHURCH.
Colorado—JAMES B. GRANT.
Connecticut—MILES B. PRESTON.
Delaware—HENRY C. PENNINGTON.
Florida—J. ED. O'BRIEN.
Georgia—B. M. DAVIS.
Idaho—WILLIAM H. DEWEY.
Illinois—CHAS. K. LADD.
Indiana—JOHN B. STOLL.
Iowa—M. H. KING.
Kansas—JAMES MCKENSTRY.
Kentucky—R. F. PEAKE.
Louisiana—PETER FARRELL.
Maine—EDWARD B. WINSLOW.
Maryland—RICHARD M. VENABLE.
Massachusetts—WM. L. DOUGLASS.
Michigan—JAMES F. MALONEY.
Minnesota—LAGUN BRACKERIDGE.
Mississippi—W. G. YERGER.
Missouri—WM. N. EADS.
Montana—S. F. HAUSER.
Nebraska—CHARLES H. BROWN.
Nevada—JOHN SPARKS.
New Hampshire—GORDON WOODBURY.
New Jersey—JAMES J. BERGEN
New York—JAMES D. BELL.
North Carolina—J. R. WEBSTER.
North Dakota—(None reported).
Ohio—JOHN H. BLACKEN.
Oregon—JOHN W. HOWARD.
Pennsylvania—B. F. MEYERS.
Rhode Island—JESSE H. METCALF.
South Carolina—JOHN G. EVANS.
South Dakota—EDW. COOK.
Tennessee—FRANK BOYD.
Texas—JOHN LOVEJOY.
Utah—R. C. CHAMBERS.
Vermont—J. W. GORDON.
Virginia—J. R. WINGFIELD.
Washington—CHAS. A. DARLING.
West Virginia—J. H. MILLER.
Wisconsin—M. C. MEAD.
Wyoming—ROBT. FOOTE.
Alaska—JAMES CARROLL.
Arizona—A. F. CORNISH.
Dist. of Columbia—WM. HOLMEAD.
Indian Terr.—HARRY CAMPBELL.
New Mexico—(None reported).
Oklahoma—J. H. MAXEY.

SECRETARIES.

Alabama—LEOPOLD STRAUSS.
Arkansas—J. N. SMITHEE.
California—H. E. WISE.
Colorado—OLNEY NEWALL.
Connecticut—WM. KENNEDY.
Delaware—DR. B. L. LEWIS.

Florida—NAT. R. WALKER.
Georgia—R. O. HOWARD.
Idaho—JOHN T. SHEELEY.
Illinois—JOSH. MARTIN.
Indiana—S. E. COOK.
Iowa—S. A. BREWSTER.
Kansas—C. W. BRANDENBURG.
Kentucky—BENJ. V. SMITH.
Louisiana—L. H. MARREN.
Maine—FRED. EMERY BEANE.
Maryland—HENRY R. LEWIS.
Massachusetts—JOHN F. O'BRIEN.
Michigan—MARTIN J. CAVANAUGH.
Minnesota—JOHN SHEEHY.
Mississippi—J. R. STOWERS.
Missouri—GEO. W. ALLEN.
Montana—(None reported).
Nebraska—F. A. THOMPSON.
Nevada—(None reported).
New Hampshire—J. J. DOYLE.
New Jersey—WM. B. EDWARDS.
New York—GEO. B. MCCLELLAN.
North Carolina—W. C. DOWD.

North Dakota—F. A. WELLSON.
Ohio—GEO. S. LONG.
Oregon—(None reported).
Pennsylvania—MILLER S. ALLEN.
Rhode Island—M. A. MCNAMEE.
South Carolina—M. B. MCSWEENY.
South Dakota—F. M. STOVER.
Tennessee—J. W. N. BURKETT.
Texas—A. S. BURLESON.
Utah—E. A. MCDANIEL.
Vermont—J. W. MCGARRY.
Virginia—W. P. BARKSDALE.
Washington—THOMAS MALONEY.
West Virginia—JOHN J. CORNWELL.
Wisconsin—LEWIS A. LANG.
Wyoming—J. W. SAMMAN.
Alaska—KARL KOEHLER.
Arizona—H. H. LOGAN.
Dist. of Columbia—GEO. KILLEEN.
Indian Terr.—W. P. THOMPSON.
New Mexico—(None reported).
Oklahoma—T. M. UPSHAW.

Milton Keynes UK
Ingram Content Group UK Ltd.
UKHW040048180324
439604UK00006B/1077